ISRAEL
ORIENTAL
STUDIES
XVII

ISRAEL ORIENTAL STUDIES

XVII

DHIMMIS AND OTHERS: JEWS AND CHRISTIANS AND THE WORLD OF CLASSICAL ISLAM

EDITED BY

URI RUBIN
DAVID J. WASSERSTEIN

EISENBRAUNS, INC.
1997

The paper in this book meets the guidelines for permanence and durability of the Committee on Production Guidelines for Book Longevity of the Council on Library Resources.

ISRAEL ORIENTAL STUDIES
Annual Publication of the Faculty of Humanities
Tel-Aviv University

Library of Congress Cataloging-in-Publication Data

LC card number 72-955546

ISSN 0334-4401
ISBN 1-57506-026-4

Typeset in Israel: 'Graphit' Ltd., Jerusalem
Printed and bound in the United States of America

CONTENTS

Book Reviews

INTRODUCTION

Islam has always had ambivalent relations with Judaism and Christianity, as also with Jews and Christians. The awkwardness of their character has been accentuated by the creation and perpetuation, on all sides, of partial and ill-intentioned images during the middle ages and by political developments in the modern period. Since the beginning of serious modern study of Islam in the west, these relations have found an important place in scholars' interest, partly because many of those in the west who have studied Islam have been Jews, with a natural attraction to an interest in those topics which affected Jews and other minorities in the Islamic environment.

These topics range broadly, including all areas and periods of the history of Islam. At the start, the mission of Muhammad himself involved him with Christians and Jews in the Arabian peninsula, an involvement which is reflected in the attitudes towards them expressed in the Qur'ān. The holy books of all three faiths, and other texts too, bear witness to a vast amount of shared interest and of common material, historical, theological, legal and more. Following the conquests of Islam, the fates of Christian and Jewish communities in the conquered territories similarly attracted concern, both for their assimilation to the new environment which the growth of Islam brought into being and for social and cultural defence mechanisms, some of them carryovers from earlier periods, which enabled them, in certain cases, to survive and even to thrive. Similarly, the contributions which such communities, or members of them, had to make to the development of Islamic societies and cultures have attracted considerable interest.

The nature of scholarly concern varied with the nature of the problems and the types of source available to meet them. This is scarcely surprising, given the great range of the subjects represented, and the immense richness of the materials available, on occasion apparently quite out of proportion to the numbers or the significance of the groups involved. And the types of scholarly attention which they have received have also, in their variation, seemed occasionally to respond to the vagaries of the political relationships between Islamic and non-Islamic polities and societies of the modern world. This variation has been much stronger in this area of Islamic studies than in others; but it has helped, a little paradoxically, to generate a fruitful discussion of the nature of the relationships over the last millennium and a half between Muslim and non-Muslim in the world of Islam and outside it.

In this volume, we have tried to assemble a collection of papers which reflect something of the diversity of the problems offered by this range of relations. We have also attempted to reflect, in the variety of the papers and the topics discussed in them, the rich variety of approach adopted by scholars over the last century and a half of such study.

The papers follow a rough chronological pattern: we begin very much at the beginning, with a study by Simon Hopkins of the words for 'Jews' in Arabic; this is succeeded by Michael Lecker on the question of Muhammad's relations with three Jewish tribes in the Arabian peninsula. Claude Gilliot then considers the ways in which the early Islamic tradition used material about Abraham, both for the internal development of an exegetical manner and as part of the creation of an independent cultural identity for Islam.

In the following section, three papers carry this further, exploring different facets of definition, of the other and, through that, of the self in the Islamic world. Uri Rubin looks at the traditions concerning the transformation of Muslims into apes and pigs, a development of earlier traditions concerning transformation of sinful Jews and Christians, and demonstrates the relationship between such changes and the attempt to resist the penetration of Judaic and Christian elements into Islam, elements whose entry was seen as a threat to Islamic identity. Hawting discusses the use of terms for idolatry, in particular the term *shirk*, and how its meaning varied with the passage of time and changes in the reality of the religious variety in Islamic societies in the early centuries; while Wasserstrom studies what Šahrastānī, in the twelfth century, knew of one particular Jewish sect and what such knowledge implies, once again, for the boundaries between Muslim and non-Muslim.

In the final section most of the articles are concerned with the Islamic West: Maribel Fierro and David Wasserstein are both concerned with the reactions of Muslims to successes of non-Muslims in different ways. Fierro looks at how Muslims in al-Andalus, Islamic Spain, reacted to Christian victories in the Iberian peninsula, with the concomitant increase in Muslim sensitivity to the dangers which they represented for Islamic polities there; Wasserstein, for an earlier period, considers Muslim awareness of the glories of Jewish cultural revival in the shadow of Islam in the peninsula. Such cultural florescence depended critically on integration into and assimilation with the Islamic environment. This was a largely one-way process, and it generated a one-sided awareness of the other. Nasir Basal's study of the surviving portion of a work of Abū al-Faraj Hārūn illustrates the complexities of the linguistic relationship between Muslims and non-Muslims, in a new world using Arabic as its major language. The use by Jews of Arabic, in different forms and at varied levels, is seen here to reflect the varying levels and types of assimilation which Jews (like other non-Muslims) underwent in the encounter with Islam. And Mercedes García-Arenal, in a study of conversion of Jews to Islam in the west, looks at the final stage in the influence of Islam on Jews in this period.

These papers all represent different approaches, and are concerned with different problems; but they are all also concerned most particularly with how Islam and Muslims looked at and understood non-Muslims; the non-Muslims — Jews and Christians — and the cultural baggage which they carried — especially biblical and similar material — exerted great influence at all periods on the formation and the perpetual re-shaping of the identities of Islam, not only in the classical and medieval periods. If we are properly to understand the nature of these identities, and the working of the forces shaping and re-forming them, then we need perhaps to lose the older, somewhat simplistic, attitude which saw Christians and Jews as minorities, however we define that word, and to begin rather to view them as full, if not therefore necessarily equal, partners in the development of a new world from the seventh century onwards. It is our hope that this volume may contribute something to that end.

Uri Rubin
David J. Wasserstein

ON THE WORDS FOR "JEW(S)" IN ARABIC*

SIMON HOPKINS

I

The words for "Jewish" and "Jew(s)" in classical Arabic are as follows:

(i) *yahūdīyun* (sg.)
(ii) *yahūdu(n)* (coll.)[1]
(iii) *hūdun* (coll.)

All three words appear in the Quran and are undoubtedly of pre-Islamic origin. (i) يَهُودِيٌّ *yahūdīy* and (ii) يَهُود *yahūd* are the normal literary Arabic terms used when speaking of contemporary or modern Jews and Judaism, as opposed to the ancient biblical Israelites, to whom the term *banū ʾisrāʾīla* is usually applied.[2] The noun (iii) هُود *hūd* is not much used outside the Quran and even there is rare. From these words are derived the denominative verbs I *hāda*, V *tahawwada* "to be(come) a Jew" and II *hawwada* "to make Jewish".[3] There are several points in the shape of these nouns for "Jews" which require explanation:

(a) The endingless *yahūd* does not occur in the meaning "Jews" in the source languages Hebrew ~ Aramaic.

* My thanks are due to M. Lecker for his helpful observations on this paper.

[1] This word usually occurs with the definite article. When indefinite it sometimes appears in classical texts with *tanwīn*, e.g. Ibn Ḥazm, *jamharat ansāb al-ʿarab*, ed. A.S.M. Hārūn (Cairo 1962) 491: *kānat ḥimyaru yahūdan*. In modern standard Arabic of the media *tanwīn* may be heard adverbially in the expression *yahūdan wa-ʿaraban* "Jews and Arabs alike", but as in the classical language *yahūd(u)* is today generally *ġayr munṣarif*.

[2] See S.D. Goitein *EI*[2] I 1020ff. *s.v.*, who also mentions the term *ʾisrāʾīlīy*. In Iraq at least, as sometimes in the English-speaking world, "Israelite" was until recently used as a (polite) variant of "Jew". Thus Iraqi Christians would refer to their Jewish compatriots as *əsġāʾīləyyīn* rather than *ya/əhūd*, dropping this practice only after 1948 when *əsġāʾīli* came to mean "Israeli"; see F. Abu-Haidar, *Christian Arabic of Baghdad* (Wiesbaden 1991) 156n.

[3] Denominative *hwd* seems to be the only verbal root in use in Muslim sources. The roots *yhwd* and *yhd* I know only from Jewish and Christian texts, e.g., translations of Esther 8:16, where Saadia uses *tayahwada*, var. *tayahhada*; see Y. Ratzaby, *A Dictionary of Judaeo-Arabic in R. Saadya's* Tafsir (Ramat-Gan 1985) 141 [Hebrew].

(b) The Hebrew ~ Aramaic etymons of these words presumably contained spirant *ḏ*, whereas Arabic tradition consistently shows plosive *d*.

(c) The base *yahūd-* contains the vowel *a* in its first syllable, a vowel hardly present in any Hebrew ~ Aramaic source.

(d) Initial *y-* is absent from *hūd*.

These matters will be briefly discussed in the present article and the suggestion will be made that the formal problems attending this family of words are best accounted for by the assumption that they reflect certain features then current in various dialects of vernacular Aramaic.

II: *yahūd*

The fact that this family of words is of non-Arabic origin is evident of itself and was well known to many of the Arab philologists, who quite rightly looked to Hebrew (~ Aramaic as the source of *yahūd* and its relatives. Others, to whom the foreign origin of the word was not apparent, or not acceptable, forced upon it an imaginary Arabic etymology based upon the root *hwd* "to return, repent", "to be calm"[4] — such midrashic speculations will not concern us here.[5]

The closest formal equivalent of *yahūd* in Hebrew/Aramaic is יְהוּד, but the north Semitic word in this endingless form does not normally mean "Jews" but rather "Judaea", a fact which does not favour a direct derivation from this source.[6] "Jew" is expressed in these languages by *yhuḏi* (Heb.) and *yhuḏāyā* (Aram.), each with the appropriate attributive *nisba*-suffix.

[4] See in general on the etymology of the word A. Jeffery, *The Foreign Vocabulary of the Qur'ān* (Baroda 1938) 293/4.

[5] For a selection of such etymological interpretations see the interesting passage adduced by I. Goldziher, *SBKAW* 67 (1871) 231/2 = *Gesammelte Schriften*, ed. J. Desomogyi, I (Hildesheim 1967) 231/2. Q 2:135 *wa-qālū kūnū hūdan aw naṣārā tahtadū* ... may also be vaguely pseudo-etymological in intent, playing on the similarity between *hūd* and *hdy*. In some dialects of Aramaic a form of "Jew" lacking initial *y-* (see below §vi) would have been very similar to, and possibly even homophonous with *hud(d)āyā* "guidance" (*hdy*). Cf. the Biblical pseudo-etymology of Judah based upon *ydy (hiphʿil)* "thank" Gen. 29:35; 49:8.

[6] As proposed by A. Fischer, *Arabische Chrestomathie*[6] (Leipzig 1953) 157a. Though one will readily admit that the distinction between *n. pr. terr.* "Judaea" and *n. pr. gent.* "Jews" may sometimes be difficult to draw, I think that, among others, K. Marti, *Kurzgefasste Grammatik der biblisch-aramäischen Sprache*[3] (Berlin 1925) §68b overstated the case in declaring Biblical Aramaic יהוד to be a collective "Juden". The word in Aramaic in general is primarily geographical, not gentilic; cf. the *n.pr.gent.* and the *n.pr.terr.* side by side in *Megillat Antiochus* 6: עמא יהודאי די ביהוד (var. בירושלים) בינתנא "the Jewish people who are among us in Judaea (var. Jerusalem)".

These are the forms from which we should start. It is not difficult to imagine that the Aramaic *-āyā* ending would have been converted into the functionally corresponding Arabic *nisba* to produce first of all *y(a)hūdīy* (sg.); from this the form *yahūd* (coll.) was then, as Brockelmann and others have observed,[7] derived by backformation. According to this view, therefore, *yahūdīy* will have preceded *yahūd*.[8] The grammatical relation between the two is the same as that obtaining elsewhere in Arabic, e.g. between *ʿarab* "Arabs" and *ʿarabīy* "(an) Arab", the singular of a collective denoting human beings being provided by the *nisba*.

III: *ḏ*/*d*

In Hebrew and Aramaic "Jew(ish)" appears as *yhuḏi* and *yhuḏāyā* respectively, in both cases with spirant *ḏ* by virtue of the well-known rule governing post-vocalic non-geminate *bgdkpt* in these languages. Since Arabic possesses a series of interdentals, there is, on the face of it, no reason why the spirant should not have been preserved: had the word entered Arabic with *ḏ* one would have expected the result to be **yahūḏīy* with ذ *ḏāl*. Nevertheless, although the philologists mention the etymological spirant *ḏ* for the word *yahūḏ(ā)* "Judah", in Muslim tradition the plosive pronunciation *yahūdīy* "Jew" is dominant, apparently exclusively so. This is stated repeatedly and explicitly, e.g., by al-Jawālīqī (d. 539 A.H. = 1144), the first part of whose entry *yahūd* reads: *aʿjamīyun muʿarrab. wa-hum mansūbūna ilā yahūḏā bni yaʿqūba fa-summū l-yahūda wa-ʿurribat bi-l-dāl*,[9] and similarly Ibn Manẓūr (d. 711 A.H. = 1311/2): *wa-qīla innamā smu hāḏihi l-qabīlati yahūḏ, fa-ʿurriba bi-qalbi l-ḏāli dālan.*[10] The contrast here between the plosive of *yahūd* and the spirant of *yahūḏ(ā)* is both striking and significant: in everyday usage, in the everyday meaning "Jew(s)", the pronunciation was with *d*; the technical, learned sense of the biblical etymon "Judah", "Judaea" was pronounced with *ḏ*.

There are two approaches to explaining the dental plosive of *yahūd*. One may suppose that the word was borrowed with *ḏ* and that the shift *ḏ* > *d* occurred within Arabic; alternatively, one could argue that when

[7] C. Brockelmann, *Grundriss der vergleichenden Grammatik der semitischen Sprachen* I (Berlin 1908) 398n. and, apparently independently, J. Horovitz, *Koranische Untersuchungen* (Berlin–Leipzig 1926) 154.

[8] For Aramaic יהוד itself as a backformation see Marti (n.6) and Brockelmann (n.7) *loc. cit.*

[9] Al-Jawālīqī, *al-muʿarrab min al-kalām al-aʿǧamī*, ed. F. ʿAbd al-Raḥīm (Damascus 1410 A.H.) 650 = ed. M.A.Šākir (Cairo 1361 A.H.) 357.

[10] Ibn Manẓūr, *lisān al-ʿarab* s.v. *hwd*

the etymon of *yahūd* reached Arabic from its north Semitic source it was already pronounced there with *d*. Since our knowledge of Aramaic and Arabic phonology during the first millennium is exiguous in the extreme,[11] the decision is a matter for delicate consideration.

The Arabic option is possible, but not without difficulty. Many urban and sedentary modern Arabic dialects are characterized by a wholesale shift of the interdental spirants to dental plosives: ث *t̲*, ذ *d̲*, ظ *ḏ̣* > *t*, *d*, *ḍ*. This shift, which is sometimes attributed to Aramaic influence, is certainly very old in colloquial Arabic and without much risk of error one may assume that in some areas and in some dialects it had already taken place in the pre-Islamic period.[12] Had *yhūd̲-* been borrowed into such a dialect, there is a good possibility that the result would have shown *d* in Arabic rather than *d̲*. The problem, however, is that the *d* of *yahūd* is not restricted to a substandard dialect spoken somewhere on the Aramaic fringes of the Arabian peninsula, but is firmly rooted within the tradition of *classical* Arabic itself. In classical Arabic, as in most bedouin dialects spoken today, preservation of the interdentals is the rule; indeed this is one of the hallmarks of the classical language. One would need, therefore, to assume that having first been borrowed into a local dialect which lacked *d̲* (and presumably the other interdentals as well), *yahūdīy* subsequently found its way in this vernacular form into classical Arabic, where it remained uninfluenced by knowledge of *yahūd̲(ā)* and unaffected by the classical interdentals. One will not claim that a development along these lines is impossible, merely that it is problematical. Even if we extend the possibilities and suppose Aramaic *yhud̲-* to have been borrowed at different times into different Arabic dialects, both those with *d̲* and those without, it is not easy to explain the preference for the non-classical pronunciation.

The other option is to approach the problem from the Hebrew ~ Aramaic side and inspect the possibility that Arabic *yahūd* appears with plosive *d* because that is the form in which it was exported from the source language. In carefully pointed written forms of Hebrew and Aramaic during the first millennium A.D. the spirantization of *bgdkpt* in post-vocalic position is ubiquitously observed according to the principles found in every grammar book. In texts which are unpointed it is entirely plausible to believe that the *bgdkpt* rules were applied by the reader, who would

[11] Moreover, some of the literature on these elusive subjects should be used with exceeding caution. E.g., the evidence produced by S. Krauss, *Griechische und lateinische Lehnwörter im Talmud, Midrasch und Targum* I (Berlin 1898) §50 in favour of spirant *d̲* in Rabbinic texts is virtually all mistaken; see S. Fraenkel, *ZDMG* 25 (1898) 295/6.

[12] See e.g. S. Hopkins, *Studies in the Grammar of Early Arabic* (Oxford 1984) §§30a, 34, 39a and the literature referred to there.

choose the plosive or spirant variant as required — lack of explicit marking of *dageš* and/or *rafe* does not, of course, mean that these variants did not exist, but simply that they were not necessarily indicated. The position was doubtless similar in principle to that prevailing in modern Hebrew, where the *b/v, k/x, p/f* alternants are realized in speech but are not usually marked in writing. This being so, to posit an unattested Aramaic etymon **yhud-* against the known phonology of this language is not an immediately attractive solution to our difficulty.

But perhaps we should bear in mind the contrast noted above between popular *yahūd* "Jews" with *d* and learned *yahūḏ(ā)* "Judah", Judaea" with *ḏ* and distinguish accordingly between vulgar and erudite usage. The latter is a literary form with a technical sense and known to savants only, who naturally learned it from literary sources in its formal pronunciation;[13] it is a bookish word and as such is of a status quite different from that of *yahūd*, which was in daily use among all sections of the population in a meaning generally known to everybody. *yahūd* is of undoubtedly popular origin and it is to colloquial rather than literary Aramaic that we should turn for its source. I should like to argue that in some forms of vernacular, as opposed to literary, Aramaic the lapse of the spirantization rule and consequent existence of plosive *bgdkpt* consonants only is a very plausible proposition. If so, one will conclude that it was precisely from one of these dialects that the Arabic *yahūd* was derived.

Very little indeed is known about the phonology of Aramaic vernaculars at the period when *yahūd* became an Arabic word, presumably during the early — middle part of the first millennium A.D. One source of information is the Aramaic loanwords in Arabic, collected in a classic work of Semitic philology, S. Fraenkel's *Die aramäischen Fremdwörter im Arabischen* (Leiden 1886), a book which, over a century after publication, has lost none whatever of its usefulness. The transference of Aramaic *bgdkpt* to Arabic is treated by Fraenkel on pp. xviii ff. of his introduction, where the discussion is based mostly upon the transcription of *nomina propria* (among them *yahūḏā*), which Fraenkel, quite rightly, supposed would reflect "am Sichersten" (p.xvii) the governing principles. The resultant picture, for various reasons, is not uniform: "wenn auch zumeist zwischen den aspirierten und harten Mutis unterschieden, so ist dies doch nicht immer der Fall" (p.xviii). When we turn to the loanwords recorded in the book itself, as opposed to the transcriptions discussed in the introduction, I have the impression that the number of "exceptions" increases. As far as Aramaic *ḏ* is concerned one should check how far this

[13] In Christian Arabic sources too "Judah", unlike *yahūd*, is often pointed with *ḏāl*; see examples in B. Knudtsson, *Studies in the Text and Language of Three Syriac-Arabic Versions of the Book of Judicum* (Leiden 1974) 98/9.

sound is regularly ("gewöhnlich" p.32) transcribed by *ḏāl*, for there is certainly a significant number of cases where this is not so. The reason for the disparity between the transcriptions, on the one hand, and the loanwords, on the other, seems to me to lie in the fact that the two groups belong to different registers: the transcriptions of many *nomina propria* are learned words found in the works of scholars, whereas the loanwords are of popular origin and belong to the language of everyday life. The former are derived from written sources (Syriac, Greek), while the latter entered Arabic from colloquial Aramaic speech. It is only natural, as Fraenkel well knew, that the transcriptions should reproduce more accurately the *bgdkpt* rules of literary Aramaic. It is equally natural that the loanwords should reflect the speech habits of the vernaculars, in some of which spirantization may no longer have existed.

A glance at the position in Neo-Aramaic is suggestive of a solution to the problem of Arabic *yahūd*. In all of the eastern Neo-Aramaic vernaculars, which continue the spoken Aramaic of old, the *bgdkpt* rule of the classical forms of the language has broken down entirely and is no longer operative as a living phonological process. Common to all dialects is the generalization of one variant to all positions, so that contrasts within the same root such as כְּתַב *kṯaḇ* "he wrote" : יִכְתֻּב *yiḵtuḇ* "he writes" no longer exist. The different dialects have abandoned the old plosive: spirant alternation in different ways, e.g. in the case of the two pairs *t*/*ṯ* and *d*/*ḏ* some dialects behave symmetrically and have generalized either both the plosives or both the spirants; others are asymmetrical and have generalized one but not the other; still others have introduced more far-reaching changes. The resultant picture is one of extreme diversity. The reflexes of earlier **ṯ* and **ḏ* in several modern eastern Neo-Aramaic dialects can be illustrated by the words for "house" and "hand":

Older Aramaic	*bēṯā*[14]	*iḏā*
	בֵּיתָא	אִידָא
Urmi (Christian)	*beta*	*ida*
Zakho (Christian)	"	"
Dehok (Jewish)	*beṯa*	*iḏa*
Zakho (Jewish)	*besa*	*iza*
Amedya (Jewish)	*beṯa*	*ida*
Urmi (Jewish)	*bela*	*ida*
Kerend (Jewish)	*bela*	*ila*

[14] This is not the place to discuss antecedent forms of this word, i.e., whether *bayṯā* (BA) or *baytā* (Syr.). For the present purpose forms without the diphthong are quite sufficient.

What is of significance here is the sheer variation of possibilities, a phenomenon quite unknown from the standard written forms of literary Aramaic. Even within the same town, e.g. Urmia or Zakho, the Christians and Jews have different reflexes. There is, as far as I know, no reason to think that, in principle, the situation in older forms of spoken Aramaic was much different. Just as today there are Aramaic dialects which have lost the interdentals and have plosives only (Urmi Christian, Zakho Christian, to which one could add others, e.g. Hertevin), we may without great risk of error assume that such dialects existed in antiquity also.[15] Recognition of their existence goes some way towards explaining some of the unexpected plosives in Aramaic loanwords in Arabic.[16] It was, I submit, from just such a dialect that the Arabic *yahūd* was borrowed.

IV: *ya-*

Another question is posed by the *a* vowel of the first syllable of *yahūd*. What is its origin? In this case we cannot with any plausibility attribute the anomaly to the source languages, neither of which show (or can show) short *a* in this position, but open with *y(ə)-*. Some varieties of Aramaic preserve initial *y(ə)-* intact; others, however, are sensitive to this combination wherever it occurs, either shifting it to *(ʾ)i-* (*ʾihuḏāyā* §v) or eliding it altogether (*huḏāyā* §vi). None of these Aramaic treatments, however, provides an explanation for the initial *ya-* of the Arabic forms, which in all probability reflects an inner-Arabic development. Since the syllable structure of classical Arabic prohibits a vowelless consonant at the beginning of a word, the vowelless Anlaut of יְהוּדָיָא *y(ə)huḏāyā* is in need of some adjustment before it can be accepted into the system, i.e. a full vowel needs to separate the initial cluster **yh-*. Were purely phonetic considerations at work here one imagines that the Arabicized form might have been **yihūd(īy)*. But not only does there seem to be no trace of such a pronunciation, there is also no Arabic pattern *fiʿūl* to which it could be adapted. Horovitz, therefore, is certainly correct in regarding the word as having been not simply borrowed, but remodelled according to Arabic

[15] A not dissimilar situation prevails in the traditional pronunciations of Hebrew in the Arabic-speaking world, some of which have lost the spirant variants of *d/t*. That there is no necessity to attribute this to the influence of the local Arabic vernaculars is shown by the case of Baghdad, where Hebrew *ḏ* ד and *ṯ* ת are rendered asymmetrically as *d* and *ṯ* against the symmetrical preservation of *ḏāl* and *ṯāʾ* in Jewish (and Muslim) Baghdadi Arabic. In Baghdad only the Christians have shifted the interdentals to stops.

[16] Such as the appearance of the Aramaic abstract ending *-uṯā* as *-ūt*, about which Nöldeke, *Neue Beiträge zur semitischen Sprachwissenschaft* (Strassburg 1910) 33 n.3 was uneasy.

morphology; he proposed[17] analogy with the pattern *yafʿulu*, a pattern often used for proper names.[18] *yahūd(u)* = *yafʿulu* implies a synchronic root *hwd*. Another possibility would be incorporation into the pattern *faʿūlu(n)*, as e.g. *ṯamūdu(n)*, in which case the implied root would be *yhd*. Hesitation as to root and pattern would have contributed to the uncertainty about the declension of *yahūdu(n)* mentioned above n.1.

REMARK: One of the Aramaic dialects which tends not to tolerate initial *y(ə)-* is Mandaic. In this language the shift **y(ə)- > (ʾ)i/e-* is the regular treatment,[19] but it so happens that two of the three relevant words in Mandaic begin with *ya-*, viz. **iahud(a)** and **iahuṭaiia**. The third Mandaic form, **hudaiia**, is treated below §vi. However, one will not be tempted to find in Mandaic the origin of the *a* vowel in the Arabic *yahūd*.

A brief discussion is necessary of these two Mandaic forms, neither of which corresponds to one's expectations from a dialect of Aramaic. **iahud(a)** can be dispensed with quickly. Despite the gloss "Judaea, Jewry" in Drower & Macuch,[20] **iahud**, as far as I see, is of geographical application only, meaning "Judaea". The word is typical of the **draša ḏ-iahia** = *Johannesbuch*, where it often appears in parallelism with "Jerusalem". **iahuda** is the Biblical Judah, son of Jacob. On semantic grounds, therefore, Mandaic **iahud(a)** is not a natural source for the Arabic *yahūd*, which refers to a people, not to a place or a person. The initial **ia-** is admittedly unexpected; perhaps it arose under the influence of the following item.

The normal word for "Jews" in classical Mandaic, from the earliest texts onwards,[21] is *yʾhwṭʾyyʾ* = **iahuṭaiia** with an *a* vowel in the first syllable. This Mandaic word, which is clearly not genetically related to other Aramaic forms for "Jews" and which contravenes the normal phonology of the language, is itself in need of explanation. That explanation is that **iahuṭaiia** is not an inherited Aramaic word but a malicious polemical modification of the expected form playing on alliterative associations with *yʾhṭʾ* "abortion, miscarriage" and $\sqrt{hṭʾ}$ "sin":[22]

[17] *Loc. cit. supra* n.7.

[18] Examples in J. Barth, *Die Nominalbildung in den semitischen Sprachen*² (Leipzig 1894) 227.

[19] Th. Nöldeke, *Mandäische Grammatik* (Halle 1875) §55; R. Macuch, *Handbook of Classical and Modern Mandaic* (Berlin 1965) §61a.

[20] E.S. Drower & R. Macuch, *A Mandaic Dictionary* (Oxford 1963) 184b. Regarding the distribution of the Mandaic words I am mostly dependent upon the information provided by this work.

[21] To the references in Drower & Macuch one may add e.g. M. Lidzbarski, *Das Johannesbuch der Mandäer* I (Giessen 1905) 131:7, 199 passim, 205:11; idem, *Mandäische Liturgien* (Berlin 1920) 121:7, 210/11 = *Johannesbuch* II (Giessen 1915) 124.

[22] Nöldeke, *Mandäische Grammatik* 43 n.2; Macuch, *Handbook* 429 n.71. Norberg's usual rendering was "Abortivi".

iahuṭaiia iahṭia unipṣia "Iudaei, abortus et excrementa";[23] **mitiqrin iahuṭaiia ḏ-hṭun** "Sie werden Juden genannt, weil sie gesündigt haben".[24] This manufactured curiosity has clearly nothing to do with Arabic *yahūd*.

V: *ʾi-*

It was mentioned above that certain varieties of Aramaic are sensitive to initial consonantal *y(ə)-* and prefer to avoid it. One of the ways by which this was achieved was to make the semi-vowel *y* fully vocalic: **y(ə)-* > *i-*, a combination which would in the nature of things often be pronounced and written *ʾi-*. This shift from non-syllabic *y* to syllabic *i* (> *ʾi*), which is frequent in many languages, is characteristic of eastern Aramaic, being quite regular in Mandaic and Syriac,[25] less so in Jewish Babylonian Aramaic,[26] and it stands to reason that this was also the norm in other dialects of Aramaic of which we have no knowledge.[27] As a result of this development יְהוּדָיָא *y(ə)huḏāyā* "Jew" appears in Syriac as ܝܗܘܕܝܐ *ihuḏāyā*, frequently written with initial *ālaph* ܐܝܗܘܕܝܐ *ʾihuḏāyā*.[28]

23 Nöldeke, *Mandäische Grammatik* 320 = M. Lidzbarski, *Ginzā. Der Schatz, oder das grosse Buch der Mandäer* (Göttingen – Leipzig 1925) 232: "die Juden, die Abortūs und Abgänge".

24 Lidzbarski, *Ginzā* 43 with n.2 and a similar passage 225:20.

25 For Mandaic see n.19; for Syriac, Th. Nöldeke, *Kurzgefasste syrische Grammatik*² (Leipzig 1898) §40C; R. Duval, *Traité de langue syriaque* (Paris 1881) §106.Ia. It so happens that in our word the stage with consonantal *y-* is still reflected in the Nestorian tradition when in close juncture with the particles *b-*, *d-*, *w-*, *l-*. Before *-yhuḏāyā* these particles are in Nestorian Syriac vocalized *ba-*, *da-*, *wa-*, *la-* as before vowelless consonants, ܠܝܗܘܕܝܐ etc., for which feature see Nöldeke, *Syrische Grammatik* §43 end; Duval, *Traité* 276; Barhebraeus trans. A. Moberg, *Buch der Strahlen. Die grössere Grammatik des Barhebräus* I (Leipzig 1913) 90. According to some, this treatment extends to other words of the same type; see R. Payne-Smith, *Thesaurus Syriacus* I (Oxford 1879) 1569a.

26 Y. Kara, *Babylonian Aramaic in the Yemenite Manuscripts of the Talmud* (Jerusalem 1983) 129; S. Morag, *Babylonian Aramaic. The Yemenite Tradition* (Jerusalem 1988) 199 n.1 [both Hebrew]. This feature is also rather common in the Babylonian tradition of Hebrew, as opposed to the Tiberian where it is quite marginal; see respectively I. Yeivin, *The Hebrew Language Tradition as Reflected in the Babylonian Vocalization* (Jerusalem 1985) I 269/70 [Hebrew]; G. Bergsträsser, *Hebräische Grammatik* I (Leipzig 1918) §17s (with t). In the western Aramaic dialects the same phonological feature is known, but is there far more sporadic than in the east; see the examples and literature in S.E. Fassberg, *A Grammar of the Palestinian Targum Fragments from the Cairo Genizah* (Atlanta 1991) 69 §19f, 98/9.

27 That this feature was commoner in spoken than in literary Aramaic is shown by the statement of Barhebraeus that initial *ālaph* is pronounced in such cases whether it is written or not; see Barhebraeus trans. Moberg, *Buch der Strahlen* II (Leipzig 1907) 27. The situation in western Aramaic is likely to have been similar, as concluded from Jerome's transcriptions by Brockelmann, *Grundriss* I 188.

28 For the sake of a fuller picture of the variation of our word in Syriac one should

This pronunciation appears not to be reflected in the mainstream of literary Arabic. The form with initial *ʾi-*, however, may possibly have reached the southern part of the Arabian peninsula, for this is perhaps what lies behind the spelling *ʾyhd* "Jews" recorded in late Sabaean.[29] This is also found on the other side of the Red Sea in Ethiopia, where in Geʿez "Jews" are referred to as *ʾayhud*. Like the Arabic *yahūd*, the Geʿez word does not reflect directly the vocalization of its north Semitic source but has been repatterned according to south Semitic morphology. In this case the borrowed *ʾyhd* < Aramaic *ʾihud-* with initial *ālaph* was matched with the (ESA and ?) Geʿez broken plural patterrn *ʾafʿul* to produce the morphologically more transparent *ʾayhud*. This interpretation receives some support from the fact that in Geʿez *ʾayhud* is morphologically isolated as a *pluralis tantum* with no corresponding singular; as in Arabic, the singular is provided by the *nisba*-form.[30]

VI: *hūd*

The typically Quranic word *hūd* "Jews" presented etymological difficulties to Muslim scholarship and its various oddities have never, as far as I know, been given a convincing explanation. As a rule, those Muslim philologists who favoured a native Arabic etymology derived *hūd* from the verb *hāda, yahūdu (hwd)* "to repent, return", "to be calm" and declared it to be the plural of the participle *hāʾid*. There are problems with both the lexicographical and morphological aspects of this view. Firstly, the development from "repent, return" > "Jews" may not be impossible,

mention that beside the usual *(ʾ)ihuḏāyā* there is another form without *h: yuḏāyā*; Nöldeke, *Syrische Grammatik* §38 end. For etymological reasons the *he* is usually preserved in writing and marked for deletion, but the phonetic spelling without *he* ܝܘܕܝܐ is not rare; it is, e.g., the only form used in the *Book of the Himyarites* and also occurs in other Aramaic dialects.

29 W. Müller *apud* W. Leslau, *Comparative Dictionary of Geʿez* (Wiesbaden 1987) 626b. A variety of forms reached South Arabia, as shown by the loan *rb-yhd, rb-h(w)d* "Lord of the Jews"; references in A.F.L. Beeston *et al.*, *Sabaic Dictionary* (Louvain – Beirut 1982) 114.

30 I gratefully acknowledge some correspondence on this subject with Prof. W.W. Müller, who kindly provided details on South Arabian *ʾyhd*. This word occurs three times in the determinate state in an unpublished late Sabaean inscription dealing with the assignment to the Jews of certain land for burial purposes. Prof. Müller, however, is not in agreement with the development tentatively put forward here. In his opinion, which may well be correct, the Sabaean word is simply a regular ESA plural of an as yet unattested *nisba* singular, and is to be vocalized as *ʾayhūd(ān)* > Geʿez *ʾayhud*. The vocalization is suggested on the basis of Yemenite Arabic plurals of the pattern *afʿūl* used as tribal names; cf. his note *apud* A.F.L. Beeston, *Sabaic Grammar* (Manchester 1984) 26 n. 44. In support of this interpretation one could add that Yemenite *afʿūl* also functions as the plural of *nisba* singulars; see S.D. Goitein, *Le Muséon* 73 (1960) 379.

but it is not immediately persuasive. According to analogy and experience, the required meaning of *hāda*, viz. "to be(come) Jewish", is in all probability derived from the primary noun "Jews", not the other way round;[31] a deverbal noun such as "Jews" is hardly to be expected. Secondly, *fuʿl* as the plural of *fāʿil* is scarcely credible; this grammatical relationship is indeed attested, but it is rare and restricted to one semantic category, viz. the characteristics of various types of beasts, relating particularly to the reproductive potential of she-camels.[32] Moreover, the posited singular **hāʾid* "Jew" does not exist in Arabic and surely never did. According to the relationship sg. *aḥmar* pl. *ḥumr* another possible singular for *hūd* would be **ahwad*, but this too is non-existent.[33]

If the derivation from *hwd* is not feasible, one might somehow think of deriving the word from the longer and semantically more suitable *yahūd*. Some of the Arab philologists, e.g. al-Farrāʾ (d. 207 A.H. = 822), indeed proposed regarding *hūd* as having developed by elision (*ḥaḏf*) from *yahūd*.[34] It need only be said that no phonological process is known in Arabic which would convincingly account for the putative development *yahūd* > *hūd*; the assumption of such a process would be purely *ad hoc* and without analogy.

A few other points in connection with *hūd* deserve notice. Unlike *yahūd*, of which the singular is *yahūdīy*, there is (except as an artefact occasionally posited by the lexicographers) no **hūdīy*; the word does not possess a singular. In fact, *hūd* "Jews"[35] is very isolated indeed in classical Arabic: it occurs only three times in the Quran (2:111, 135, 140),[36] always in the expression *kwn hūdan aw naṣārā*, "to be Jews or Christians", and one has the impression that it has been obsolete in the language ever since.[37] The normal way of referring to "Jews" in Arabic, in the Quran and

31 Horovitz, *Koranische Untersuchungen* 153.

32 Cf. e.g. G.H.A. Ewald, *Grammatica critica linguae arabicae* I (Leipzig 1831) 191; Barth, *Nominalbildung* 455. *ḥāʾik* pl. *ḥūk* adduced as an example in some sources is an error for *ḥāʾil* pl. *ḥūl*.

33 Horovitz, *Koranische Untersuchungen* 154.

34 Al-Farrāʾ, *maʿānī al-qurʾān*, ed. A.Y. Najātī & M.A. al-Najjār I (Cairo 1955) 73 *ad* Q2:111, often quoted in later sources.

35 I do not deal here with any connection, real or otherwise, between our word and the name of the Arabian prophet Hūd, the hero of the eponymous Quranic sūra 11. One could also mention the personal name *hūd* and the tribal group *hūḏ*.

36 That is in the ʿUṯmānic recension. In Ubayy's version of Q2:111, and possibly in other versions as well, the reading was *yahūdīyan*; see G. Bergsträsser & O. Pretzl, *Geschichte des Qorāns von Th. Nöldeke* III (Leipzig 1938) 83; A. Jeffery, *Materials for the History of the Text of the Qurʾān* (Leiden 1937) 27, 119.

37 Wehr's *Dictionary* lists *al-hūd* "the Jews, the Jewry" (sic), but I do not know in what context this occurs. I think it is generally true to say that from classical Arabic onwards *hūd*

elsewhere, then as now, is as *yahūd*.[38] The Quranic verb *hāda* "to be Jewish" strikes one no less as being a linguistic fossil. This denominative verb appears eleven times in scripture, only in the perfect, and only in the set phrase *allaḏīna hādū* "those who are Jews". In extra-Quranic Arabic it appears not to be productive at all.

It does not seem to me that anything yet suggested can provide a satisfactory etymology for *hūd*, or explain its peculiarly arrested development. The natural way out of these difficulties is to identify *hūd* as a primary substantive, and the analogy of *yahūd* would suggest that *hūd* also be a substantive of non-Arabic, viz. Aramaic, origin. An Aramaic solution to the problem, in my opinion, is in fact quite possible.

It has been mentioned that many Aramaic dialects were sensitive to initial *y(ə)-* and shifted this combination to the corresponding vowel *(ʾ)i-*. Another possible treatment, as we shall now see, was to elide initial *y(ə)-* altogether.

The shift of *y(ə)-* > *(ʾ)i-* contributed significantly to the merger on a rather wide scale of roots I*y* and Iʾ, thus that already in classical Syriac these two root categories begin to share a common conjugation, Iʾ becoming absorbed within I*y*.[38] In the course of time the similarity between the two conjugations grew, particularly at those points where *y* and ʾ were vowelless in initial position. In this position both original consonants came to partake of a similar fate. Within the history of Aramaic vowelless initial ʾ - (which in Syriac > *ʾe/a-*) and, following it, initial *y-* (Syriac > *ʾi-*) become increasingly unstable and prone to elision. In Syriac and some other older dialects aphaeresis of vowelless initial ʾ- is a common, but not yet regular, feature.[40] By the time we reach the modern dialects, however, not only has this become a regular phonological process, but has been extended to include vowelless initial *y-* also.[41] This means e.g. that whereas in the present stem, based upon **qāṭil*, forms of I*y* and Iʾ roots will generally be separate, in the preterite, based upon **qṭil-* with vowelless *q-*, they will often be identical (not only with each other, but also with

has not been employed in ordinary Arabic prose. For its occurrences in Sabaean *v. supra* n.29.

[38] These matters were clearly pointed out long ago by H.L. Fleischer in the *Literaturblatt* section no.12, 20 March 1841, col.171 of Fürst's *Der Orient* 2 (1841) = *Kleinere Schriften* II (Leipzig 1888) 135.

[39] Nöldeke, *Syrische Grammatik* §§174E–F, 175A; less clearly Duval, *Traité* §§203, 205, 207.

[40] Nöldeke, *Syrische Grammatik* §32; Duval, *Traité* §107a; Brockelmann, *Grundriss* I 110.

[41] Suffice it here to refer to Th. Nöldeke, *Grammatik der neusyrischen Sprache am Urmia-See und in Kurdistan* (Leipzig 1868) 55.

derivatives of II*y*). This identity of treatment may be illustrated by the Christian Urmi forms (Soviet orthography) in the following table:

	I*y*		Iʾ		II*y*
Root	*ytb* "sit"		*ʾmr* "say"		*qym* "stand"
Present (subjunctive)	*yətiv*		*əmir*		*qəyim*
Preterite	*tivli*	=	*mirri*	=	*qimli*
	**ytib-li*		**ʾmir-li*		**qim-li*

Now there exists a very great deal of variation in the manner, distribution and extent of these developments, but the principle is found in one form or another in all known dialects of eastern Neo-Aramaic and is so thoroughly rooted in them that there is no doubt that the elision of vowelless initial *y*- and ʾ- in Aramaic must be very old indeed. That the shift *y*C- > *ø*C- is not well attested from earlier recorded stages of the language is due simply to the paucity of the sources, their predominantly literary nature and their orthographical conservatism. In the spoken language the phenomenon was surely very common.

In these circumstances it will be no surprise to discover that in most, and probably all,[42] modern dialects of Aramaic the word for "Jews" harks back to **hudāye*, i.e. < **yhudāye* with aphaeresis of initial *y*- in accordance with the principle just described:

Older Aramaic	*yhuḏāye*
Aradhin (Christian)	*huḏāye*
Ṭuroyo	*huḏoyo*
Zakho (Jewish)	*huzāye*
Hertevin (Christian)	*hudāye*
Kerend (Jewish)	*hulāe*

Such a form is also attested in Mandaic: **hudaiia**.[43]

I should like to offer the suggestion that an early colloquial Aramaic form of this type without initial *y*- provides a more plausible background to the Arabic *hūd* than the assumption that *hūd* arose autonomously within Arabic, whether from the root *hwd* (in any of its meanings) or as an unmotivated truncation of *yahūd*. In other words, I think there is good

[42] Some of the Christian dialects, e.g. Urmi, retain, possibly under the influence of classical Syriac, reflexes of the *ihud-, yud-* type, but most (all?) such dialects also have forms opening with *h*-. In the spoken language these are doubtless the normal forms; examples in H.J. Polotsky, *JSS* 6 (1961) 14 top.

[43] Drower & Macuch, *Mandaic Dictionary* 135a. It is apparently known only from post-classical Mandaic sources. Similar forms also occur in colloquial Mandaic (in addition to those mentioned above §iv).

reason to subscribe in this matter to the succinct judgment of Jawālīqī: *al-hūd: al-yahūdu, aʿǧamīyun muʿarrab.*[44] The assumption of a direct Aramaic loan would also tally quite well with the marginality of the word in classical Arabic. One could plausibly argue that the word "Jews" entered Arabic, doubtless at different places and at different times, as a doublet from different Aramaic dialects, one form with initial *y*-, the other with initial *h*-. For some time both forms would have existed side by side. In the course of time, however, the *y*- form gained the upper hand and the *h*- form fell into desuetude. This stage, it seems, is reflected in the text of the Quran, where *yahūd* is the normal word and *hūd* survives only vestigially in one fossilized locution. In subsequent Arabic *hūd* disappeared altogether, ousted by, or rather absorbed into, the rival member of the doublet. The process envisaged here is perfectly normal in linguistic history.[45]

VII: MODERN ARABIC DIALECTS

Three Aramaic types of the word for "Jews" have been mentioned in the preceding discussion and they may be presented schematically (and with a little over-simplification) as *yhuḏāyā*, *ihuḏāyā* and *huḏāyā*, viz. (i) *y*-forms, (ii) *i*-forms and (iii) *h*-forms. Of these only (i) and (iii) occur in classical Arabic, as *yahūd* and *hūd* respectively. In colloquial Arabic dialects, however, we quite probably have forms of type (ii) also. A few illustrations of these types in eastern Arabic follow.

(i) *yahūd* is the form that is continued in most modern dialects of Arabic. This is a very common word and requires no particular exemplification. It is sometimes pronounced with a lengthened first syllable: *yāhūd*.[46] It also appears with a reduced *a* vowel, *yəhūd*,[47] and when in such cases the reduced vowel is elided > *yhūd*, the result is not always neatly distinguishable, particularly in non-differential dialects,[48] from (ii).

[44] *muʿarrab* ed. ʿAbd al-Raḥīm 638 = ed. Šākir 350.

[45] See e.g. H. Paul, *Prinzipien der Sprachgeschichte*[5] (Tübingen 1920) §279 and for English J.B. Greenough & G.L. Kittredge, *Words and their Ways in English Speech* (London 1914) 206ff. (lexical fossils); M. Serjeantson, *A History of Foreign Words in English* (London 1935) 5 (loanwords as doublets).

[46] H. Grotzfeld, *Laut- und Formenlehre des Damaszenisch-Arabischen* (Wiesbaden 1964) §107c; A. Bloch & H. Grotzfeld, *Damaszenisch-arabische Texte* (Wiesbaden 1964) 78:9.

[47] E.g. O. Jastrow, *Der arabische Dialekt der Juden von ʿAqra und Arbīl* (Wiesbaden 1990) 430.

[48] Non-differential dialects are those in which all three short vowels *a, i, u* are elided in open unstressed syllables. In differential dialects *a* is preserved in this position and elision affects only *i* and *u*.

(ii) We also find forms lacking the *a* vowel of the first syllable, opening either with vocalic *i*- or, what amounts to the same thing, with vowelless consonantal *y*-. The forms *ihūd* ~ *yhūd* present a delicate problem of interpretation. In basically differential dialects such as Aleppo or Damascus, where there is no compelling reason for the elision of *a*, we expect, and we find, unaltered reflexes of *yahūd*.[49] But we also find there forms opening with *i*- ~ vowelless *y*-: Aleppo *īhūd* "Juifs", *līhūd* "les Juifs";[50] Damascus *īhūdi msāfer* "travelling Jew" = the name of a dish made from eggplants and rice.[51] In other words, as in classical Arabic, we are again in the presence of a doublet. It is natural (though perhaps not strictly necessary) to suppose that here too the forms are different in shape precisely because they are different in origin. Rather than derive *ihūd* ~ *yhūd* by irregular development from classical *yahūd*, it is tempting to think that at least some such cases are reflexes of Aramaic types (i) and/or (ii) in which there was no *a* vowel to elide.

(iii) Colloquial Arabic examples of the *hūd* type are rather rarer. The form was noted, alternating as a doublet with the usual *yahūd*, in some Galilean Druze dialects by H. Blanc: *hūd* "Jews", *bint hudiyyi* "a Jewish girl".[52] That this form should be an inner-Arabic continuation of the Quranic *hūd* is intrinsically unlikely; that Arabic word was already an obsolete relic by the middle of the 1st millennium. I prefer to attribute the Galilean *hūd* to the Aramaic substrate of Palestinian Arabic, a supposition somewhat strengthened by the fact that a type (iii) form is to this day in use in the western Aramaic vernacular of Maᶜlūla, viz. **huḏāy(ā)* > *ūḏay*.[53]

[49] Also in metaphorical senses: *yähūdi* "Geizkragen" in O. Jastrow & S. Kazzarah, *ZAL* 5 (1980) 98 n.10 (Aleppo).

[50] A. Barthélemy, *Dictionnaire Arabe-Français. Dialectes de Syrie: Alep, Damas, Liban, Jérusalem* (Paris 1935 – 1969) 918, who gives only this form (thus, with long *ī*): *dīn līhūdi* "religiosité d'un juif" 291.

[51] J. Malinjoud, *JA* 204 (1924) 287 ult. From I. Hasson I learn that Jewish Damascene has *ihūdi* = *yhūdi* as against Muslim *yahūdi*; accordingly the form in Malinjoud's text will reflect Jewish pronunciation.

[52] H. Blanc, *Studies in North Palestinian Arabic* (Jerusalem 1953) 33, 130 n.83. Further afield and more problematical is Maltese *Lhud*.

[53] A. Spitaler, *Grammatik des neuaramäischen Dialekts von Maᶜlūla (Antilibanon)* (Leipzig 1938) 91; W. Arnold, *Das Neuwestaramäische V. Grammatik* (Wiesbaden 1990) 374.

VIII: CONCLUSION

The names for "Jew(s)" in classical Arabic, viz. *yahūdīy*, *yahūd* and *hūd*, present a number of formal difficulties which are here studied in the light of the Aramaic etymons of the three words. Since יְהוּד means "Judaea" rather than "Jews" it will not be the direct source of Arabic *yahūd*. The starting point was rather the *nisba*-form יהודיא > *y(a)hūdīy*, from which *yahūd* was derived by backformation (§ii). In Hebrew and Aramaic there is a clear relationship between יהודה "Judah, Judaea" and its *nisba*- form יהודי(א) "Jew"; the one is derived from the other. In Arabic, however, the two are not parallel, for the former is *yahūḏā* with *ḏāl* ذ while the latter is *yahūdīy* with *dāl* . This is because *yahūḏā* is a learned form, a *mot savant* with a technical meaning, unlike the popular loan *yahūdīy*, which was in everyday use among the unlettered. These two forms reached Arabic through different channels; the one derives from literary sources preserving the interdental spirant, the other from a colloquial Aramaic dialect which, like certain Neo-Aramaic dialects spoken today, no longer observed the *bgdkpt* rule and had plosives only (§iii). The *a* vowel in the initial syllable of *yahūd(īy)*, on the other hand, is not of Aramaic but of Arabic origin (§iv). Instead of vowelless initial *y-* some old Aramaic dialects show *i-* > *ʾi-*, i.e. *yhuḏāyā* > *ʾihuḏāyā*. Forms of this kind opening with a glottal stop do not appear in classical Arabic, but quite conceivably did reach the south Semitic world, viz. southern Arabia and Ethiopia (§v). The word for "Jews" was borrowed into Arabic (at least) twice. *hūd* and *yahūd* form a doublet in classical Arabic, each being loaned from different Aramaic dialects. *hūd* is not to be derived from the root *hwd*, nor to be seen as an irregular abridgement of *yahūd*; it is derived from an Aramaic dialect in which *yhud-* > *øhud-* was a regular phonological process, as it is in many Neo-Aramaic dialects of today. *hūd* survived as an archaism in the Quran, but in later Arabic disappeared (§vi). Reflexes of both *yahūd* and, more rarely, of *hūd* occur in modern Arabic dialects. This dialectal *hūd* is an Aramaic substrate feature, not a continuation of the Quranic form. In modern Arabic dialects we also find forms of the shape *yhūd* ~ *ihūd*, reminiscent of Aramaic forms beginning with *y-* ~ *(ʾ)i-*; many of these too may be attributed to the Aramaic substrate of eastern colloquial Arabic (§vii).

The philological minutiae presented here may not individually and of themselves be of great significance. The picture that cumulatively they depict, however, is by no means without interest. We have seen that in order to express the notion "Jew(s)" the Arabs used, and still use, a family of loanwords of heterogeneous yet related origin. These words did not reach the Arabic language from a single source, nor, in all probability, were they adopted at the same time; they were borrowed from Aramaic via various routes and at different periods. Nor, having reached Arabia, did they develop in the same way; according to time and place the number and identity of the members of the family have differed. If it is true that language and culture, Wörter und Sachen, proceed hand in hand and illumine one the other, the close study of the linguistic details may well be able to tell us something about the way in which knowledge of Jews and Judaism spread in the Arabian peninsula. Reflected in the composite Arabic nomenclature for "Jews" is the complexity of the contact between the north and south Semitic worlds, of which the major manifestations are the linguistic meeting of Aramaic and Arabic and the cultural encounter of Judaism with Islam.

DID MUḤAMMAD CONCLUDE TREATIES WITH THE JEWISH TRIBES NAḌĪR, QURAYẒA AND QAYNUQĀʿ?*

MICHAEL LECKER

ABSTRACT: This article examines an episode in the diplomatic history of the Prophet Muḥammad, namely the non-belligerency treaties he is said to have concluded after the Hijra with the main Jewish tribes of Medina, the Naḍīr, Qurayẓa and Qaynuqāʿ. I argue that the reports on these treaties, their obvious weaknesses notwithstanding, are on the whole reliable. The treaties were based on a reciprocal undertaking of each party not to cause harm to the other party. This obligation characterized the first stage of Muḥammad's relationship with the Jews of Medina. Due to contradicting claims, it seems impossible to determine the precise terms of the treaties beyond the essential security clause.

For obvious reasons, the encounter between the Prophet Muḥammad and the Jewish tribes of Medina continues to attract scholarly attention. On the popular level it is still alive in the minds of contemporary Muslims some of whom are inspired by Muḥammad's brilliant military successes.

Two decades ago, Moshe Gil published in this journal an article which looked into the position of the Jews according to the most important document preserved from the time of Muḥammad, namely the *ʿAhd al-ʾUmma* or "The Constitution of Medina".[1] In the following pages, some of the relevant evidence is scrutinized, much in the footsteps of Professor Gil's pioneering study.[2]

1. Most detailed and important is a report (which belongs to the type of *dalāʾil al-nubuwwa* or "proofs of Muḥammad's prophethood") by Abū

* I am indebted to the editors of this volume, Professors David Wasserstein and Uri Rubin, for commenting on an earlier draft of this paper.

1 M. Gil, "The constitution of Medina: a reconsideration", in *IOS* 4 (1974), 44–66.

2 The sources quoted below are often late, because few early sources survived; quotations from lost sources partially make up for the loss; cf. M. Lecker, "The death of the Prophet Muḥammad's father: did Wāqidī invent some of the evidence? in *ZDMG* 145 (1995), 9–27, at 16–20.

ʿAlī al-Faḍl b. al-Ḥasan al-Ṭabrisī (d. ca. 550/1155).[3] He says that the Jews of the Qurayẓa, Naḍīr and Qaynuqāʿ (i.e., their leaders) went to Muḥammad. Unwilling to embrace Islam, they proposed a truce (*hudna*), the provisions of which were as follows: they would neither take Muḥammad's side nor act against him; and, they would not provide assistance to anyone against him. For his part, Muḥammad would not attack any of them or their friends. This truce was to remain in force until the Jews saw what evolved between Muḥammad and his tribe (i.e., the Qurayš).[4] The proposed provisions of this temporary agreement do not exceed a reciprocal *ʾamān* or guarantee of security. However, the following passages in Ṭabrisī's report which purport to relate the actual contents of the treaty (or treaties) are problematic because of the unusual detail they include on the Jews' undertaking not to harm Muḥammad or his Companions, and because they include what appears to be an uncommon sanctions clause. The treaty with the Jews reportedly stipulated that they would not aid an enemy against Muḥammad or his Companions in speech, action, or by providing him with weapons or horses. Neither secretly nor openly, at night or in daylight were the Jews to give aid to the enemies of the Prophet. God is witness to their fulfilment of the treaty. If they fail to carry out the terms of the agreement, Muḥammad would be at liberty to kill them, enslave their women and children, and take their property. Muḥammad wrote separate documents addressed to each tribe (*wa-kataba li-kull qabīla minhum kitāban ʿalā ḥida*). Ḥuyayy b. Aḫṭab signed on behalf of the Naḍīr,[5] Kaʿb b. Asad signed for the Qurayẓa, and Muḫayrīq signed for the Qaynuqāʿ.

[3] C. Brockelmann, *Geschichte der arabischen Litteratur, Supplementbände*, Leiden 1937–42, I, 708–709; Gil, "Constitution", 59, n. 108=Ṭabrisī, *ʾIʿlām al-warā*, Beirut 1985, 99–100 (=45–46 of the lithograph, [Tehran] 1312 AH, used by Gil), quoting ʿAlī b. Ibrāhīm b. Hāšim al-Qummī who fl. in the second half of the 3rd century AH and the first half of the 4th; M.M. Bar-Asher, *Studies in Early Imāmī-Shīʿī Qurʾān Exegesis (3rd–4th/9th–10th Centuries)* (in Hebrew), Ph.D. dissertation, Hebrew University of Jerusalem, 1981, 40–41; cf. F. Sezgin, *Geschichte des arabischen Schrifttums*, Leiden 1967ff., (=*GAS*), I, 45–46. Gil sums up this report in a footnote: "The Jews come to the Prophet requesting a *hudna* [=truce], then he wrote them a *kitāb*".

[4] The duration of Muḥammad's treaty with Hilāl b. ʿUwaymir al-Aslamī was stated in an expression which, according to M.J. Kister, ("The massacre of the Banū Qurayẓa: a re-examination of a tradition", in *JSAI*, 8 [1986], 61–96 [reprinted in *idem, Society and Religion from Jāhiliyya to Islam*, Aldershot: Variorum, 1990, no. VIII], 84, n. 83), is "slightly enigmatic": *ḥattā yarā wa-yurā*. Kister remarks that it is so vowelled in the text and renders, "until he would consider (the matter) and things would be considered". However, *ḥattā tarā wa-narā*, "until you and us reconsider our positions", seems to be a smoother reading. Cf. al-Balāḏurī, *Ansāb al-ʾašrāf*, IVb, ed. M. Schloessinger, Jerusalem 1938, 13:4: *kuffa ḥattā nanẓura wa-tanẓurū wa-narā wa-taraw*.

[5] At this point Ṭabrisī digresses to describe an alleged conversation between Ḥuyayy and his brothers, Ǧudayy and Abū Yāsir.

The mention of Ḥuyayy and Muḫayrīq as the respective signatories of the Naḍīr and Qaynuqāʿ is of special interest although for the time being it cannot be corroborated by other evidence. As to Kaʿb b. Asad, he is known from elsewhere as "the owner [i.e., signatory] of the treaty of the Qurayẓa which was breached in the Year of the Combined Forces" [i.e., the parties which fought against Muḥammad in the Battle of the Ditch].[6]

2. A report by al-Mawṣilī on the same topic belongs to the category of *ʾawāʾil*:[7]

> "The first treaty which the Messenger of God concluded with the Jews of Medina took place when he concluded a truce with the Naḍīr, Qurayẓa, and Qaynuqāʿ in Medina, stipulating that they refrain from supporting the pagans and help the Muslims. This was the first of his treaties" [i.e., with the Jews].[8]

3. The Prophet concluded a treaty (*ʿāhada*) with the Qaynuqāʿ which was identical to his treaty with the Qurayẓa (literally: "like the Banū Qurayẓa") and the Naḍīr, namely, that they would neither fight him nor assist (*yuẓāhirū*) his enemy against him.[9]

4. Three kinds of stances were adopted by different groups towards the Prophet after the Hijra. One group concluded a *muwādaʿa* or non-belligerency treaty with the Prophet, prescribing that they were neither to fight him nor rally (*yuʾallibū*) his enemies against him, i.e., that they would not support his enemy. This group was made up of the three Jewish tribes (*ṭawāʾif*), Qurayẓa, Naḍīr and Qaynuqāʿ. The second group included the Qurayš and others who fought against the Prophet and acted with hostility towards him (*wa-naṣabū lahu l-ʿadāwa*). The third group included those who left him unmolested (*tārakūhu*) and anticipated the outcome of his affair (*mā yaʾūlu ʾilayhi ʾamruhu*). The last-mentioned category included the bedouin tribes (*ṭawāʾif*). Some of them, e.g. the Ḫuzāʿa, desired his

[6] *Ṣāḥib ʿaqd banī Qurayẓa llaḏī nuqiḍa ʿāma l-ʾaḥzāb*; Ibn Hišām, *al-Sīra al-nabawiyya*, ed. al-Saqqā, al-Abyārī and Šalabī, Beirut 1391/1971 (reprint), II, 162:4. Also al-Wāqidī, *al-Maġāzī*, ed. Marsden Jones, London 1966, II, 455:1: *wa-kāna Kaʿb ṣāḥiba ʿaqd banī Qurayẓa wa-ʿahdihā.*

[7] See *The Encyclopaedia of Islam*², s.v. (F. Rosenthal).

[8] Cf. Gil, "Constitution", 59, n. 108=al-Mawṣilī, *Ġāyat al-wasāʾil ʾilā maʿrifat al-ʾawāʾil*, MS Cambridge, Or. Qq 33, fol. 160: *ʾAwwalu ʿahdin ʿahidahu rasūlu llāhi (ṣ) li-yahūdi l-Madīna kāna lammā wādaʿa banī l-Naḍīr wa-banī Qurayẓa wa-banī Qaynuqāʿ bi-l-Madīna li-yakuffū ʿan maʿūnati l-mušrikīna wa-yakūnū ʿawnan li-l-muslimīna. Wa-kāna ḏālika ʾawwala ʿuhūdihi (ṣ).* The wording suggests the existence of other treaties with the Jews.

[9] Fāʾid b. al-Mubārak, *Mawrid al-ẓamʾān*, MS Kılıç Ali 766, I, 225b. Regarding the use of the verb *ẓāhara* cf., e.g., Quran, 33,26.

appearance at heart (*man kāna yuḥibbu ẓuhūrahu fī l-bāṭin*), while others, such as the Bakr, wanted the opposite. Yet others among them [i.e., among the people of the third category], the *munāfiqūn*, pretended to be on Muḥammad's side while in fact backing his enemy.[10]

5. The Prophet wrote a treaty of security (*kitāb ʾamn*) between himself and the three main Jewish tribes.[11]

6. An obligation of the Jews to provide military support for the Muslims (cf. no. 2 above) also appears in an eloquent speech ascribed to ʿAmr b. Suʿdā, a member of the Qurayẓa (or rather of their brother-tribe, the Hadl) who left the besieged fortress of the Qurayẓa unharmed on the eve of their surrender. ʿAmr accused his fellow-tribesmen of breaking their treaty with the Prophet, referring to their undertaking not to support his enemy, and to assist the Prophet against a force taking him by surprise (...*ʾallā tanṣurū ʿalayhi ʾaḥadan min ʿaduwwihi wa-ʾan tanṣurūhu mimman dahamahu*).[12] While the speech is no doubt apocryphal, the treaty of the Qurayẓa may have included a clause on succour against an attacking enemy. However, perhaps the treaty in question did not belong to the period immediately following the Prophet's Hijra.[13]

7. Muḥammad b. Kaʿb al-Quraẓī (d. ca. 118/736),[14] who was the son of a boy from the Qurayẓa spared from death because he had not reached the age of puberty, became a famous Muslim scholar and was interested, among other topics, in the history of the Arabian Jews. In the context of the Prophet's expedition against the Qaynuqāʿ he provides further details on the agreements between the Prophet and the Jews which he dates to the period immediately following the Hijra: When the Prophet arrived at Medina, he reports, all the Jews concluded with him a non-belligerency treaty (*wādaʿathu yahūdu kulluhā*).[15]

[10] ʿAlī al-Qārī, *Sayr al-bušrā fī l-siyar al-kubrā*, MS Süleymaniye 836, 80a.

[11] Ibn al-Qayyim al-Ǧawziyya, *Zād al-maʿād fī hady ḫayr al-ʿibād*, on the margin of Muḥammad b. ʿAbd al-Bāqī al-Zurqānī, *Šarḥ ʿalā l-mawāhib al-laduniyya*, Cairo 1329/1911, III, 388:10.

[12] Al-Wāqidī, *al-Maġāzī*, II, 503–504.

[13] Cf. Kister, "The massacre of the Banū Qurayẓa", 82–83.

[14] Al-Mizzī, *Tahḏīb al-kamāl fī ʾasmāʾ al-riǧāl*, ed. Baššār ʿAwwād Maʿrūf, Beirut, 1405/1985–1413/1992, XXVI, 340–48; *GAS*, I, 32.

[15] In Gil's translation: "...all the Jews met him..."; Gil, "Constitution", 58=al-Wāqidī, *al-Maġāzī*, I, 176. Cf. Abū Hilāl al-ʿAskarī, *al-ʾAwāʾil*, ed. Muḥammad al-Miṣrī and Walīd Qaṣṣāb, Damascus 1975, I, 188, quoting al-Wāqidī: [...] *wādaʿathu l-yahūd kulluhā*; al-Saraḫsī, *Šarḥ kitāb al-siyar al-kabīr li-Muḥammad b. al-Ḥasan al-Šaybānī*, V, ed. ʿAbd al-ʿAzīz Aḥmad, Cairo 1972, 1690, quoting Muḥammad b. Kaʿb: [...] *wādaʿathu yahūduhā kulluhā*.

8. Gil also cites the following report: "When the Prophet arrived (in Medina) he reached an agreement with the Qurayẓa and Naḍīr and the other Jews in Medina that some of them should help him if he were attacked, while maintaining their former ties (*maʿāqil*) with the ʾAws and Ḫazraǧ". However, in the source which he quotes there are two specifically separate records: one speaks of a treaty which confirmed the Jews' neutrality (*wa-kāna rasūlu llāhi [ṣ] ḥīna qadima ṣālaḥa Qurayẓa wa-l-Naḍīr wa-man bi-l-Madīna mina l-yahūd ʾallā yakūnū maʿahu wa-lā ʿalayhi*); and the other refers to their obligation to provide military aid while confirming their former agreements regarding the payment of blood-wit with the ʾAws and Ḫazraǧ (*wa-yuqālu: ṣālaḥahum ʿalā ʾan yanṣurūhu mimman dahamahu minhum, wa-yuqīmū ʿalā maʿāqilihimi l-ʾūlā llatī bayna l-ʾAws wa-l-Ḫazraǧ*).[16] Gil seems to have skipped the phrase *ʾallā yakūnū maʿahu wa-lā ʿalayhi*; "some of them" in his translation is presumably the rendering of the unsmooth preposition *minhum* in the phrase *mimman dahamahu minhum*. It could be understood to indicate that the Jews undertook to aid the Prophet against *any of them* who might attack him unexpectedly; but a variant version with *min ʿaduwwihi* instead of *minhum* probably includes the correct reading.[17]

9. Gil writes: "The *sīra ḥalabīya* says that the Prophet wrote a book between the *Muhājirūn* and the *Anṣār* in which he addressed (*dāʿā*) the Jews... and made a treaty with them, that he would not fight nor harm them, and they should not help his opponents; if he were attacked they should assist him. He also made an agreement with them establishing their rights of religion and property".[18] In fact, the text is not from the *Sīra Ḥalabiyya*, but from Aḥmad Zaynī Daḥlān's (d. 1304/1887) *al-Sīra al-nabawiyya wa-l-ʾāṯār al-muḥammadiyya* printed on the margin of the *Sīra Ḥalabiyya*.[19] Daḥlān's text includes the corrupt verb *wa-daʿā* (not *wa-dāʿā*) rendered by Gil as "he addressed". But this is obviously a scribal error; read: *wādaʿa*, "he concluded a treaty of non-belligerency".

There is more to be said about the text in point, which is transliterated

[16] Gil, "Constitution", 59=al-Wāqidī, *al-Maġāzī*, II, 454.

[17] Al-Zurqānī, *Šarḥ ʿalā l-mawāhib al-laduniyya*, I, 456:22: *wa-qīla: ʿalā an lā yakūnū maʿahu wa-lā ʿalayhi, wa-qīla: ʿalā ʾan yanṣurūhu mimman dahamahu min ʿaduwwihi*. See also al-Ṭabarī, *Taʾrīḫ al-rusul wa-l-mulūk*, ed. Muḥammad Abū l-Faḍl Ibrāhīm, Cairo 1380/1960–1387/1967, II, 479 [=I, 1359 of the Leiden edition]: *wa-kāna qad wādaʿa ḥīna qadima l-Madīna yahūdahā ʿalā ʾan lā yuʿīnū ʿalayhi ʾaḥadan wa-ʾannahu ʾin dahamahu bihā ʿaduwwun naṣarūhu*.

[18] Gil, "Constitution", 59.

[19] ʿAlī b. Burhān al-Dīn al-Ḥalabī, *ʾInsān al-ʿuyūn fī sīrat al-ʾamīn al-maʾmūn*, Cairo 1320 AH, I, 337:8.

below in three distinct passages:

> *wa-kataba rasūlu llāhi (ṣ) kitāban bayna l-muhāǧirīna wa-l-ʾanṣār wa-daʿā [=wādaʿa] fīhi yahūda / banī Qaynuqāʿ wa-banī Qurayẓa wa-banī l-Naḍīr wa-ṣālaḥahum ʿalā tarki l-ḥarb wa-l-ʾaḏā, an lā yuḥāribahum wa-lā yuʾḏiyahum wa-ʾan lā yuʿīnū ʿalayhi ʾaḥadan, wa-ʾannahu ʾin dahamahu bihā ʿaduww yanṣurūhu / wa-ʿāhadahum wa-ʾaqarrahum ʿalā dīnihim wa-ʾamwālihim* ("And the Messenger of God wrote a document between the Muhāǧirūn and the ʾAnṣār in which he concluded a treaty of non-belligerency with the Jews — / Banū Qaynuqāʿ, Banū Qurayẓa and Banū l-Naḍīr, and he made peace with them on the condition that they [i.e., both parties] would give up warlike activities and molestation, he would neither fight against them nor harm them and they would not aid anyone against him, and if an enemy suddenly attacked him in it [i.e., in Medina], they would assist him — / and he made a pact with them and permitted them to hold on to their religion and estates").

A comparison between Daḥlān's text and Ibn Isḥāq's introduction to the *ʿAhd al-ʾUmma* or "Constitution of Medina" shows that Daḥlān took the opening and concluding passages from Ibn Isḥāq:

> *wa-kataba rasūlu llāhi (ṣ) kitāban bayna l-muhāǧirīna wa-l-ʾanṣār wādaʿa fīhi yahūda / wa-ʿāhadahum wa-ʾaqarrahum ʿalā dīnihim wa-ʾamwālihim.*

The middle passage from *banī Qaynuqāʿ* to *yanṣurūhu* was incorporated by Daḥlān between the fragments taken from Ibn Isḥāq without any comment whatsoever.

The interpolation perhaps indicates that Daḥlān assumed the treaties with the main Jewish tribes and the *ʿAhd al-ʾUmma* to be two sides of the same coin. This — in my opinion wrong — assumption which is common in Islamicist research[20] should be discarded: the Naḍīr and Qurayẓa were not part of the *ʿAhd al-ʾUmma* and the same is probably true for the Qaynuqāʿ as well.[21]

[20] See, e.g., J. Wellhausen, *Medina vor dem Islam*, Berlin 1889 (*Skizzen und Vorarbeiten*, IV), 73–74; A.J. Wensinck, *Muhammad and the Jews of Medina*, trans. and ed. by W. Behn, Freiburg im Breisgau 1975 (=*Mohammed en de Joden te Medina*, Leiden 1908), 61–64, 68; W.M. Watt, *Muhammad at Medina*, Oxford 1956, 196–97; Gil, "Constitution", 58–60; R.B. Serjeant, "The *sunnah jāmiʿah* ...", in *BSOAS* 41 (1978), 1–42, *passim*. Cf., however, U. Rubin, "The 'Constitution of Medina': some notes", in *Studia Islamica* 62 (1985), 5–23, at 6, 9, 10; A. Goto, "The Constitution of Medina", in *Orient* (Report of the Society for Near Eastern Studies in Japan) 18 (1982), 1–17, at 12–13.

[21] I studied the question of the Jewish participation in this treaty in my Ph.D. dissertation

The passages discussed above reflect the unanimity of Muslim scholars regarding the first stage in Muḥammad's relations with the main Jewish tribes of Medina in the period following the Hijra. What do we make of this unanimity? According to Gil, the evidence does not reflect historical fact:

> It seems obvious that the position of the Muslim sources is that there was a treaty between the Jews and the Prophet; they took upon themselves certain obligations, which they broke; thus their later fate is explained as a *suum cuique*.[22]

Gil also argues that:

> It is therefore as an obvious alibi that Muslim sources have developed a tradition about a treaty between Muḥammad and the Jews, be it this document [= the *ʿAhd al-ʾUmma*] or a lost one, as presumed by some modern scholars.[23]

I wish to disagree with Gil and argue that his suspicions are unwarranted. While it is true that the chapters in Muḥammad's biography which deal with his struggle against the Jewish tribes of Medina are often apologetic, particularly when they deal with the circumstances in which hostilities broke out, on the whole the evidence about the conclusion of treaties shortly after the Hijra is reliable.

My suggestion is based on two main arguments, one of which is source-critical and the other historical. First, the weight of the evidence is overwhelming, the more so since the sources are sometimes at variance concerning the contents of the treaties beyond the reciprocal guarantee of security. Paradoxically, their differences strengthen their claim for historical veracity when they agree.[24] It can be said that the richness and complexity of Islamic historiography which speaks to us in many different voices simultaneously excludes the presumed plot.

Second, the assumption that there was no treaty with the Jews does not relate to the state of affairs in Medina shortly after the Hijra. At that time the main Jewish tribes were still the strongest element in its population

(*On the Prophet Muḥammad's activity in Medina* [in Hebrew], Hebrew University of Jerusalem, 1982) and hope to publish a revised version of my findings.

22 Cf. N.A. Stillman, *The Jews of Arab Lands*, Philadelphia 1979, 14–15, according to whom a treaty between the Qurayẓa leader Kaʿb b. Asad and Muḥammad "seems doubtful... and is probably the invention of later Muslim writers who wished to justify the harsh punishment that was meted out to the Qurayẓa".

23 Cf. Gil, "Constitution", 59, 65.

24 M. Lecker, "Wāqidī's account on the status of the Jews of Medina: a study of a combined report", in *JNES* 54 (1995), 15–32, at 28–29.

both militarily[25] and economically.[26] In order to establish himself, Muḥammad was bound to conclude a series of non-belligerency treaties with the Jewish tribes; it was not a matter of tolerance but of expediency. In sum, this short-lived honeymoon in Muḥammad's relations with the Jews of Medina, before he secured his position there, is a solid historical fact.

[25] Lecker, *op.cit.*; idem, *Muslims, Jews and Pagans: Studies on Early Islamic Medina*, Leiden 1995, 10–15.

[26] Cf. M.J. Kister, "The market of the Prophet", in *JESHO* 8 (1965), 272–76; reprinted, with additional notes, in idem, *Studies in Jāhiliyya and Early Islam*, London: Variorum Reprints, 1980, no. IX.

LES TROIS MENSONGES D'ABRAHAM DANS LA TRADITION INTERPRÉTANTE MUSULMANE
REPÈRES SUR LA NAISSANCE ET LE DÉVELOPPEMENT DE L'EXÉGÈSE EN ISLAM*

CLAUDE GILLIOT

I. INTRODUCTION. GENRE LITTÉRAIRE DU *TAFSĪR* ET CHRONOLOGIE

1. Dans une contribution récente, Norman Calder[1] a mis en valeur "l'organisation structurelle complexe" du genre littéraire qu'est le *tafsīr* en islam. Y interviennent, en effet, différentes "disciplines", des genres littéraires variés: l'histoire prophétique, les histoires des prophètes, la théologie, l'eschatologie, le droit, la mystique, sans oublier la grammaire et la sémantique. Cela dit, chaque commentateur, ou presque, a ses propres intérêts et ses objectifs particuliers, en fonction desquels il puise plus ou moins dans les domaines sus-cités. N. Calder a illustré ce point de vue notamment par l'exemple des "mensonges" d'Abraham surtout dans les commentaires de Ṭabarī et de Qurṭubī,[2] et il est parvenu ainsi à des résultats dignes d'intérêt, mais qui ne paraîtront pas toujours convaincants, faute d'avoir pris en considération la genèse de l'exégèse coranique, de sorte que des choix exégétiques anciens sont attribués à des auteurs plus

* Que notre collègue de l'I.R.E.M.A.M., Mustapha Khayati, soit remercié, qui a bien voulu examiner avec nous, tout en dégustant le nectar du divin roi Gambrinus/Cambrinus, le dieu-roi de la bière, maintes apories philologiques posées par les textes ici étudiés. Grâces soient rendues également à Andrew Rippin de l'Université de Calgary qui nous a envoyé, *recto tramite* du Canada, une copie de la contribution de Norman Calder mentionnée ci-après. Merci enfin à Pierre Larcher de notre département d'arabe de l'Université de Provence pour une discussion sur le *miʿrāḍ* en rhétorique.

1 N. Calder, 'Tafsīr' from Ṭabarī to Ibn Kathīr: problems in the description of a genre, illustrated with reference to the story of Abraham (*v.* nos réf. *infra*), p. 106, et le résumé de A. Rippin, 'Tafsīr', *in EI* IX (à paraître).

2 *Art. cit.*, p. 106–10, *passim*.

récents, alors que ceux-ci ne font que les citer ou, dans le meilleur des cas, les reprendre à leur compte.

2. En effet, la plupart des choix de ces deux exégètes, même s'ils sont significatifs, ne remontent pas à eux, et la seule description synchronique d'un commentaire coranique, ou même de plusieurs, sans que l'on s'inscrive dans une diachronie plus longue, ne permet guère la "description d'un genre" littéraire comme le *tafsīr*. C'est pourquoi nous voudrions reprendre ce dossier en allant plus avant dans le temps, non pas pour décrire ce genre, mais pour tenter d'établir des jalons chronologiques, doctrinaux et littéraires sur la genèse et le développement de l'exégèse coranique à travers l'exemple d'Abraham. Nous nous limiterons à la littérature interprétante des périodes classique et post-classique, le dernier auteur pris en considération étant al-Šawkānī (m. 1250/1832). Cependant les exégètes ou auteurs postérieurs au IVe/Xe siècle n'ont été consultés et utilisés ici que dans la mesure où ils sont des témoins précieux d'états plus anciens de l'exégèse. Il ne saurait être question dans le présent cadre de traiter de l'ensemble de l'herméneutique abrahamique en islam, car cela requérrait que l'on écrive un volume entier sur le sujet. C'est pourquoi l'on s'est imposé ici une limite thématique, celle du "*logion* des trois mensonges d'Abraham". Nous n'avons abordé d'autres aspects de la légende abrahamique dans le Coran et dans la tradition interprétante que dans la mesure où ils pouvaient être utiles à la présente recherche. Les résultats auxquels nous parviendrons pourront être confirmés ou affinés, voire infirmés, par l'étude d'autres cas d'exégèse.

3. Les deux lieux reçus du Coran à propos desquels les exégètes citent le logion prophétique des "trois mensonges" du patriarche — en islam, le prophète, intime de Dieu (*al-ḫalīl*) — sont deux de ceux où ce dernier est montré aux prises avec les idolâtres: 21, *Anbiyā'*, 62–63: "Ils dirent: 'Est-ce toi, Abraham, qui as fait cela à nos dieux?' Il dit: 'Non! c'est le plus grand d'entre eux. Interrogez-les donc s'ils peuvent parler'",[3] et 37, *Ṣaffāt*, 88–89: "Il jeta un regard sur les étoiles[4] et déclara: 'Je suis malade!'".[5]

4. Au fil du temps, l'exégèse de ces versets a été marquée et influencée par la doctrine musulmane de "l'impeccabilité des prophètes", avec ses différentes thèses; mais cela ne se fit qu'à l'issue d'un assez long

[3] Traduction de Denise Masson.

[4] Nous avons partout traduit *nuǧūm* par "étoiles", on pourrait aussi traduire par "astres". Les commentateurs et les lexicographes glosent, en général, *naǧm* par *kawkab*; *v.* Yaḥyā b. Sallām (al-Baṣrī, m. 200/815), *al-Taṣārīf*, p. 292.

[5] Traduction de Si Hamza Boubakeur. D. Masson a: "Il regarda attentivement les étoiles (*naẓara naẓratan fī l-nuǧūm*) [...] Oui je vais être malade (*innī saqīm*)".

cheminement théologique dont la littérature exégétique, que ce soit dans les commentaires coraniques, dans le *ḥadīṯ* ou encore en historiographie, conserve les vestiges. Même s'il est désormais quasiment impossible de retracer avec une exactitude sûre une chronologie des évolutions de la l'exégèse musulmane à ce sujet, on peut au moins tenter de poser quelques jalons. C'est ce que l'on voudrait faire ici pour l'un des "prophètes", dont il est dit qu'il a menti à trois reprises.[6] S'en tenir, il est vrai, à la seule chronologie n'offrirait qu'un intérêt réduit. Le voudrait-on d'ailleurs, on ne le pourrait, tant de facteurs divers ayant contribué à l'innocenter de ces fautes ou tout au moins à l'en excuser: motifs théologiques, raisons juridiques, recours aux grammairiens, voire à l'explication par une figure rhétorique.

5. La chronologie ici ne saurait s'entendre des seuls "auteurs" de "commentaires coraniques", en l'état où il nous sont parvenus, et qui déjà font problème pour les plus anciens d'entre eux. Il faut également tenir compte d'exégèses plus anciennes dont des commentaires plus récents sont les témoins, même si les chaînes de garants qu'ils contiennent ne sont pas toujours fiables. Cela dit, il peut être utile de ranger ici selon l'ordre chronologique, entendu de la date du décès de leurs auteurs, les commentaires coraniques que nous avons consultés pour le sujet qui nous occupe:

Commentaires coraniques ou assimilés:[7] sur 21, 62–63 et sur 37, 8

6. COMMENTAIRES "SUNNITES"

Muǧāhid b. Ǧabr al-Makkī (m. 104/722), *Tafsīr*, I, p. 412 (sur 21,63; Tab, XIX, p. 39, l. 3–6, sur 21,58); II, p. 542, sur 37,89, absent, mais sur 21,57, I, p. 411–12, présent; de même Tab, XIX, p. 37, sur 21,57;

Muqātil (m. 150/767), III, p. 85 (21,63); 611–612 (37,89);

Abū ʿUbayda (m. 207/822), *Maǧāz*, 121,63 et 37,89, non commentés;

[6] R. Firestone, *Journeys in Holy Lands*, p. 31–38, a regroupé une partie des matériaux exégétiques où figure le logion des trois mensonges.

[7] Par assimilés, nous entendons, les ouvrages qui s'intéressent à la grammaire et à la sémantique du texte coranique (*iʿrāb al-Qurʾān, maʿānī l-Qurʾān*, etc.). Ils ont été disposés ici chronologiquement, selon la date du décès des auteurs. Nous nous sommes très peu référé aux ouvrages du genre des *qiṣaṣ al-anbiyāʾ* qui ne comportent guère de chaînes de garants et qui, pour cette recherche du moins, sont largement an-historiques. A ce propos, N. Calder utilise (notamment p. 116 de sa contribution) les *Qiṣaṣ al-anbiyāʾ* d'Ibn Kaṯir, publiées à Beyrouth en un ouvrage à part, comme s'il s'agissait d'une œuvre indépendante. Ce texte a été en réalité extrait par l'éditeur du début de son *Histoire, al-Bidāya wa l-nihāya*, I, p. 68*sqq.*, *i. e.* à partir de la création d'Adam. Les noms complets des auteurs figurent dans nos références bibliographiques *infra*.

— Farrā᾽ (m. 207/822), *Maʿānī*, II, 206-207 (21,62-63); II, 388 (37,89; *miʿrāḍ*);

ʿAbd al-Razzāq (m. 211/827), *Tafsīr*, II, p. 153/II, p. 125, n°. 2534 (sur 37,89);

— Aḫfaš al-Awsaṭ (m. 215/830), *Maʿānī l-Qurʾān*: 21,63 et 37,89 non commentés;

Hūd (2ème moitié IIIe s.), III, p. 77 (21,62-63); III, p. 454 (37,89), ne revient pas sur le sujet;

Abū ʿAlī al-Ǧubbāʾī (m. 303/915), *in* Gimaret, p. 613 (21,63); p. 309, sur 76-79: “Lorsque la nuit l’enveloppa, il vit une étoile et dit: voici mon Seigneur...”: cela se passait avant qu’il n’eût atteint la plénitude de l’intelligence...;

— Ṭabarī (310/923), XVIII, p. 40-41 (21,63); XXIII, 70-72 (37,89);

— Zağğāğ (311/323), III, p. 396-97 (21, 63): il veut dire la très grande idole (*ʿaẓīm*); IV, p. 308-09 (37,89, mais il donne aussi la tradition sur les trois mensonges: 21,63 et avec Sarah);

Abū Muslim (M. b. Baḥr al-Iṣfahānī al-Muʿtazilī, m. 322/934), sur 37,68, interprétation *in* Ṭūṣī, VIII, p. 509 et Ṭabarsī, XXIII, p. 68: “Il les [les étoiles] examina en réfléchissant[8] et il en conclut qu’elles n’étaient pas des dieux, comme Dieu dit: ‘Lorsque la nuit l’enveloppa, il vit une étoile et il dit: c’est mon Seigneur’ (6,76). Cela se passa dans le court instant où il examinait” (ici d’après Ṭūsī). Les deux commentateurs chiites rejettent cette interprétation comme ne correspondant pas au contexte, car il est dit: “Il vint à son Seigneur avec un cœur sain” (37,84), c’est-à-dire: “sain par rapport à l’associationnisme”.

Abū l-Layṯ al-Samarqandī (m. 375/985), *Tafsīr*, II, p. 371 (21,63): “Il a dit cela par mode de moquerie (*ʿalā wağh al-istihzāʾ*) et non sous le mode du sérieux”; III, p. 117-18 (37,89);

— Māwardī (m. 450/1058), *Tafsīr*, III, 451-52 (21,63); V, 56 (37,89);

— Wāḥidī (m. 468/1076), *Wasīṭ*, III, p. 242 (21,63); 528 (37,89), cite Muqātil;

— Baġawī (m. 516/1122), III, 249 (21,63); IV, 30-31 (37,89);

— Zamaḫšarī (m. 538/1144), II, 577; III, 344;

Ibn ʿAṭiyya (m. 541/1147 ou 542), *Tafsīr*, IV, p. 87 (21,63); V, p. 478 (37,89);

— Rāzī (m. 606/1210), *Tafsīr*, XXII, p. 182-86 (21,56-63); XXVI, p. 146-49 (37,83-94);

— Qurṭubī (m. 671/1272), XI, 299-301 (21,63); XV, 93 (37,89); XXVI, 147-48;

[8] L’interprétation de *naẓara* comme “réfléchir” (*tafakkara, mufakkiran*) est attribuée à Ḥasan al-Baṣrī, mais dans une autre direction; *v. infra sub* § 13.

Ibn al-Naqīb (m. 698/1299), *Muqaddimat al-Tafsīr [fī ʿulūm al-bayān wa-l-maʿānī wa-l-badīʿ wa-iʿǧāz al-Qurʾān]*, p. 276 (*taʿrīḍ*, sur 21,62–63);
— Bayḍāwī (*ob. prob.* 716/1316–7 ou 708),[9] *Tafsīr*, II, p. 36, l. 4–7 (21,63); II, p. 158, l. 10–14;
— Nīsābūrī (Niẓām al-Dīn, *prob. med.* VIII/XIVe s.),[10] *Tafsīr*, XVII, p. 31–34; XXIII, p. 63–64;
Abū Ḥayyān al-Ġarnāṭī (m. 745/1344), *Tafsīr*, VI, p. 324–25 (21,63); VII, p. 366 (37,89);
Ibn Kaṯīr (m. 774/1373), V, p. 343–44; VII, p. 21;
— Suyūṭī (911/1505), IV, *Durr*, p. 321, l. 24–29 (21,63); V, p. 279, l. 5 *sqq.* (37,89); *Itqān*, *cap.* 54, II, p. 164, 165 (21,63: *taʿrīḍ*);
— Šawkānī (m. 1250/1832), *Tafsīr*, III, p. 414–16 (21,63); IV, p. 401–02 (37,88–89).

7. COMMENTAIRES CHIITES[11]

— Ayyāšī (*ob. ca.* 320/932), *Tafsīr*, versets non commentés, car la partie retrouvée et éditée de ce commentaire s'arrête à la sourate *al-Kahf*, tout au moins dans l'édition que nous en avons;
— Qummī (*viv. med.* IV/Xe s.), *Tafsīr*, II, p. 71–72 (21,51–63);
— Ṭūsī (m. 460/1067) (muʿtazilite), *Tafsīr*, VII, p. 259–60 (21,63); VIII, p. 509–11;
— Ṭabarsī (m. 548/1153) (muʿtazilite), *Tafsīr*, XVII, p. 38–40 (21,63); XXIII, p. 68–70 (37,89);
— Baḥrānī (m. 1107/1696), *al-Burhān fī tafsīr al-Qurʾān*, III, p. 62–65 (21,57–63); IV, p. 25 (37,89).

II. LES EXÉGÈSES ANCIENNES. L'INTÉGRATION DU TEXTE CORANIQUE DANS UN RÉCIT LÉGENDAIRE "CONTINU"

8. Deux exégètes anciens au moins, Muǧāhid b. Ǧabr (m. 104/722) et Muqātil b. Sulaymān (m. 150/767) ne paraissent pas être gênés par ces

[9] Pour ces dates, *v.* Gl. Gilliot, Textes arabes anciens..., *MIDEO* 21 (1993), n° 142, d'après J. van Ess, *in Die Welt des Orients* 9 (1978), p. 268.

[10] *V.* Guy Monnot, Islam: exégèse coranique, *in Annuaire EPHE*, Ve Section, *Résumés des conférences et travaux* LXXXIX (1980–81), p. 369–73.

[11] *V.* Guy Monnot, Islam: exégèse coranique, *in Annuaire EPHE*, Ve Section, *Résumés des conférences et travaux* XCI (1982–83), p. 309–18; Meir Michael Bar-Asher, *Studies in Early Imāmī-Šīʿī Qurʾān Exegesis* (3rd–4th/9th–10th centuries), traduction anglaise de la thèse DPh, Université de Jérusalem, janvier 1991, à paraître, p. 13–65 du manuscrit. Que Monsieur Bar-Asher soit remercié, qui a bien voulu nous envoyer le tapuscrit de sa traduction.

deux reparties d'Abraham qui pourront passer par la suite pour "mensongères", ce pour quoi on s'est évertué à montrer qu'elles ne le sont pas; ils n'emploient d'ailleurs pas ici le terme mensonge. Le premier déclare: "'Par Dieu, je jouerai un mauvais tour à vos idoles' (21,57). Il dit (*i.e.* Muğāhid): c'est ce que dit Abraham lorsque leurs gens lui demandèrent de le suivre pour aller à leur fête; mais [il refusa et][12] dit: 'Je suis malade' (37,89). Or l'un d'entre eux qui était resté en arrière avait entendu la menace qu'il avait proférée contre leurs idoles, et c'est lui qui déclara:[13] 'Nous avons entendu un jeune homme nommé Abraham parler [mal] d'elles' (21,60)."[14]

Ou encore, sur 21,63: "Non, dit-il, c'est le plus grand d'entre eux qui l'a fait": "Abraham posa la pioche avec laquelle il avait détruit leurs idoles appuyée contre la poitrine de la plus grande qu'il avait laissée [sans la briser]".[15]

9. Quand à Muqātil, il interprète 21,63 comme suit: "C'est-à-dire la plus importante des idoles qui a en main la pioche; elle s'est courroucée lorsque vous l'avez mise au même rang que les petites, et elle les a brisées".[16]

A propos de 37,89, il déclare:[17] "Ils s'en allaient à leur fête. 'Je suis malade', c'est-à-dire j'ai mal (*wağīʿ*); ils adoraient en effet les idoles". Suit une courte description des soixante-douze idoles et des rites de cette fête, puis de reprendre: "Lorsqu'ils partirent pour se rendre à leur fête, Abraham

[12] En Ṭabarī seulement.

[13] Dans le Coran, il est écrit, 21,60: "Ils dirent", ce qui devrait rendre impossible l'attribution de cette parole à un seul homme, mais les anciens exégètes ne faisaient pas toujours une distinction précise entre le texte coranique et leur propre récit.

[14] Muğāhid, *Tafsīr*, I, p. 411–12; Tab, XIX, p. 37, l. 17–20. Dans les deux cas, il s'agit du "*Tafsīr* de Warqāʾ": Warqāʾ b. ʿUmar al-Yaškurī al-Šaybānī al-Kufī (m. 160/776; *San*, VII, p. 419–22)/Ibn a. Nağīḥ (ʿAbd Allāh b. Yasār, m. 131/749 ou 132, qadarite de La Mecque; *v.* van Ess, *TG*, II, p. 643–47)/Muğāhid). Mais dans le *Tafsīr* dit de Muğahid, édité à part, la recension est de Ādam b. a. Iyās (m. 220/835; *v. infra* n. 191); en Ṭabarī, la recension est de Abū ʿĀṣim (al-Ḍaḥḥāk b. Maḫlad al-Nabīl al-Šaybānī al-Bāsrī, m. 212/827; *San*, IX, p. 480–85) et d'al-Ḥasan b. Mūsā al-Ašyab al-Baġdādī, m. à Rayy, rabīʿ I 209/juillet 824. Il fut cadi de Homs, de Mossoul et du Tabaristan; *San*, IX, p. 559–60: à Mossoul, des chrétiens ayant rassemblé de une importante somme pour réparer une église, il leur dit de la remettre à des témoins musulmans; une fois ceux-ci venus à la mosquée, il déclare qu'il a décidé qu'elle ne serait pas reconstruite, il rend l'argent aux chrétiens et les expulse. Tab, XIX, p. 37, l. 21, donne également une autre recension du même récit (*miṯlahu*): Ibn Ğurayğ (ʿAbd al-Malik b. ʿAbd al-ʿAzīz al-Qurašī al-Umawī [*mawlā*] al-Makkī, m. 150/767 ou 151, à Bagdad; *GAS*, I, p. 91; *San*, VI, p. 325–36)/Muğāhid.

[15] Muğāhid, I, p. 412, dans la même version du *Tafsīr*. La partie entre crochets est en Tab, XIX, p. 39, l. 3–5. Chacun des deux textes est respectivement dans les mêmes recensions du *Tafsīr* que pour la tradition précédente. Même texte, d'après Ibn Ğurayğ/Muğāhid, en Tab, XIX, p. 39, l. 1–2, mais sans la partie entre crochets.

[16] Muqātil, III, p. 85.

[17] Muqātil, III, p. 612.

fut frappé de la peste. Ils examinaient, en effet, les étoiles, et Abraham examina aussi les étoiles (*naẓara fī*) et dit: "Je suis malade". Al-Farrā' a dit: 'Tout homme en qui l'imperfection est à l'œuvre, en qui la caducité se répand et qui s'attend à mourir, est malade'".[18]

Comme on l'a compris, la citation d'al-Farrā' est une interpolation provenant d'un des transmetteurs du commentaire de Muqātil. A la page précédente, on trouve d'ailleurs une autre interpolation introduite par deux garants: "Abū Muḥammad a dit: j'interrogeai Abū l-ʿAbbās à ce sujet...". Il s'agit, à n'en pas douter, respectivement de Abū Muḥammad ʿAbd Allāh b. Ṯābit al-Tawwāzī al-Muqri' (m. 308/920)[19] et de Abū l-ʿAbbās Aḥmad b. Yaḥyā, c'est à dire Ṯaʿlab (291/904).[20] L'interpolation de l'interprétation d'al-Farrā' est le fait d'al-Tawwāzī.

10. Si nous nous tournons maintenant vers des savants ou des exégètes, parfois plus anciens, qui figurent dans diverses chaînes de garants, la mention d'un mensonge ou des tentatives d'innocenter Abraham d'une faute qui pourrait lui être imputée en l'espèce n'apparaissent pas non plus, tout au moins dans l'état de nos propres connaissances.

Ainsi al-Suddī (m. 128/745):[21] "[...] Abraham partit avec eux; mais en chemin, il se jeta par terre et dit: 'Je suis malade'. J'ai mal au pied. En effet, ils lui marchèrent[22] sur le pied alors qu'il était par terre (*wa huwa ṣarīʿ*)". Après ce stratagème, Abraham revient au temple et brise les idoles, hormis la grande.[23] Dans le même sens, Ḥasan al-Baṣrī (m. 110/728)[24] aurait

18 *Kullu man ʿamila fīhi l-naqṣu wa dabba fīhi l-fanā'u wa kāna muntaẓiran li-l-mawti fa-huwa saqīm*. Farrā', II, p. 388, a: *kullu man fī ʿunuqihi l-mawtu fa-huwa saqīm*. Pour Farrā', *v. infra* § 14.

19 *V.* Gilliot, Muqātil, p. 49–50, 41.

20 *V.* Gilliot, Muqātil, p. 49 et n. 53.

21 Abū Muḥammad Ismāʿīl b. a. Karīma al-Kūfī al-Suddī al-Kabīr; *v.* Gilliot, *Baqara*, p. 216, 232–33, 239–41, 247, 250; Kohlberg, *Ibn Ṭāwūs*, p. 348, n° 574: Ibn Ṭāwūs soutient qu'il était sunnite, mais Ṭihrānī souligne que c'était un disciple des Imams 4–6; van Ess, *TG*, I, p. 301–02, pour al-Suddī al-Ṣaġīr, mais aussi pour le nôtre.

22 *Fa-tawāṭa'ū*. En *Annales*, I, p. 259/I, p. 238: *fa-tawaṭṭa'ū*. En Qurt, XV, p. 93, *fa-waṭṭa'ū*. Nous ne comprenons pas comme W. M. Brinner *in History*, II, p. 55, qui traduit: "They sat down by his feet". La séquence logique de la phrase est la suivante: Abraham se jette par terre, ils lui marchent alors sur le pied, et il dit qu'il a mal. De même, deux lignes en dessous, corriger: "for two of the people had remained" (*fa-qad baqiya ḍaʿfā l-nāsī*, sur le schème *faʿlā*) (d'autres versions ont *ḍuʿafā'*; Rāzī, XXII, p. 182, l. 18, sur 21, 57): "alors que les gens faibles (ou malades) étaient restés". Ou encore, *in* Nīsābūrī, *Tafsīr*, XVII, p. 31, l. 24: *fa-lammā baqiya huwa wa ḍuʿfā'u l-nās*, dans la recension d'al-Suddī.

23 Tab, XIX, p. 38, l. 15–16; l'ensemble du récit de Suddī, l. 12–24, sur 21,57–58; Qurt, XV, p. 93, l. 5–10, sur 37,89, mais la chaîne de garants remonte plus avant: Suddī/Abū Ṣāliḥ (Bāḏām)/Ibn ʿAbbās; et également avec une chaîne abrégée qui va jusqu'à Ibn Masʿūd, d'après al-Tirmiḏī et al-Ḥākim al-Nīsābūrī. De plus, le récit y est plus court.

24 Cependant, *v. infra sub* § 13 une autre interprétation attribuée à Ḥasan al-Baṣrī.

déclaré: "Il se coucha sur le dos et dit: 'Je suis malade'; je ne peux pas partir. Il regarda alors dans le ciel, et lorsqu'ils furent partis, il s'en prit à leurs dieux et les brisa".[25]

De même Qatāda (m. 118/736),[26] commentant 21,63: "C'est cette façon[27] par laquelle il les a circonvenus".[28] Ou encore, le même, citant Saʿīd b. al-Musayyab:[29] "Il vit une étoile se lever, et il dit: 'Je suis malade'. Le prophète de Dieu usa d'un stratagème pour défendre sa religion (*kāyada nabiyyu Llāhi ʿan dīnihi*), et il dit: 'Je suis malade'".[30] Ou dans le *Tafsīr* de ʿAbd al-Razzāq[31] (m. 211/827) par la voie Maʿmar[32]/Qatāda: "Il vit une étoile montante et dit: je serai malade demain. Ibn al-Musayyab dit: 'Le prophète de Dieu usa d'un stratagème pour défendre sa religion'".[33]

Derrière son *Tafsīr*, il faut probablement voir des notes de leçons prises par divers personnages et exploitées par la suite. La rédaction la plus importante remonte à ʿAmr b. ʿUbayd; *v.* van Ess, *TG*, II, p. 55; 298–300.

[25] Suyūṭī, *Durr*, p. 239, l. 18–20, d'après ʿAbd b. Ḥamīd [al-Kissī, m. 249/863, auteur d'un *Tafsīr* et d'un *Musnad*; *GAS*, I, p. 113; Gilliot, Textes arabes anciens..., *MIDEO* 20 (1991), nº 104, pour l'éd. de l'abrégé de son *Musnad*], Ibn al-Mundir (m. 318/930; *GAS*, I, 495–16; dans son *Tafsīr*) et Ibn a. Ḥātim (m. 327/938; *GAS*, I, p. 178–79; dans son *Tafsīr*). Ṭabarī, *Annales*, I, p. 254–59/I, p. 236–38/*History*, II, p. 50–53, transforme en un récit continu des données qu'il emprunte à Suddī: *ʿan* Abū Ṣāliḥ (Bāḏām) et *ʿan* Abū Mālik (al-Ġifārī Ġazwān al-Kūfī)/Ibn ʿAbbās, et à Murra al-Hamdānī (b. Šarāḥīl al-Kūfī, Murra al-Ḫayr)/Ibn Masʿūd; *v.* l'analyse des chaînes de Suddī *in* Gilliot, *Baqara*, p. 211–240, où tous ces personnages sont présentés. Suyūṭī, *Durr*, IV, p. 321, l. 5–10, donne la tradition d'Ibn Masʿūd d'après le *Tafsīr* d'Ibn a. Ḥātim: "Il dit: 'Je suis malade'. Il avait dit la veille: 'Par Dieu, je jouerai un mauvais tour à vos idoles dès que vous aurez rebroussé chemin' (21,57) [...]."

[26] Abū l-Ḫaṭṭāb b. Diʿāma al-Sadūsī al-Baṣrī al-Ḍarīr al-Akmah (l'aveugle de naissance); il aurait tenu ses idées qadarites de Ḥasan al-Baṣrī, et il allait même au-delà; *v.* *San*, V, p. 269–83; Gilliot, *Baqara*, p. 262–70; van Ess, *TG*, II, p. 135–46.

[27] *Ḫaṣla*, qualité, action bonne ou mauvaise, mais aussi coup qui atteint son but.

[28] *Wa hiya hāḏihi l-ḫaṣlatu llatī kādahum bihā*; Tab, XIX, p. 41, l. 4. *Cf.* Suyūṭī, IV, p. 321, l. 17–22, d'après Ṭabarī, Ibn al-Mundir et Ibn a. Ḥātim.

[29] B. Ḥazn al-Qurašī al-Maḫzūmī, m. à Médine, 94/712–3 (93, 95); *San*, IV, p. 217–46; *GAS*, I, p. 276.

[30] Tab, XXIII, p. 71, l. 1–2, avec la chaîne Bišr (b. Muʿāḏ al-Baṣrī, m. 245/859)/Yazīd (b. Zurayʿ al-Baṣrī, m. 182/798)/Saʿīd b. a. ʿArūba al-ʿAdawī al-Baṣrī, qadarite, m. 156/773; *v. infra* n. 145); pour cette chaîne, *v.* Gilliot, *Baqara*, p. 268–70. En Suyūṭī, *Durr*, V, p. 279, l. 4–6, de Sayyid b. al-Musayyab seul: le début de la tradition est corrompu dans le texte (*kāyada īnī fī l-nuǧūm*): "[...] Il dit un mot de la langue des Arabes, Dieu dit que sa religion soit puissante" (?), d'après ʿAbd al-Razzāq, ʿAbd b. Ḥamīd et Ibn Ǧarīr (Ṭabarī).

[31] ʿAbd al-Razzāq b. Hammām al-Ḥimyarī, m. 211/827; *GAS*, I, p. 99.

[32] B. Rāšid al-Azdī al-Baṣrī, m. 154/770 à Sana; il suivit entre autres les leçons de Qatāda; *San*, VII, p. 5–18; *GAS*, I, p. 290–91.

[33] ʿAbd al-Razzāq, *Tafsīr*, II, p. 153/II, p. 125, nº 2534. *Cf.* Ibn Kaṯīr, VII, p. 21, d'après Qatāda seul.

Ou encore, selon le Suivant Zayd b. Aslam (m. 136/753),[34] dans la recension du commentaire d'Ibn Wahb (m.197/812):[35] "Cette étoile ne s'est jamais levée sans m'annoncer que je serai malade, et il dit: 'Je suis malade'".[36]

Pour d'autres, Abraham dit qu'il était atteint d'une maladie pour les faire fuir (Ibn Isḥāq, m. 150/767),[37] ou de la peste (al-Ḍaḥḥāk b. Muzāḥim[38] et al-Kalbī[39]).

Al-Kalbī[40] explique la parole d'Abraham de façon plus détaillée encore: "Ils étaient dans une localité entre Bassorah et Coufa qui s'appelle Hurmuzgard,[41] où l'on pratiquait l'examen des étoiles. Il examina les étoiles et dit: 'Je suis malade', c'est-à-dire atteint de la peste".[42] Ou selon une autre version: "Abraham était d'une famille dans laquelle on examinait les étoiles. S'ils se rendaient à leur fête, ils ne laissaient que les malades à la maison. Quand l'idée vint à Abraham de briser les idoles, il examina le ciel le jour qui précédait la fête, et il dit à ses compagnons: 'Je me vois malade demain', c'est pourquoi il est dit: 'Il jeta un regard sur les étoiles et déclara: Je suis malade!' Le lendemain matin, il se leva, la tête entourée d'un

34 Pour la chaîne dans laquelle il apparaît chez Ṭabarī, *v.* Gilliot, *Baqara*, p. 277–78.

35 ʿAbd Allāh b. Wahb b. Muslim al-Fihrī al-Miṣrī; *GAS*, I, p. 466; *cf.* ʿAbd Allāh b. Wahb, *al-Ǧāmiʿ. Tafsīr al-Qurʾān* (Die Koranexegese), Herausgegeben und kommentiert von Miklos Muranyi, Wiesbaden 1993; *al-Ǧāmiʿ. Tafsīr al-Qurʾān.* Die Koranexegese 2, Teil I, Wiesbaden 1995. Ce passage n'y est pas commenté.

36 Tab, XXIII, p. 71, l. 6–8. *cf. Annales*, I, p. 256/I, p. 236/*History*, II, p. 52; *cf.* Suyūṭī, *Durr*, V, p. 279, l. 11–12.

37 Tab. XXIII, p. 71, l. 9–11.

38 Tab, XXIII, p. 71, l. 3–5, dans la recension de ʿUbayd b. Sulaymān al-Bāhilī al-Kūfī qui habita Merv; *v.* TT, VII, p. 67; Gilliot, *Baqara*, p. 171–72. Pour al-Ḍaḥḥāk b. Muzāḥim al-Balḫī al-Ḫurāsānī al-Hilālī (m. 105/723) et les recensions de son "commentaire" ou la transmission de ses traditions, *v. GAS*, I, p. 29–30; Gilliot, *Baqara*, p. 168–78; van Ess, *TG*, II, p. 509.

39 D'après Hūd b. Muḥakkam, III, *Tafsīr*, p. 453–54. Ou encore selon Ibn ʿAbbās dans "la chaîne des al-ʿAwfī" qui aboutit chez Tabarī à Muḥammad b. Saʿd al-ʿAwfī (m. 276/889). Pour cette chaîne, *v.* Gilliot, *Baqara*, p. 136–45.

40 Sur Muḥammad b. al-Sāʾib al-Kalbī al-Kūfī (m. 146/763) et son exégèse, *v.* Gilliot, *Baqara*, p. 141–45; Kohlberg, *Ibn Ṭāwūs*, p. 343, n° 564; van Ess, *TG*, I, p. 298–301. Nous avons écrit à plusieurs reprises que Ṭabarī ne citait jamais Kalbī dans son commentaire, depuis nous avons trouvé un lieu où il y figure, sur 7,172, *in* Tab, XIII, p. 243, n° 15374: Muḥammad b. ʿAbd al-Aʿlā/Muḥammad b. Ṯawr/Maʿmar/al-Kalbī.

41 Terme qui signifie le lieu ou le cercle de Hurmurz. Nous remercions notre collègue de l'Université de Provence, Parviz Abolgassemi, qui nous a aidé à rétablir la graphie de ce mot. *In* Yāqūt, *Buldān*, V, p. 402b: Hurmuzǧird ou Hurmuzǧurd, le *ǧīm* n'y étant pas vocalisé. L'éditeur du commentaire de Hūd b. Muḥakkam lit Hurmuzḫurrid d'après l'un des manuscrits; un autre a: Mūrmarḫid (ou autre vocalisation). *Cf.* Ṭabarī, *Annales*, I, p. 346/I, p. 310/*History*, II, p. 127: Hurmuzǧird dans al-Ahwāz.

42 Hūd b. Muḥakkam, *Tafsīr*, III, 453–54; Qurṭubī, *Tafsīr*, XV, p. 92.

bandeau (*maʿṣūban raʾsuhu*). Ils allèrent tous à la fête, sauf lui qui resta là [...]".[43]

Parmi les exégètes anciens, nous n'avons trouvé qu'une seule explication dans laquelle le terme mensonge apparaît, et qui est attribuée à al-Ḥasan al-Baṣrī, sur 21,62–63: "Il est acquitté de son mensonge à propos du stratagème dont il a usé contre eux (*inna kaḏibahu fī makīdatihi iyyāhum mawḍūʿun ʿanhu*)".[44]

III. L'INTERVENTION DE LA PHILOLOGIE ET DE LA RHÉTORIQUE. DES TENTATIVES POUR QU'UNE FAUTE NE SOIT PAS IMPUTÉE À ABRAHAM?

11. Certains commentateurs rapportent qu'al-Kisāʾī (ʿAlī b. Ḥamza, m.189/805) faisait une pause après *faʿalahu* (21,63).[45] De la sorte, le sujet est sous-entendu, et il faudrait comprendre: "L'a fait qui l'a fait (*faʿalahu man faʿalahu*).[46] Le plus grand d'entre eux, c'est celui-là. Interrogez-les s'ils parlent". La suite, *kabīruhum hāḏā*, est donc le début d'une nouvelle phrase nominale constituée d'un sujet (*kabīr*) et d'un attribut (*hāḏā*).

Une autre possibilité retenue par les commentateurs est que l'énoncé assertorique (*ḫabar*) d'Abraham doive être compris comme une injonction (*ilzām*), dans la mesure où une injonction peut être exprimée soit sous la forme d'une question, soit sous celle d'un ordre, soit sous celle d'une

[43] Rāzī, *Tafsīr*, XXII, p. 182, l. 19–23. Une tradition approchante selon Qatāda, *in* Tab, XXIII, p. 70, l. 19–20: "Son peuple pratiquait l'astrologie (*ahl al-tanǧīm*). Il vit une étoile qui se levait, alors il s'enveloppa la tête et dit: 'J'ai la peste'".

[44] Hūd b. Muḥakkam, *Tafsīr*, III, p. 77. Cet exégète ibāḍite a dû emprunter cette tradition à Yaḥyā b. Sallām (m. 200/815; *GAS*, I, p. 39), dans la mesure où son ouvrage est une sorte d'abrégé du *Tafsīr* de ce dernier, mais évidemment avec ses propres idées ḫāriǧites à l'opposé des tendances murǧiʾites de l'exégète de Bassorah. *V.* Gilliot, "Der koranische Kommentar des Ibāḍiten Hūd b. Muḥakkam/Muḥkim", à paraître dans les actes du XXVI. Deutscher Orientalistentag (*ZDMG Suppl.*), Leipzig, 25–29 septembre 1995, et dans une version française beaucoup plus développée: "Le commentaire coranique de Hūd b. Muḥakkam/Muḥkim", à paraître dans *Arabica*, 1997. Nous y avons relevé quelques-unes des chaînes de garants de Yaḥyā b. Sallām, placées par l'éditeur du Commentaire de Hūd dans ses notes.

[45] Abū l-Baqāʾ al-ʿUkbarī, *Tibyān*, II, p. 921 (sans mention de Kisāʾī): *al-waqf ʿalā faʿalahu, wa l-fāʿil maḥḏūf, ay faʿlahu man faʿalahu, wa hāḏā baʿīdun li-anna ḥadfu l-fāʿili lā yasūġu*; Qurt, XI, p. 300, l. 14–15; Abū Ḥayyān, VI, p. 325, l. 15–16; Ibn al-Ǧawzī, *Tabṣira*, I, p. 107; Ṭabarsī, XVII, p. 38: *man waqafa ʿalā faʿalahu fa-fāʿiluhu muḍmarun wa taqdīruhu faʿlahu man faʿlahu wa kabīruhum mubtadaʾun wa hāḏā ḫabar*; p. 38: *inna taqdīrahu faʿalahu man faʿlahu*; Nīsābūrī, *Tafsīr*, XVII, p. 33, l. 28–31, 4ème solution.

[46] Ce que Rāzī, XXII, p. 185, 4e solution, a qualifié plus tard de "métonymie d'anonymat" (*kināya ʿan ġayr maḏkūr*).

assertion. C'est à dire qu'il incombe à ceux qui adorent des idoles d'établir qu'elles agissent, en l'occurrence: c'est la grande idole qui l'a fait, c'est ce que vous êtes obligés de croire; si elles parlent, interrogez-les donc.[47] On ne sait malheureusement pas à qui remonte cette interprétation.

12. Certains mentionnent la lecture "irrégulière" d'Ibn al-Samayfaʿ (al-Samayqaʿ) qui lisait *bal faʿallahu*, avec gémination du *lām*, dans le sens de *fa-laʿallahu kabīruhum*, puis il y eut assimilation (*taḫfīf*)[48] d'un des deux *lāms*. Cette leçon est déjà mentionnée par al-Farrāʾ qui ne donne pas l'identité du lecteur.[49] Elle est en général rejetée comme absurde.[50]

Le nom, l'identité et les dates de ce lecteur, Ibn al-Samayfaʿ (al-Samayqaʿ), font problème. Selon Ibn al-Ǧazarī: Abū ʿAbd Allāh Muḥammad b. ʿAbd al-Raḥmān b. al-Samayfaʿ al-Yamanī al-Makkī,[51] donc al-Samayfaʿ, comme en plusieurs commentaires édités. Mais ailleurs, on trouve: Ibn al-Samayqaʿ (qui a une petite tête).[52] Al-Sumayqaʿ (en diminutif), donné par Calder,[53] ne semble pas devoir être retenu. Considéré comme bon en arabe, il avait des lectures qui lui étaient propres (*lahu iḫtiyār*), mais dont plusieurs sont classées parmi les "irrégulières". Il suivit les leçons de lectures d'Ibn Kaṯīr (m. 120/738) et de Ṭāwūs b. Kaysān (m. 106/724); tous trois étaient d'origine yéménite. Ibn al-Samayfaʿ/Samayqaʿ s'établit par la suite à Bassorah.[54] Ismāʿīl b. Muslim al-Maḫzūmī al-Makkī (m. *ca.* 160)[55] transmit de ses choix de lectures. Si l'on tient compte de ces données, sa mort devrait se situer autour de 140 h. et il appartiendrait donc à la quatrième classe des lecteurs selon la division de Ḏahabī dans ses *Ṭabaqāt al-qurrāʾ* (où il n'apparaît pas); toutefois, Ḏahabī[56] déclare,

47 Qurt, XI, p. 300, l. 15–16: *qīla: ay li-mā yunkirūna an yakūna faʿalahu kabīruhum? Fa-hāḏā ilzāmun bi-lafẓi l-ḫabari, ʾay mani ʿtaqada ʿibādatahum yalzamuhu an yuṯbita lahā fiʿlan; wa l-maʿnā bal faʿalahu kabīruhum fīmā yalzamukum*; Ṭūsī, *Tafsīr*, XVII, p. 259; Ṭabarsī, XVII, p. 39.

48 *V. LA*, IV, p. 3082c, un vers avec *laʿalnā* pour *laʿallanā*.

49 Farrāʾ, II, p. 206–07: *qāla baʿḍu l-nāsi...*

50 Abū Ḥayyān, VI, p. 325, l. 16–17: [...] *wa huwa al-Farrāʾ, mustadillan bi-qirāʾati Bni l-Samayfaʿi, fa-hum buʿadāʾu ʿan ṭarīqi l-faṣāḥa*. En fait, Farrāʾ mentionne cette lecture, mais ne prend pas position en sa faveur. Zamaḫšarī, II, p. 577, l. 14–15, sans la juger; de même, Šawkānī, III, p. 414, l. 24–25. Ibn ʿAṭiyya, *Tafsīr*, IV, p. 87, mentionne cette lecture, mais non le lecteur; Nīsābūrī, *Tafsīr*, XVII, p. 33, l. 40–41, 5ème solution, commentant: "C'est là [une interprétation] forcée (ou arbitraire) (*wa fīhi taʿassuf*)".

51 Ibn al-Ǧazarī, *Ġāyat al-nihāya fī ṭabaqāt al-qurrāʾ*, nº 3106.

52 *LA*, III, p. 2099b, d'après Ibn Barrī; Zabīdī, *Tāǧ*, XXI, p. 238–39, et id., *al-Takmila wa l-ḏayl wa l-ṣila*, IV, p. 372a–b, reprenant Ibn Manẓūr. Al-Samayfaʿ est également donné comme existant (*GdQ*, III, p. 151, nº 3), mais non pour notre lecteur, par *Tāǧ*, XXI, p. 238.

53 Calder, *art. cit.*, p. 108.

54 *V. GdQ*, III, p. 169, d'après la liste de Abū ʿUbayd.

55 *Ġāya*, nº 788.

56 Ḏahabī, *Mīzān*, nº 7649 (*sub* Muḥammad b. al-Samayfaʿ).

d'après Sibṭ al-H̱ayyāṭ,[57] qu'il serait mort en 90, sous le califat d'al-Walīd b. ʿAbd al-Malik. D'autres disent encore qu'il aurait suivi les leçons de lectures de Nāfiʿ (m. 169/785), voire de Abū Ḥaywa Šurayḥ b. Yazīd al-Haḍramī (m. ṣafar 203/), et D̲ahabī de conclure sa notice par ces paroles: "Voyez ce méli-mélo!" (*fa-nẓur ilā hād̲ā l-balāʾ*).

13. Il convient de mentionner ici une interprétation ancienne qui, bien que ne portant pas directement sur les versets qui nous occupent, n'est pas sans relation avec eux, car elle vise, semble-t-il, à innocenter Abraham d'avoir consulté les astres. En effet, selon al-H̱alīl b. Aḥmad[58] ou al-Layṯ (b. al-Muẓaffar, *ob. prob.* 190/805),[59] ami du précédent, on dit de quelqu'un qui réfléchit sur une affaire qui le concerne afin de pouvoir la régler: il examine les étoiles (ou les astres) (*naẓara fī l-nuǧūm*), et de citer al-Ḥasan al-Baṣrī sur 37,88: "C'est-à-dire qu'il réfléchit au moyen de s'en sortir, car ils lui avaient imposé de partir avec eux; [il dit alors]: 'Je suis atteint'. Ils prirent la fuite par crainte de la peste".[60]

14.1. Même si le mot mensonge n'est toujours pas employé, on trouve chez al-Farrāʾ (m. 204) une explication rhétorique sur 37,89 dont on peut penser qu'elle vise à barrer la route à l'interprétation de la parole d'Abraham comme un mensonge: "'Je suis malade', c'est-à-dire atteint de la peste (*maṭʿūn min al-ṭāʿūn*).[61] On dit que c'est une parole dans laquelle il y a une manière indirecte de parler (*kalima fīhā miʿrāḍ*). Tout homme, enclin qu'il est à la mort (*fī ʿunuqihi l-mawt*), est malade, même si au moment où il dit cela (à savoir qu'il est malade) il n'a pas une maladie déclarée. C'est là une bonne interprétation".[62] Cette explication de Farrāʾ est suivie dans le texte d'un chaîne de garants qui est l'une des voies de

[57] Abū Muḥammad ʿAbd Allāh b. ʿAlī b. Aḥmad (m. 22 rabīʿ II 541 / 1er oct. 1146), petit-fils de Abū Manṣūr al-H̱ ayyāṭ. C'était un grammairien et un spécialiste des lectures sur lesquelles ils composa plusieurs ouvrages dont *al-Mubhiǧ*, *al-Īǧāz* et *al-Kifāya*. Ce fut l'un des maîtres d'Ibn ʿAsākir, d'al-Samʿānī et d'Ibn al-Ǧawzī; *v.* *San*, XX, p. 130–34.

[58] Al-Farāhīdī al-Yaḥmadī al-Baṣrī, m. entre 160/776 et 175, ibāḍite; van Ess, *TG*, II, p. 220–24.

[59] *GAS*, VIII, p. 189.

[60] Al-H̱ alīl, *Muʿǧam al-ʿAyn*, VI, p. 154, d'après Khan, *Die exegetischen Teile des Kitāb al-ʿAyn*, p. 291; *cf.* *TA*, VI, p. 4358a, avec al-Layṯ et al-Ḥasan. *Cf. supra sub* § 10, une autre interprétation attribuée à al-Ḥasan.

[61] En Tab, XXIII, l. 4: *maṭʿūn* seul, et cette interprétation y est attribuée à Ibn ʿAbbās avec la chaîne suivante: *ḥuddiṯtu ʿan* Yaḥyā b. Zakarriyā (*sic*)/*ʿan baʿḍi aṣḥābihi*/ Ḥakīm b. Ǧubayr (al-Asadī al-Kufī; *TT*, II, p. 445–46; il passe pour "faible"; *cf.* Tab, VIII, p. 268, nº 9257)/ Saʿīd b. Ǧubayr/ Ibn ʿAbbās. Nous pensons qu'il faut corriger le début de la chaîne et que l'autorité de Ṭabarī ici est Yaḥyā b. Ziyād Abū Zakariyyā, *i. e.* Farrāʾ.

[62] Farrāʾ, II, p. 388.

transmission des *Maʿānī l-Qurʾān*: Abū l-ʿAbbās[63] nous a rapporté: Muḥammad[64] nous a rapporté: al-Farrāʾ nous a rapporté: Yaḥyā b. al-Muhallab Abū Kudayna[65] m'a rapporté: d'al-Ḥasan b. ʿUmāra:[66] d'al-Minhāl b. ʿAmr (*ʿan*):[67] de Saʿīd b. Ǧubayr:[68] d'Ibn ʿAbbās: d'Ubayy b. Kaʿb: "Ne me reproche pas mon oubli" (18, *Kahf*, 73; c'est Moïse qui parle): "Il n'avait pas oublié. Mais cela fait partie des manières indirectes de parler. C'est ainsi que ʿUmar a dit: 'Dans les manières indirectes de parler nous avons un moyen de nous dispenser de mentir'."

Mais si l'on se reporte à l'exégèse de 18,73 chez Farrāʾ, on trouve: Abū l-ʿAbbās nous a rapporté: Muḥammad nous a rapporté: al-Farrāʾ nous a rapporté: Yaḥyā b. al-Muhallab, homme des plus distingués [en science] (*min afāḍil*) de Coufa, m'a rapporté: de quelqu'un (*ʿan raǧul*): d'al-Minhāl b. ʿAmr: de Saʿīd b. Ǧubayr: d'Ibn ʿAbbās: d'Ubayy b. Kaʿb: "Il n'avait pas oublié. Mais cela fait partie des manières indirectes de parler".[69]

Les chaînes de garants de cette tradition paraîtront bien tourmentées. La première est démesurément longue,[70] avec un grand nombre de transmetteurs; y figure al-Ḥasan b. ʿUmāra, chargé par la critique musulmane du *ḥadīṯ* de toutes les tares qui se peuvent concevoir; la seconde, beaucoup plus courte, comporte un anonyme. De plus, s'il s'agit bien dans les deux cas de la recension connue des *Maʿānī l-Qurʾān* par Muḥammad b. Ǧahm. La présence d'une chaîne, justement pour cette tradition semble être liée aux avatars de la transmission de cet ouvrage, d'autant plus que dans la recension utilisée par Ṭabarī il y a des variantes dans les chaînes[71] comme dans le texte. Enfin on notera que la maxime est tantôt attribuée directement à Ubayy (chez Ṭabarī), tantôt à ce dernier par le canal d'Ibn ʿAbbās. On pourra supposer qu'une interprétation attribuée à Kaʿb a été fondue avec une autre attribuée à Ibn ʿAbbās pour constituer

63 Ṯaʿlab, m. ǧumāda I, 291/mars-avr. 904.

64 Ibn Ǧahm al-Simmarī al-Kātib, m. ǧumāda II 277/sept–oct. 890, à l'âge de 89 ans, élève de Farrāʾ et transmetteur de ses *Maʿānī l-Qurʾān*; *San*, XIII, p. 163–64.

65 Al-Kūfī; *TT*, XI, p. 289.

66 B. al-Muḍarrib al-Baǧalī Kūfī, m. 153/770; *TT*, II, p. 304–08: il passait pour "menteur" (dans sa transmission des *ḥadīṯ*s); il est accusé de forgerie et blasonné des pires qualificatifs pour un traditionniste (*matrūk*, *sāqiṭ*, *ḍaʿif*). Il fut cadi de Bagdad durant le califat d'al-Manṣūr.

67 Al-Asadī al-Kūfī, *ob. ca.* 110/728–9; *San*, V, p. 184.

68 Al-Asadī al-Wālibī al-Kūfī, m. 95/714.

69 Farrāʾ, II, p. 155. En Tab, XV, p. 285, l. 15–16: *ḥudditu ʿan* Yaḥyā b. Ziyād (Farrāʾ)/Yaḥyā b. al-Muhallab: de quelqu'un (*ʿan raǧul*), de Saʿīd b. Ǧubayr, d'Ubayy b. Kaʿb.

70 Chaîne "basse" (*nāzil*) (de plus, ici avec *ʿan* et non pas *ḥaddaṯanī*), opposée à la chaîne "haute" (*ḥadīṯ ʿālin, min al-aḥādīṯ al-ʿawālī*).

71 On ne peut exclure évidemment que cela soit le fait d'erreurs de copistes.

une tradition exégétique unique: "Je suis malade" signifie je suis atteint de la peste, c'est là une manière indirecte de parler.

La parole de ʿUmar sur les manières indirectes de parler n'est pas là au hasard, homme de pouvoir, attaché à la mise sur pied d'un droit "d'État", il savait ce que parler par allusion veut dire. Les restrictions mentales sont bien utiles en droit et en politique!

14.2. L'interprétation des paroles d'Abraham comme *miʿrāḍ* est reprise dans la plupart des commentaires sunnites postérieurs, mais elle a un écho particulièrement favorable chez Zamaḫšarī dont l'illustration qu'il donne à ce propos reçut à son tour bon accueil chez les commentateurs qui vinrent après lui, non seulement chez les sunnites,[72] mais chez l'exégète chiite muʿtazilite qu'est Ṭabarsī[73] dont la structure du commentaire est à bien des égards semblables à celle des commentaires sunnites.

15. La façon oblique, détournée, de parler occupe une place non négligeable dans la littérature du *ḥadīṯ* dont nous donnons ici quelques-uns des éléments, mais aussi dans les ouvrages de rhétorique dont il sera moins question.[74]

Ainsi Ibn al-Aṯīr a rassemblé un certain nombre de traditions à ce sujet:[75]

1. Le *ḥadīṯ*: "En vérité, dans les manières indirectes de parler, on a toute latitude de ne pas user du mensonge. C'est le pluriel de *miʿrāḍ*, cela vient de *taʿrīḍ*, qui est le contraire de l'expression directe."[76]

2. On dit: "C'est ce que j'ai compris de sa manière indirecte de parler, avec ou sans *alif (miʿrāḍ/miʿraḍ)*".[77] Ibn al-Aṯīr continue: "Il [*i.e.*, le *ḥadīṯ* et non l'expression] est cité par Abū ʿUbayd et autres, et il fait partie les

[72] Bayḍāwī, II, p. 36, l. 5–7, sur 21,63: "[...] ou l'attribution de cet acte à lui-même sous le mode ironique [*cf. supra* § 6 *sub* Abū l-Layṯ al-Samarqandī], ou une réfutation (*tabkīt*) de façon allusive (*uslūb taʿrīḍī*)", suit l'illustration abrégée de Zamaḫšarī. Pour les autres commentaires sunnites, *v.* nos références *supra sub* § 6.

[73] Ṭabarsī, XVII, p. 39–40: *wa yağūzu an yakūna mina l-maʿārīḍi, fa-qad ubīḥa ḏālika ʿinda l-ḍarūra...*

[74] *V.* Ibn al-Naqīb, *Muqaddimat al-Tafsīr, fann* I, *cap.* 18, *al-Taʿrīḍ*, p. 275–80, p. 277, sur 21,63; Suyūṭī, *Itqān*, *cap.* 54, *Fī kināyātihi wa taʿrīḍihi*, III, p. 156–65, mais sans les deux cas qui nous occupent. Ibn Qutayba (m. 276/889), *Taʾwīl muškil al-Qurʾān*, p. 266–69, a rassemblé les expressions du Coran considérées comme des manières indirectes de s'exprimer, notamment pour Abraham, p. 267–68.

[75] Ibn al-Aṯīr (Mağd al-Dīn, m. 606/1210), *Nihāya*, III, p. 212.

[76] *Inna fī l-maʿārīḍi la-manduḥatan ʿani l-kaḏibi): ğamʿ miʿrāḍ, mina l-taʿrīḍ, wa huwa ḫilāfu l-taṣrīḥi mina l-qawli. Cf.* Lane, II, p. 2780b: "*Verily, in oblique, indirect, ambiguous, or equivocal, modes of speech, is ample scope, freedom, or liberty, to avoid lying: or, that which renders one in no need of lying*".

[77] *ʿAraftu ḏālika min miʿrāḍi kalāmihi, wa miʿraḍi kalāmihi, bi-ḥadfī l-alifi.*

hadīṯs rapportés par ʿImrān b. Ḥusayn (Abū Nuǧayd al-Ḫuzāʿī);[78] c'est un *ḥadīṯ* remontant au Prophète (*marfūʿ*)".

3. Le *ḥadīṯ* de ʿUmar: "N'y a-t-il pas dans les façons indirectes de parler un moyen qui dispense les musulmans de mentir?"[79]

4. Le *ḥadīṯ* d'Ibn ʿAbbās: "Je n'échangerais pas volontiers les manières indirectes de parler contre des chamelles de couleur fauve".[80]

Zamaḫšarī, pour sa part, donne d'abord la définition comme en 1., suivie de l'expression 2., puis le *ḥadīṯ* 1., avec l'explication: *la-saʿatan wa fusḥatan*, sans aucune mention de Abū ʿUbayd.[81]

Abū ʿUbayd,[82] cite 1. d'après Ḥuṣayn b. ʿImrān, et commente: "*Mandūḥa*, c'est-à-dire le fait d'être ample et large. On dit à un homme dont le ventre est énorme et a de l'ampleur: 'Ton ventre est bien large'.[83] Il veut dire ici que par les manières indirectes de parler on se dispense d'avoir absolument besoin de mentir."[84] "Les manières indirectes de parler

[78] Il se fit musulman, tout comme Abū Hurayra, l'année de Ḫaybar (7 h.); c'est lui qui portait l'étendard des Ḫuzāʿa lors de la conquête de La Mecque. Envoyé par ʿUmar à Bassorah pour y prêcher l'islam, il fut y nommé cadi par Ziyād. Il se "retira" (*iʿtazala*) lors de la bataille de Ṣiffīn. Il mourut en 52.

[79] *A-mā fī l-maʿārīḍi mā yuġnī l-muslima ʿani l-kaḏibi. V.* Ṭabarī, *Tahḏīb al-āṯār, Musnad ʿAlī*, p. 145, n° 244, même tradition de ʿUmar, mais avec *mā yuġnīkum*; Bayhaqī, *al-Sunan al-kubrā*, X, p. 199, l. 4–5; la même parole est attribuée à Mahomet par la voie de ʿImrān b. Ḥuṣayn, *ibid.*, l. 6–15. Ou de ʿUmar à nouveau: "*A-mā inna fī l-maʿārīḍi mā yakfī l-rağula ʿani l-kaḏibi*", Ṭabarī, *Tahḏīb al-āṯār*, *op. cit.*, p. 144, n° 242, à la suite des propos suivants attribués à Abū ʿUṯmān al-Nahdī (ʿAbd al-Raḥmān. b. Mill b. ʿAmr; il se convertit du vivant de M., mais ne le rencontra pas. Il transmit des traditions de ʿUmar sur lui, *v. infra* n. 150): *ḥasbu mriʾin mina l-kaḏibi an yuḥaddiṯa bi-kulli mā samiʿa*. En Muslim, *Muqaddima, Bāb al-nahī ʿan al-ḥadīṯ bi-kulli mā sumiʿa*, I, p. 11, l. 1–2: [...] Abū ʿUṯmān al-Nahdī/ʿUmar: *Bi-ḥasbi l-marʾi...*, mais sans *A-mā fī l-maʿārīḍi....* De même encore de Abū Hurayra/le Prophète: *Kafā bi-l-marʾi iṯman an yuḥaddiṯa...*, Abū Dāwūd, 40, *Adab, Bāb fī l-kaḏib*, IV, p. 298, n° 4992. Ou encore: Abū ʿUṯmān al-Nahdī/une de ses autorités: *Mā yasurrunī anna lī bi-maʿārīḍi l-kalāmi ka-ḏā wa ka-ḏā*, Ṭabarī, *op. cit.*, p. 145, n° 246; Ṭabarī, *op. cit.*, p. 145, n° 243: Sulaymān al-Taymī (Abū l-Muʿtamir Sulaymān b. Ṭarḫān al-Baṣrī, m. ḏū l-qaʿda 143/févr. 761, auteur d-un *K. al-Maġāzī*; *GAS*, I, p. 285–86; van Ess, *TG*, II, p. 367–70): *aḥsibu Abū ʿUṯmāna ḏakara ʿan ʿUmara annahu qāla: Inna fī l-maʿārīḍi la-manduḥatan ʿani l-kaḏibi.* Des propos semblables sont mis dans la bouche de Ḥumayd b. ʿAbd al-Raḥmān (al-Ḥimyarī al-Baṣrī): *Mā uḥibbu anna lī bi-naṣībī min al-maʿārīḍi miṯlu ahlī wa mālī*, ou encore: *Mā yasurrunī bi-l-maʿārīḍi miʾatu alfin*, Ṭabarī, *op. cit.*, p. 145, n° 247–48.

[80] *Mā uḥibbu bi-maʿārīḍi l-kalāmi ḥumra l-naʿami. Cf. Nihāya*, V, p. 35, où 1. est également expliqué (*s. rad. ndḥ*).

[81] Zamaḫšarī (m. 538/1144), *Faʾiq*, II, p. 419.

[82] Abū ʿUbayd (al-Qāsim b. Sallām, m. 224/839), *Ġarīb al-ḥadīṯ*, IV (éd. de Hyderabad), p. 286–87/II (Beyrouth, Dār al-Kutub al-ʿilmiyya, 1406/1986), p. 332–33.

[83] C'est à dessein que nous retenons cette traduction pour *indaḥā*, afin de garder en français dans l'expression "avoir toute latitude pour ne pas", utilisée pour traduire *al-mandūḥa ʿan*, l'idée de largeur (latin *latitudo*) contenue dans la racine arabe.

[84] *Yaʿnī saʿatan wa fusḥatan. Wa minhu qīla li-l-rağuli iḏā ʿaẓuma baṭnuhu wa ttasaʿa:*

consistent à s'exprimer de sorte que si on le faisait de manière directe ce serait un mensonge, ce pour quoi on substitue [à l'expression directe] une autre expression (*fa-yuʿāriḍahu bi-kalāmin āḫara*)[85] qui correspond mot à mot à cette dernière, mais dont le sens est tout à fait autre. Dès lors, votre auditeur s'imagine que c'est ce que l'on veut dire.[86] Ce procédé est très fréquent dans les traditions rapportées [*ḥadīṯ*][87] Ainsi Ibrāhīm[88] qui a raconté qu'un homme venu le voir lui dit [suit un exemple d'expression à double sens utilisée dans un cadre juridique]."[89]

Al-Buḫārī consacre un chapitre aux "propos à mots couverts (grâce auxquels on a toute latitude pour ne pas mentir"),[90] mais il ne contient aucune des traditions ici mentionnées.[91] Ibn Ḥağar déclare que l'une des

qadi ndāḥa baṭnuhu wa-ndahā (avec *alif maqṣūra*), *luġatān. Fa-arāda anna fī l-maʿārīḍi mā yastaġnī bihi l-rağulu ʿani li-ḍṭirāri ilā l-kaḏibi.*

[85] *ʿĀraḍtuhu bi-miṯli mā ṣanaʿa / bi-miṯli ṣanīʿihi*: je lui ai fait comme il m'a fait, rendre la pareille; Lane, II, p. 2004c, l. 10–11, d'après le *Qāmūs*. D'où *muʿāraḍa*: vendre un produit pour un autre, échange, troc, synonyme *taʿrīḍ*, voire *iʿtirāḍ*. Mais ici, c'est l'une des formes de la syllepse de sens; Dupriez, *Gradus*, p. 434–35; *v. infra* n. 209.

[86] Depuis: "Les manières indirectes de parler" jusqu'ici, l'explication de Abū ʿUbayd est reprise par Bayhaqī, *al-Sunan al-kubrā*, X, p. 199, l. 15–17.

[87] Ainsi Qurt, XV, p. 93, cite: "Il te suffit de la santé comme remède" (*kafā bi-l-salāma dāʾan*); *v.* Daylamī (a. Šuğāʿ Šīrawayh b. Šahradār Ilkiyā, m. 509/1115), *al-Firdaws*, Beyrouth, Dār al-Kutub al-ʿilmiyya, 1986, III, p. 290, nº 4871, d'après Anas. Ou encore le Coran 39,30: *innaka mayyitun wa innahum mayyitūn.*

[88] Ibrāhīm b. Yazīd al-Naḫaʿī, m. 96/714–5, l'un des plus important *fuqahāʾ* de Coufa; *GAS*, I, p. 403–04. On rapporte de lui qu'il aurait dit: *Kāna lahum kalāmun yatakallamūna bihi fī l-maʿārīḍi*; Ṭabarī, *Tahḏīb al-āṯār, Musnad ʿAlī*, p. 141, nº 235.

[89] Ibrāhīm al-Naḫaʿī semble avoir été très intéressé en tant que juriste par les expressions à double sens comme en témoigne Ṭabarī, *Tahḏīb al-āṯār, Musnad Ibn ʿAbbās*, nº 230–31, 233–35, notamment: "Ils disposaient de certaines expressions qu'ils utilisaient pour parler aux gens lorsqu'ils craignaient quelque chose, et ce pour se protéger eux-mêmes, tout en se prémunissant du mensonge" (*kāna lahum kalāmun yatakallamūna bihi, iḏā ḫašū min šayʾin, yukallimūna bihi l-nāsa, yadraʾūna ʿan anfusihimi ttiqāʾa l-kaḏibi*, nº 234). Ou encore: "Ils disposaient de certaines expressions pour parler, puisées dans les manières indirectes de s'exprimer" (*kāna lahum kalāmun yatakallamūna bihi fī l-maʿārīḍi*, nº 235).

[90] Buḫārī, 78, *Adab*, 116, *Bāb al-maʿārīḍ al-mandūḥa ʿan al-kaḏib* / Trad. Houdas, IV, p. 207–208 / *Fatḥ*, X, p. 489. On corrigera le contresens de Houdas qui a: "Des propos à mots couverts pris pour des mensonges", non relevé par M. Hamidullah, *Introductions et notes correctives de la traduction française de O. Houdas et W. Marçais*, El-Bokhari, *Les traditions islamiques*, Paris, Association Culturelle Islamique, 1981, p. 219.

[91] Non plus que Qast, VIII, p. 120–21, ni Abū Dāwūd, 40, *Adab*, *Bāb fī l-maʿārīḍ*, IV, p. 293, nº 4971. Dans les deux cas, celui-ci et celui d'al-Buḫārī, il s'agit de traditions qui contiennent des façons détournées de s'exprimer. Par ailleurs, l'une des tournures employée par le Prophète pour désigner ses femmes, et rapportée par Buḫārī sous ce chapitre: "Du calme, ô Anğaša, gare aux poteries, malheureux", est plus une métaphore qu'une façon détournée de parler, comme le souligne d'ailleurs Qasṭallānī. Au contraire, Bayhaqī, *al-Sunan al-kubrā*, X, p. 199, dans son chapitre qui porte le même titre que celui de Buḫārī; *v. supra* ce que nous en avons mentionné.

questions souvent traitées est la différence entre le *taʿrīḍ* et la *kināya* ("métonymie")[92] et que Taqī l-Dīn al-Subkī a écrit un petit livret (*ǧuzʾ*) à ce sujet.

16. Jusqu'ici nous avons traduit *miʿrāḍ* par "manière indirecte de parler" pour ne pas mettre dans la bouche des compagnons de Mahomet qui sont censés avoir employé ce terme une terminologie de rhétoricien. Pourtant cette figure de style entre dans la catégorie plus générale de l'allusion ou de l'insinuation, pour être plus précis, c'est une métalepse qui, selon Fontanier, ne doit pas être confondue avec la métonymie, car elle: "n'est jamais un nom seul, mais toujours une proposition, [elle] consiste *à substituer l'expression indirecte à l'expression directe*, c'est-à-dire à faire entendre une chose par une autre, qui la précède, la suit ou l'accompagne, en est un adjoint, une circonstance quelconque, ou enfin s'y rattache ou s'y rapporte de manière à le rappeler aussitôt à l'esprit."[93]

Pour: "Non! C'est le plus grand d'entre eux qui l'a fait" (21,63), on peut penser à une métastase, "figure de dialectique par laquelle on rejette sur le compte d'autrui ou sur des circonstances jugées impérieuses la faute que l'on est contraint d'avouer".[94]

Quant à l'expression "Je suis malade" (37,89), l'une des interprétations est que tous les hommes étant sujets à la mort, ils sont "malades"; elle serait, dans ce contexte où l'on veut éviter à Abraham la tare du mensonge, également une métalepse, "figure par laquelle on prend l'antécédent pour le conséquent: il a vécu, pour il est mort; ou le conséquent pour l'antécédent: nous le pleurons, pour il est mort."[95]

IV. "ABRAHAM N'A DIT QUE TROIS MENSONGES". CORAN, EXÉGÈSE, *ḤADĪṮ* ET PROPHÉTOLOGIE

17. Les §8–10 ci-dessus nous montrent que jusque vers 150 h., le logion prophétique des trois mensonges d'Abraham n'avait pas encore

[92] *V.* Ch. Pellat, 'Kināya', *EI*, V, p. 119b; Abū Hilāl al-ʿAskarī, *K. al-Ṣināʿatayn*, *cap.* 12, p. 368–70: *Fī l-kināya wa l-taʿrīḍ*. V. Iyāḍ, *Šifāʾ*, II, p. 140/ʿAlī Qārī, *Šarḥ al-Šifāʾ*, II, p. 251.

[93] Pierre Fontanier, *Les figures du discours* (*v.* notre bibliographie), p. 127–28; *cf.* Bernard Dupriez, *Gradus*. Les procédés littéraires (Dictionnaire), p. 285: "elle doit être rattachée à l'allusion. Elle est aussi parfois une forme de l'euphémisme".

[94] Henri Morier, *Dictionnaire de poétique et de rhétorique*, p. 742. Ainsi en Genèse 3, 12–13, Adam déclare: "C'est la femme que tu m'as donnée..." et Ève: "C'est le serpent qui m'a trompée". On parle également alors de réjection, Dupriez, *Gradus*, p. 289.

[95] Émile Littré, *Dictionnaire de la langue française*, Paris, Hachette, 1863, II/1, p. 536c, d'après Du Marsais; *v.* Du Marsais (César Chesneau, sieur), *Traité des tropes*, p. 80: selon Quintilien: *ex alio in aliud viam prœstat* (m. à m. "Elle ouvre la voie d'une chose à une autre", elle permet de passer d'une idée à une autre).

"contaminé" l'exégèse coranique *stricto sensu*. Faute d'avoir pu consulter les manuscrits du *Tafsīr* de Yaḥyā b. Sallām (m. 200/815),[96] nous ignorons s'il s'y trouve. En tout cas, par la voie de l'ibāḍīte des Aurès, Hūd b. Muḥakkam (*viv. sec. med.* III/IXe s.), nous savons que l'idée du mensonge d'Abraham y était présente, au moins dans une tradition exégétique attribuée à Ḥasan al-Baṣrī qui, par ailleurs, excuse le patriarche de cette faute.[97]

Toutefois cette absence ou quasi-absence de l'idée de mensonge et surtout du logion prophétique des trois mensonges en exégèse *ut sic*, c'est-à-dire en des segments de traditions appliqués à l'interprétation du texte coranique en tant que tel, ne signifie pas qu'il était inconnu et ne circulait pas. Le problème est de savoir si c'était bien un logion en soi, ou bien s'il a été détaché et isolé d'un ensemble plus important, et de donner une date approximative de son entrée dans l'exégèse coranique.

18. Voici tout d'abord quelques-unes des versions de ce logion, qui étaient en circulation dès la première moitié du IIe/VIIIe siècle, et même avant, spécialement dans la tradition historiographique parmi les transmetteurs de *maġāzī*, notamment par le canal d'Ibn Isḥāq (m. 150/767):

18.1. Ibn Ḥumayd[98]/Salama[99]/Muḥammad b. Isḥāq/ʿAbd al-Raḥmān b. a. l-Zinād[100]/son père (Abū l-Zinād)[101]/ʿAbd al-Raḥmān al-Aʿraǧ[102]/Abū Hurayra: "J'ai entendu l'ED dire: "Abraham n'a jamais rien dit qui ne fût, hormis trois choses:[103] 'Je suis malade', alors qu'il ne l'était pas; 'Non! c'est le plus grand d'entre eux. Interrogez-les donc s'ils peuvent parler'; enfin, lorsque Pharaon lui demanda au sujet de Sarah: 'Qui est

[96] *GAS*, I, p. 39, avec indication du manuscrit de Tunis et de l'abrégé d'Ibn a. l-Zamanīn (m. 399/1008), p. 47, l. 1–2; cf. Gilliot, "Le commentaire coranique de Hūd b. Muḥakkam/Muḥkim", § 4, à paraître.

[97] *V. supra* § 10 et 13, et n. 24.

[98] Muḥammad b. Ḥumayd b. Ḥayyān al-Rāzī, m. 248/862; Gilliot, *Elt*, p. 21–22.

[99] B. al-Faḍl al-Rāzī al-Abraš, m. 191/806–7; *San*, IX, p. 49–50; Gilliot, *ibid.*

[100] Al-Madanī, m. 174/790. Il vint s'établir à Bagdad; *San*, VIII, p. 167–70. La critique des traditions lui fait une mauvaise réputation. Mālik l'aurait notamment critiqué pour sa transmission des "sept *fuqahā*ʾ" [de Médine] (*i. e.* Saʿīd b. al-Musayyab, ʿUrwa b. al-Zubayr, al-Qāsim b. Muḥammad, Ḫāriǧa b. Zayd, Abū Bakr b. ʿAbd al-Raḥmān b. al-Ḥāriṯ b. Hišām, Sulaymān b. Yasār, et ʿUbayd Allāh b. ʿAbd Allāh b. Masʿūd), par le canal de son père Abū l-Zinād.

[101] ʿAbd Allāh b. Ḏakwān al-Qurašī al-Madanī, m. 130 ou 131/748; *San*, V, p. 445–51; *GAS*, I, p. 405.

[102] Ibn Hurmuz, m. 110/735; *GAS*, I, p. 82, n. 1.

[103] *Lam yaqul Ibrāhīmu šayʾan qaṭṭu lam yakun illā ṯalāṯan.*

cette femme avec toi?' et qu'il répondit: 'C'est ma sœur'. Hormis ces trois choses, Abraham n'a jamais rien dit qui ne fût."[104]

18.2. Ou dans une version où le terme "mensonge" (*kiḏba, kaḏba*) figure: Saʿīd b. Yaḥyā al-Umawī[105]/son père[106]/Muḥammad b. Isḥāq/Abū l-Zinād[107]/ʿAbd al-Raḥmān al-Aʿraǧ/Abū Hurayra: "Abraham n'a jamais menti en rien, si ce n'est [qu'il a commis] trois mensonges [deux sur l'être de Dieu, en disant: 'Je suis malade' et 'Non! C'est le plus grand d'entre eux qui l'a fait', et aussi à propos de Sarah: 'C'est ma sœur'."[108]

Ou encore Yaʿqūb b. Ibrāhīm[109]/Ibn ʿUlayya[110]/Ayyūb[111]/Muḥammad (b. Sīrīn) [/Abū Hurayra].[112]

18.3. Ou encore: Muḥammad b. Ḥumayd Abū Sufyān al-ʿAbdī[113]/Maʿmar (b. Rāšid)[114]/Ayyūb[115]/Ibn Sīrīn/Abū Hurayra:[116] avec

[104] Ṭabarī, *Annales*, I, p. 269/I, p. 247/*History*, II, p. 64.

[105] Saʿīd b. Yaḥyā b. Saʿīd b. Abān b. Saʿīd b. al-ʿĀṣ b. Saʿīd b. al-ʿĀṣ al-Umawī al-Baġdādī, m. 249/863; *TT*, IV, p. 97–98. On lui attribue des *Maġāzī*, ou du moins, il s'en était fait une spécialité (*ṣāḥib al-maġāzī*); *San*, IX, p. 139 (notice sur son père).

[106] Yaḥyā b. Saʿīd b. Abān [...] al-Umawī, m. 194/809–10; *v. San*, IX, p. 139–40.

[107] *V. supra* n. 101.

[108] *Annales*, *ibid.*, où la tradition s'arrête avant les crochets et est conclue par: "ensuite, il a mentionné à peu près la même chose", *i. e.* que la tradition précédemment traduite ici. La partie entre crochets, se trouve, en revanche en Tab, XXIII, p. 71, l. 18–20. *Cf.* Wāḥidī, *Wasīṭ*, III, p. 242, par le canal de l'auteur de *maġāzī*, Mūsā b. ʿUqba (m. 141/758; *v. GAS*, I, p. 286)/Abū l-Zinād, et le reste semblable; Tirmiḏī, 44 [48], *Tafsīr*, 22, *Anbiyāʾ*, V, p. 321, n° 2166, même chaîne qu'en Ṭabarī, avec un ordre différent pour les trois mensonges (tradition qualifiée de *ḥasan ṣaḥīḥ*)/Mubārakfūrī, *Tuḥfat al-aḥwaḏī*, IX, p. 6–7; Ibn Ḥanbal, *Musnad*, II, p. 403 *antepen.*-404/éd. Šākir, XVIII, p. 34–36, n° 9230, même chaîne à partir de Abū l-Zinād, et avec un texte légérement différent.

[109] Al-Dawraqī, m. 252/866; *v.* Gilliot, *Elt*, p. 28.

[110] Ismāʿīl b. Ibrāhīm b. Miqsam al-Asadī al-Baṣrī al-Kūfī (*al-aṣl*), né à Bassorah l'année où mourut Ḥasan al-Baṣrī (en 110 h.), m. ḏū l-qaʿda 193/août 809; *San*, IX, p. 107--20; van Ess, *TG*, II, p. 419.

[111] Abū Bakr b. a. Tamīma Kaysān al-Saḫtiyānī al-ʿAnazī al-Baṣrī, m. 131 à Bassorah; *San*, VI, p. 15–27. Il est compté au nombre des "petits suivants" (*ṣiġār al-tābiʿīn*); van Ess, *TG*, II, p. 343–52, qui met en doute les tentatives de faire de lui un disiciple et continuateur de Ḥasan. Il serait mieux placé dans le cercle des disciples d'Ibn Sīrīn.

[112] Tab, XXIII, l. 24–26. La chaîne s'arrête à Ibn Sīrīn chez Ṭabarī (chaîne "coupée" *maqṭūʿ*). Abū Hurayra ne figure pas chez Ṭabarī, mais chez Buḫārī (tradition "arrêtée", *mawqūf*), où les deux premiers garants sont Muḥammad b. Maḥbūb et Ḥammād b. Zayd; *v.* Buḫārī, 60, *Anbiyāʾ*, 8_9/Trad., II, 475–6/*Fatḥ*, VI, 301–04/Qast, V, 347–48.

[113] Al-Yaškurī al-Maʿmarī al-Baṣrī, m. 182/798; il fut appelé al-Maʿmarī pour être allé recueillir les traditions de Maʿmar au Yémen; *TB*, II, p. 257–59, n° 732; *San*, IX, p. 39–40.

[114] M. 154/740; *GAS*, I, p. 290–91.

[115] Al-Saḫtiyānī.

[116] Ibn Saʿd, *Ṭabaqāt*, (éd. Sachau)I/1, p. 23/(éd. I. ʿAbbās), I, 49–50.

une version longue sur l'histoire d'Abraham et Sarah auprès du souverain.

18.4. On trouvera encore d'autres lieux parallèles chez Buḫārī:[117] [...] Ḥammād b. Zayd[118] [ou Ibn Wahb/Ǧarīr b. Ḥāzim[119]]/Ayyūb/ Muḥammad [b. Sīrīn]/Abū Hurayra: "Abraham n'a jamais menti, sauf trois fois"; suit l'énumération des trois mensonges et un long développement sur le mensonge à propos de Sarah. Ou encore: [...] Abū l-Zinād/al-Aʿraǧ/Abū Hurayra: seulement l'histoire d'Abraham et de Sarah: "Abraham étant parti avec Sarah [...]. 'Ne va pas me démentir...[...]", sans la mention des deux autres mensonges.[120] De même chez Abū Yaʿlā al-Mawṣilī:[121] Hišām b. Ḥassān[122]/Ibn Sīrīn/Abū Hurayra: *Lam yakḏib Ibrāhīmu illā ṯalāṯa kaḏabātin, kulluhunna fī Llāhi* [verset cité, puis récit sur Abraham, Sarah et le souverain] *wa anti uḫtī fī l-islām*. Enfin chez Ibn Ḥanbal:[123] ʿAlī b. Ḥafṣ/Warqā'[124]/Abū Zinād/al-Aʿraǧ/Abū Hurayra: [...] *innakī uḫtī, in ʿalā l-arḍi mu'minun ġayrī wa ġayruki*.

18.5. Dans une autre version, on note que l'un des transmetteurs est intervenu dans le texte pour atténuer l'aspect mensonger des deux premiers mensonges: Ibn Ḥumayd/Ǧarīr[125]/Muġīra[126]/al-Musayyab b. Rāfiʿ[127]/ Abū Hurayra: "Abraham n'a commis que trois mensonges: lorsqu'il a dit: 'Je suis malade' et lorsqu'il a dit: 'Non! C'est le plus grand d'entre eux qui

[117] Buḫārī, 60, *Anbiyā'*, 8_9/Trad., II, p. 475–76/*Fatḥ*, VI, p. 301–04/Qast, V, p. 347–48; Buḫārī, 67, *Nikāḥ*, 13 (*bāb ittiḫāḏ al-sarārī*) (absent de l'éd. Krehl), abrégé de la précédente/Trad. III, 550/*Fatḥ*, IX, 104–05/Qast, VIII, 16; Muslim, 43, *Faḍā'il*, 41 n° 154 (2371), IV, p. 1840–41 ([...] ʿAbd Allāh b. Wahb/Ǧarīr b. Ḥāzim/Ayyūb, etc.)/Nawawī, XV, 123–25.

[118] B. Dirham al-Azdī al-Baṣrī al-Azraq al-Ḍarīr, originaire du Siǧistān, où son grand-père avait été fait captif; il était client de la famille de Ǧarīr b. Ḥāzim, m. ram. 179/nov.–déc. 795; *San*, VII, p. 456–66.

[119] B. Zayd al-Azdī al-Baṣrī, m. 170/786; *San*, VII, p. 98–103.

[120] Buḫārī, 34, *Buyūʿ*, 100/trad. II, p. 49–50 (/*Fatḥ*, IV, 326–27 (il renvoie à son com. du Livre des prophètes); Baġawī (m. 516), *Maṣābīḥ al-sunna*, IV, p. 18–19, n° 4429: d'après Abū Hurayra, sans chaîne.

[121] Abū Yaʿlā al-Mawṣilī, *Musnad*, X, p. 426–28 (n° 199), n° 6039.

[122] Abū ʿAbd Allāh Hišām b. Ḥassān al-Azdī al-Qurdūsī al-Baṣrī, m. 1 ṣafar 148/28 mars 765; *San*, VI, p. 355–63.

[123] Ibn Ḥanbal, *Musnad*, II, 403 *antepen*.-404/IX (éd. A. M. Šākir, Ḥamza A. al-Zayn *et alii*), p. 148–49, n° 9213.

[124] Warqā' b. ʿUmar al-Yaškurī al-Šaybānī al-Kufī, m. 160/776; *San*, VII, p. 419–22.

[125] B. ʿAbd al-Ḥamīd al-Ḍabbī al-Kūfī, m. 188/804. Il séjourna à Rayy où diffusa son savoir; *San*, IX, p. 9–18.

[126] B. Miqsam al-Ḍabbī al-Kūfī, m. 133/750; *San*, VI, p. 1013.

[127] Al-Asadī al-Kāhilī al-Kūfī, m. 105/723–4; *San*, V, p. 102–03. Le seul compagnon dont il aurait entendu des traditions est al-Barrā'.

l'a fait'. En fait, il a dit cela sous le mode de l'exhortation (*innamā qālahu mawᶜiẓatan*), puis, lorsqu'interrogé par le roi, il dit de Sarah 'ma sœur', alors que c'était son épouse."[128]

18.6. Cette tradition courte est souvent intégrée au début d'un récit plus long qui est une réminiscence du récit yahviste de Genèse 12,10–20, et dans lequel Abraham et Sarah rencontrent le roi-tyran (le Pharaon dans la Genèse):[129] Abū Kurayb[130]/ Abū Usāma[131]/ Hišām[132]/ Muḥammad[133]/ Abū Hurayra: "Abraham n'a dit que trois mensonges: deux à l'endroit de Dieu,[134] lorsqu'il a dit: 'Je suis malade' et lorsqu'il a dit: 'Non! C'est le plus grand d'entre eux qui l'a fait'. Lorsqu'il cheminait sur les terres de certain tyran [...]."[135]

18.7. On remarque, sauf oubli de notre part, que la plupart de ceux des auteurs ou des transmetteurs qui sont morts autour de 150/767 ou avant ne cherchent pas à interpréter les trois mensonges d'Abraham, en les atténuant de quelque façon, pour l'innocenter d'une faute. Tout au plus, trouve-t-on, dans certaines versions: "Tu es ma sœur en islam",[136] ou encore: "Nous sommes frère et sœur (*aḫawāni*) dans le Livre de Dieu; il n'y a, en effet, sur terre par d'autre croyant et croyante que nous",[137] ou enfin un commentaire attribué à Mahomet lui-même: "Il n'y a aucun des

[128] Tab, XXIII, p. 71, l. 21–23; *Annales*, I, p. 270/I, p. 247/*History*, II, p. 64.

[129] Tab, I, p. 228/I, p. 245/*History*, II, p. 63–64. Le récit sur Sarah est abrégé en Abū Dāwūd, 13, *Ṭalāq*, 16, *Fī l-waswasa bi-l-ṭalāq*, II, p. 264–65, n° 2212.

[130] Muḥammad b. al-ᶜAlā' al-Hamdānī al-Kūfī, m. 247/861 ou 243; *v.* Gilliot, *Elt*, p. 20, 24, etc.

[131] Ḥammād b. Usāma b. Zayd al-Kūfī, m. 201/817; *San*, IX, p. 277–79.

[132] *V. supra* n. 122.

[133] Abū Bakr Muḥammad b. Sīrīn al-Anṣārī al-Baṣrī, m. 110/729; *GAS*, I, p. 633–34.

[134] *Fī ḏāti Llāhi*; *v.* la discussion de cette expression *in* Lane, I, p. 985c: *in, in respect of, that which is the right of, or due; of, or in, or in respect of, obedience of God.* A comparer avec *fī ǧanbi Llāhi.*

[135] Suit le récit de la rencontre d'Abraham et de Sarah avec le souverain, le mensonge d'Abraham sur Sarah, la paralysie du souverain dès qu'il veut la toucher, le don d'Agar comme servante à Sarah. Le tout se termine par une remarque d'Ibn Sīrīn qui déclare que lorsque Abū Hurayra rapportait cet épisode, il terminait en disant: "C'est votre mère, ô fils de l'eau du ciel" (*banī mā' al-samā'*). Plusieurs interprétations sont données à cette expression qui désigne les Arabes: 1. parce qu'ils parcourent des déserts sans eau (*falawāt*) à la recherche d'un point d'eau pour leur bétail. 2. Parce qu'Ismaël fut nourri par Agar avec l'eau de Zamzam. 3. A cause de l'extrême pureté de leur lignage (*li-ḫulūṣ nasabihim wa ṣafā'ihi*), etc.; v. *Fatḥ*, VI, p. 304, l. 19–26, commentaire de Buḫārī, 60, *Anbiyā'*, 8_9/Trad., II, p. 49–50; *cf.* Ḥakīm Tirmiḏī, *Nawādir al-uṣūl*, II, p. 61, *cap.* 157; p. 410, *cap.* 256.

[136] Abū Yaᶜlā, *Musnad*, X, p. 427, n° 6039: Hišām b. Ḥassān/Ibn Sīrīn/Abū Hurayra.

[137] En Nasā'ī, *v. infra* § 20.11; Ibn Qutayba, *Ta'wīl muškil al-Qur'ān*, p. 268 qui commente: "Parce que les fils d'Adam descendent des [mêmes] parents; ils sont donc frères; et parce que les croyants sont frères, Dieu a dit: 'Les croyants sont frères' (49, *Ḥuǧurāt*, 10)."

mensonges [d'Abraham] qui n'ait été une astuce pour défendre la religion de Dieu (*mā minhā min kaḏibatin illā māḥala biḥā ʿan dīni Llāhi*)."[138]

19. Jusqu'ici nous n'avons donné que le logion lui-même, parfois, il est vrai, intégré dans un récit plus long sur la rencontre entre Abraham et Sarah, et le "tyran", mais il l'était également dans des récits plus amples, notamment dans le "tradition prophétique de l'intercession" (*ḥadīṯ al-šafāʿa*). Le récit-cadre est le suivant: au jour de la résurrection, Dieu rassemblera les croyants qui cherchent un intercesseur en la personne d'un prophète. Mais chacun des prophètes, hormis Jésus, a quelque chose à se reprocher et renvoie le quémandeur à l'un de ses pairs, jusqu'à ce que Jésus lui-même renvoie à Mahomet, le seul intercesseur, puisque Dieu lui a pardonné toutes ses fautes, passées et futures. Même s'il y a des variantes, la formule la plus utilisée par ces prophètes pour éconduire le demandeur peut être rendue par: "Je ne puis rien pour vous" ou "Je ne suis pas ce qu'il vous faut" (*lastu hunākum*),[139] voire, plus rarement: "Je ne suis pas votre homme" (*mā anā bi-ṣāḥibikum hāḏā*). C'est cette expression qu'utilise aussi Abraham avant de renvoyer à Moïse. Selon des versions, il dit ensuite: "J'ai menti trois fois", selon d'autres, cette même formule est accompagnée de la mention de ces trois mensonges ou de ses trois fautes (*ḫaṭāyā*).

20. Le logion des trois mensonges dans la tradition de l'intercession (*ḥadīṯ al-šafāʿa*) est on ne peut plus fréquent. Nous donnons ci-après un aperçu des principaux lieux:[140]

20.1. Ainsi chez Ibn a. Šayba:[141] [...] Abū Ḥayyān[142]/Abū Zurʿa Ibn ʿAmr[143]/Abū Hurayra: [...] "Mon Seigneur est en grand courroux aujourd'hui comme il ne l'a jamais été et comme il ne le sera plus", puis: *wa ḏakara kaḏabātihi, nafsī, nafsī ḏhabū ilā ġayrī*; sans l'énumération des

[138] Abū Yaʿlā al-Mawṣilī, *v. infra* § 20.12, première tradition.

[139] Avec le "*kāf* d'allocution", *kāf al-ḫiṭāb*; *v.* Murādī (al-Ḥasan b. al-Qāsim), *al-Ǧānī l-dānī fī ḥurūf al-maʿānī*, éd. Faḫr al-Dīn Qabāwa et M. Nadīm Fāḍil, Beyrouth, Dār al-kutub al-ʿilmiyya, 1992, p. 91–95. Dans certains contextes, et c'est le cas ici, l'opposition *ḏāk/hunāk* est équivalente à l'opposition *ille/iste*, laudatif/péjoratif, en latin. Ici aptitude/inaptitude, voire dignité/indignité: *innī lastu ahlan li-ḏālika*.

[140] Plusieurs classements de ces traditions eussent été possibles: selon le Compagnon transmetteur, selon les variantes communes, etc. Nous les avons classées finalement par ordre chronologique des ouvrages, mais en indiquant à chaque fois les premiers transmetteurs et les thèmes qui importent pour ce sujet. Nous avons fait également une place à part pour trois séries de thèmes (§ 20.11–14), comme on le verra.

[141] Ibn a. Šayba (Abū Bakr ʿAbd Allāh b. Muḥammad al-ʿAbsī al-Kūfī, m. 235/849), *Muṣannaf*, 27, *Faḍāʾil*, 1, éd. Šāhīn, Beyrouth, 1995, VI, p. 311, nº 31665.

[142] Abū Ḥayyān Yaḥyā b. Saʿīd b. Ḥayyān al-Taymī al-Kūfī; *TT*, XI, p. 214–15.

[143] Al-Baǧalī al-Kūfī; *San*, V, p. 8.

mensonges. Ou encore:[144] Saʿīd b. a. ʿArūba[145]/Qatāda/Anas:[146] seulement: *lastu hunākum*. Ou enfin:[147] Abū Muʿāwiya[148]/ʿĀṣim[149]/Abū ʿUṯmān[150]/Salmān (al-Fārisī): *lastu hunāk wa lastu bi-ḏāk*: "cela ne m'est pas possible (ou: je n'en suis pas digne), je ne suis pas l'homme qu'il faut"; ici il ne renvoie pas à Moïse, mais à Jésus.

20.2. Chez Ibn Ḥanbal:[151] [...] Ḥammād b. Salama[152]/ʿAlī b. Zayd[153]/Abū Naḍra,[154] qui rapporte le sermon d'Ibn ʿAbbās dans la mosquée de Bassorah, au cours duquel il transmet l'une des versions longues de la tradition de l'intercession; Abraham déclare: "J'ai commis trois mensonges sur l'islam", avec leur mention.[155]

20.3. Chez Ibn Ḥanbal toujours:[156] ʿAffān/Ḥammād b. Salama/Ṯābit[157]/Anas: *lastu hunākum*, sans plus. Ou enfin:[158] ʿAffān[159]/

144 Ibn a. Šayba, *Muṣannaf*, 27, *Faḍāʾil*, 1, VI, p. 312–13, n° 31668.

145 Saʿīd b. a. ʿArūba Mihrān al-ʿAdawī al-Baṣrī, qadarite, m. 156/773; *V. supra* n. 30; *GAS*, I, p. 91–92; van Ess, *TG*, II, p. 62–65.

146 Anas b. Mālik al-Anṣārī al-Ḫazraǧī al-Naǧǧārī al-Madanī; m. 91, 92 ou 93 h., à 103 ou 107 ans, dit-on! *San*, III, 395–406.

147 Ibn a. Šayba, *Muṣannaf*, VI, p. 312, n° 31666.

148 Muḥammad b. Ḫāzim (*mawlā* des Banū Saʿd) al-Saʿdī al-Kūfī al-Ḍarīr, m. ṣafar 195/nov. 810 ou 194; *San*, IX, p. 73–78.

149 ʿĀṣim b. Sulaymān al-Aḥwal al-Baṣrī, agoranome de Ctésiphon (*muḥtasib al-Madāʾin*), m. 141 ou 142; *San*, VI, p. 13–15.

150 ʿAbd al-Raḥmān b. Mill [nous vocalisons comme Zabīdī, *al-Takmila wa l-ḏayl wa l-ṣila*, VI, p. 282a; *qīla*: Ibn Mallī, vocalisé ainsi par l'éditeur de Ḏahabī] al-Nahdī al-Baṣrī, m. 95 ou autres dates; *San*, IV, p. 175–78; *cf. supra* n. 79.

151 Ibn Ḥanbal, *Musnad*, I, 281–82/IV (éd. A. M. Šākir), p. 187–89, n° 2546/III (éd. A. M. Šākir, Ḥamza A. al-Zayn *et alii*), p. 152–4, n° 2546.

152 Ḥammād b. Salama b. Dīnār al-Baṣrī al-Naḥwī al-Bazzār, m. ḏū l-ḥiǧǧa 167/juin–juil. 784; *San*, VII, p. 444–56; van Ess, *TG*, II, p. 376–79: il aurait composé le premier recueil de *judaica* (*isrāʾīliyyāt*), *Aḫbār Banī Isrāʾīl*, d'après M. J. Kister, *in CHAL*, I, p. 354.

153 ʿAlī b. Zayd b. Ǧudʿān al-Qurašī al-Taymī al-Baṣrī al-Aʿmā, m. 131/748–9; *San*, V, p. 206–08.

154 Al-Munḏir b. Mālik b. Quṭaʿa al-ʿAbdī al-ʿAwaqī al-Baṣrī, m. 108/726–7 ou 107; *San*, IV, p. 529–31

155 *Cf.* Ibn Ḥanbal, *Musnad*, I, 295/IV (éd. Šākir), p. 241–43, n° 2692/IV (éd. [Šākir, al-Zayn *et alii*), p. 202–4, n° 2692, même chaîne, même occasion, contenu presque identique.

156 Ibn Ḥanbal, *Musnad*, III, p. 247 *antepen.*-248, l. 16/XI (éd. Šākir, al-Zayn *et alii*), p. 223–24, n° 13524.

157 Ṯābit b. Aslam al-Bunānī (*mawlā*) al-Baṣrī, m. 127/744–5 (86 ans) ou 123; *San*, V, p. 220–25. Sur cette chaîne et les problèmes qu'elle pose, *v.* Juynboll, *Muslim Tradition*, p. 67, 144; *cf. infra* n. 287.

158 Ibn Ḥanbal, *Musnad*, III, p. 244, l. 11–245 l. 1/XI (éd. Šākir, al-Zayn *et alii*), p. 214–15, n° 13496.

159 ʿAffān b. Muslim Abū ʿUṯmān al-Baṣrī al-Ṣaffār ("le dinandier"), m. rabīʿ II 220/avr. 835 ou avant, à l'âge de 85 ans; *San*, X, p. 242–54.

Hammām[160]/Qatāda/Anas: [...] *lastu hunākum wa yaḏkuru ḫaṭīʾatahu llatī aṣāba ṯalāṯa kaḏabātin kaḏabahunna.*

20.4. Chez al-Buḫārī:[161] Muʿāḏ b. Faḍāla[162]/Hišām[163]/Qatāda/Anas: *lastu hunākum wa yaḏkuru lahum ḫaṭāyāhu llatī aṣābahā.* Ou encore:[164] [...] Hišām[165]/Qatāda/Anas: *lastu hunākum*, sans la mention d'une faute. Et enfin:[166] [...] Abū ʿAwāna[167]/Qatāda/Anas: *lastu hunākum wa yaḏkuru ḫaṭīʾatahu.*[168]

20.5. Chez Muslim:[169] Abū ʿAwāna/Qatāda/Anas: *lastu hunākum wa yaḏkuru ḫaṭīʾatahu llatī aṣābahā fa-yastaḥī rabbahu minhā.*[170] Chez al-Dārimī:[171] Abraham envoie les hommes (*yadulluhum ʿalā*) à Moïse sans faire de commentaire.

20.6. Chez Ibn a. l-Dunyā:[172] [...] Muḥammad b. Kaʿb al-Quraẓī[173]/un Auxiliaire (*ʿan rağulin min al-anṣār*)/Abū Hurayra: *fa-yaḏkuru ḏanban wa yaqūlu: mā anā bi-ṣāḥibikum ḏālika.*

20.7. Chez Abū Yaʿlā al-Mawṣilī:[174] [...] Abū ʿAwāna/Qatāda/Anas: *wa yaḏkuru ḫaṭīʾatahu llatī aṣābahā fa-yastaḥī min rabbihi*, mais sans l'énumération des fautes.

160 Hammām b. Yaḥyā b. Dīnār al-ʿAwḏī al-Muḥallimī al-Baṣrī, qadarite, m. 163 ou ram. 164/mai 781; *San*, VII, p. 296–301; van Ess, *TG*, II, p. 70–71.

161 Buḫārī (m. 256/870), 97, *Tawḥīd*, 19/Trad., IV, p. 590–91/*Fatḥ*, XIII, p. 335–36.

162 Abū Zayd al-Zahrānī (al-Ṭufāwī) al-Baṣrī, *ob. post* 200 ou 210; *TT*, X, p. 193.

163 Abū Bakr Hišām b. a. ʿAbd Allāh Sanbar al-Dastuwāʾī al-Rabaʿī al-Baṣrī (qadarite), m. 154; *San*, VII, p. 149–56; van Ess, *TG*, II, p. 60–62.

164 Buḫārī, 65, *Tafsīr*, 2,1/Trad., III, p. 250–51/*Fatḥ*, VIII, p. 130–31.

165 Al-Dastuwāʾī, *v. supra* n. 163.

166 Buḫārī, 81, *Riqāq*, 51_{17}/Trad., IV, p. 310–11/*Fatḥ*, XI, p. 362–71.

167 Abū ʿAwāna al-Waḍḍāḥ b. ʿAbd Allāh al-Wāsiṭī al-Baṣrī al-Bazzār, m. rabīʿ I 176/juin–juil. 792; *San*, VIII, p. 217–22. Il serait né *ca.* 90, *mawlā*, fit partie des captifs de Ğurğān. Il "vit" encore (*raʾā*) al-Ḥasan et Ibn Sīrīn.

168 Sur cette version, Ibn Ḥağar, *Fatḥ*, XI, p. 366, l. 6–15, donne les variantes de la réponse d'Abraham selon les diverses recensions que l'on trouve chez Buḫārī ou chez Muslim.

169 Muslim (m. 261/875), 1, *Īmān*, 322, éd. ʿAbd al-Bāqī, I, p. 180–81.

170 *V.* Tor Andrae, *Die Person*, p. 236–38, où la tradition de Muslim est en partie traduite et commentée.

171 Dārimī (ʿAbd Allāh b. ʿAbd al-Raḥmān. b. al-Faḍl, m. 255/869), 30, *Raqāʾiq*, *Šafāʿa*, II, p. 327.

172 Ibn a. l-Dunyā (m. 281/894), *K. al-Ahwāl*, p. 169, n° 255.

173 Al-Madanī, m. 108, ou 117 (à l'âge de 78 ans), ou 119, ou 120. Son père, captif des Qurayẓa, habita Coufa, puis Médine. Le grand écart entre les dates extrêmes de sa mort provient probablement du fait que certains ont voulu le faire naître du vivant de Mahomet, ce que Ḏahabī rejette. Il était prédestinationniste. Ṭabarī a transmis beaucoup de ses traditions exégétiques; *San*, V, p. 65–68, *GAS*, I, p. 32; Gilliot, *Elt*, p. 267–68.

174 Abū Yaʿlā al-Mawṣilī (m. 307/919), V, p. 279, n° 2899.

20.8. Ibn Manda:[175] [...] Muslim b. Ibrāhīm[176]/Hišām b. a. ʿAbd Allāh[177]/Qatāda/Anas: *lastu hunākum wa yaḏkuru ḫaṭīʾatahu llatī aṣābahā*, sans la mention des trois mensonges. Ou encore:[178] Hammām b. Yaḥyā/Qatāda/Anas: *lastu hunākum wa yaḏkuru ḫaṭāyāhu llatī aṣābahā*, suit la mention des trois fautes. [...] Šaybān b. ʿAbd al-Raḥmān[179]/Qatāda/Anas: *lastu hunākum wa yaḏkuru kaḏabātihi l-ṯalāṯa*, suivent les trois mensonges.[180] [...] ʿAffān b. Muslim/Ḥammād b. Salama/Ṯābit/Anas: *innī lastu hunākum*, sans plus.[181] Ou enfin:[182] [...] Ḥammād b. Zayd/Maʿbad b. Hilāl:[183] ce dernier se rend chez Anas en compagnie d'un groupe de Bassoriens; c'est Ṯābit [al-Bunānī] qui les introduit et qui reste-là durant la séance. Ils interrogent Anas sur la tradition de l'intercession des prophètes; il la leur confirme et la leur rapporte, avec des variantes, pour Abraham: *lastu lahā, wa lākin ʿalaykum bi-Mūsā fa-huwa kalīmu Llāh.*

20.9. Chez al-Bayhaqī:[184] [...] Hišām/Qatāda/Anas: *lastu hunākum wa yaḏkuru lahum ḫaṭāyāhu llatī aṣāba*. Ou encore:[185] [...] Yūnus b. Ḥabīb[186]/Abū Dāwūd[187]/Hišām/Qatāda/Anas: *lastu hunākum wa yaḏkuru lahum ḫaṭāyāhu*, sans plus.

20.10. Chez al-Ġazālī:[188] "Mon Seigneur est en grand courroux...", avec la réponse *nafsī, nafsī*, au rapport de Abū Hurayra.[189]

175 Ibn Manda (Muḥammad b. Isḥāq b. Yaḥyā, m. 395/1005), *K. al-Īmān*, II, 830–32; n° 861.

176 Abū ʿAmr al-Azdī al-Farāhīdī (leur *mawlā*) al-Baṣrī al-Qaṣṣāb, m. ṣafar 222/janv.–févr. 837; *San*, X, p. 314–18.

177 Al-Dastuwāʾī.

178 Ibn Manda, *K. al-Īmān*, II, p. 833–34, n° 863; p. 834–35, n° 864: [...] Abū ʿAwāna/Qatāda/Anas: *lastu hunākum wa yaḏkuru ḫaṭīʾatahu llatī aṣāba wa yastaḥī rabbahu minhā.*

179 Abū Muʿāwiya al-Naḥwī al-Tamīmī (*mawlā*) al-Baṣrī al-Muʾaddib, m. 164/780–1; *San*, VII, p. 406–08; van Ess, *TG*, II, p. 140 (*sub* Qatāda)

180 Ibn Manda, *K. al-Īmān*, II, p. 836–37, n° 865.

181 Ibn Manda, *K. al-Īmān*, II, p. 837–38, n° 866.

182 Ibn Manda, *K. al-Īmān*, II, p. 841–42, n° 873.

183 Al-ʿAnazī al-Baṣrī; *TT*, X, p. 225.

184 Bayhaqī (m. 458/1066), *al-Asmāʾ wa l-ṣifāt, Mā ǧāʾa fī iṯbāt ṣifāt al-taklīm*, p. 250.

185 Bayhaqī, *Šuʿab*, II, p. 123–24, n° 303.

186 Abū Bišr Yūnus b. Ḥabīb al-ʿIǧlī (*mawlā*) al-Iṣfahānī, m. 267; *San*, XII, p. 596–97.

187 Sulaymān b. Dāwūd al-Ṭayālisī al-Asadī al-Zubayrī (*mawlā*) al-Baṣrī, m. rabīʿ I 204/août–sept. 819, l'auteur du célèbre *Musnad*; *San*, IX, p. 378–84.

188 Ġazālī (m. 505/111), *Iḥyāʾ, Ḏikr al-mawt wa mā baʿdahu, pars secunda, Ṣifat al-šafāʿa*, IV, p. 448, l. 7–450, l. 5/Trad. T. J. Winter, *The Remembrance of Death and the Afterlife*, p. 212–14/Zabidī, *Itḥāf*, Beyrouth, Dār al-Kutub al-ʿilmiyya, 1989, XIV, p. 504–07.

189 Tradition identique à la première de § 20.1. *supra*.

20.11. Plusieurs versions des traditions sur l'intercession comportent une justification par Abraham lui-même du mensonge à propos de Sarah, ainsi:[190] [...] Ādam[191] / Šaybān Abū Muʿāwiya[192] / Qatāda / Anas: *innī lastu hunākum, wa yaḏkuru kaḏabātihi l-ṯalāṯ*; à propos de Sarah: "Nous sommes frère et sœur (*aḫawāni*) dans le Livre de Dieu; il n'y a, en effet, sur terre par d'autre croyant et croyante que nous". Ou encore chez Abū Yaʿlā al-Mawṣilī:[193] *lastu hunākum wa yaḏkuru kaḏabātihi l-ṯalāṯa*; avec énumération des mensonges, puis à propos de l'épisode avec Sarah: "Nous sommes frère et sœur (*aḫawāni*) dans le Livre de Dieu; il n'y a, en effet, sur terre pas d'autre croyant et croyante que nous".

20.12. Plusieurs de ces versions contiennent une justification du mensonge par Mahomet. Ainsi chez Abū Yaʿlā al-Mawṣilī:[194] [...] Sufyān b. ʿUyayna[195] / ʿAlī b. Zayd / Abū Naḍra / Abū Saʿīd: six lignes extraites de la tradition sur l'intercession des prophètes, Abraham dit: *innī kaḏabtu ṯalāṯa kaḏabāt*, et le Prophète de déclarer: "Il n'y a aucun des mensonges qui n'ait été une astuce pour défendre la religion de Dieu (*mā minhā min kaḏibatin illā māḥala biḥā ʿan dīni Llāhi*)."[196] Ou encore:[197] [...] Ḥammād b. Salama / ʿAlī b. Zayd / Abū Naḍra / Ibn ʿAbbās: ce dernier transmet la tradition de l'intercession alors qu'il prêche à Bassorah: *lastu hunākum innī kaḏabtu fī l-islāmi ṯalāṯa kaḏabātin*, suit la mention des deux mensonges habituels, le troisième étant évoqué par la formule: "ce qu'il a dit au roi lorsqu'il passa chez lui". Et Mahomet de commenter: "Par Dieu! En les utilisant il n'avait en vue que la puissance pour la religion de Dieu" (*mā arāda bihi illā ʿizzatan li-dīni Llāhi*).

20.13. La tradition de l'intercession renferme également parfois la

190 Nasāʾī (m. 303/915), *al-Sunan al-kubrā*, VI, 82, *Tafsīr*, *ad* 21, *Anbiyāʾ*, 88–89, VI, p. 440–41, n° 11433/ou Nasāʾī, *Tafsīr* (édité cette fois à part), II, p. 209–12, n° 298.

191 Abū l-Ḥasan Ādam b. a. Iyās [Nāhiya b. Šuʿayb ou ʿAbd al-Raḥmān] al-Ḫurāsānī al-Marrūḏī al-Baġdādī al-ʿAsqalānī, m. ǧumāda II 220/juin 835, transmetteur du *tafsīr* de Muǧāhid; *v. supra* n. 14; *San*, X, p. 335–38.

192 *V. supra* n. 179.

193 Abū Yaʿlā al-Mawṣilī, *Musnad*, V, p. 396–98 (*musnad* de Anas, Qatāda *ʿan* Anas, n° 309), n° 3064.

194 Abū Yaʿlā al-Mawṣilī, *Musnad*, II, p. 310 (*musnad* de Abū Saʿīd al-Ḫuḏrī, n° 67), n° 1040.

195 Al-Hilālī al-Kūfī al-Makkī, né en 107/725 à Coufa, il grandit à La Mecque où il mourut à la mi-šaʿbān 196/1er mai 812. Il était le *mawlā* de Muḥammad b. Muzāḥim, frère d'al-Ḍaḥḥāk b. Muzāḥim; *GAS*, I, p. 96; *San*, VIII, p. 454–74.

196 Repris par Suyūṭī, *Durr*, IV, p. 321, l. 26–29, et par Ibn Qutayba, *Taʾwīl muškil al-Qurʾān*, p. 268 qui a: *illā wa huwa yumāḥilu bihā ʿani l-islām*. On dit *miḥāl*, ruse, astuce.

197 Abū Yaʿlā al-Mawṣilī, IV, p. 213–16, n° 2328.

mention de 6, *An'ām*, 76.[198] Ainsi chez Ibn a. l-Dunyā:[199] Abū Ḫaytama[200]/Ǧarīr[201]/ʿUmāra[202]/Abū Zurʿa[203]/Abū Hurayra, comme en Ibn a. Šayba,[204] avec mention des deux mensonges et de 6, *Anʿām*, 76: "Il vit une étoile et dit: Voici mon Seigneur![205] [mais il dit lorsqu'elle eut disparu: je n'aime pas ceux qui disparaissent]."

Ṭabarī[206] s'exprime sur ce même verset, d'après une tradition d'Ibn Isḥāq; selon une tradition d'Ibn ʿAbbās[207] (p. 480, nº 13462), Abraham adora l'étoile jusqu'à ce qu'elle disparût. C'est la solution que retient Ṭabarī, rejetant la position de ceux[208] qui disent que cela n'est pas possible pour un prophète qui a atteint l'âge mûr, et qui ne peut être qu'unitariste (*muwaḥḥid*), mais qu'il a dit cela en niant que c'était son Seigneur, blâmant ainsi son peuple idolâtre, recourant à une expression à double sens (*muʿāraḍatan*),[209] ou que cela s'est passé dans son enfance, ou encore que le *alif* a été élidé (*a-hāḏā rabbī*).

Avant lui, al-Farrā',[210] avait proposé deux solutions, introduites par *yuqāl*, si bien qu'on ne sait pas laquelle est la sienne: 1. *istidrāǧan li-l-*

198 Nous avons ajouté les interprétations de ce verset données par plusieurs exégètes, en dehors de la tradition de l'intercession. *V.* également *infra* § 26.5.

199 Ibn a. l-Dunyā, *K. al-Ahwāl*, p. 166–67, nº 154.

200 Zuhayr b. Ḥarb b. Šaddād [Aštāl] al-Ḥarašī (*mawlā*) al-Nasā'ī al-Baġdādī, m. šaʿbān 234/mars 849; *San*, XI, p. 489–92.

201 Ǧarīr b. ʿAbd al-Ḥamīd b. Yazīd al-Ḍabbī al-Kūfī. Il naquit dans le gouvernorat d'Ispahan, vécut à Coufa et séjourna à Rayy; m. ǧumāda I 188/avr.–mai 804, à l'âge de 99 ans! *San*, IX, p. 9–18.

202 ʿUmāra b. al-Qaʿqāʿ b. Šubruma al-Ḍabbī al-Kūfī; il était plus âgé que son oncle paternel, ʿAl. b. Šubruma, lequel est mort en 144 (*San*, VI, p. 347–48); *San*, VI, p. 140.

203 Ibn ʿAmr; *v. supra sub* § 20.1.

204 *Cf. supra* § 20.1, première tradition.

205 C'est à cette tradition que fait référence Ġazālī (*v. supra* § 20.10.), p. 449, l. 4–7/Zabīdī, *Itḥāf*, XIV, p. 507.

206 Tab, XI, p. 480–82, nº 13464.

207 Tab, XI, p. 480, nº 13462.

208 *Wa ankara qawmun min ġayri ahli al-riwāyati hāḏā l-qawla llaḏī ruwiya ʿani bni ʿAbbās*, Tab, XI, p. 483, 484. Derrière cette appellation ("des gens qui ne sont pas des transmetteurs de traditions"), on peut peut-être reconnaître, entre autres, les muʿtazilites et les ḫāriǧites (*v. infra* § 25, pour ces derniers); *cf. infra* n. 236 V. L'exégèse de Abū ʿAlī al-Ǧubbā'i, *in* Gimaret, p. 309. *Cf.* ci-après la première solution mentionnée par Farrā'; Zaǧǧāǧ, II, p. 266: "Lorsqu'Abraham atteignit l'âge de raison où il faut la réflexion et auquel l'homme a besoin de preuves [...], il dit: 'C'est mon Seigneur!', c'est-à-dire à ce que vous prétendez."

209 *I. e.* l'une des formes de la syllepse de sens; *v. supra* n. 85 et *infra* n. 222. Pour appuyer notre traduction de *muʿāraḍa*, qui ne signifie pas ici une simple "objection", nous nous référons à Tab, XI, p. 484, l. 1–3, qui donne comme exemple: opposer à un argument faux (*baṭil*) employé par l'un un [autre] argument faux. Mais ici, il s'agit d'une reprise de la même expression employé par l'adversaire.

210 Farrā', I, p. 341.

ḥuǧǧati ʿalā qawmihi li-yaʿība ālihatahum annahā laysat bi-šayʾ. 2. Abraham "l'a dit dans un sens différent du premier (*ʿalā l-waǧhi l-āḫari*), comme Dieu a dit à Muḥammad (93, *Ḍuḥā*, 6–7): "Ne t'a-t-il pas trouvé orphelin [...]. Il t'a trouvé dans l'errance (*ḍāllan*) et il t'a guidé". [Ceux qui soutiennent cette interprétation] citent ici comme argument la parole suivante d'Abraham: "Si mon Seigneur ne me dirige pas, je serai au nombre des égarés" (6,77). On ne trouve rien en Muqātil, I, p. 571.

20.14. La tradition de l'intercession figure également comme une occasion de polémique anti-ḫāriǧite, ainsi à l'occasion de la "conversion" de Yazīd al-Faqīr ("celui qui a mal aux vertèbres"),[211] selon al-Āǧurrī:[212] [...] al-Ḥasan b. Muḥammad al-Zaʿfarānī[213]/Saʿīd b. Sulaymān[214]/ʿAbd al-Wāḥid b. Salīm[215]/Yazīd al-Faqīr: "Nous étions une groupe de gens séjournant à La Mecque (*min wuṭṭānihā*), et il avait avec moi un frère du nom de Ṭalq b. Ḥabīb,[216] et nous professions la doctrine des ḥarūrites. Nous apprîmes que Ǧābir b. ʿAbd Allāh (al-Anṣārī) qui venait à chaque pèlerinage était arrivé, et nous vînmes le voir, lui disant: Nous avons appris que tu avais dit quelque chose sur l'intercession (*qawl fī l-šafāʿa*)" etc.

V. L'INTÉGRATION DU LOGION DES TROIS MENSONGES DANS L'EXÉGÈSE

21. Pour montrer la façon dont le logion des trois mensonges a été intégré dans l'exégèse coranique, nous partirons de Zaǧǧāǧ,[217] même si cette

[211] Abū ʿUṯmān Yazīd b. Ṣuhayb al-Kūfī, Coufien qui vint s'établir à La Mecque; il transmit des traditions de Ǧābir b. ʿAbd Allāh et d'Ibn ʿUmar. D'après Ḏahabī, il fut l'un des maîtres de Abū Ḥanīfa. Selon le même, il fut surnommé *al-faqīr* parce qu'il avait mal aux vertèbres (*faqār*); Ibn Saʿd, VI, p. 305; *TT*, XI, p. 338; *San*, V, p. 227–28; *cf.* van Ess, *ZHT*, p. 177 et n. 15 (*ubi leg.* b. Ṣuhayb, *non* ʿUṯmān, corrigé en *TG*); id., *TG*, I, p. 163: il fit partie d'une délégation de cinq murǧiʾites coufiens qui se rendirent à Damas auprés de ʿUmar II. Dans la tradition qui suit en Āǧurrī, p. 3344, Yazīd al-Faqīr entend Ǧābir parler de "gens qui sortent de l'enfer", Yazīd déclare: "A l'époque, je niais cela". Grâce à cette "conversion", on ne fait plus mention de son murǧiʾisme dans les ouvrages d'onomastique, où il est placé parmi les autorités dignes de confiance!

[212] Āǧurrī (m. 360), *Šarīʿa*, p. 333–34. *Cf.* Tor Andrae, *Die Person*, p. 242.

[213] Al-Zaʿfarānī, élève d'al-Šāfiʿī, m. à Bagdad en 260/874; *GAS*, I, p. 491–92; *San*, XII, p. 262–65.

[214] Saʿduwayh al-Ḍabbī al-Wāsiṭī al-Baġdādī, m. 4 ḏū l-ḥiǧǧa 225/4 oct. 840; *TT*, IV, p. 43–44; *San*, X, p. 481–83.

[215] ʿAbd al-Wāḥid b. Salīm al-Mālikī al-Baṣrī; *TT*, VI, p. 435–36.

[216] Murǧiʾite, coufien, originaire de Bassora, m. *ca.* 95/714, *v. Lrs*, I, p. 432; van Ess, *TG*, I, p. 158–60.

[217] Abū Isḥāq Ibrāhīm b. Muḥammad b. al-Sarī al-Baġdādī, m. 19 ǧumāda II 311/3 oct. 923 (310, 316); *v.* Ibn Ḫallikān, I, p. 49–50; *San*, XIV, p. 360.

intégration a été faite bien avant lui, car la façon dont il procède nous paraît significative d'un processus plus ancien qui remonte peut-être au début du IIIe siècle. A propos de 21,63, il déclare: "Certains disent que le sens est le suivant: 'Non! c'est la plus grande d'entre elles qui l'a fait, si elles peuvent parler.'[218] Il est dit en exégèse[219] qu'Abraham a prononcé trois paroles dont le sens est différent du mot à mot, avec ce que cela comporte de probité [et de mentionner les trois paroles]. Ces trois paroles renferment une vérité évidente: 'Je suis malade' peut être compris de plusieurs façons, en particulier, je suis affligé (*muġtamm*) de votre errance jusqu'à en être comme malade, mais aussi je suis malade pour vous, sans compter qu'il avait pu contracter une maladie à ce moment-là."[220] Il revient sur le même sujet à propos de 37,89,[221] citant le logion des trois mensonges, reprenant l'interprétation de manière approchante, et considérant que dans les trois cas, il s'agit d'une expression à double sens (*muʿāraḍa*)[222] opposée aux idolâtres.[223] Abraham est donc en quelque sorte innocenté de ces fautes.

Or Zağğāğ nous donne ses sources à ce sujet: "[...] la plus grande partie de ce que j'ai rapporté en exégèse (*min al-tafsīr*) dans ce livre provient du Commentaire transmis (*min K. al-Tafsīr ʿan*) de Aḥmad b. Ḥanbal,"[224] dont on sait par ailleurs qu'il a reçu la licence de transmission du fils de ce dernier, ʿAbd Allāh.[225]

[218] Cette interprétation par l'antéposition/postposition est déjà signalée par Farrāʾ, II, p. 207, qui ne la prend pas à son compte, mais qui retient l'interprétation de la "majorité" (*al-ʿawāmm*) des exégètes qui comparent cette repartie à celle du "crieur" (*muʾaḏḏin*) en 12, *Yūsuf*, 70: Ô vous les caravaniers! Vous êtes des voleurs", alors qu'ils n'avaient pas volé. Nous n'avons pas retrouvé à qui remonte l'interprétation par antéposition/postposition; Qurt, XI, p. 300, la mentionne introduite par *qīlā*; Rāzī, XXII, p. 185, 6e solution, mentionne l'antéposition/postposition, mais également de façon anonyme; de même Ṭabarsī, XVII, p. 39, 1ère solution; Nīsābūrī, XVII, p. 33, l. 35–40, 6e solution, etc. Il semblerait qu'elle soit d'origine muʿtazilite; c'est en tout cas l'interprétation de Abū ʿAlī al-Ǧubbāʾī qui n'en est probablement pas l'initiateur; *v.* Gimaret, *Une lecture muʿtazilite du Coran*, p. 613. L'anonymat observé à propos de cette interprétation semblerait confirmer notre hypothèse sur son origine.

[219] *Ǧāʾa fī l-tafsīr*. Cette expression très fréquente chez Zağğāğ ne semble pas viser un ouvrage particulier, un commentaire, mais l'exégèse de l'un ou l'autre verset chez les exégètes. En certains cas, elle peut être un renvoi au *Tafsīr* d'Ibn Ḥanbal. Cette expression ainsi que *qālū fī l-tafsīr* (les commentateurs disent) se retrouve aussi dans le genre des *qiṣaṣ al-anbiyāʾ*; *v.* récemment Roberto Tottoli dans son excellente édition commentée de Ṭarafī (a. ʿAl. M. b. A., m. 454/1062), p. 141, 144, *et passim*.

[220] Zağğāğ, III, p. 397.

[221] Zağğāğ, IV, p. 309.

[222] *V. supra* n. 209 et 85.

[223] *Cf. supra sub* § 20.13.

[224] Zağğāğ, III, p. 166.

[225] Zağğāğ, III, p. 8. Abū ʿAbd al-Raḥmān ʿAbd Allāh b. Aḥmad b. Muḥammad b. Ḥanbal, m. 290/903; *GAS*, I, p. 511.

22. Excursus sur le *Tafsīr* d'Ibn Ḥanbal. Cette dernière remarque mérite une explication. En effet, si Ibn al-Ǧawzī déclare que le *Tafsīr* d'Ibn Ḥanbal contenait 120,000 *ḥadīṯs*,[226] Ḏahabī, lui, considère qu'il n'a jamais eu aucune existence et que, s'il en avait été autrement, les savants auraient fait l'impossible pour l'acquérir. "De plus, il aurait contenu tout au plus dix mille traditions (*aṯar*) en cinq volumes. Par mode de comparaison, le *Tafsīr* d'Ibn Ǧarīr renferme environ vingt mille traditions. Le seul à mentionner de *Tafsīr* de Aḥmad est Abū l-Ḥusayn Ibn al-Munādī.[227] Nul n'a plus rapporté de traditions de son père que ʿAbd Allāh, son fils. Il a, en effet, entendu de lui le *Musnad* qui comporte trente mille traditions. Il en a entendu les deux tiers[228] sous le mode de l'audition, le reste lui vient de la plume de son père (*wiǧāda*)." Ḏahabī reparle plus longuement de ce *Tafsīr* dans sa notice sur ʿAbd Allāh b. Aḥmad b. Muḥammad b. Ḥanbal, ajoutant que s'il avait eu une existence quelconque Ṭabarī en aurait transmis des traditions. Mais la façon dont il décrit la manière dont a été fait le *Musnad* peut nous aider à comprendre: Ibn Ḥanbal ne l'a pas composé lui-même, mais il transmettait (oralement) un exemplaire ou une partie à son fils et lui ordonnait de placer telle ou telle tradition dans le *musnad* d'un tel. On peut supposer que ʿAbd Allāh a regroupé des traditions ordonnées par ailleurs dans le *Musnad* pour en faire un *Tafsīr*. Quant au nombre des traditions mentionné par Ibn al-Munādī, il est évidemment exagéré. L'affirmation de Zaǧǧāǧ selon qui il a reçu une licence de transmission de ce *Tafsīr* de ʿAbd Allāh ne nous semble pas devoir être rejetée. Ce n'est pas le lieu d'émettre ici des hypothèses sur les raisons de sa non-circulation dans le milieu des savants.

23. Si nous nous sommes arrêté si longuement sur ces déclarations de Zaǧǧāǧ et sur le *Tafsīr* d'Ibn Ḥanbal, c'est parce que nous avons là, venant de l'auteur d'un ouvrage consacré à la grammaire et à la sémantique du Coran, une reconnaissance du rôle important que jouent dans certaines de ses interprétations les traditions prophétiques ou non prophétiques qu'il puise non pas chez les exégètes anciens, mais parmi des traditions extraites de celles qui furent à la base du *Musnad* d'Ibn Ḥanbal, regroupées par le

[226] Ibn al-Ǧawzī, *Manāqib al-Imām Ibn Ḥanbal*, Le Caire 1349/1941, reprise à Beyrouth, Ḫanǧī et Ḥamdān, s. d., p. 195; Abū Yaʿlā Ibn al-Farrāʾ, *Ṭabaqāt al-Ḥanābila*, I, p. 183: "J'ai lu dans le livre de Abū l-Ḥusayn Ibn al-Munādī..."

[227] Aḥmad b. Ǧaʿfar b. Muḥammad al-Baġdādī, m. muḥarram 336/juil.-août 947, spécialiste en sciences coraniques et auteur d'un *Taʾrīḫ*, *San*, XV, p. 361–62; *GAS*, I, p. 44. Il passe pour avoir écrit une centaine d'ouvrages. Son tempérament insociable et peut-être ses mœurs (*šaris al-aḫlāq*) auraient été la cause que ses œuvres n'ont pas été transmises.

[228] En *San*, XIII, p. 521: "Il en [*i. e.* traditions] entendit huit mille sous le mode de l'audition, et le reste lui vient de la plume de son père (*wiǧādatan*) (ou sans en avoir reçu la licence).

fils de ce dernier pour constituer un *Tafsīr* ʿ*an* Ibn Ḥanbal. Cela signifie que dès au moins la première moitié du IIIe siècle,[229] voire la seconde moitié du IIe siècle, on pouvait interpréter le Coran essentiellement à l'aide de traditions qui ne sont pas "purement" exégétiques.[230] Cela correspond tout à fait à ce qu'a fait Buḫārī dans le *K. al-Tafsīr* de son *Ṣaḥīḥ*, et plusieurs auteurs de recueils canoniques à son instar. Cette reconnaissance, surtout venant d'un grammairien de tradition bassorienne, est riche de conséquences pour l'évolution de l'exégèse. Cela ne veut pas dire que tous les exégètes de cette période ont procédé ainsi. En effet, Ṭabarī, par exemple, s'il puise également dans le même réservoir, cite aussi des traditions exégétiques empruntées aux anciens exégètes.

24. Si nous mettons en relation les trois exégètes ou assimilés que sont Farrāʾ, Zaǧǧāǧ et Ṭabarī, à quelles conclusions pouvons-nous parvenir? Ils ont en commun de prendre au sérieux la parole coranique d'Abraham: "C'est la plus grande d'entre elles qui l'a fait". Farrāʾ ne mentionne pas le logion des trois mensonges, bien qu'il le connût à n'en point douter, comme semble l'indiquer l'expression: "L'opinion de la majorité est: Non! Elle l'a fait [*i.e.*, la plus grande des idoles];[231] c'est comme ce qu'a dit Joseph: 'Ô vous, les caravaniers! Vous êtes des voleurs!', alors qu'il n'avait pas volé. Dieu a aidé ses prophètes en des choses bien plus grandes".

Pour ce qui est de Ṭabarī et de Zaǧǧāǧ, le logion des trois mensonges vient, en quelque sorte, renforcer leur interprétation "littérale" des paroles d'Abraham.

Ṭabarī, pour sa part, cite le logion des trois mensonges qu'il oppose à la solution de l'antéposition/postposition, et il déclare: "Il n'est pas impossible que Dieu ait permis cela [*i.e.*, les trois "mensonges"] à son intime comme moyen de réprimander son peuple, d'argumenter contre eux et de leur signaler où se trouve leur faute et leur mauvaise façon de réfléchir sur eux-mêmes. Comme a dit Joseph...".[232] En fait, il reprend la solution de Farrāʾ, mais en plus, il part en guerre contre ceux qui parlent ici d'antéposition/postposition, ces gens qui: "n'ajoutent pas foi aux

[229] Nous procédons par approches successives en fonction de témoignages certains ou, du moins, d'une grande probabilité. Nous considérons le témoignage de Zaǧǧāǧ sur le *Tafsīr* en question comme assuré. Mais cela ne signifie pas que le processus décrit ici a commencé avec lui. Ibn Ḥanbal, rappelons-le, est mort en 241.

[230] Nous ne sommes pas satisfait de cette expression, mais nous n'en avons pas trouvé d'autre. Nous voulons dire par là des traditions empruntées aux anciens exégètes, tels Muǧāhid, Muqātil et autres, c'est-à-dire antérieures à l'établissement de la "science du *ḥadīṯ*". Elles peuvent évidemment être influencées par des traditions non exégètiques, mais elles sont d'abord appliquées au texte coranique *ut sic*.

[231] Encore que ce soit là bien le sens littéral de cette parole.

[232] Tab, XVII, p. 41.

traditions (*āṯār*) et qui n'acceptent des récits en tradition (*aḫbār*) que ceux qui ont été transmis de façon ininterrompue[233] par la majorité des savants (*ʿawāmm*)."[234] Dans sa terminologie, *āṯār* désigne, en général, des traditions des Compagnons ou même des Suivants, et *aḫbār* des traditions qui remontent au Prophète.[235] On peut supposer que ce sont les muʿtazilites ou des ḫāriǧites qui sont ici visés.[236]

Dès lors, le jugement de N. Calder sur Ṭabarī nous paraît peu convaincant, voire erroné: "Ṭabarī characteristically, as we shall see, prefers narrative to theology and considers this theological subtlety overruled by the plain meaning of the prophetic *ḥadīth*."[237] Bien évidemment, Ṭabarī fait appel à des récits en tradition comme à l'accoutumée, notamment au logion des trois mensonges, mais en tenant compte et du Coran et de la théologie dont il est un grand connaisseur. Pour ce qui est du Coran, après tout, il prend le texte au sérieux, dans la mesure où Abraham dit bien que c'est la plus grande des idoles qui a brisé les autres; de plus le logion des trois mensonges vient renforcer la compréhension littérale de ce verset et de l'autre. Quant à l'intérêt théologique de Ṭabarī, nous en parlerons plus loin, mais pour lors on remarque déjà que, comme Farrāʾ, il voit dans que nous appelons un "mensonge" un moyen que Dieu a accordé à Abraham pour confondre les idolâtres.

VI. LES TROIS MENSONGES, L'INTERCESSION DU PROPHÈTE ET L'IMPECCABILITÉ DES PROPHÈTES

25. Il pourra sembler paradoxal de prétendre comme nous le faisons maintenant que le logion des trois mensonges a contribué à l'élaboration

[233] Ce dernier principe est aussi l'un de ceux de Ṭabarī pour l'acceptation des traditions prophétiques, mais des traditions approchantes peuvent servir d'argument en faveur de l'acceptation d'une tradition non transmise de façon ininterrompue. C'est d'ailleurs l'un des objets principaux de son *Tahḏīb al-āṯār*. On traduit parfois *istifāḍa* par "commune renommée"; v. Gilliot, *Elt*, p. 141–42.

[234] *Ibid.*

[235] *V.* Gilliot, *Elt*, p. 58, œuvre n° 020; id., "Le traitement du *ḥadīṯ* dans le *Tahḏīb al-āṯār* de Tabari".

[236] *V. supra* n. 208, pour une expression proche. Cette interprétation par l'antéposition, même si le terme n'est pas utilisé, est attestée également chez les chiites pour barrer la route à l'idée du mensonge d'Abraham, ainsi Baḥrānī, III, p. 65, sur 21,63, d'après Muḥammad b. Yaʿqūb, *i. e.* al-Kulīnī (m. 328/939 à Bagdad) avec une chaîne qui aboutit à Abū ʿAbd Allāh, *i. e.* Ǧaʿfar b. Muḥammad al-Ṣādiq (148/765), mis également en parallèle avec 12,70. De même Qummī, *Tafsīr*, II, p. 72, selon Ǧaʿfar al-Ṣādiq, sans la mention de 12,70.

[237] Calder, "*Tafsīr* from Ṭabarī to Ibn Kathīr", p. 108; *cf.* p. 117*sqq.*

de la doctrine de l'impeccabilité des prophètes et de l'intercession du Prophète,[238] tout au moins en islam sunnite. Nous commencerons par le plus simple: l'intercession du Prophète. Il suffira, en effet, pour s'en convaincre de se reporter à notre § 20 où l'on constatera que les "fautes" des prophètes, et notamment d'Abraham,[239] furent une bonne aubaine pour asseoir la doctrine de l'intercession de Mahomet. Il fallait que Mahomet apparût le seul digne d'intercéder en faveur des musulmans afin que Dieu les fît sortir de l'enfer.

A *contrario*, les ḫariǧites, et notamment les ibāḍites, pour qui la damnation du pécheur est éternelle, et qui donc ont moins besoin de l'intercession, s'attachent à démontrer qu'Abraham n'a pas menti. C'est ainsi que Hūd b. Muḥakkam déclare à propos de la tradition de l'intercession:

> "Cela ne peut être dit par les musulmans, et il n'y a pas d'accord sur cette version, car on rejette l'idée que l'ami du Miséricordieux ait menti. Pour ce qui est de 'Je suis malade', c'est-à-dire des péchés (*al-maᶜāṣī*) qu'ils commettent, car Abraham leur avait ordonné de ne pas faire cela. C'est ainsi que l'on dit: cela me rend malade, si quelqu'un fait le contraire de ce qu'on lui a ordonné. Pour ce qui est de ce qu'Abraham a dit à Sarah: 'S'ils t'interrogent, dis que tu es ma sœur', elle est bien sa sœur en religion, elle est également sa sœur parce qu'elle est fille d'Adam, et lui aussi est fils d'Adam. Enfin, la parole d'Abraham: 'C'est le plus grand d'entre eux qui l'a fait', c'est un blâme (*tawbīḫ*), et il ne saurait y avoir de mensonge dans un blâme. Telle est la meilleure interprétation des paroles du Prophète transmises par les transmetteurs, disant qu'Abraham avait commis trois péchés."[240]

[238] Dans l'état actuel de la recherche, nous ne pouvons établir s'il a été forgé en fonction de ces deux objectifs théologiques. Il est également quasi impossible de décider s'il y eut d'abord le logion qui fut intégré dans la tradition de l'intercession ou dans d'autres, ou bien s'il fut extrait de traditions plus longues. Pour des raisons de longueur, nous ne pouvons traiter ici des influences du judaïsme et du christianisme dans le sujet qui nous occupe. Le texte de Genèse 12,10–13 et surtout les traditions de ces deux religions ont été exploitées sans aucun doute par la tradition musulmane. *V.* G. Weil, *Biblische Legenden der Muselmänner*, p. 69–71; M. Grünbaum, *Beiträge zur semitischen Sagenkunde*, p. 102–103; A. Geiger, *Was hat Mohammed aus dem Judenthume aufgenommen?*, p. 120–26; H. Speyer, *Die biblischen Erzählungen im Qoran*, p. 138–40; D. Sidersky, *Les origines des légendes musulmanes*, p. 35–39. Pour des études sur la traditions juives à ce sujet, *v.* R. Firestone, *Journeys in Holy Lands*, p. 190 (*i. e.* n. 9 de la p. 32), ainsi que p. 188 (n. 20 de la p. 27), renvoi à l'article en hébreu de Moshe Zucker sur l'infaillibilité des prophètes, et notamment leur immunité par rapport au péché et à l'erreur, dans les littératures juives et musulmanes.

[239] Ce n'est pas le lieu de traiter ici du cas spécial de Jésus qui est le seul à n'avoir rien à se reprocher.

[240] *V.* Gilliot, "Le commentaire coranique de Hūd b. Muḥakkam", § 42, à paraître.

26. Pour ce qui est du rapport entre le logion des trois mensonges et l'impeccabilité des prophètes, nous commencerons par voir quelle est la doctrine des chiites à ce sujet, car l'on peut penser qu'elle n'a pas été sans influencer la position sunnite,[241] non pas tant pour l'interprétation des "mensonges" d'Abraham que pour l'impeccabilité elle-même.

26.1. Si nous nous tournons tout d'abord vers deux auteurs chiites muʿtazilites, Ṭūsī et Ṭabarsī,[242] nous les voyons rejeter absolument le logion des trois mensonges comme étant dénué de tout fondement. Pour innocenter Abraham d'une semblable faute, ils ont recours à des interprétations que nous avons rencontrées chez Zaǧǧāǧ ou ailleurs, y compris, la manière indirecte de parler.[243]

26.2. Mais des commentateurs ou des savant chiites antérieurs plus "classiques" dans le cadre chiite, tels Kulīnī[244] et Ibn Bābuyā,[245] ne mentionnent pas le logion des trois mensonges, mais citent une tradition qu'ils font remonter à Ǧaʿfar al-Ṣādiq selon laquelle aucune des trois paroles d'Abraham n'est un mensonge. Ainsi d'après Kulīnī: [...] al-Ḥasan al-Ṣayqal[246]/Ǧaʿfar al-Ṣādiq: Joseph (12,70) n'a pas menti, sur 21,63: "Elles ne l'on pas fait [*i.e.*, les autres idoles n'ont pas répondu à la question, parce qu'elles ne peuvent parler] et Abraham n'a pas menti [...]. Il a voulu ainsi les réformer et leur démontrer qu'ils ne pensent pas raisonnablement [...]."

Des paroles presque identiques sont même attribuées à Mahomet par Ǧaʿfar al-Ṣādiq.[247] On trouve des explications semblables sur 37,62–63,[248] mais avec en plus une interprétation typiquement chiite: si Abraham a dit qu'il était malade, c'est qu'il examina les étoiles et vit par anticipation ce qui allait arriver à al-Ḥusayn.[249] Quant au regard d'Abraham sur les

241 *V.* Amir-Moezzi, la longue n. 204, p. 103–04, qui pense qu'il semble que ce soit surtout la tradition hāšimite, pro-šīʿite, mais surtout pro-ʿabbāside, qui a glorifié l'excellence des ancêtres de Mahomet. *Cf.* Rubin, "Prophets and progenitors...", p. 50, qui montre que des traditions chiites sur la "*waṣiyya* universelle" ont été intégrées dans les sommes sunnites de traditions.

242 *V.* les références *supra sub* §7.

243 *V. supra* § 14.2.

244 Baḥrānī, III, p. 65, n° 1, sur 21,63, chaîne introduite par Muḥammad b. Yaʿqūb, *i. e.* Kulīnī. *Cf.* Kulīnī, *Rawḍa*, p. 303, n° 559, seulement sur 37,89.

245 Ibn Bābuyā, *Maʿānī l-āṯār*, p. 209–10; Baḥrānī, IV, p. 65, n° 3, tradition abrégée du précédent.

246 Ḥasan b. Ziyād al-Šayqal; *Muʿǧam riǧāl al-hadīṯ*, IV, p. 366.

247 Baḥrānī, III, p. 65, n° 2.

248 Baḥrānī, IV, p. 25, n° 2–5.

249 Baḥrānī, IV, p. 25, n° 1, d'après Kulīnī.

étoiles, ce fut une seul regard (*naẓra wāḥida*), ce qui n'est pas un péché.[250] Quant à la rencontre entre Abraham et Pharaon (ou le tyran), le mensonge à propos de Sarah, n'apparaît pas dans certaines légendes chiites, dans la mesure où le patriarche dissimule son épouse dans un coffre, essaye par tous les moyens qu'il ne soit pas ouvert, tout d'abord en présence d'un "douanier" (ou mieux: dîmeur-péager, *āšir*), puis de Pharaon.[251]

26.3. Mais il est au moins un autre lieu, 6, *ʿAnʿām*, 74, qui est l'occasion d'affirmer l'impeccabilité des prophètes: "Lorsque Abraham dit à son père Āzar (*li-abīhi*): Prendras-tu comme divinités des idoles?"[252] Ṭūsī,[253] entre autres, s'arrête longuement sur la question du nom du père d'Abraham, important pour les chiites pour qui aucun des ancêtres de Mahomet, tout au moins du côté paternel,[254] ne peut être polythéiste. Le père d'Abraham n'était pas Āzar, mais Térah (Tāraḫ), et de prendre à témoin al-Zağğāğ qui déclare: "Il n'y pas de désaccord parmi les généalogistes pour qui le nom du père (*abī*) d'Abraham est Térah (Tāriḫ)..."[255] Ṭabarsī[256] reprend pratiquement ce que dit Ṭūsī, et d'appuyer cela par une tradition: "Dieu m'a toujours fait passer des lombes des pères dans les matrices des [mères] purifiées jusqu'à ce qu'il me fît sortir en ce monde, sans que je fusse souillé par la souillure de l'ignorance."[257]

250 Baḥrānī, IV, p. 25, n° 6.

251 Kulīnī, *Rawḍa*, p. 304–06; repris par Mağlisī, *Biḥār*, XII, p. 44–47; *Cf.* Weil, p. 80–83; Sidersky, p. 42–44, qui montre que tous les détails sont repris du *Midrash Tanḥuma* (Genèse, *Lekh Lekha*, 5).

252 *V.* le commentaire de Hamza Boubakeur, p. 460 de l'éd. de 1995; *cf.* Calder, p. 102–04.

253 Ṭūsī, *Tibyān*, IV, p. 175–76.

254 *V.* Ḥalabī (Nūr al-Dīn Abū l-Farağ ʿAlī b. Ibrāhīm, m. 1044/1635), *al-Sīra al-Ḥalabiyya*, I, p. 45: *al-nasab al-šarʿī fī l-abāʾ*.

255 V. Zağğāğ, *Maʿānī l-Qurʾān wa-iʿrābuhu*, II, p. 265. Nous ne reprenons pas ici les débats en exégèse pour savoir comment s'appelait le père d'Abraham, ils sont exposés par Calder, p. 102–03. Certains exégètes distinguent ici entre *ab* et *wālid*. Peu importe que le *ab*, ancêtre ou même oncle, de plus, du côté des femmes (!), ait été idolâtre, l'important c'est que le géniteur (*wālid*) ne l'ait pas été! Cela dit, même dans la tradition chiite, il n'y a pas une unanimité totale à ce sujet; *v.* Qummī, *Tafsīr*, I, 266, selon Ğaʿfar al-Ṣādiq, Āzar, le père d'Abraham (*ab*) était astronome de Nemrod.

256 Ṭabarsī, VII, p. 105–06.

257 Ṭabarsī, IV, p. 106; Ḥalabī, I, p. 45, 47, 49, 70, avec les deux versions: *Lam azal unqalu min aṣlāb al-ṭāhirīn* et *lam yazali Llāhu yanqulunī...* Abū Nuʿaym al-Iṣfahānī (m. 430), *Dalāʾil al-nubuwwa*, p. 57, d'après ʿIkrima/Ibn ʿAbbās: *Lam yaltaqi abawāya fī l-sifāḥ, lam yazali Llāhu yanqulunī min aṣlābin ṭayyibatin ilā arḥāmin ṭāhiratin ṣafiyan muhaḏḏiban, tatašaʿʿabu šuʿbatāni illā kuntu fī ḫayrihimā.* Ibn a. Šayba, *Muṣannaf*, 27, *Faḍāʾil*, 1, éd. Šāhīn, Beyrouth, 1995, VI, p. 307, n° 31632: *ḫarağtu min nikāḥin, lam aḫruğ min sifāḥin min laduni Ādama, lam yuṣibnī sifāḥu l-ğāhiliyya.* ʿAlī/le Prophète: *ḫarağtu min nikāḥin, wa lam aḫruğ min sifāḥin, min ladun Ādama ilā an waladanī abī wa ummī*, Ṭabarānī (Abū l-Qāsim Sulaymān b. Aḥmad, m. 360), *al-Muʿğam al-awsaṭ*, V, p. 80, n° 4728, repris par Abū

Bref, tous les ancêtres du Prophète étaient des unitaristes (*muwaḥḥidūn*).[258] Nous ne nous étendrons pas plus sur ce sujet qui a été traité exhaustivement par U. Rubin, M. M. Bar-Asher et A. M. Amir-Moezzi.[259]

26.4. Ce type de tradition est souvent cité à propos de 26, *Šuʿarāʾ*, 219: "et quand tu changes de position[260] parmi ceux qui se prosternent" (*wa taqallubuka fī l-sāǧidīna*).[261] Muǧāhid (m. 104) et Muqātil (m. 150) prennent ce passage à la lettre; chez le premier: "parmi ceux qui prient; on disait qu'il voyait ceux qui étaient derrière lui à la prière",[262] ce qui est également le commentaire de ʿAbd al-Razzāq (m. 211);[263] chez le second: "Il te voit te prosterner, t'incliner et le te lever, c'est cela le *taqallub*."[264] L'ibāḍite Hūd b. Muḥakkam (*viv.* 2ème moitié IIIe s.) s'en tient lui aussi à l'interprétation rituelle sur la prière.[265] De même encore al-Ṭabarī (m.

Nuʿaym, *ibid.*/Qasṭallānī (Šihāb al-Dīn Aḥmad b. Muḥammad, m. 923/1517), *al-Mawāhib*, I, p. 86. *V.* des traditions identiques ou approchantes *in* Ibn al-Ǧawzī, *al-Wafāʾ bi-aḥwāl al-muṣṭafā*, I, p. 79; Suyūṭī, *Ḫaṣāʾiṣ*, I, p. 37, l. 23–27; p. 38, l. 1–2 /éd. Harās, p. 94; Abū Ḥātim al-Rāzī, *Aʿlām al-nubuwwa [The Peaks of Prophecy]*, éd. Salāḥ al-Ṣāwī et Ġulām-Riḍā Aʿwānī, Téhéran, 1977, p. 88, l. 16–17: *nuqiltu min ṭuhrin ilā ṭuhrin, mā massanī sifāḥu al-ǧāhiliyya.*

258 Maǧlisī, *Biḥār*, XII, p. 48–49.

259 Uri Rubin, Pre-existence and Light. Aspects of the concept of Nūr Muḥammad, *IOS* V (1975), p. 81–82, *passim*; M. M. Bar-Asher, *Studies in Early Imāmī-Shīʿī Qurʾān Exegesis* (3rd–4th/9th–10th centuries), traduction anglaise à paraître, *cap.* 4; Moezzi, p. 101–03, *passim.*

260 Traduction personnelle.

261 *V.* les traditions rassemblées sur ce thème par U. Rubin, Pre-existence and Light, p. 77–79.

262 Muǧāhid, *Tafsīr*, II, p. 467; Tab, XIX, p. 124, donne deux versions de l'interprétation de Muǧāhid, l'une d'après le *tafsīr* de Warqāʾ, l'autre d'après Ibn Ǧurayǧ. Le fait de voir derrière lui, en se retournant (Ibn ʿAṭiyya, *Muḥarrir*, IV, p. 246), ceux qui prient devient ensuite une "preuve de la prophétie: il les voit sans se retourner; Bayhaqī, *Dalāʾil*, VI, p. 74, d'après Muǧāhid: "Il voyait les rangées derrière lui, aussi bien qu'il voyait quelqu'un devant lui". Version différente, mais ayant le même sens *in* Qurt, XIII, p. 144, qui déclare que "cela est authentiquement établi, mais improbable pour l'interprétation du verset" (*ṯābit fī l-ṣaḥīḥ wa fī taʾwīl al-āya baʿīd*). Cela dit, on attribue également à Muǧāhid (et à Ibn ʿAbbās) l'interprétation suivante de ce verset: "de prophète en prophète jusqu'à ce je fusse extrait prophète (*ḥattā uḫriǧtu nabiyyan*), Suyūṭī, *Durr*, V, p. 98, l. 24–26, d'après les *Musnads* d'Ibn a. ʿUmar al-ʿAdanī et d'al-Bazzār, d'après Ibn a. Ḥātim, al-Ṭabarānī, Ibn Mardawayh et al-Bayhaqī dans les *Dalāʾil.*

263 ʿAbd al-Razzāq, *Tafsīr*, III, p. 77/II, p. 65–66, n° 2139, d'après Maʿmar/Qatāda; puis tradition n° 2140, d'après Maʿmar/Qatāda/ʿIkrima: "Te levant, te prosternant, t'inclinant, t'asseyant"; même tradition avec la même chaîne en Tab, XIX, p. 124, l. 3–4.

264 Muqātil, III, p. 282.

265 Hūd b. Muḥakkam, *Tafsīr*, III, p. 243.

310)[266] qui en appelle au rapport de Muǧāhid, d'Ibn ʿAbbās et autres, toujours sans citer une seule tradition sur la préexistence de Mahomet dans les lombes des prophètes. Il faut attendre Abū l-Layṯ al-Samarqandī (m. 375) et al-Wāhidī (m. 428) pour voir apparaître, tout au moins pour ce lieu du Coran, la "tradition des lombes des prophètes", même s'ils privilégient l'explication rituelle. Le premier l'introduit par: "on dit que";[267] le second, après avoir dit que l'explication matérielle est celle de la majorité des exégètes, déclare qu'Ibn ʿAbbās a dit: "Il veut dire dans les lombes des prophètes unitaristes, de prophète en prophète, jusqu'à ce qu'il te fît sortir dans cette communauté, ainsi l'Envoyé de Dieu [est toujours passé dans les lombes des prophètes jusqu'à ce que sa mère le mît au monde]."[268]

Zamaḫšarī (m. 538/1144) ne donne qu'une explication rituelle avec également une tradition de Abū Ḥanīfa qui, interrogé par Muqātil (*uterque ob.* 150/767) sur le lieu du Coran où il est question de l'office religieux communautaire, aurait répondu qu'il ne le lui en venait pas à l'esprit (*lā yaḥḍurunī*), mais aurait récité ce verset.[269]

Rāzī qui tient à l'explication rituelle s'en prend aux rāfiḍites qui utilisent la "tradition des lombes des prophètes" pour donner à ce verset un sens qu'il n'a pas, déclarant que la tradition d'un seul (*ḫabar wāḥid*) ne saurait contredire le Coran.[270]

26.5. La question de "l'examen" des étoiles par Abraham ou du "regard" qu'il a porté sur elles (37,63) a inquiété aussi l'exégèse sunnite. Nous en avons deux témoignages fort intéressants et significatifs chez Qurṭubī,[271] mais que nous n'avons malheureusement pas retrouvés ailleurs avec une chaîne de garants pour savoir approximativement quant ils étaient en

[266] Tab, XIX, p. 124–25.

[267] Abū al-Layṯ al-Samarqandī, *Tafsīr*, II, p. 486: "C'est à dire le fait que tu es passé des lombes des pères aux matrices des mères depuis Adam jusqu'à Noé, puis Abraham, puis ceux qui sont venus après lui".

[268] Wāḥidī, *Wasīṭ*, III, p. 325, Ibn ʿAbbās par la voie de ʿAṭāʾ/ʿIkrima. La partie entre crochets se trouve à la fois chez Wāḥidī et chez Abū Nuʿaym, *Dalāʾil al-nubuwwa*, p. 58, nº 17; Hayṯamī (Nūr al-Dīn ʿAlī b. a. Bakr, m. 807), *Maǧmaʿ al-zawāʾid, K. ʿAlāmāt al-nubuwwa, Bāb fī Karāmat aṣlihi*, Beyrouth, Muʾassasat al-Maʿārif, VIII, p. 217, d'après Ibn ʿAbbās: *min ṣulbi nabiyyin ilā ṣulbi nabiyyin ḥattā ṣirtu nabiyyan*, rapporté par al-Bazzār (Abū Bakr A. b. ʿAmr, m. 292/905, dans son *Musnad*; *v. GAS*, I, p. 162); en Qasṭallānī (Šihāb al-Dīn Aḥmad b. Muḥammad, m. 923/1517), *Mawāhib, cap. al-Nasab al-šarīf*, I, p. 86–87, également d'après al-Bazzār, mais: *ḥatta aḫraǧtuka nabiyyan*. Abū l-Baqāʾ Hibat Allāh al-Ḥillī (*viv.* 2ᵉ moitié Vᵉ ou 1ère moitié VIᵉ s. h.), *K. al-Manāqib al-mazyadiyya*, p. 358: *Nuqiltu mina l-aṣlābi l-ṭāhirati ilā l-arḥāmi l-ṭāhirati nikāhan wa lā sifāḥan. Cf.* les traditions semblables rassemblée par U. Rubin, Pre-existence and Light, p. 80*sqq.*

[269] Zamaḫšarī, III, p. 132.

[270] Rāzī, XXIV, p. 173–74.

[271] Qurt, XV, p. 92.

circulation: selon Ibn ʿAbbās: “L’astronomie/astrologie (*ʿilm al-nuǧūm*) faisait partie [des attributs] de la prophétie, mais lorsque Dieu arrêta le soleil pour Josué fils de Nūn,[272] cela fut supprimé. L’examen qu’Abraham fit des étoiles était donc une science prophétique”, et Qurṭubī de poursuivre immédiatement: “On raconte que Ǧuwaybir[273] qui tenait cela d’al-Ḍaḥḥāk[274] a dit: L’astronomie/astrologie demeura en vigueur [selon la Loi divine] jusqu’à l’époque de Jésus jusqu’à ce qu’ils[275] vinssent voir ce dernier en un lieu duquel ils n’avaient pas été informés. Marie dit alors: D’où tenez-vous la connaissance du lieu où il se trouve? Ils répondirent: Des étoiles [des astres]. Il [Jésus] pria alors son Seigneur en disant: Ô Dieu, ne leur fais pas comprendre la science des étoiles (*ʿilmahā*). Et c’est ainsi qu’aucun ne sut plus cette science, que son statut devint légalement interdit et qu’elle fut ignorée des gens”.

On voit là comment un récit légendaire peut à la fois être utilisé pour rester fidèle à la littéralité du texte coranique qui dit qu’Abraham a jeté un regard sur les étoiles et pour satisfaire aux exigences d’une doctrine théologique naissante sur l’impeccabilité des prophètes.

VII. CONCLUSIONS

27. Ce parcours exégétique conduit à quelques conclusions sur la genèse, l’évolution et la circulation de plusieurs thèmes exégétiques jusqu’au début du IVe/Xe siècle, ici, il est vrai, dans un cadre défini et réduit, puisque le cas retenu ne porte pas sur une question de droit, hormis un point annexe, la licéité du mensonge en certaines occasions.[276] Il s’agit

[272] Sur cette légende, *v.* Jos 10, 12–15; Grünbaum, p. 184–85; Sidersky, 106–08; ʿUmāra b. Waṯīma al-Fārisī (m. 289/902), *in* Khoury, *Légendes*, p. 54; Muqātil, I, p. 468, sur 5,25; Tab, X, *ca.* p. 176, sur 5, 23; Ṭabarī, *Annales*, I, p. 513/*History*, III, p. 95; Šahrastānī, *in Lrs*, I, p. 632, II, p. 164–65; Baġawī, *Tafsīr*, II, p. 27–28, sur 5, 26, *Faṣl fī ḏikr wafāt Hārūn; Livre de la création*, III, p. 90; Sibṭ Ibn al-Ǧawzī, *Mirʾāt al-zamān*, I, p. 452. Il est dit notamment d’Idrīs/Enoch: *naẓara fī ʿilmi l-nuǧūmi*; Rāzī, XXI, p. 233.

[273] B. Saʿīd al-Balḫī (*ob. ca.* 150/767, ou entre 140 et 150); *v.* Gilliot, *Baqara*, p. 172–73.

[274] Pour lui, *v. supra* n. 38.

[275] Il s’agit de la légende la la visite des rois mages. *V.* Ṭabarī, *Annales*, I, p. 728–29/I, p. 596–97/Trad. A. Ferré, *in Islamochristiana*, 5 (1979), p. 19.

[276] Pour satisfaire sa femme, pour rétablir la concorde entre deux personnes, pour tromper l’ennemi au cours d’une guerre; *v.* Ibn a. l-Dunyā, *K. al-Ṣamt wa ādāb al-lisān*, éd. Naǧm ʿAbd al-Raḥmān Ḫalaf, Beyrouth, Dār al-Ġarb al-islāmī, 1986, n° 501, 503. Ou selon Zuhrī: la guerre, la concorde entre les gens, l’homme qui parle à sa femme et vice versa [toujours pour éviter la discorde], n° 502, avec les traditions parralèles dans les recueils canoniques indiquées par l’éditeur; Ṭabarī, *Tahḏīb al-āṯār, Musnad ʿAlī*, n° 216–21, selon le principe énoncé par Mahomet: “N’est pas menteur qui veut rétablir la concorde entre les gens et souhaite le bien”.

donc essentiellement de la façon dont les premiers exégètes et ceux qui les ont suivis ont procédé lorsqu'ils se sont trouvés face à l'aporie suivante: comment honorer le texte coranique dans sa littéralité et satisfaire aux exigences d'une doctrine théologique qui se mettait en place dans une ambiance de débats et de conflits d'idées. Car si l'impeccabilité des prophètes n'était pas encore établie au Ier siècle et dans la première moitié du IIe siècle, il n'en restait pas moins qu'un homme juste, a fortiori un prophète, ne devait pas mentir, si toutefois mensonge il y avait.

28. Les récits coraniques sur Abraham sont eux-mêmes des bribes éclatées de la légende abrahamique qui circulait dans le Moyen-Orient et en particulier dans une péninsule Arabique qui n'était pas un milieu fermé, comme en témoignent notamment les liens avec Ḥīra et avec la Perse,[277] mais aussi les récits d'origine yéménite. Ils s'inscrivent dans un topos coranique récurrent, celui de l'affrontement entre l'homme pieux, en l'occurrence un "prophète", et un souverain, potentat "tyran", qu'il soit babylonien, pharaonique ou autre. Le "prophète-devin" s'y montre plus malin que ce dernier, déjouant ses stratagèmes, sa magie, voire son recours aux astres.[278]

Les exégètes des premières générations retrouvaient dans les légendes prophétiques rapportées par le Coran des condensés de récits qui ne leur étaient pas étrangers et dont le caractère allusif suscitait en eux non seulement des réminiscences, mais aussi la mise en branle de l'imagination et de l'art du conteur. Ces histoires évoquées dans les versets coraniques étaient l'occasion de remarques brèves destinées à les "désambiguïser" (*taʿyīn al-mubham*), expression probablement plus tardive, mais bienvenue ici, parce que correspondant bien à une société marquée par l'oralité. Mais elles pouvaient aussi servir de prétexte ou d'occasion pour établir des récits plus importants, parsemés de versets coraniques, ordonnés en séquences "chronologiques". En somme, c'était déjà une forme de mise en ordre, de "rationalisation" du texte coranique, dans la mesure où l'introduction de la chronologie, même à l'intérieur de récits mythiques, est l'une des manifestations du *logos*.

29. A ce premier stade, il n'est pas encore question de mensonges d'Abraham. Quoi d'étonnant d'ailleurs, puisque le Coran ne donne pas *ut*

277 *V.* Gilliot, Muḥammad, le Coran et les "contraintes de l'histoires", *in* Stefan Wild (ed.), *The Qurʾān as Text*, Leyde, Brill, 1996, p. 23–24, n. 87, sur al-Naḍr b. al-Ḥāriṯ, avec référence à l'étude de M. J. Kister sur Hīra; Gilliot, Les "informateurs" juifs et chrétiens de Muḥammad. Reprise d'un problème traité par Aloys Sprenger et Theodor Nöldeke, à paraître in *JSAI*, § 25 et n. 108.

278 *V.* H. T. Norris, "*Qiṣaṣ* elements in the Qurʾān", *in CHAL*, I, p. 247–50.

sic à penser qu'Abraham ait menti! Ces exégètes ou conteurs se contentent de trouver une raison à la parole d'Abraham: "Je suis malade": une maladie quelconque, la peste, ou encore le fait qu'on lui a marché sur le pied, mais avec l'idée coranique que le patriarche était décidé à jouer un mauvais tour aux idolâtres.[279] Cela dit, certains déjà, probablement dès la fin du Ier ou le début du IIe siècle ont des intepértations qui sembleraient indiquer qu'ils veulent innocenter Abraham de son "mensonge", notamment al-Ḥasan à Bassorah.[280] Les moins sensibles à l'aspect possiblement mensonger des reparties d'Abraham sont certainement les conteurs, ou encore des transmetteurs ou des auteurs du genre des *maġāzī/siyar*, entendus ici dans le sens général d'une historiographie des temps mythiques (*qiṣaṣ al-anbiyā'* anciennes) et de l'époque prophétique (*sīra*).[281]

30. Le logion des trois mensonges[282] ne semble avoir commencé à "contaminer" l'exégèse des versets 21,63 et 37,89 qu'à partir de la première moitié du IIIe/IXe siècle, non pas tant sous l'effet de la doctrine de l'impeccabilité des prophètes, à tout le moins en islam "sunnite", que de celle de l'intercession du Prophète. La première, en effet, a probablement son origine dans la théologie chiite qui soutenait, tout au moins depuis la première moitié du IIe siècle, que l'Imam désigné doit être exempt de l'erreur et du péché.[283] Ṭabarī, et il n'est pas le seul, admet que les prophètes peuvent commettre des fautes mineures (*ṣaġā'ir*).[284] Dès lors, il

[279] *V. supra* § 8–10. Nous n'encombrons plus ici notre texte de dates, on les trouvera en ces lieux dans le texte ou dans les notes.

[280] *V.* § 10 *in fine*. Si nous mentionnons ici Bassorah, ce n'est pas par hasard, comme on le verra plus loin.

[281] Cela inclut non seulement Wahb b. Munabbih (m. 114/732 ou 110/728; *v.* Khoury, *Wahb b. Munabbih*, I, p. 232, n° 11), Ibn Isḥāq, mais encore des exégètes comme Kalbī, Muqātil, etc., dont des segments exégétiques entiers auraient leur place dans les *qiṣaṣ al-anbiyā'* anciennes. Nous n'avons pas pris en considération les ouvrages tardifs sur les légendes prophétiques pour des raisons et pour des motifs de méthode. *Cf.* Ṯaʿlabī (a. Isḥ. A. b. M. b. Ibr., m. 427/1035), *ʿArā'is al-maǧālis*, Le Caire 1332, p. 45, l. 33–34 ("Abraham n'a dit que trois mensonges"); 47, l. 27–28 ("C'est ma sœur")/Beyrouth, Šarikat Šamarlī, 1980, p. 80, 84; Ṭarā'ifī (Abū ʿAbd Allāh Muḥammad b. Aḥmad b. Muṭarrif al-Kinānī, m. 464/1062), *Qiṣaṣ al-anbiyā'*, éd. R. Tottoli, p. 147, n° 128–30, notes de Totolli, p. 408–09; Kisā'ī, éd. Eisenberg, p. 138, 142/trad. W. M. Thackston, p. 146, 150–51 (mais le mot mensonge n'est pas utilisé).

[282] *V. supra* § 18.

[283] *V.* W. Madelung, 'Iṣma', *EI*, IV, p. 190b: pour le théologien chiite Hišām b. al-Ḥakam (m. 179/795–6), les Imams sont impeccables, mais les prophètes pouvaient désobéir aux ordres de Dieu, quitte à être tancés ensuite par Dieu. *Cf.* Gimaret, *in Lrs*, I, p. 536 et n. 180.

[284] ʿIyāḍ, *Šifā'*, p. 144, après avoir dit que c'est la position des "pieux anciens". C'est également la position de Ǧuwaynī et du muʿtazilite Abū Hāšim; *v.* ʿAlī al-Qarī, *Šarḥ al-Šifā'*, II, p. 257, l. 26–28. *V.* Gimaret, *in Lrs*, I, p. 286, n. 98, sur la position de Ǧubbā'ī, pour qui il

n'est pas étonnant qu'à la suite de plusieurs exégètes antérieurs il prenne au sérieux les deux versets du Coran selon lesquels Abraham semblerait mentir, s'appuyant aussi sur le logion des trois mensonges.[285]

31. Mais il nous paraît que le logion a surtout était transmis dans le cadre de la "tradition de l'intercession" (*ḥadīṯ al-šafāʿa*), et plus spécialement à Bassorah, mais aussi à un moindre degré à Coufa. Nous inclinerions même à penser que cette tradition prophétique aurait pu voir le jour à Bassorah: le sermon d'Ibn ʿAbbās dans la mosquée de cette métropole,[286] les chaînes bassoriennes conduisant à Anas[287] par la voie de Qatāda.[288] La présence du logion des trois mensonges ou des fautes d'Abraham, ainsi que la mention de celles des autres "prophètes", hormis Jésus qui n'a rien à se reprocher, fut bien utile pour asseoir la doctrine de l'intercession du Prophète.[289]

32. Mais entre la diffusion ou l'invention de la tradition de l'intercession et sa prise en compte dans l'exégèse, il s'est écoulé du temps. C'est pourquoi nous pensons pouvoir dire que le logion des trois mensonges a "contaminé" l'exégèse de nos deux versets coraniques seulement dès la première moitié du IIIe siècle.[290] Toutefois cela ne s'opposait pas à ce que l'on trouvât des

est impossible que les prophètes pèchent intentionnellement. Quant à la position d'Ašʿarī sur ce point, elle est pour l'essentiel celle de Ǧubbāʾī: antérieurement à leur mission prophétique "les prophètes sont peccables et susceptibles même de fautes graves", Gimaret, *La doctrine d'al-Ashʿarī*, Paris, Cerf, 1990, p. 459.

285 *V. supra* § 24.

286 *V. supra* § 20.2, 20.12.

287 *V.* les remarques critiques de G. H. A. Juynboll, *Muslim Tradition*, Cambridge, 1983, p. 144–45, qui, de plus, parle de "véritables armées de soi-disant élèves d'Anas". *Cf. supra* n. 157, sur le cas de Ṯābit étudié par Juynboll. Depuis un débat est engagé sur certaines des positions de Juynboll, *v.* G. H. A. Juynboll, Nāfiʿ, the *mawlā* of Ibn ʿUmar, and his position in Muslim *Ḥadīth* Literature, *Der Islam* 70 (1993), p. 207–44; id., 'Nāfiʿ', *EI* VII, p. 877–78, et la remise en question de certaines de ses thèses par Harald Motzki, *Quo vadis, Ḥadīṯ*-Forschung. Eine kritische Untersuchung von G. H. A. Juynboll: 'Nāfiʿ, the *mawlā* of Ibn ʿUmar, and his position in Muslim *Ḥadīṯ* Literatures', *Der Islam* 73 (1996), p. 40–80 (à suivre dans la prochaine livraison).

288 *V. supra* § 20.7–9, 20.11. Toutefois en 20.14, c'est une délégation coufienne, composée, semble-t-il, de ḫāriǧites de de murgi'ites qui se rend à La Mecque auprès de Ǧābir b. ʿAl. lors du pèlerinage, avec en plus dans la chaîne de garants un Bassorien et un murǧiʾite coufien, originaire de Bassorah.

289 *V. supra* § 25.

290 *V. supra* § 21–23, surtout avec la mention du *Tafsīr* d'Ibn Ḥanbal par Zaǧǧāǧ. Encore une fois, ce *Tafsīr* devait être une suite de traditions telles qu'on les trouve dans son *Musnad* qui contient de nombreuses voies de transmission de la tradition de l'intercession. Muḥāsibī (m. 243/857) connaissait cette tradition, mais il n'en tire pas les mêmes conclusions qu'Ašʿarī; *v.* van Ess, *Gedankenwelt*, p. 125–26. Il nous manque un commentaire contemporain des

solutions plus ou moins ingénieuses pour innocenter Abraham de ses trois fautes, ou du moins pour en atténuer la gravité, non seulement par le recours aux anciennes légendes,[291] mais aussi aux nouveaux moyens qu'offrait une théologie plus rationnelle.[292] voire la rhétorique.[293] Abraham a menti sans mentir, tout en mentant!

Dans la tradition chiite, pour des raisons que nous avons expliquées,[294] l'idée qu'Abraham ait pu mentir est inacceptable. Paradoxalement, c'est pourtant la doctrine chiite qui semble bien avoir influencé indirectement une grande partie de l'exégèse sunnite des deux versets ici retenus, au moins dès la première moitié du IIIe/IXe siècle.

Maʿāni l-Qurʾān de Farrāʾ ou de peu postérieur à eux pour nous prononcer avec plus de certitude; *v. supra* § 17, nos remarques sur le *Tafsīr* de Yaḥyā b. Sallām.

291 *V. supra* § 8–10.

292 *V. supra* § 6 *sub* Abū Muslim.

293 *V. supra* § 14–16.

294 *V. supra* § 26.1–3.

RÉFÉRENCES BIBLIOGRAPHIQUES ET ABRÉVIATIONS*

ʿAbd al-Razzāq (Abū Bakr b. Hammām al-Ḥimyarī al-Ṣanʿānī, m. 211/827), *Tafsīr*, I–III en 4, éd. Muṣṭafā Muslim Muḥammad, Riyad, Maktabat al-Rušd, 1410/1989/I–II, éd. ʿAbd al-Muʿṭī Amīn Qalʿaǧī, Beyrouth, Dār al-Maʿrifa, 1411/1991, 350+338 p.

Abū ʿAlī al-Ǧubbāʾī (m. 303/915), *v.* Gimaret.

Abū l-Baqāʾ Hibat Allāh al-Ḥillī (*viv.* 2e moitié Ve ou 1ère moitié VIe s. h.), *K. al-Manāqib al-mazyadiyya [fī aḫbār al-mulūk al-asadiyya]*, éd. Ṣāliḥ Mūsā Darāka et ʿAbd al-Qādir Ḫuraysāt, Amman, al-Ǧāmiʿa al-ʾurdunniyya, 1404/1984, 682 p.

Abū l-Baqāʾ al-ʿUkbarī (Muḥibb al-Dīn ʿAbd Allāh b. al-Ḥusayn al-Baġdādī al-Ḍarīr al-Naḥwī, m. 616/1219), *al-Tibyān fī iʿrāb al-Qurʾān*, I–II, éd. ʿAlī Muḥammad al-Biǧāwī, Le Caire, ʿĪsā l-Bābī l-Ḥalabī, 1396/1976, 11+1362 p.

Abū Ḥayyān al-Ġarnāṭī (Aṯīr al-Dīn Muḥammad b. Yūsuf, m. ṣaf. 745/juil. 1344), *Tafsīr al-Baḥr al-muḥīṭ*, I–VIII, Le Caire 1328–29/1911, réimpr. Beyrouth, Dār al-Fikr, 1983.

Abū Hilāl al-ʿAskarī (al-Ḥasan b. ʿAbd Allāh b. Sahl, *ob. post* 400/1010), *K. al-Ṣināʿatayn*, éd. ʿAlī Muḥammad al-Biǧāwī et Muḥammad Abū l-Faḍl Ibrāhīm, Le Caire 1952, réimpr. Sidon/Beyrouth, al-Maktaba al-ʿaṣriyya, 1986, 528 p.

Abū l-Layṯ al-Samarqandī (Naṣr b. Muḥammad b. Ibrāhīm al-Ḥanafī, m. ǧumāda II 375/oct.–nov. 985), *Tafsīr [Baḥr al-ʿulūm]*, I–III, éd. ʿAlī Muḥammad Muʿawwaḍ *et al.*, Beyrouth, Dār al-Kutub al-ʿilmiyya, 1413/1993.

Abū Nuʿaym al-Iṣfahānī (Aḥmad b. ʿAbd Allāh b. Aḥmad b. Isḥāq, m. muḥ. 430/oct. 1038), *K. al-Asmāʾ wa l-ṣifāt*, Beyrouth, Dār al-Kutub al-ʿilmyya, 1405/1985 (reprise de l'éd. du Caire 1358/1939, Maṭbaʿat al-Saʿāda), 664 p.

Id., *Dalāʾil al-nubuwwa*, I–II en 1, éd. M. Rawwās Qalʿaǧī et ʿAbd al-Barr ʿAbbās, Beyrouth, Dār al-Nafāʾis, 1406/1986,694 p.

Abū Yaʿlā al-Mawṣilī (Aḥmad b. ʿAlī b. al-Muṯannā al-Tamīmī, m. 307/919), *Musnad*, I–XIV, éd. Ḥusayn Salīm Asad, Damas, Dār al-Maʾmūn li-l-turāṯ, 1405–10/1985–90.

* Ne sont données ici, sauf exception, que les références complètes qui ne se trouvent pas dans Gilliot, *Elt (v. infra)*, p. 283–307, liste des abréviations, p. 308. On y trouvera notamment les références des grands recueils de traditions "authentiques" (Muslim, Abū Dāwūd, Tirmiḏī, etc.), ou moins "authentiques", des ouvrages d'onomastique, etc., qui ne sont pas reprises ici.

Aḫfaš al-Awsaṭ (Abū l-Ḥasan Saʿīd b. Masʿada al-Muǧāšiʿī, m. 215/830), *Maʿānī l-Qurʾān*, I–II, éd. Fāʾiz Fāris, al-Ṣafāt (Koweït), à compte d'auteur, 1981^{2} (1979^{1}), 667+2/p. I–II, éd. ʿAbd al-Amīr M. Amīn al-Ward, Beyrouth, ʿĀlam al-kutub, 1405/1985, 858 p.

ʿAlī al-Qārī al-Harawī, *v. sub* ʿIyāḍ.

Andrae (Tor), *Die Person Muhammeds in Lehre und Glauben seiner Gemeinde*, Stockholm ("Archives d'Études Orientales", 16), 1918, VI+401 p.

ʿAyyāšī (Abū al-Naḍr Muḥammad b. Masʿūd b. Muḥammad al-Sulamī al-Samarqandī, *ob. ca.* 320/932), *Tafsīr*, I–II, Téhéran 1380/1961, 403+368 p.

Baġawī (Abū Muḥammad al-Ḥusayn b. Masʿūd b. Muḥammad al-Farrāʾ al-Šāfiʿī, m. 516/1122), *Maṣābīḥ al-sunna*, I–IV, éd. Yūsuf ʿAbd al-Raḥmān al-Marʿašlī *et al.*, Beyrouth, Dār al-Maʿrifa, 1407/1987.

Id., *Tafsīr al-Baġawī al-musammā bi-Maʿālim at-tanzīl*, I–IV, éd. Ḫālid ʿAbd al-Raḥmān al-ʿAk et Marwān Sawār [éd. non critique; texte établi à partir de l'une des éd. anciennes], Beyrouth, Dār al-Maʿrifa, 1992^{3} (1983^{1}).

Baḥrānī (al-Sayyid Hāšim b. Sulaymān, m. 1107/1696), *al-Burhān fī tafsīr al-Qurʾān*, I–IV, Téhéran, 1375/1956, réimpr. Beyrouth, al-Wafāʾ, 1403/1983.

Bar-Asher (Meir Michael), *Studies in Early Imāmī-Shīʿī Qurʾān Exegesis* (3rd–4th/9th–10th centuries), thèse DPh, Université de Jérusalem, janvier 1991 (en hébreu). Nous en avions consulté la table des matières et le résumé en anglais, XX p. Depuis, l'auteur nous a envoyé la traduction anglaise de cette thèse qui devrait paraître en 1997: *Studies in Early Imāmī-Shīʿī Qurʾān Exegesis* (3rd–4th/9th–10th centuries), temporary title, 297 p., *pro manuscripto*.

Bayḍāwī (al-Qāḍī Nāṣir al-Dīn Abū Saʿīd ʿAbd Allāh b. ʿUmar b. Muḥammad, m. 716/1316–17 ou 708), *Anwār al-tanzīl wa asrār al-taʾwīl*, I–II, Le Caire, Muṣṭafā l-Bābī al-Ḥalabī, $1375/1955^{2}$, 302+320 p.

Bayhaqī (Abū Bakr Aḥmad b. al-Ḥusayn, m. 458/1066), *Dalāʾil al-nubuwwa*, I–VII, éd. ʿAbd al-Muʿṭī Qalʿaǧī, Beyrouth, Dār al-Kutub al-ʿilmiyya, 1405/1985.

Id., I–X, *al-Ǧāmiʿ li-šuʿab al-īmān*, éd. ʿAbd al-ʿAlī ʿAbd al-Ḥamīd Ḥamīd, Bombay/Le Caire, al-Dār al-Salafiyya/Dār al-Rayyān, 1406–10/1986–90, éd. inachevée.

Buḫārī (Abū ʿAbd Allāh Muḥammad b. Ismāʿīl al-Ǧuʿfī, m. 256870), 00, titre arabe, 00/Trad., II, p. 00/*Fatḥ*, VI, p. 00/Qast, V, p. 00, se lit Buḫārī, *al-Ṣaḥīḥ*, n° du livre, titre arabe du livre, n° du chapitre (*bāb*)/Ibn Ḥaǧar al-ʿAsqalānī, *Fatḥ al-bārī bi-šarḥ Ṣaḥīḥ al-Buḫārī*,

I-XIII, Le Caire, al-Maṭbaʿa al-Bahiyya al-miṣriyya, 1348–52/1929–33; réimpr. Beyrouth, Dār Iḥyāʾ al-turāṯ al-ʿarabī, 1402/1981/
Qasṭallānī (Šihāb al-Dīn Abū al-ʿAbbās Aḥmad b. Muḥammad b. a. Bakr), *Iršād al-sārī li-šarḥ Ṣaḥīḥ al-Buḫārī*, I–X, Boulac, al-Maṭbaʿa al-Amīriyya, 1323–27/1905–09; réimpr. Beyrouth, Dār Iḥyāʾ al-turāṯ al-ʿarabī, s. d.

Calder (Norman), *Tafsīr* from Ṭabarī to Ibn Kathīr: problems in the description of a genre, illustrated with reference to the story of Abraham, *in* G. R. Hawting and Abdul-Kader A. Shareef (ed.), *Approaches to the Qurʾān*, Londres 1993, p. 101–40.

Coran: 1. *Le Coran*, Traduction française et commentaire d'après la tradition, les différentes écoles de lecture, d'exégèse, de théologie, les interprétations mystiques, les tendances schismatiques et les doctrines hérétiques de l'Islâm, et à la lumière des théories scientifiques, philosophiques et politiques modernes, par le Cheikh Si Hamza Boubakeur, Paris, Maisonneuve & Larose, 1995 (Paris, I-I, 1965[1]; ici éd. revue et augmentée, en un vol.), 2131 p. 2. Traduction par Denise Masson, revue par Sobhi El Saleh (avec le texte arabe, pagination doublée pour le texte arabe et la traduction), *Essai d'interprétation du Coran inimitable*, Beyrouth, Dār al-Kitāb al-lubnānī, 1967, LXIV+889 p.

Du Marsais (César Chesneau, sieur; + 1756), *Traité des tropes*, suivi de J. Paulhan, Traité des figures, Paris, Le Nouveau Commerce, 1977 (1730[1]), 322 p.

Dupriez (Bernard), *Gradus*. Les procédés littéraires (Dictionnaire), Paris, Union générale d'éditions ("10/18", nº 170; Ottawa, 1977[1]), 542 p.

Eisenberg (Isaac) (ed.), *Vita prophetarum, auctore Muḥammed ben ʿAbdallah al-Kisaʾi*, ex codicibus qui in Monaco, Bonna, Lugd. Batav., Lipsia et Gothana asservantur edidit Dr. Isaac Eisenberg, I–II, Lugduni Batavorum (Leyde), E. J. Brill, 1922, XII+309 p. / *The Tales of the Prophets of al-Kisaʾi*, Translated from the Arabic with notes by W. M. Thackston, Boston, Twayne Publishers, 1978, XXXIV+377 p.

Elt, v. Gilliot

Ess (Josef van), *TG* = *Theologie und Gesellschaft im 2. und 3. Jahrhundert Hidschrah*. Eine Geschichte des religiösen Denkens im frühen Islam, I–VI, Berlin/New York, Walter de Gruyter, 1991–97.

Fatḥ, v. sub Buḫārī.

Fayyūmī (Abū ʿAbbās Aḥmad b. Muḥammad b. ʿAbd Allāh, *ob. post* 770/1368), *Miṣbāḥ* = Fayyūmī, *al-Miṣbāḥ al-munīr fī ġarīb al-Šarḥ al-waǧīz li-l-Rāfiʿī*, Le Caire, al-Maṭbaʿa al-Amīriyya, 1921[4], 16+979 p.

Firestone (Reuven), *Journeys in Holy Lands*. The Evolution of the Abraham-Ishmael Legends Islamic Exegesis, Albany, SUNY, 1990, XV+265 p. *Cf.* le c. r. critique de Uri Rubin, in *JSAI* 17 (1994), p. 245–49.

Fontanier (Pierre, + *post* 1830), *Les figures du discours*, Paris, Flammarion ("Science. Flammarion"), introduction par Gérard Genette, 1968, 505 p. [contient: *Manuel classique pour l'étude des tropes*, Paris 1821, ici *Manuel des tropes*, 1830[4], et les *Figures autres que les tropes*, Paris 1827].

Ġazālī (Abū Ḥāmid Muḥammad b. Muḥammad, m. 505/111), *Iḥyā' ʿulūm al-dīn*, I–IV, Boulac, al-Maṭbaʿa al-Amīriyya, 1289/1872, réimpr., Le Caire 1353/1933/Zabidī, *Itḥāf al-sāda bi-šarḥ Iḥyā' ʿulūm al-dīn*, Beyrouth, Dār al-Kutub al-ʿilmiyya, 1989, I–XIV/ *The Remembrance of Death and Afterlife*. Kitāb Dhikr al-mawt wa-mā baʿdahu. Book XL of the Revival of the religious sciences, Iḥyā' ʿulūm al-dīn, translated with an introduction and notes by T. J. Winter, Cambridge, The Islamic Texts Society, 1989, XXX+ 347 p.

Gilliot (Claude), *Elt = Exégèse, langue et théologie en islam*. L'exégèse coranique de Tabari, Paris, Vrin ("Études musulmanes", XXXII), 1990, 320 p.

Id., Der koranische Kommentar des Ibāḍiten Hūd b. Muḥakkam/ Muḥkim, à paraître dans les actes du XXVI. Deutscher Orientalistentag (*ZDMG Suppl.*), Leipzig, 25–29 septembre 1995, et dans une version française beaucoup plus développée: "Le commentaire coranique de Hūd b. Muḥakkam/ Muḥkim", à paraître dans *Arabica*, 1997.

Id., Le traitement du *ḥadīṯ* dans le *Tahḏīb al-āṯār* de Tabari, *Arabica* XLI (1994), p. 309–51.

Id., Les débuts de l'exégèse coranique, *R.E.M.M.M.* 58 (1990/4), p. 82–100.

Id., Muqātil, grand exégète, traditionniste et théologien maudit, *JA* CCLXXIX (1991), p. 39–92.

Id., *La sourate al-Baqara dans le commentaire de Ṭabarī*. Le développement et le fonctionnement des traditions exégétiques à la lumière du commentaire des versets 1 à 40 de la sourate, thèse pour le troisième cycle, Université Paris III, 1982, 414+138 p.

Gimaret = Gimaret (Daniel), *Une lecture muʿtazilite du Coran*. Le *Tafsīr* d'Abū ʿAlī al-Djubbā'ī (m. 303/915) partiellement reconstitué à partir de ses citateurs, Louvain/Paris, Peeters ("Bibliothèque de l'École Pratique des Hautes Études. Section des sciences religieuses", CI), 1994, 889 p.

Grünbaum (Max), *Beiträge zur semitischen Sagenkunde*, Leyde, E. J. Brill, 1893, 292 p.

Ḥakīm Tirmiḏī, *Nawādir al-uṣūl* = Ḥakīm Tirmiḏī (Abū ʿAbd Allāh Muḥakkam b. ʿAlī b. al-Ḥasan b. Bišr, *adhuc viv.* 318/930), *Nawādir al-uṣūl fī maʿrifat aḥādīṯ al-rasūl*, I–II, éd. Aḥmad ʿAbd al-Raḥīm al-Sāyiḥ et al-Sayyid al-Ǧamīlī, Le Caire, Dār al-Rayyān, 1408/1988, 720+704 p.

Ḥalabī (Nūr al-Dīn Abū l-Faraǧ ʿAlī b. Ibrāhīm, m. 1044/1635), *al-Sīra al-Ḥalabiyya*, I–III, Beyrouth, Dār al-Maʿrifa, s. d., 520+796+509 p.

Hamza Boubakeur, *v.* Coran.

Hayṯamī/Haytamī (Nūr al-Dīn Abū l-Ḥasan ʿAlī b. a. Bakr b. Sulaymān al-Qāhirī, m. 807/1405), *Maǧmaʿ al-zawāʾid [wa manbaʿ al-fawāʾid]*, I–X en 5, Beyrouth, Muʾassasat al-Maʿārif, 1406/1986 (reprise de l'éd. du Caire, Maktabat al-Qudsī, 1932–34).

Hūd b. Muḥakkam (/Muḥkim al-Huwwārī, *viv. sec. med.* IIIᵉ/Xᵉ s.), *Tafsīr*, I–IV, éd. Belḥāǧǧ Saʿīd Šarīfī, Beyrouth, Dār al-Ġarb al-islāmī, 1990.

Ibn a. l-Dunyā (a. Bakr ʿAbd Allāh b. Muḥammad b. ʿUbayd al-Qurašī al-Baġdādī, m. 281/894), *K. al-Ahwāl*, éd. Maǧdī Fatḥī al-Sayyid, Guizéh, Maktabat Āl Yāsīn, 1413/1993, 319 p.

Ibn a. Šayba (Abū Bakr ʿAbd Allāh b. Muḥammad b. Ibrāhīm al-ʿAbsī al-Kūfī, m. 235/849), *al-Muṣannaf fī l-aḥādīṯ wa l-āṯār*, I–IX, texte revu par M. ʿAbd al-Salām Šāhīn, Beyrouth, Dār al-Kutub al-ʿilmiyya, 1416/1995.

Ibn ʿAṭiyya (Abū Muḥammad ʿAbd al-Ḥaqq b. Ġālib al-Ġarnāṭī, m. 25 ram. 541/28 févr. 1147 ou 542), *al-Muḥarrir al-waǧīz*, I–V, éd. ʿAbd al-Salām ʿAbd al-Šāfī Muḥammad, Beyrouth, Dār al-Kutub al-ʿilmiyya, 1413/1993.

Ibn Bābawayh (Abū Ǧaʿfar Muḥammad b. ʿAlī b. al-Ḥusayn al-Qummī al-Ṣadūq, m. 381/991), *Maʿānī l-aḫbār*, Beyrouth, Muʾassasat al-Aʿlamī, 1410/1990.

Ibn al-Ǧawzī (Abū l-Faraǧ ʿAbd al-Raḥmān. b. ʿAlī, m. 597/1200), *K. al-Tabṣira*, I–II, éd. Muṣṭafā ʿAbd al-Wāḥid, Le Caire, Muṣṭafā l-Bābī l-Ḥalabī, 1390/1970, 17+508+344 p.

Ibn Ḥanbal (a. ʿAl. A. b. M. b. Ḥanbal, m. 241/855), *al-Musnad*, I–VI, éd. M. al-Zuhrī al-Ġamrāwī, Le Caire, al-Maymaniyya, 1313/1895; réimpr. Beyrouth, al-Maktab al-islāmī, 1978/I–XX, éd. A. M. Šākir, Ḥamza A. al-Zayn *et alii*, Le Caire, Dār al-Ḥadīṯ, 1416/1995.

Ibn Kaṯīr (ʿImād al-Dīn Ismāʿīl b. ʿUmar, m. 774/1373), *Tafsīr*, I–VIII, éd. ʿAbd al-ʿAzīz Ġunaym, M. A. ʿĀšūr, M. Ibrāhīm al-Bannā, Le Caire, Dār al-Šaʿb, 1390/1971.

Ibn Manda (Abū ʿAbd Allāh Muḥammad b. Isḥāq b. Muḥammad b. Yaḥyā al-ʿAbdī al-Iṣfahānī, m. ḏū l-q. 395/sept. 1005), *K. al-Īmān*, I–II, éd. ʿA. b. M. b. Nāṣir al-Faqīhī, Beyrouth, Muʾassasat al-Risāla ("ʿAqāʾid al-salaf", 1), 1407/1987[3], 6+1095 p.

Ibn al-Naqīb (Ǧamāl al-Dīn Abū ʿAbd Allāh Muḥammad b. Sulaymān b. al-Ḥasan al-Balḫī al-Maqdisī, m. 698/1299), *Muqaddimat al-Tafsīr [fī ʿulūm al-bayān wa l-maʿānī wa l-badīʿ wa iʿǧāz al-Qurʾān]*, éd. Zakariyyāʾ Saʿīd ʿAlī, Le Caire, al-Ḫānǧī, 1415/1995, 687 [Cet ouvrage avait été attribué par erreur à Ibn Qayyim al-Ǧawziyya et publié sous le titre: *al-Fawāʾid al-mušawwaq*...].

ʿIyāḍ (al-Qāḍī Abū l-Faḍl b. Mūsā al-Yaḥṣubī, m. 544/1149), *al-Šifāʾ bi-taʿrīf ḥuqūq al-muṣṭafā*, I–II en 1 [avec Aḥmad b. Muḥammad al-Šummunī al-Qāhirī, m. 872/1467, *Muzīl al-ḫafāʾ ʿan alfāẓ al-Šifāʾ*], Beyrouth, Dār al-Fikr, s. d., 8+376+318 p./ʿAlī l-Qārī (al-Mullā al-Harawī, m. 1014/1605), *Rafʿ al-ḫafāʾ ʿan ḏāt al-Šifāʾ*, I–II, Istamboul, al-Maṭbaʿa al-ʿUṯmāniyya, 1316/1898, réimpr. Beyrouth, Dār al-Kutub al-ʿilmiyya, s. d., 764+4+536+4 p.

Khan (Mohammad-Nauman), *Die exegetischen Teile des Kitāb al-ʿAyn*. Zur ältesten philologischen Koranexegese, Berlin, Klaus Schwarz ("IQTdB", 7), 1994, 397 p.

Kisāʾī, *v.* Eisenberg.

Kohlberg (Etan), *Ibn Ṭāwūs = A Medieval Muslim scholar at work*. Ibn Ṭāwūs & his library, Leyde, Brill ("IPTS", XII), 1992, IX+470 p.

Kulīnī (Ṯiqat al-Islām Abū Ǧaʿfar Muḥammad b. Yaʿqūb, m. 329/940), *Rawḍat al-Kāfī*, éd. ʿA. Akbar al-Ġifārī, Beyrouth, Dār al-Aḍwāʾ, s. d., 351 p. (éd. originale, Najaf 1395/1966).

Lrs, I–II, *v.* Šahrastānī.

Madelung (Wilferd), 'Iṣma', *EI* IV, p. 190–92.

Maǧlisī (Muḥammad Bāqir, m. 1110/1698), *Biḥār al-anwār [al-ǧāmiʿa li-durar aḫbār al-aʾimma al-aṭhār]*, XII et XV, Beyrouth, Muʾassasat al-Wafāʾ, 1403/1983[2].

Māwardī (Abū l-Ḥasan ʿAlī b. Muḥammad b. Ḥabīb, m. 450/1058), *al-Nukat wa l-ʿuyūn (fī l-tafsīr) [corr. : al-Nukat wa l-ʿuyūn fī tafsīr al-Māwardī, leg. : (...) fī l-tafsīr li-l-Māwardī]*, I–VI, éd. al-Sayyid b. ʿAbd al-Maqṣūd b. ʿAbd al-Raḥīm, Beyrouth, Dār al-Kutub al-ʿilmiyya/Muʾassasat al-Kutub al-ṯaqāfiyya, 1412/1992.

Morier (Henri), *Dictionnaire de poétique et de rhétorique*, Paris, PUF, 1981[3] augmentée (1961[1]), 1263 p.

Mubārakfūrī (Abū l-ʿAlī Muḥammad b. ʿAbd al-Raḥmān, m. 1353/1934), *Tuḥfat al-aḥwaḏī = Tuḥfat al-aḥwaḏī bi-šarḥ Ǧāmiʿ al-Tirmiḏī*, I–II (en 1)+I–X, texte revu par ʿAr. M. ʿUṯmān, Médine, al-Maktaba al-Salafiyya (M. ʿAbd al-Muḥsin al-Kutubī), 1406/1986[2] (Le Caire 1387/1967[1]).

Muǧāhid (b. Ǧabr al-Makkī; m. 104/722), *Tafsīr*, I–II, éd. ʿAr. b. Ṭāhir b. M. al-Sūratī, Qatar 1976, 898+5 p.

Muqātil b. Sulaymān (Abū l-Ḥasan al-Baǧalī al-Azdī al-Balḫī al-Ḫurāsānī al-Marwazī, m. 150/765), *Tafsīr*, I–V, éd. ʿAl. Maḥmūd Šaḥāta, Le Caire, al-Hay'a, 1980–89.

Naḥḥās (Abū Ǧaʿfar Aḥmad b. Muḥammad b. Ismāʿīl al-Murādī al-Miṣrī, m. 338/950), *Iʿrāb al-Qur'ān*, I–V, éd. Zuhayr Ġāzī Zāhid, Beyrouth, ʿĀlam al-kutub et Maktabat al-Nahḍa al-ʿarabiyya, 1405/1985[2].

Nasā'ī (Abū ʿAbd al-Raḥmān Aḥmad b. Šuʿayb b. ʿAlī al-Ḫurāsānī, m. šaʿbān 303/févr. 916), *al-Sunan al-kubrā*, I–VI, éd. ʿAbd al-Ġaffār Sul. al-Bandārī et al-Sayyid Kisrawī Ḥasan, Beyrouth, Dār al-Kutub al-ʿilmiyya, 1411/1991.

Id., *Tafsīr*, I–II, éd. Ṣabrī ʿAbd al-Ḫāliq al-Šāfiʿī et Sayyid ʿAbbās al-Ǧalīmī, Beyrouth, Mu'assasat al-Kutub al-ṯaqāfiyya, 1410/1990, 687+894 p. Ce *Tafsīr* se trouve également dans le vol. VI, d'*al-Sunan al-kubrā* (livre 82), p. 282–526.

Nīsābūrī (Niẓām al-Dīn Abū l-Qāsim al-Ḥasan b. Muḥammad b. Ḥabīb ou Ḥusayn al-Qummī, *prob. med* VIII/XIVe s.), *Tafsīr ġarā'ib al-Qur'ān wa raġā'ib al-furqān*, en marge de Ṭabarī, *Ǧāmiʿ al-bayān...*, I–XXX, Boulac, al-Maṭbaʿa al-Amīriyya, 1323–29/1905–11; réimpr. Beyrouth, Dār al-Maʿrifa, 1392/1972.

Opeloye (M. O.), An exegetical study of the sins of the prophets, *IC* LXIX (1995/3), p. 21–35 [ne traite pas d'Abraham].

Qast = Qasṭallānī (Šihāb al-Dīn Aḥmad b. Muḥammad, m. 923/1517), *v. sub* Buḫārī.

Qasṭallānī, *Mawāhib* = Qasṭallānī (Šihāb al-Dīn Aḥmad b. Muḥammad, m. 923/1517), *al-Mawāhib al-laduniyya bi-l-minaḥ al-muḥammadiyya*, I–IV, éd. Ṣāliḥ A. al-Šāmī, Beyrouth/Damas/Amman, al-Maktab al-islāmī, 1412/1991.

Qummī (Abū l-Ḥasan ʿAlī b. Ibrāhīm, *viv. med.* IV/Xe s.), *Tafsīr*, I–II, éd. Ṭayyib al-Mūsawī al-Ǧazā'irī, Najaf 1387/1967[2], 395+456 p.

Rāzī (Faḫr al-Dīn Abū ʿAbd Allāh Muḥammad b. ʿUmar, m. 606/1210), *ʿIṣmat al-anbiyā'*, introd. de ʿAbd al-ʿAzīz ʿUyūn al-Sūd, Homs, Maktabat al-Iršād (ʿĀrif al-Nakdalī), s. d. (*ca.* 1970), 10+137+5 p.

Id., *Tafsīr* = *Mafātīḥ al-ġayb*, I–XXXII en 16, éd. M. Muḥyī l-Dīn ʿAbd al-Ḥamīd, ʿA. Ism. al-Ṣāwī *et al.*, Le Caire, Mu'assasat al-Maṭbūʿāt al-ʿarabiyya, Maktabat ʿAr. Muḥammad, 1933–62.

Rippin (Andrew), Literary Analysis of *Qur'ān*, *Tafsīr*, and *Sīra*: The Methodologies of John Wanbrough, *in* Richard C. Martin (ed.), *Approaches to Islam in Religious Studies*, Tucson, The University of Arizona Press, 1985, p. 151–63.

Id., 'Tafsīr', in *EI* IX (à paraître).

Rubin (Uri), Pre-existence and Light. Aspects of the concept of Nūr Muḥammad, *IOS* V (1975), p. 62–119.

Id., Prophets and progenitors in the early Shᶜīa tradition, *JSAI* 1 (1979), p. 41–65.

Id., *The Eye of the Beholder*. The Life of Muḥammad as viewed by the Early Muslims. A Textual Analysis, Princeton, The Darwin Press, 1995, IX+289 p.

Šahrastānī (Tāğ al-Dīn Abū l-Fatḥ Muḥammad b. ᶜAbd al-Karīm, m. 548/1153), *K. al-Milal wa l-niḥal*, I–II, éd. William Cureton, Londres 1842, 1846. *Le Livre des religions et des sectes*, I, Trad. Daniel Gimaret et Guy Monnot, Louvain/Paris, Peeters/UNESCO, 1986; II, Trad. Jean Jolivet et G. Monnot, 1993.

Šāmī (Šams al-Dīn Abū ᶜAbd Allāh Muḥammad b. Yūsuf al-Ṣāliḥī; m. 942/1536), *Subul al-hudā wa l-rašād* [ou: *wa l-iršād*] *fī sīrat ḫayr al-ᶜibād [i.e., al-Sīra al-Šāmiyya]*, I–XII, éd. ᶜĀdil A. ᶜAbd al-Mawğūd et ᶜA. M. Muᶜawwaḍ, Beyrouth, Dār al-Kutub al-ᶜilmiyya, 1414/1993.

San = Ḏahabī, *Siyar aᶜlām al-nubalā*ʾ.

Šawkānī (Abū ᶜAbd Allāh Muḥammad b. ᶜAlī, m. 1250/1832), *Tafsīr — Fatḥ al-qadīr al-ğāmiᶜ bayna fannay l-riwāya wa l-dirāya fī ᶜilm al-tafsīr*, I–V, Le Caire, Muṣṭ. l-Bābī l-Ḥalabī, 1349/1930; réimpr. Beyrouth, Dār al-Fikr, 1973[3].

Šummunī, *v. sub* ᶜIyāḍ.

Sibṭ Ibn al-Ğawzī (Šams al-Dīn Abū l-Muẓaffar Yūsuf b. Qizoğlu, m. 654/1257), *Mirʾāt al-zamān fī taʾrīḫ al-aᶜyān*, I, éd. Iḥsān ᶜAbbās, Beyrouth, Dār al-Šurūq, 1405/1985, 604 p.

Suyūṭī, *al-Ḫaṣāʾiṣ al-kubrā*, Hyderabad 1320/1902, réimpr. Beyrouth, Dār al-Kutub al-ᶜilmiyya, s. d.

Ṭabarānī (Abū l-Qāsim Sulaymān b. Aḥmad, m. 28 ḏū l-qaᶜda 360/21 sept. 971), *al-Muᶜğam al-awsaṭ*, I–X, éd. Ṭāriq b. ᶜAwaḍ Allāh b. M. et ᶜAbd al-Muḥsin Ibr. al-Ḥusaynī, Le Caire, Dār al-Ḥaramayn, 1415/1995.

Id., *al-Muᶜğam al-kabīr*, I–XII, XVII–XX, XXII–XXV, éd. Ḥamdī ᶜAbd al-Mağīd al-Silafī, Mossoul, Wizārat al-Awqāf, Maṭbaᶜat al-Zahrāʾ, 1401/1983[2] (Bagdad, 1398–1404/1977–83[1]).

Tab = Ṭabarī, *Tafsīr*: jusqu'à 14, *Ibrāhīm*, 27, éd. Maḥmūd M. Šākir et A. M. Šākir, I–XVI, Le Caire, Dār al-Maᶜārif, 1954–68 (2ème éd., 1969, pour quelques vol.); au-delà, éd. A. Saᶜīd ᶜAlī, Muṣṭ. al-Saqqā *et al.*, XIII, p. 219 (14, *Ibrāhīm*, 28)–XXX, Le Caire, Muṣṭafā l-Bābī l-Ḥalabī, 1373–77/1954–57. La réimpression de Beyrouth, Dār al-Fikr, 1984, comporte un vol. d'index. Nous nous référons, quant à nous, à l'éd. d'origine. Pour les vol. XIII–XVI où il y a concurrence de tomaison entre les deux éd., les tomes de cette dernière sont marqués de 2 en exposant, soit XIII²–XVI².

Ṭabarī, *Annales*, I, p. 000 (= éd. De Goeje)/ I, p. 000 (= éd. M. Abū l-Faḍl Ibrāhīm)/ *History*, II, p. 000 (= *The History of al-Ṭabarī*, II, *Prophets and Patriarchs*, Translated and annotated by William M. Brinner, Albany, SUNY, 1987, XII+207 p.

Ṭabarī, *Tahḏīb al-āṯār, Musnad ʿAlī*, éd. Maḥmūd M. Šākir, Le Caire, Maṭbaʿat al-Madanī, 1982, 24+490 p.

Ṭabarsī (Amīn al-Dīn Abū ʿAlī al-Faḍl b. al-Ḥasan, m. 548/ 1153), *Tafsīr [Maǧmaʿ al-bayān fī tafsīr al-Qurʾān]*, I–XXX en 6, Introduction de Muḥsin al-Amīn al-Ḥusaynī al-ʿĀmilī, Beyrouth, Dār Maktabat al-Ḥayāt, s. d. (réimpr. de l'éd. de Beyrouth 1380/ 1961).

Ṯaʿlabī (Abū Isḥāq Aḥmad b. Muḥammad b. Ibrāhīm, m. 427/ 1035), *Qiṣaṣ al-anbiyāʾ al-musammā bi-ʿArāʾis al-maǧālis* [en marge: Yāfiʿī, *Rawḍ al-rayāḥīn fī ḥikāyāt al-ṣāliḥīn]* Le Caire 1322, 256 p., réimpr. Beyrouth, al-Maktaba al-Šaʿbiyya li-l-ṭibāʿa wa l-našr, s. d./ Beyrouth, Šarikat Šamarlī, 1980, 477 p.

TB = Ḫaṭīb Baġdādī, *Taʾrīḫ Baġdād*.

TG, *v.* van Ess.

Tottoli (Roberto), *Le* Qiṣaṣ al-anbiyāʾ *di Ṭarafī*, Dottorato di ricerca, Naples, Istituto Universitario di Napoli, 1996, 735 p.

TT = Ibn Ḥaǧar al-ʿAsqalānī, *Tahḏīb al-tahḏib*.

Ṭūsī (Šayḫ al-Ṭāʾifa Abū Ǧaʿfar Muḥammad b. al-Ḥasan, m. 460/ 1067), *Tafsīr [al-Tibyān fī tafsīr al-Qurʾān]*, I–X, Introduction de Āġā Buzrak al-Ṭahrānī, Beyrouth, Dār Iḥyāʾ al-turāṯ al-ʿarabī, s. d. (réimpr. de l'éd. de Najaf 1367–83/ 1957–63).

Wāḥidī, *Wasīṭ* = Wāḥidī (Abū l-Ḥasan ʿAlī b. Aḥmad al-Nīsābūrı, m. ǧumādā II 468/ janvier 1076), *al-Wasīṭ fī tafsīr al-Qurʾān*, I–IV, éd. ʿĀdil A. ʿAbd al-Mawǧūd *et al.*, Beyrouth, Dār al-Kutub al-ʿilmiyya, 1415/ 1994.

G. Weil (Gustav), *Biblische Legenden der Muselmänner*. Aus arabischen Quellen zusammengetragen und mit jüdischen Sagen verglichen, Francfort sur le Main, Literarische Anstalt (J. Rütten), 1845, VI+ 298 p.

Yaḥyā b. Sallām (al-Baṣrī, m. 200/ 815), *al-Taṣārīf*. Tafsīr al-Qurʾān mimmā štabahat asmāʾuhu wa taṣarrafat maʿānīhi, éd. Hind Šiblī, Tunis, al-Šarika al-Tūnisiyya li-l-tawzīʿ, 1979, 410 p.

Zaǧǧāǧ = Zaǧǧāǧ (Abū Isḥāq Ibrāhīm b. Muḥammad b. al-Sarī al-Baġdādī, m. 19 ǧumāda II 311/ 3 oct. 923, ou 310, ou 316), *Maʿānī l-Qurʾān wa iʿrābuhu*, I–V, éd. ʿAbd al-Ǧalīl ʿAbduh Šalabī, Beyrouth, ʿĀlam al-kutub, 1408/ 1988.

APES, PIGS, AND THE ISLAMIC IDENTITY

URI RUBIN

That Jews and Christians were once transformed into apes and pigs by way of punishment, is a well-known Islamic idea. It is based on the Quran and is elaborated in Islamic literature.[1] The aim of the present article is to illuminate a less explored aspect of the theme, namely, transformation into apes and pigs as a punishment meted out to Muslims.[2]

In what follows the process of the adaptation of this Jewish-Christian type of punishment to Muslims will be traced, and its role within the Islamic context will be elucidated. It will become clear that the punishment was not applied to Muslim sinners at random, but rather to sinners whose deeds had a Jewish or a Christian connotation. It will be demonstrated that the traditions adapting the punitive transformation to Muslims were designed to confront Jewish and Christian elements which penetrated Islamic society and were considered a threat to the genuine Islamic identity.

ESCHATOLOGICAL *MASḪ*

As a punishment inflicted on Jews and Christians, transformation into apes and pigs is an event of the historical past. With the adaptation of the theme to Muslims, it has been changed from historical to eschatological; the traditions imposing this punishment on Muslims are all cast as apocalypses anticipating future disasters for sinful Muslims, including transformation.

As an eschatological event, the transformation has become associated with the idea of *masḫ* — the usual Arabic term for metamorphosis. The

[1] Ilse Lichtenstaedter, "And Become Ye Accursed Apes", *Jerusalem Studies in Arabic and Islam* 14 (1991), 153–75; Michael Cook, "Early Muslim Dietary Law", *Jerusalem Studies in Arabic and Islam* 7 (1986), 222–23; idem, "Ibn Qutayba and the Monkeys", *Paper presented at the Seventh International Colloquium: From Jāhiliyya to Islam*, Jerusalem 1996.

[2] Occasional reference to some relevant traditions has already been made in Cook, "Ibn Qutayba and the Monkeys", note 32.

link between the two themes is secondary, and in its historical form the punitive transformation into apes and pigs has little to do with the idea of *masḫ*. This is very clear in the Quran in which the punishment of sinners becoming apes and pigs is not described as *masḫ* at all.[3] In fact, the root *m.s.ḫ.* is employed in the Quran only once, and in a strict eschatological context. It occurs in a passage (36:63–67) describing the day on which the [non-Muslim] sinners will be shown the hell (*ǧahannam*) that was promised to them. On that day God will set a seal on their mouths, and if God wills, He will obliterate their eyes so that they will not find their way on the path (*ṣirāṭ*). Or He may change them (*la-masaḫnāhum*) where they are, so that they will not be able to proceed, or to go back.

The earliest Quran exegetes differ as to the exact significance of the eschatological *masḫ* awaiting the sinners, and suggest different possibilities: Changing them into stones,[4] making them lame, or crippled in the legs and the arms (*kusḥ*),[5] or changing their outer appearance (*ḫalq*),[6] or destroying (*ahlaka*) them where they stand.[7] Two basic meanings can be detected here: transformation (including deformation) and destruction. They remind one of the Hebrew root *h.f.k.*, which in the Bible has the same range of connotations. It signifies destruction (by overthrowing),[8] as well as transformation.[9] A variant form of the root found its way into the Quran in passages reflecting the biblical story of the destruction of Sodom,[10] and in early *ḥadīṯ* this root (*ʾ.f.k.*) is sometimes interchangeable with the root *m.s.ḫ.* (see below).

As for *m.s.ḫ.* in the sense of transformation, it is significant that the above exegetes have offered various possibilities, but none with apes and

[3] Quran 2:65; 5:60; 7:166.

[4] Muqātil, III, 584; Samarqandī, *Tafsīr*, III, 105; Wāḥidī, *Wasīṭ*, III, 518; Baġawī, *Tafsīr*, IV, 550; Zamaḫšarī, *Kaššāf*, III, 329; Ibn al-Ǧawzī, *Zād al-masīr*, VII, 33; Ibn Kaṯīr, *Tafsīr*, III, 578; Suyūṭī, *Durr*, V, 268. Šīʿī *tafsīr*: Ṭabarsī, *Maǧmaʿ*, XXIII, 37.

[5] ʿAbd al-Razzāq, *Tafsīr*, II, 145. The *isnād*: ʿAbd al-Razzāq < Maʿmar < Qatāda. See also Suyūṭī, *Durr*, V, 268. The same is also the sense of the interpretation of *masaḫahu* as *aqʿadahu*. See Huwwārī, III, 439; Ṭabarī, *Tafsīr*, XXIII, 18 (al-Ḥasan al-Baṣrī; Qatāda); Māwardī, *Nukat*, V, 29; Zamaḫšarī, *Kaššāf*, III, 329; Ibn al-Ǧawzī, *Zād al-masīr*, VII, 33; Qurṭubī, *Aḥkām*, XV, 50; Ibn Kaṯīr, *Tafsīr*, III, 578. Šīʿī *tafsīr*: Ṭūsī, *Tabyān*, VIII, 473.

[6] Māwardī, *Nukat*, V, 29 (al-Suddī); Ibn Kaṯīr, *Tafsīr*, III, 578.

[7] Ṭabarī, *Tafsīr*, XXIII, 18 (Ibn ʿAbbās); Māwardī, *Nukat*, V, 29; Ibn al-Ǧawzī, *Zād al-masīr*, VII, 33; Qurṭubī, *Aḥkām*, XV, 50; Ibn Kaṯīr, *Tafsīr*, III, 578; Suyūṭī, *Durr*, V, 268. The best-known example of the changing of sinners into stones is the case of the Meccan idols Isāf and Nāʾila who are said to have originally been a man and a woman who had fornicated in the Kaʿba, and therefore were turned into stones. See, e.g., Ibn al-Kalbī, *Aṣnām*, 9; Ibn Abī l-Dunyā, *ʿUqūbāt*, nos. 304–305; Azraqī, 49, 74.

[8] Genesis 19:29 (Sodom); Jonah 3:4 (Nineveh).

[9] Exodus 7:15 (the rod of Moses).

[10] Quran 9:70; 69:9; 53:53.

pigs. Only relatively late Quran commentaries interpret *masḫ* as metamorphosis into apes and pigs.[11] This is a clear indication that the idea of transformation into apes and pigs and the punishment of *masḫ* awaiting the sinners in the eschatological future were only linked at a secondary stage.

The evidence of *ḥadīṯ* material seems to confirm the impression that the idea of the eschatological *masḫ* was not always linked to the idea of punitive metamorphosis into apes and pigs. There are several traditions describing the eschatological *masḫ* in which there is no mention of apes or of pigs. Let us take a look at these traditions.

Most of the traditions about the eschatological *masḫ* describe a triple calamity which portends the Hour, i.e., the eschatological phase of world history. Such traditions emerged as a result of the civil wars (*fitan*) which occurred among Muslims during the Umayyad period. The tribulations triggered an apocalyptic mood which gave rise to traditions predicting the impending end of the world, and the triple calamity is mentioned frequently among the apocalyptic events.

One of the three events of which the calamity consists is *masḫ*, while the other two are usually *ḫasf* and *qaḏf*. The latter two, like the event of *masḫ*, have a Quranic basis, signifying divine retribution. The root *ḫ.s.f.* is used quite frequently in the Quran,[12] denoting the act of God in causing the earth to engulf the sinners, either in past history or in the eschatological future. An event of an army being swallowed up (*ḫasf*) on its way to Mecca is often described in apocalyptic visions alluding to the military clash in Arabia between ʿAbdallāh b. al-Zubayr and the Umayyads.[13] The act of *qaḏf* is less frequent in the Quran; it denotes the pelting of devils with shooting stars.[14] Sometimes another event replaces one of the three, or appears as a fourth, namely *raǧf*: "earthquake". This, too, is a Quranic eschatological calamity.[15]

The earliest traditions in which the triple calamity is predicted were circulated in Syria, and mainly in Ḥimṣ, where messianic and apocalyptic

[11] Samarqandī, *Tafsīr*, III, 105 (al-Kalbī); Baġawī, *Tafsīr*, IV, 550; Zamaḫšarī, *Kaššāf*, III, 329 (Ibn ʿAbbās); Ibn al-Ǧawzī, *Zād al-masīr*, VII, 33 (Ibn al-Kalbī). Šīʿī *Tafsīr*: Ṭabarsī, *Maǧmaʿ*, XXIII, 37. Cf. Ṭūsī, *Tabyān*, VIII, 473.

[12] Quran 16:45; 28:81; 29:40; 34:9; 67:16.

[13] For these traditions see Wilferd Madelung, "ʿAbd Allāh b. al-Zubayr and the Mahdī," *Journal of Near Eastern Studies* 40 (1981), 291–305 (repr. in Wilferd Madelung, *Religious and Ethnic Movements in Medieval Islam*, Variorum Reprints, 1992); *idem*, s.v. 'Mahdī', *EI*[2] (p. 1232a). Cf. Michael Cook, "Eschatology and the Dating of Traditions", *Princeton Papers in Near Eastern Studies* 1 (1992), 32–33.

[14] 37:8.

[15] 73:14; 79:6.

expectations were nurtured especially in connection with holy war against the nearby Byzantine empire.[16] They are all recorded by Nuʿaym b. Ḥammād (d. AH 229) in his *Kitāb al-fitan*. The triple calamity is included in a series of events which are usually foreseen by the Prophet himself. They are about to happen at various stages of the history of the Islamic *umma*, and specific dates are provided, which serve to authenticate the apocalypse.

One of these traditions is quoted from three Ḥimṣī traditionists: Šarīḥ b. ʿUbayd, Abū ʿĀmir al-Hawzanī and Ḍamra b. Ḥabīb (d. AH 130). In it the Prophet predicts disastrous events which are to befall the Muslims between AH 210–300. The triple calamity (*qadf-ḫasf-masḫ*) will be the first.[17] In the tradition of Ǧubayr b. Nufayr (Ḥimṣī d. AH 75), the events predicted by the Prophet take place between AH 133–200. The triple calamity (pelting with stones, *ḫasf* and *masḫ*) is scheduled to occur in AH 172.[18] In the Ḥimṣī tradition of the Meccan Companion ʿAbdallāh b. ʿUmar (d. AH 73), the Prophet does not provide dates, but merely surveys a series of anticipated earthquakes, which are accompanied in one instance by the triple calamity. This tradition also refers to the stubbornness of the Muslim sinners, who do not repent.[19] Finally, there is also a short non-prophetic apocalypse, transmitted by the Ḥimṣī Arṭāt b. al-Mundir (d. AH 163), referring only to the triple calamity. In it Arṭāt provides a somewhat obscure indication of the time of the event. He states that it will occur after the emergence of the *mahdī*, in the days of the Hāšimī who will behave insolently in Jerusalem.[20]

In the apocalyptic visions which were circulated outside Syria, the triple calamity figures alone, with no other disasters. Here, too, the *masḫ* remains vague, with no mention of apes and pigs. These traditions are usually based on a short uniform pattern. They open with the word *yakūn*: "there will be", and proceed to specify the triple calamity. The utterance is made by the Prophet in the first person, and he specifically declares that

[16] Wilferd Madelung, "Apocalyptic Prophecies in Ḥimṣ in the Umayyad Age", *Journal of Semitic Studies* 31 (1986), 141–85 (repr. in Wilferd Madelung, *Religious and Ethnic Movements in Medieval Islam*, Variorum Reprints, 1992); Josef Van Ess, *Theologie und Gesellschaft im 2. und 3. Jahrhundert Hidschra: Eine Geschichte des religiösen Denkens im frühen Islam* (6 vols. Berlin, New York, 1991–95), I, 65–69.

[17] Nuʿaym b. Ḥammād, *Fitan*, 427. See an abridged version *ibid.*, 376. See also Cook, "Ibn Qutayba and the Monkeys", note 32.

[18] Nuʿaym b. Ḥammād, *Fitan*, 422. See also Cook, "Ibn Qutayba and the Monkeys", note 32 (where he suggests emending the reading from 172 to 192).

[19] Nuʿaym b. Ḥammād, *Fitan*, 374. See also Suyūṭī, *Durr*, VI, 326. The *isnād*: Ḥudayr b. Kurayb (Ḥimṣī d. AH 129) < Kaṯīr b. Murra Abū Šağara (Ḥimṣī) < Ibn ʿUmar < Prophet.

[20] Nuʿaym b. Ḥammād, *Fitan*, 378. The *isnād*: al-Ǧarrāḥ b. Mulayḥ (Ḥimṣī) < Arṭāt b. al-Mundir (Ḥimṣī d. AH 163). Cf. Cook, "Ibn Qutayba and the Monkeys", note 32.

the triple calamity will occur in "my community". Some versions of the utterance appear in certain canonical *ḥadīṯ* compilations. Thus Ibn Māğa (d. AH 275) has recorded in *Kitāb al-fitan* of his *Sunan* some prophetic utterances of this kind. One is quoted from the Prophet by the Qurašī Companion ʿAbdallāh b. ʿAmr b. al-ʿĀṣ (d. AH 63),[21] and the other by the Medinan Companion Sahl b. Saʿd al-Anṣārī (d. AH 88).[22] A third version, of ʿAbdallāh b. Masʿūd, provides a specific apocalyptic designation of the time of the triple calamity: "Just before the Hour".[23] Outside the canonical compilations there are more such versions, quoted from the Prophet by the Companions Anas b. Mālik (Baṣran d. AH 91–95),[24] and by Saʿīd b. Abī Rāšid.[25] A version of the Companion Abū Hurayra (d. AH 57) opens with the standard formula of the traditions about the portents of the Hour: "The Hour shall not come until there is in my community *ḫasf* and *masḫ* and *qaḏf*".[26]

ESCHATOLOGICAL APES AND PIGS

The meaning of *masḫ* in the above traditions is no clearer than it is in the Quran, but the range of possible interpretations of the term is narrowed down considerably in further versions in which this term has been glossed by an explicit mention of apes and pigs. Sometimes the term is simply replaced by the statement about the apes and the pigs; this is the case in the following Syrian version of ʿAṭāʾ al-Ḫurasānī (d. AH 135) in which the Prophet declares: "There will be in my community *ḫasf*, and *rağf* and apes and pigs".[27]

[21] Ibn Māğa, II, no. 4062 (36:29). See also Aḥmad, *Musnad*, II, 163. The *isnād*: Abū l-Zubayr (Muḥammad b. Muslim b. Tadrus, Meccan d. AH 126) < ʿAbdallāh b. ʿAmr < Prophet.

[22] Ibn Māğa, II, no. 4060 (36:29). The *isnād*: ʿAbd al-Raḥmān b. Zayd b. Aslam (Medinan d. AH 182) < Abū Ḥāzim al-Aʿrağ (Salama b. Dīnār, Medinan d. AH 140) < Sahl b. Saʿd < Prophet.

[23] Ibn Māğa, II, no. 4059 (36:29). See also Abū Nuʿaym, *Ḥilya*, VII, 121. The *isnād*: Sayyār Abū l-Ḥakam al-Wāsiṭī < Ṭāriq b. Šihāb (Kūfan d. AH 82) < ʿAbdallāh b. Masʿūd < Prophet.

[24] Abū Yaʿlā, VII, no. 3945; Dānī, *Fitan*, no. 338; *Kašf al-astār*, IV, no. 3404. The *isnād*: Mubārak b. Suḥaym (Baṣran) < ʿAbd al-ʿAzīz b. Ṣuhayb (Baṣran d. AH 130) < Anas < Prophet.

[25] *Kašf al-astār*, IV, no. 3402; Ṭabarānī, *Kabīr*, VI, no. 5537. The *isnād*: ʿAbd al-Raḥmān b. Sābiṭ (Meccan Successor) < Saʿīd b. Abī Rāšid < Prophet.

[26] Ibn Ḥibbān, *Ṣaḥīḥ*, XV, no. 6759. The *isnād*: Kaṯīr b. Zayd (Medinan d. AH 158) < al-Walīd b. Rabāḥ (Medinan d. AH 117) < Abū Hurayra < Prophet.

[27] Suyūṭī, *Durr*, II, 295 (from Ibn Abī l-Dunyā's *Ḏamm al-malāhī*). The *isnād*: ʿUṯmān b. ʿAṭāʾ al-Ḫurasānī (d. AH 155) < his father ʿAṭāʾ al-Ḫurasānī < Prophet.

Such modified versions are the result of a process in which the theme of the apes and the pigs was transformed from its original Jewish-Christian (historical) denotation to an Islamic (eschatological) one. This process began independently of the idea of the triple calamity, and deserves to be examined more closely.

The adaptation of the theme of the punitive metamorphosis into apes and pigs to Muslim sinners in the eschatological future is connected with the general idea of a common sin linking Israelites and Muslims. The latter are accused of following the ways (*sunna*, *sunan*) of their sinful predecessors. The traditions conveying this idea reflect the aversion of Sunnī Muslims to the spread of the Israelite (Jewish-Christian) heritage in Islamic society,[28] which challenged the Islamic identity of the believers. This aversion gave rise to a series of traditions denouncing the assimilation of the *sunan* of the Children of Israel into the Islamic *sunna*.[29] A typical presentation of the idea is given in the following statement attributed to the Companion Ḥuḏayfa b. al-Yamān (Medinan/Kūfan d. AH 36) on whose authority many apocalypses were circulated. The present one was recorded by ʿAbd al-Razzāq.[30] It runs as follows:

> You (i.e., the Muslims) will follow the ways (*sunan*) of the Children of Israel (in precise symmetry), as one feather of an arrow matches another, and as one strap of a sandal matches another — if a man of the Children of Israel did this or that, a man of this community would surely do it as well.

The tradition goes on to relate that upon hearing this, someone reminded Ḥuḏayfa that there had been apes and pigs among the Children of Israel, and Ḥuḏayfa retorted that apes and pigs would also be among this community. Thus the common fate shared by Israelites and Muslims involves not only identity of sin but also of punishment.

This version of the statement was transmitted on the authority of Ḥuḏayfa by the Baṣran Successor Qatāda b. Diʿāma (d. AH 117), but there is also a slightly different version of the same Companion transmitted by Abū l-Baḫtarī Saʿīd b. Fayrūz (Kūfan d. AH 83). Here the statement is plain, with no similes. Ḥuḏayfa merely confirms that each act of the

[28] See M.J. Kister, "Do not Assimilate Yourselves...", *Jerusalem Studies in Arabic and Islam* 12 (1989), 321–71.

[29] Cf. *idem*, "*Ḥaddithū ʿan banī isrāʾīla wa-lā ḥaraja*", *Israel Oriental Studies* 2 (1972), 232 (repr. in M.J. Kister, *Studies in Jāhiliyya and Early Islam*, Variorum Reprints, London 1980).

[30] ʿAbd al-Razzāq, *Muṣannaf*, XI, no. 20765; *idem*, *Tafsīr*, I, 235; Ibn Baṭṭa, *Ibāna*, II, no. 715.

Children of Israel will be repeated by the Muslims, and that apes and pigs will be among them as well.[31]

There is also a Syrian version of the statement predicting a fate of transformation into apes and pigs for Muslims imitating the sins of their Jewish and Christian predecessors. The tradition describes a dialogue between the Syrian Companion ʿUbāda b. al-Ṣāmit (Anṣārī, d. AH 34–45) and another Muslim (Abū ʿAṭāʾ al-Yaḥbūrī). The former tells the latter that scholars and Quran experts will be persecuted, and that they will seek refuge with the beasts on the mountains, because Muslims will want to kill them. The latter does not believe it, claiming that such a sin could not be committed as long as the Quran exists among the Muslims. To this ʿUbāda replies:

> Had not the Jews been given the Torah, but they went astray and abandoned it later on, and had not the Christians been given the Gospel, but they went astray and abandoned it later on? These are the ways (*sunan*) that are followed everywhere, and by God, nothing happened among those who were before you, which will not take place among you as well.[32]

In an extended version of the same dialogue, Abū ʿAṭāʾ al-Yaḥbūrī meets a few days later with the same ʿUbāda b. al-Ṣāmit and tells him that there were apes and pigs among "those before us". ʿUbāda replies that he heard an unnamed person (*fulān*) relating a tradition to the effect that before long, a group of this community will be transformed (*tumsaḫ*).[33]

Just as the apes and the pigs were turned from historical into eschatological, so the eschatological *masḫ* became a historical one. This event — together with the other calamities — was built into some versions describing the transformation of the ancient Jews into apes and pigs. Thus a tradition of ʿIkrima (Medinan d. AH 105) relates that on the evening before the sinful Israelites were turned into apes and pigs, their righteous brethren had already warned them that God might kill them by *masḫ* or *ḫasf* or *qaḏf*.[34]

QADARĪS

But let us stay in the eschatological domain, which is reserved for the Muslims. There are more traditions which specify the exact group among

31 Ibn Abī Šayba, XV, 103 (no. 19227).

32 Marwazī, *Sunna*, nos. 62, 107.

33 Ibn Abī l-Dunyā, *ʿUqūbāt*, no. 347.

34 *Ibid.*, no. 226.

the Muslims to whom the eschatological punishment of metamorphosis into apes and pigs will be meted out. They are the Qadarīs. This label stands for heretics who discuss the problem of the *qadar* (*allaḏīna yaqūlūna fī l-qadari*), and deny (*yukaḏḏibūna*) the totality of its effect.[35] The term *qadar* itself means "destiny", "decree", and those who doubted its existence actually rejected the idea of predestination.

That heretics are likely to become apes and pigs has already been observed,[36] but the reason why this fate shall affect them and not other Muslims has not yet been clarified. The reason seems to be connected with the fact that the views of the Qadarīs were condemned by their Muslim opponents as Jewish and Christian by origin. The evidence as to these accusations is abundant, contrary to the observation of Van Ess.[37] Thus there are utterances attributed to the Prophet himself criticising the Qadariyya for their Christian-oriented views. One of them is of Ibn ʿAbbās who is quoted by his *mawlā* ʿIkrima. In it the Prophet warns the Muslims against conducting debates on the *qadar*, because this kind of deliberation is a branch (*šuʿba*) of Christianity.[38] In another Meccan tradition the Prophet predicts the emergence of people who will deny that God decreed the sins of man, and declares that they will have borrowed their views from the Christians.[39] There is also a statement of the Kūfan Saʿīd b. Ǧubayr (d. AH 95) to the effect that the Qadarīs are "Jews".[40] These are only a few examples out of many more.

Whether or not the association of the Qadarīs with Jews and Christians is historically justified, the mere association reflects the contempt of the Sunnīs for these heretics who shattered the unity of the Islamic community. The damage they caused to Islamic solidarity was blamed on their Jewish and Christian orientation.

Orthodox contempt for the heretics is demonstrated further in traditions attaching to them the most typical Jewish-Christian stigma: apes and pigs. This is indicated in a series of traditions condemning heretics in general, in which the heretics are on a par with Jews and Christians, as well as with apes and pigs. In some of these traditions the Baṣran Abū l-Ǧawzāʾ (Aws

[35] On the Qadarīs, see J. Van Ess, "Ḳadariyya", *EI*², and the bibliography therein.

[36] Cook, "Ibn Qutayba and the Monkeys", note 32.

[37] In art. "Ḳadariyya", *EI*² (p. 371b), he says that the traditions against the Qadarīs "speak of the 'Magians' instead of the 'Christians' of this community". Cf. also *idem*, *Theologie und Gesellschaft*, II, 53.

[38] Ibn Abī ʿĀṣim, *Sunna*, no. 332; Ṭabarānī, *Kabīr*, XI, no. 11680; Lālikāʾī, II, no. 1128; *Maǧmaʿ al-zawāʾid*, VII, 205.

[39] Ṭabarānī, *Kabīr*, XI, no. 11179; *Maǧmaʿ al-zawāʾid*, VII, 208. The *isnād*: ʿAmr b. Dīnār (Meccan d. AH 126) < ʿAbd al-Raḥmān b. Sābiṭ (Meccan Successor) < Prophet.

[40] Lālikāʾī, II, no. 1267.

b. ʿAbdallāh al-Rabaʿī d. AH 83) states that being a neighbour to apes and pigs is more desirable for him than to be a neighbour to heretics (*ahl al-ahwāʾ*).[41] A similar statement is reported in a Kūfan tradition on the authority of Abū Mūsā al-Ašʿarī (ʿAbdallāh b. Qays, Companion d. AH 42–53); he says that he prefers to have Jews and Christians and apes and pigs as neighbours, rather than to live next to a heretic.[42]

The association of heretics with apes and pigs seems also to be demonstrated in traditions placing the apes and the pigs in the context of resurrection. The Syrian Šahr b. Ḥawšab (d. AH 100) quotes an apocalypse heard from the Prophet by ʿAbdallāh b. ʿAmr b. al-ʿĀṣ. The Prophet states that the evil-doers (*širār*) among the people will be resurrected by a cataclysmic fire together with the apes and the pigs.[43] A more detailed Ḥimṣī apocalypse of Kaʿb al-Aḥbār (d. AH 32) says that the evil ones will be resurrected in Palestine (*al-Šām*), and they will be those who have forgotten the Quran and the *sunna*, abandoned the worship of God, indulged in fornication, and said that there is no god in heaven.[44] The title "evil ones" (*širār*) is usually attached to Islamic heretical groups.[45] Therefore, the present traditions, too, seem to point to the association of heretics with apes and pigs.

The anti-Qadarī traditions also predict for them actual transformation into apes and pigs. Such traditions are numerous. A realistic description of the fate awaiting the Qadarīs is found in a Ḥijāzī tradition of the Anṣārī Companion Abū Saʿīd al-Ḫudrī (d. AH 65); the Prophet says that at the end of time a bride shall come into her canopy and find her groom there metamorphosed (*musiḫa*) into an ape, because he denied the *qadar*.[46]

There is another tradition describing a similar event, but the sin for which the person has become an ape is not stated explicitly. Ḥuḏayfa b. al-Yamān says: "What will you do if one of you goes out of his tent (*ḥağala*) to his garden (*ḥišš*), and comes back metamorphosed (*wa-qad musiḫa*) into an ape; he will look for his family, but they will run away from him."[47]

[41] Ibn Baṭṭa, *Ibāna*, II, nos. 466–68; Lālikāʾī, I, no. 231.

[42] Ibn Baṭṭa, *Ibāna*, II, nos. 469, 471. The *isnād*: Layṯ b. Abī Sulaym (Kūfan d. AH 143) < anonymous < Abū Mūsā.

[43] Abū Dāwūd, II, 4 (15:3). See also Nuʿaym b. Ḥammad, *Fitan*, 381, 382, 383, 383–84 (from ʿAdan); Aḥmad, *Musnad*, II, 84 (Ibn ʿUmar), 198–99, 209; Ibn Ṭāwūs, *Malāḥim*, 81.

[44] Nuʿaym b. Ḥammad, *Fitan*, 379–80.

[45] E.g., Ibn Abī ʿĀṣim, *Sunna*, no. 350; Ṭabarānī, *Awsaṭ*, VI, no. 5905; *Mağmaʿ al-zawāʾid*, VII, 202.

[46] Ṭabarānī, *Awsaṭ*, VIII, no. 7146. See also Damīrī, *Ḥayawān*, II, 203; *Mağmaʿ al-zawāʾid*, VII, 209 (from Ṭabarānī, *Awsaṭ*).

[47] Ibn Abī l-Dunyā, *ʿUqūbāt*, no. 284 (printed: *ḥabšihi*); Dānī, *Fitan*, no. 349.

As sinners doomed to metamorphosis (*masḫ*) into apes and pigs, the Qadarīs also became a natural target for the triple calamity, in which *masḫ* figures as one of the events. The triple calamity is meted out to the Qadarīs in a lengthy Ḥiǧāzī tradition transmitted on the authority of the Anṣārī Companion Rāfiʿ b. H̬adīǧ (d. *ca.* AH 59–74). The Prophet describes the basic tenets of the Qadarīs, and emphasizes that they are like the Jews and the Christians who already before them denied the sacredness of their own scriptures and discredited whole parts of them. Then the Prophet predicts the triple calamity which will strike the Qadarīs, and this time it consists of *ṭāʿūn* (plague), *ḫasf* and *masḫ*. The latter event is glossed by an explanation to the effect that God will metamorphose (*yamsaḫu*) them into apes and pigs. In the second part of his statement, the Prophet says that the main reason why the Children of Israel perished was that they denied the *qadar*. Finally, the Prophet explains the dogmatic meaning of the *qadar*.[48]

There is one more tradition in which the triple calamity is linked to the Qadarīs, but this time without explicit mention of apes and pigs. This is a Medinan prophetic version of Ibn ʿUmar (d. AH 73), in which the Prophet declares: "There will be in my community (or: in this community) *masḫ* and *ḫasf* and *qaḏf*". This is glossed by the words: "and this will happen among the people of the *qadar*".[49] The gloss is also available in an extended version including the Zindīqiyya as well.[50] With such a gloss the term *masḫ* has evidently come to mean transformation into apes and pigs.

The eschatological curse of the apes and the pigs was applied not only to groups, but to places as well. Baṣra was renowned for the prevalence of Qadarī thinking in it,[51] and therefore it was presented as a zone in which people are particularly likely to be transformed into apes and pigs. The triple calamity was linked to this place, too. Thus the Prophet tells the Baṣran Companion Anas b. Mālik (d. AH 91–95) that the Baṣrans will be hit by *ḫasf* and *qaḏf* and *raǧf*, and that some people will go to bed and will wake up in the morning as apes and pigs.[52] In another version of the same warning, the apes and the pigs are not mentioned explicitly, but the term *masḫ* evidently conveys the idea. The Prophet warns Anas not to enter the

[48] Āǧurrī, *Šarīʿa*, no. 363; Ṭabarānī, *Kabīr*, IV, no. 4270; *Maǧmaʿ al-zawāʾid*, VII, 200–201. The *isnād*: ʿAmr b. Šuʿayb (Medinan d. AH 118) < Saʿīd b. al-Musayyab (Medinan d. AH 94) < Rāfiʿ b. H̬adīǧ < Prophet. For another version see Lālikāʾī, II, no. 1100.

[49] Ibn Māǧa, II, no. 4061 (36:29); Tirmiḏī/ *Tuḥfa*, VI, 367–68 (30:16). The *isnād*: Abū Ṣaḫr al-Ḫarrāṭ (Ḥumayd b. Ziyād, Medinan d. AH 189) < Nāfiʿ the *mawlā* of Ibn ʿUmar (Medinan d. AH 117) < Ibn ʿUmar < Prophet.

[50] Aḥmad, *Musnad*, II, 108 (*masḫ* only), 137; Lālikāʾī, II, no. 1135. See also *Maǧmaʿ al-zawāʾid*, VII, 206.

[51] On the Qadariyya and Baṣra, see Van Ess, *Theologie und Gesellschaft*, I, 23.

[52] Abū Dāwūd, II, 428 (36:10).

public places in Başra, telling him that at the end of days some of its inhabitants will suffer *ḫasf* and *masḫ* and *qaḏf*. This will take place when there is no more justice there, and when oppression, prostitution and false testimony prevail.[53]

SLAVE-GIRLS, WINE, ETC.

The eschatological metamorphosis into apes and pigs did not always remain confined to heretics accused of Israelite orientation. Other kinds of sin — outside the sphere of dogma — were also linked to the same punitive metamorphosis. The sins are wine (*ḫamr*) drinking, as well as playing music in the company of singing slave-girls. Occasionally, wearing silk (*ḥarīr*) clothes is added to the list, as well as false testimony and taking usury. At least some of these types of sin were associated with Jews and Christians (usury, wine, music), as well as with non-Arabs in general (silk[54]). These practices were considered a threat to the distinctive Islamic identity, and in order to diminish their prevalence Muslim tradition linked them to the classical Jewish-Christian type of punishment.

A group of traditions linking the punishment of the apes and the pigs to these sins was circulated by Farqad b. Yaʿqūb al-Sabaḫī (Başran d. AH 131). His traditions are traced back to the Prophet through Syrian and Iraqi *isnāds* of Abū Umāma al-Bāhilī (Syrian Companion d. AH 81–86), ʿUbāda b. al-Şāmit (Syrian Anşārī Companion, d. AH 34–45), ʿAbd al-Raḥmān b. Ġanm al-Ašʿarī (Syrian d. AH 78) and Ibn ʿAbbās. In all of these versions the Prophet states in the first person that people of "my community" will spend the night rejoicing and exulting (*ʿalā ašar wa-baṭar*) and enjoying themselves playfully, and will wake up in the morning as apes and pigs. This will happen because they desecrated forbidden women and slave-girls, drank wine (*ḫamr*), took usury, and wore silk clothes.[55]

Another version of Farqad links the same statement of the Prophet to the triple calamity. Farqad quotes the statement in response to a question of whether the tradition about the *ḫasf* and the *qaḏf* was uttered by the

[53] Ṭabarānī, *Awsaṭ*, VII, no. 6091. The *isnād*: ʿAbd al-Ḫāliq Abū Hāniʾ < Ziyād b. al-Abraş < Anas b. Mālik < Prophet.

[54] For silk clothes and the manners of the *Aʿāǧim* (non-Arabs), see Abū Dāwūd, II, 371 (31:8); Nasāʾī, *Kubrā*, V, no. 9366 (80:25); Aḥmad, *Musnad*, IV, 134.

[55] Aḥmad, *Musnad*, V, 329. See also Ṭabarānī, *Kabīr*, VIII, no. 7997; *idem*, *Şaġīr*, I, 62. A similar statement is contained in a tradition of the Companion ʿAbdallāh b. Bišr. See *Maǧmaʿ al-zawāʾid*, VIII, 14 (Ṭabarānī).

Prophet himself. In the version quoted by Farqad on this occasion, the sinners are not only turned into apes and pigs, but their families are carried away by wind.[56] However, there is no explicit *ḫasf* or *qadf* here.

Elements of the triple calamity are present more explicitly in the version of Qabīṣa b. Ḏu'ayb (Medinan Successor d. AH 86) as recorded by Nuʿaym b. Ḥammād. In it the Prophet describes transformation (conveyed here by the root *'.f.k.*) of people into apes and pigs, as well as their being engulfed by the earth (*ḫasf*). This is a punishment inflicted for drinking wine, wearing silk clothes and playing music.[57]

The same combination of disasters (transformation into apes and pigs and *ḫasf*) appears in a Syrian tradition in which the Prophet predicts that people will drink wine (*ḫamr*) while calling it otherwise, and will enjoy singing and music. God will cause the earth to engulf them, and will turn them into apes and pigs. This tradition is of the Companion Abū Mālik al-Ašʿarī and was recorded in several *ḥadīṯ* compilations, including canonical ones.[58]

The sin of enjoying the above unlawful kinds of pleasure was also built into independent statements about the triple calamity in which no explicit mention of apes and pigs is made. Such versions appear in the canonical compilations. Al-Tirmiḏī has recorded a tradition of the Meccan Companion ʿImrān b. Ḥuṣayn (d. AH 52) in which the Prophet states: "[There will be] in this community *ḫasf* and *qadf* and *masḫ*". Someone asks the Prophet: "When will it be?" The Prophet: "When slave-girls and musical instruments appear, and when wine is drunk."[59] A very similar dialogue is described in traditions of the Companion Abū Mālik al-Ašʿarī,[60] and the Anṣārī Companion Abū Saʿīd al-Ḫudrī (d. AH 65).[61] The same discourse appears in an extended version of the triple calamity of the above-mentioned Sahl b. Saʿd al-Anṣārī.[62] A version of Abū Hurayra adds homosexuality to the list, and also the sin of false testimony.[63]

However, the apes and the pigs did not always retain their Jewish-

[56] Aḥmad, *Musnad*, V, 259.

[57] Nuʿaym b. Ḥammād, *Fitan*, 371–72.

[58] The *isnād*: ʿAbd al-Raḥmān b. Ġanm al-Ašʿarī (Syrian d. AH 78) < Abū Mālik al-Ašʿarī < Prophet. See Ibn Abī Šayba, VII, no. 3810; Ibn Māǧa, II, no. 4020 (36:22); Ibn Ḥibbān, *Ṣaḥīḥ*, XV, no. 6758; Bayhaqī, *Sunan*, VIII, 295, X, 221. See also Buḫārī, *Tārīḫ kabīr*, I, no. 967; Ṭabarānī, *Kabīr*, III, no. 3419. And see a parallel version in Buḫārī, *Ṣaḥīḥ*, VII, 138 (74:6); Abū Dāwūd, II, 369 (31:6); Bayhaqī, *Sunan*, X, 221; *Kanz*, XI, no. 30926.

[59] Tirmiḏī/ *Tuḥfa*, VI, no. 2309 (31:38). See also Dānī, *Fitan*, no. 340.

[60] Ṭabarānī, *Kabīr*, III, no. 3410.

[61] *Idem*, *Awsaṭ*, VII, no. 6901.

[62] *Idem*, *Kabīr*, VI, no. 5810.

[63] *Kašf al-astār*, IV, no. 3405.

Christian connotation, and they eventually became a general metaphor for desecration, beastliness and corruption. This seems already to be the case with respect to some of the above sins, but it comes out far more clearly in the political sphere. There is a series of anti-Umayyad utterances of the Prophet in which this dynasty is likened to monkeys as well as to pigs. These traditions describe a dream of the Prophet in which he sees the Umayyads use his own *minbar* (pulpit) for their public addresses, and he is deeply grieved by the sight. There are numerous versions of the dream,[64] and in a Medinan one of Abū Hurayra the Umayyads [the Marwānids] are seen jumping up and down on Muḥammad's *minbar* like monkeys.[65] The monkeys here illustrate the desecration of the *minbar* of the Prophet by the Umayyads. In another very rare version of Saʿīd b. al-Musayyab (Medinan d. AH 94), the Umayyads climbing the *minbar* are seen by the Prophet in the form of "apes and pigs".[66]

CONFIRMING VERSIONS

Finally, some versions about the above kinds of unlawful pleasure contain additional remarks designed to confirm that the punitive transformation into apes and pigs will indeed befall Muslims. Such expanded versions were needed because the notion that a Jewish-Christian type of punishment could befall good obedient Muslims just for not drinking the right beverage or wearing the right cloth looked absurd to people still convinced of the unique virtues of the Islamic community, and of its superiority to non-Muslim communities.

Thus in a version of the Companion Abū Hurayra, the Prophet declares that at the end of days people of his community will be metamorphosed into apes and pigs. Someone asks him whether this will be the fate of those who profess the *šahāda* and observe the duty of fasting, and the Prophet confirms it. He then goes on to explain that this will be their fate because of the pleasure they used to take in music and in slave-girls, and because

[64] E.g., Ṭabarī, *Tafsīr*, XXX, 167 (on *Sūrat al-Qadar*); Aḥmad, *Musnad*, II, 385, 522; Bayhaqī, *Dalāʾil*, VI, 509–510 (with editor's references); Ṭabarānī, *Kabīr*, I, no. 1425.

[65] Bayhaqī, *Dalāʾil*, VI, 511; Ǧawrakānī, *Abāṭīl*, I, nos. 236, 237; Ibn Kaṯīr, *Bidāya*, VI, 243. The *isnād*: al-ʿAlāʾ b. ʿAbd al-Raḥmān al-Ḥuraqī (Medinan d. AH 132) < his father < Abū Hurayra < Prophet.

[66] *Tārīḫ Baġdād*, IX, 44; Ǧawrakānī, *Abāṭīl*, I, no. 238. The *isnād*: Sufyān al-Ṯawrī (Kūfan d. AH 161) < ʿAlī b. Zayd b. ʿAbdallāh b. Ǧudʿān (Baṣran d. AH 131) < Saʿīd b. al-Musayyab < Prophet. But in a parallel version of the same tradition no mention is made of apes and pigs. See *Tārīḫ Baġdād*, IX, 44; Ibn Kaṯīr, *Bidāya*, VI, 243.

they drank wine. They will spend the night enjoying these things, and will become apes and pigs in the morning.[67]

A similar confirmation was offered in connection with the triple calamity. A version of the Meccan Successor ʿAbd al-Raḥmān b. Sābiṭ (d. AH 118) contains an additional remark of the Prophet to the effect that indulgence in the above unlawful pleasures will result in the triple calamity, even if the sinful Muslims stick to the *šahāda*, i.e., the initial tenet of the Islamic creed.[68]

The same message is conveyed in the version of ʿĀʾiša of the dialogue appended to the announcement about the triple calamity. This version was recorded by al-Tirmiḏī.[69] The Prophet here stresses that the calamity will not be prevented even if the Muslims have righteous individuals (*ṣāliḥūn*) among them. This means that Muslim sinners will not enjoy the intercession of the righteous.

CONCLUSION

In conclusion, the existence of so many versions of traditions applying to Muslims the Jewish-Christian type of punitive metamorphosis, including some which gained entrance into canonical *ḥadīṯ* compilations, indicates fear for the unique Islamic identity. This identity was supposed to be based on unity and on morality, and both were threatened by Muslims imitating Jewish and Christian ways. Unity was shattered by heretics suspected of following Jewish and Christian dogma, and morality was corrupted by people assimilating profane aspects of Jewish and Christian culture. To confront these trends, traditions were circulated which were designed to expose their Jewish and Christian backgrounds, and thus help eliminate them from Islamic society. This was also the aim of the traditions about the apes and the pigs, the most characteristic symbols of Jewish-Christian historical punishment.

[67] Abū Nuʿaym, *Ḥilya*, III, 119–20. The *isnād*: Sulaymān b. Sālim < Ḥassān b. Abī Sinān (Baṣran) < Abū Hurayra < Prophet.

[68] Ibn Abī Šayba, XV, no. 19391; Nuʿaym b. Ḥammād, *Fitan*, 375; Dānī, *Fitan*, no. 339.

[69] Tirmiḏī/ *Tuḥfa*, VI, no. 2280 (31:21). See also Dānī, *Fitan*, no. 341.

REFERENCES

ʿAbd al-Razzāq, Abū Bakr b. Hammām al-Ṣanʿānī. *Al-Muṣannaf*. Ed. Ḥabīb al-Raḥmān al-Aʿẓamī. 11 vols. Beirut 1970.

—. *Tafsīr al-Qurʾān*. Ed. Muṣṭafā Muslim Muḥammad. 3 vols. Riyadh 1989.

Abū Dāwūd. *Al-Sunan*. 2 vols. Cairo 1952.

Abū Nuʿaym, *Ḥilyat al-awliyāʾ*, Cairo 1357/1938, repr. Beirut 1967.

Abū Yaʿlā, Aḥmad b. ʿAlī al-Mawṣilī. *Al-Musnad*. Ed. Ḥusayn Salīm Asad. 13 vols. Damascus-Beirut 1984–1990.

Aḥmad b. Ḥanbal. *Al-Musnad*. 6 vols. Cairo 1313/1895, repr. Beirut n.d.

al-Āğurrī, Muḥammad b. al-Ḥusayn. *Kitāb al-šarīʿa*. Ed. Muḥammad b. al-Ḥasan Ismāʿīl. Beirut 1995.

al-Azraqī, Abū l-Walīd. *Aḫbār Makka*. In F. Wüstenfeld (ed.), *Die Chroniken der Stadt Mekka* (Göttingen 1858, repr. Beirut n.d.), vol. I.

al-Baġawī, al-Ḥusayn b. Masʿūd. *Maʿālim al-tanzīl fī l-tafsīr wa-l-taʾwīl*. 5 vols. Beirut 1985.

al-Bayhaqī, Aḥmad b. al-Ḥusayn. *Dalāʾil al-nubuwwa*. Ed. ʿAbd al-Muʿṭī Qalʿağī. 7 vols. Beirut 1988.

—. *Al-Sunan al-kubrā*. 10 vols. Hyderabad 1355/1936, repr. Beirut n.d.

al-Buḫārī, Muḥammad b. Ismāʿīl. *Al-Ṣaḥīḥ*. 9 vols. Cairo 1958.

—. *al-Tārīḫ al-kabīr*. 8 vols. Hyderabad 1360/1941, repr. Beirut 1986.

Cook, Michael. "Early Muslim Dietary Law," *Jerusalem Studies in Arabic and Islam* 7 (1986), 217–77.

—. "Ibn Qutayba and the Monkeys." Paper presented in the *Seventh International Colloquium: From Jāhiliyya to Islam*, Jerusalem 1996.

al-Damīrī, Kamāl al-Dīn. *Ḥayāt al-ḥayawān*. Cairo 1970.

al-Dānī, Abū ʿAmr ʿUṯmān b. Saʿīd. *Al-Sunan al-Wārida fī l-fitan wa-ġawāʾilihā wa-l-sāʿati wa-ʾašrāṭihā*. Ed. Riḍāʾullāh al-Mubārakfūrī, 6 vols. Riyadh 1995.

al-Huwwārī, Hūd b. Muḥakkam. *Tafsīr kitāb Allāh al-ʿAzīz*. Ed. Belḥāğ Šarīfī. 4 vols. Beirut 1990.

Ibn Abī ʿĀṣim al-Šaybānī. *Kitāb al-sunna*. Ed. Muḥammad Nāṣir al-Dīn al-Albānī. Beirut-Damascus 1985.

Ibn Abī l-Dunyā, ʿAbdallāh b. Muḥammad. *Al-ʿUqūbāt al-ilāhiyya li-l-afrād wa-l-ğamāʿāt wa-l-umam*. Ed. Muḥammad Ḫayr Ramaḍān Yūsuf. Beirut 1996.

Ibn Abī Šayba, ʿAbdallāh b. Muḥammad. *Al-Muṣannaf fī l-aḥādīṯ wa-l-āṯār*. Ed. ʿAbd al-Ḫāliq al-Afġānī. 15 vols. Bombay 1979–83.

Ibn Baṭṭa, ʿUbaydallāh b. Muḥammad. *Al-Ibāna ʿan šarīʿati l-firqati l-nāǧiya wa-muǧānabati l-firaqi l-maḏmūma: kitāb al-īmān*. Ed. Riḍā b. Naʿsān Muʿṭī. 2 vols. Riyadh 1994.
Ibn Ḥibbān, Muḥammad b. Aḥmad al-Bustī. *Al-Iḥsān fī taqrīb Ṣaḥīḥ Ibn Ḥibbān, tartīb ʿAlāʾ al-Dīn al-Fārisī*. Ed. Šuʿayb al-Arnaʾūṭ. 16 vols. Beirut 1988.
Ibn al-Ǧawzī, Abū l-Farağ ʿAbd al-Raḥmān. *Zād al-masīr fī ʿilm al-tafsīr*. 9 vols. Beirut 1984.
Ibn al-Kalbī, Hišām b. Muḥammad. *Kitāb al-aṣnām*. Ed. Aḥmad Zakī. Cairo 1924, repr. Cairo n.d.
Ibn Kaṯīr, Ismāʿīl b. ʿUmar. *Al-Bidāya wa-l-nihāya*. 14 vols. Repr. Beirut 1974.
—. *Tafsīr al-Qurʾān al-ʿaẓīm*. 4 vols. Cairo n.d.
Ibn Māğa, Muḥammad b. Yazīd, *al-Sunan*, ed. ʿAbd al-Bāqī, Cairo 1952.
Ibn Ṭāwūs, ʿAlī b. Mūsā. *al-Malāḥim wa-l-fitan*. Beirut 1988.
al-Ǧawrakānī, al-Ḥusayn b. Ibrāhīm al-Hamaḏānī. *Al-Abāṭīl wa-l-manākīr wa-l-ṣiḥāḥ wa-l-mašāhīr*. Ed. ʿAbd al-Raḥmān al-Faryuwāʾī. 2 vols. Benares 1403/1983, repr. Riyadh 1994.
Kanz = ʿAlāʾ al-Dīn al-Muttaqī b. Ḥusām al-Dīn al-Hindī. *Kanz al-ʿummāl fī sunan al-aqwāl wa-l-afʿāl*. Ed. Ṣafwat al-Saqqā and Bakrī Ḥayyānī. 16 vols. Beirut 1979.
Kašf al-astār = al-Hayṯamī, Nūr al-Dīn. *Kašf al-astār ʿan zawāʾid al-Bazzār*. Ed. Ḥabīb al-Raḥmān al-Aʿẓamī. 4 vols. Beirut 1979.
al-Lālikāʾī, Hibatullāh b. al-Ḥasan. *Šarḥ uṣūl iʿtiqād ahl al-sunna wa-l-ǧamāʿa*. Ed. Aḥmad Saʿd Ḥamdān. 4 vols. Riyadh 1988.
Lichtenstaedter, Ilse. "And Become Ye Accursed Apes," *Jerusalem Studies in Arabic and Islam* 14 (1991), 153–75.
Mağmaʿ al-zawāʾid = al-Hayṯamī, Nūr al-Dīn. *Mağmaʿ al-zawāʾid wa-manbaʿ al-fawāʾid*. 10 vols. Repr. Beirut 1987.
al-Marwazī, Muḥammad b. Naṣr. *Al-Sunna*. Ed. Sālim al-Salafī. Beirut 1988.
al-Māwardī, ʿAlb b. Muḥammad. *Al-Nukat wa-l-ʿuyūn fī tafsīr al-Qurʾān*. Ed. ʿAbd al-Maqṣūd b. ʿAbd al-Raḥīm. 6 vols. Beirut 1992.
Muqātil b. Sulaymān. *Tafsīr al-Qurʾān*. Ed. ʿAbdallāh Maḥmūd Šiḥāta. 5 vols. Cairo 1979.
al-Nasāʾī, Aḥmad b. Šuʿayb. *Al-Sunan al-kubrā*. Ed. ʿAbd al-Ġaffār al-Bandārī, and Sayyid Ḥasan. 6 vols. Beirut 1991.
Nuʿaym b. Ḥammād. *Kitāb al-fitan*. Ed. Suhayl Zakkār. Beirut 1993.
al-Qurṭubī, Muḥammad b. Aḥmad. *Al-Ǧāmiʿ li-aḥkām al-Qurʾān*. 20 vols. Cairo 1967.
al-Samarqandī, Abū l-Layṯ Naṣr b. Muḥammad. *Tafsīr al-Qurʾān*. Ed. ʿAlī Muʿawwaḍ, ʿĀdil ʿAbd al-Mawǧūd, and Zakariyyā al-Nawtī. 3 vols. Beirut 1993.

al-Suyūṭī, Ǧalāl al-Dīn. *Al-Durr al-manṯūr fī l-tafsīr bi-l-maʾṯūr*. 6 vols. Cairo 1314/1869, repr. Beirut n.d.

al-Ṭabarānī, Sulaymān b. Aḥmad. *Al-Muʿǧam al-awsaṭ*. Ed. Maḥmūd al-Ṭaḥḥān. 10 vols. Riyadh 1985–95.

—. *Al-Muʿǧam al-kabīr*. Ed. Ḥamdī ʿAbd al-Maǧīd al-Salafī. 25 vols. Baghdad 1980–85.

—. *Al-Muʿǧam al-ṣaġīr*. Ed. ʿAbd al-Raḥmān Muḥammad ʿUṯmān. 2 vols. Cairo 1981–83.

al-Ṭabarī, Muḥammad b. Ǧarīr. *Ǧāmiʿ al-bayān fī tafsīr al-Qurʾān*. 30 vols. Būlāq 1323/1905, repr. Beirut 1972.

al-Ṭabarsī, al-Faḍl b. al-Ḥasan. *Maǧmaʿ al-bayān fī tafsīr al-Qurʾān*. 30 vols. Beirut 1957.

Tārīḫ Baġdād = Al-Ḫaṭīb al-Baġdādī, Aḥmad b. ʿAlī. *Tārīḫ Baġdād*. Ed. Muḥammad Saʿīd al-ʿUrfī and Muḥammad Ḥāmid al-Faqiyy. 14 vols. Cairo *ca*. 1932, repr. Beirut n.d.

Tirmiḏī/*Tuḥfa* = ʿAbd al-Raḥmān al-Mubārakfūrī. *Tuḥfat al-aḥwaḏī šarḥ Ǧāmiʿ al-Tirmiḏī*. Ed. ʿAbd al-Raḥmān Muḥammad ʿUṯmān. 10 vols. Cairo 1979.

al-Ṭūsī, Muḥammad b. al-Ḥasan. *Al-Tabyān fī tafsīr al-Qurʾān*. Ed. Aḥmad al-ʿĀmilī. 10 vols. Beirut n.d.

Van Ess, Josef. *Theologie und Gesellschaft im 2. und 3. Jahrhundert Hidschra: Eine Geschichte des religiösen Denkens im frühen Islam*. 6 vols. Berlin, New York, 1991–95.

al-Wāḥidī, ʿAlī b. Aḥmad. *al-Wasīṭ fī tafsīr al-Qurʾān al-maǧīd*. Ed. ʿĀdil Aḥmad ʿAbd al-Mawǧūd and others. Beirut 1994.

al-Zamaḫšarī, Ǧārullāh Maḥmūd b. ʿUmar. *Al-Kaššāf ʿan ḥaqāʾiq al-tanzīl*. 4 vols. Cairo 1966.

ŠIRK AND "IDOLATRY" IN MONOTHEIST POLEMIC

GERALD R. HAWTING

In Muslim texts of different sorts the accusation is frequently made against opponents that they are *mušrikūn*, that is, that they commit the sin of *širk*. That charge has been made by Muslims against opponents both within and outside the tradition of monotheism. On different occasions, *širk* has been imputed, whether explicitly or implicitly, to Christians, Jews, and other Muslims, as well as to, for example, Hindus and adherents of traditional African religions. My aim here is to discuss the content and function of the charge, to relate it to the idea of idolatry in monotheist thought more generally, and to suggest that its use against monotheists is more basic (and probably more frequent) than against non-monotheists.

The charge of *širk* is generally equivalent in its content and function, it will be argued, to that of "idolatry". It functions primarily as an item of polemic within monotheism and its application to peoples such as Hindus and Africans is probably secondary. That might imply even that the concept of *širk* originated in early Muslim polemic against other monotheists and not, as is usually assumed, in arguments against "real" idolaters, the Arab pagans of the time of the Prophet. To substantiate this last suggestion would involve discussion which would not seem immediately relevant to the theme of this volume, and it will not, therefore, be followed up in detail here. In view of its importance in polemic between Muslims, Jews and Christians, however, an attempt to elucidate the concept of idolatry/*širk* does not seem out of place. Most of the examples adduced here are quite well known, and they are not intended to be comprehensive. It seems worthwhile, however, to present them together in a comparative discussion.[1]

* * * *

[1] This is not the place for a detailed bibliography of polemic and apologetic between Jews, Christians and Muslims. Further to the fundamental works of M. Steinschneider (1877) and E. Fritsch (1930), the articles s.vv. 'Polemic' and 'Apologetic' in the *Encyclopaedia Judaica*,

Semantically and etymologically, of course, *širk* is not exactly equivalent to English "idolatry" and the various related words in European languages which derive from Greek *eidōlatreia*. Literally, *širk* means something like "associationism" and a *mušrik* is someone who, allegedly, recognizes or attributes to someone else an associate, companion or friend (*šarīk*). *Širk* is most frequently translated into English as "polytheism" since it is the sin imputed to those who are said to associate other gods or beings with God, who alone should be the object of worship. Applied to peoples such as Hindus or Africans, this charge relates to beliefs understood as polytheistic or to practices understood as idolatrous in a quite literal sense. Applied to Jews, Christians, or (other) Muslims, the charge seems to be made usually because some belief (or, less frequently, practice) of the opponent is held to compromise or dilute the absolute unity or uniqueness of God. From the point of view of the Muslim who is accusing a monotheist opponent of *širk*, the opponent's doctrines (or acts) are inconsistent with true monotheism and make the opponent the equivalent of a polytheist or idolater.

Even though the idea of polytheism usually remains an ingredient of the word, it also often has connotations of "idolatry". This is especially evident in the Quran and the tradition of interpreting that work as reflecting conditions in central Arabia at the beginning of the 7th century. In the scripture itself the words *širk*, *mušrik* and other derivations from the same Arabic root occur frequently in attacks on opponents, and the opponents are referred to in ways which associate them with the use of idols as well as with acceptance of more than one god. The association with polytheism is most explicit in those passages where they are charged with having other gods before (*min dūni*; cf. *ʿal-pənē* in Deut, 5:7) God,[2] while that with idolatry appears in the accusation that they follow the *ṭāġūt* and (in one instance) the *ǧibt*. Although the origin and significance of these two latter words is not completely clear, it seems likely that they have been taken over from earlier monotheistic usage where they have associations with the idea of idolatry.[3]

and 'Polemic' in M. Eliade (ed.), *The Encyclopaedia of Religion*, London and New York, 1987, vol. 11 are useful. Note too G.C. Anawati, 'Polémique, apologie et dialogue islamo-chrétiens', in *Euntes Docete* xxii (1969), 380–92; David Thomas, *Anti-Christian Polemic in Early Islam*, Cambridge 1992; Muḥammad al-Ḥawārī, *Al-Ǧadal al-yahūdī ḍidda-l-masīḥiyya fī ḍawʾ al-ǧanīza*, Cairo 1994.

[2] E.g., Quran 21: 98–99 (which denies that those whom the opponents worship besides God are in reality gods — if they were, they would not be in hell) and 25:3 (which again denies the reality of those whom the opponents take as gods before Him).

[3] For the *ṭāġūt*, see Quran 2:256, 257; 4:54, 60, 76; 16:36; 39:17; for *al-ǧibt*, see 4:51. For discussion of etymology and meaning, see A. Jeffery, *The Foreign Vocabulary of the Qurʾān*,

On the assumption that the language used against opponents in the Quran should be understood as polemic, it is not necessary to take these associations of *širk* literally. Just because the Quran accuses its opponents of taking gods before God and of following after *ṭāġūt* and *ǧibt* we do not have to envisage that those opponents were in fact polytheists or idolaters in a real sense (whatever that might be given the relativity of concepts such as monotheism and polytheism). Here it is only intended to show that readers or hearers of the Quran would associate *širk* with polytheism and idolatry, especially once the original polemical context which the Quran reflects had passed away. It is noticeable that in spite of its frequent translation as polytheism, some translations of the Quran do supply "idolatry" and "idolater" for *širk* and *mušrik*.[4]

In so far as one can detect a concept opposite to *širk* in the Quran it seems to be something like *iḫlāṣ*, "devoting oneself to God alone", and not merely *tawḥīd*, "insistence on the oneness of God".[5] It may also be worth pointing out that the common Arabic words for idol, *ṣanam* and *waṯan*, seem rare in the Quran in the context of attacks against the opponents: when these words do occur in the Quran it tends to be in connexion with earlier peoples and prophets — the contemporaries of Abraham or the Children of Israel when they entered the Promised Land, for example.

The linkage of *širk* with idolatry can also be seen outside the Quran in the *tafsīr*, *sīra* and associated types of literature. This is done in a general way by the systematic identification of the Quranic *mušrikūn* as the idolatrous (and polytheistic) pagan Arabs of the time of Muḥammad and by the elaboration of descriptions of the idols and practices of those Arabs. This gives rise to the lists of pre-Islamic idols, the best known of which is the "Book of Idols" (*Kitāb al-Aṣnām*) attributed to Hišām Ibn al-Kalbī (d. 204/819 or 206/821).[6] The tradition's establishment of the identity between *širk* and idolatry may be illustrated further by two specific examples.

Baroda 1938, 99–100, 202–3; R. Köbert, Das koranische 'ṭāġūt', *Orientalia*, n.s. xxx (1961), 415–16; R. Paret, *Der Koran: Kommentar und Konkordanz*, Stuttgart, etc. 1971, 96.

4 E.g., the well known translations of Pickthall and Dawood. Jane Dammen McAuliffe in her *Qur'ānic Christians*, Cambridge 1991, regularly glosses *mušrikūn*, *allaḏīna ašrakū*, etc. as idolaters.

5 See, e.g., Quran 29:65, which contrasts the *iḫlāṣ* of the opponents when they feel that they are in peril on the sea with their *širk* when they feel secure on dry land. And see further the passage recounting the arguments of Ibn ʿAbd al-Wahhāb, below (pp. 118–120).

6 See Rosa Klinke-Rosenberger (tr.), *Das Götzenbuch. Kitâb al-Aṣnâm des Ibn al-Kalbî*, Leipzig 1941; H.S. Nyberg, "Bemerkungen zum 'Buch der Götzenbilder' von Ibn al-Kalbī," in *ΔΡΑΓΜΑ Martino P. Nilsson...dedicatum*, Lund 1939, 346–66; F. Stummer, "Bemerkungen zum Götzenbuch des Ibn al-Kalbî," *ZDMG* xcviii (1944), 377–94.

In his history of Mecca al-Azraqī has a chapter about the destruction of the idols (*aṣnām*) around the Kaʿba at the time when the Prophet conquered Mecca. In the middle of reports referring to idols like Isāf and Nāʾila, a man and a woman who in ancient times had been turned into stone by God for sexual misconduct inside the Kaʿba and who had then been set up and worshipped as idols by the Meccans, we have a report about the distress of Satan at the time of the destruction of the idols. He gave up all hope that "the *umma* of Muḥammad will return to *širk* after this day of theirs". In this report *širk* is clearly understood to be the equivalent of idolatry, literally *ʿibādat al-aṣnām*.[7]

Quran 6: 136 reads "They assign to God, from the crops and cattle which He has created, a portion, saying, 'This is for God' — so they claim (*bi-zamʿihim*) — 'and this is for our associates (*li-šurakāʾinā*)'. That which is for their associates does not come to God, but that which is for God does come to their associates. Theirs is an evil arrangement (*sāʾa mā yaḥkumūna*)." The meaning of the verse is debatable but the significant thing here is that the *tafsīr* tradition consistently identifies the associates (*šurakāʾ*) mentioned in it with the idols or gods of the pagan Arabs. Ibn Isḥāq relates the verse to an idol of the tribe of Ḫawlān: "Ḫawlān had an idol called ʿUmyānis in their territory. According to what they claimed (*bi-zamʿihim*), they used to divide part of their cattle and crops between it and God. If any of the portion which they had assigned for God came into that assigned for ʿUmyānis, they would leave it for the latter; but, if any of the share of ʿUmyānis came into that which had been assigned to God, they would retrieve it for [the idol]. This was a clan of Ḫawlān called al-Adīm. It is said that it was regarding them that God revealed Quran 6:136."[8] Here the identification of the *šarīk* with the idol reflects the wider identification of *širk* with idolatry.

In the Quran the words *kufr* and *kāfir* are of a frequency comparable with *širk* and *mušrik* in their application to the opponents. The content of *kufr* seems rather less specific than that of *širk* and it is usually translated simply as "infidelity" or "unbelief", sometimes "ingratitude". It is tempting to relate *kāfir* to *kōfēr* in Rabbinic usage, especially in the phrase *kōfēr bā-ʿiqqār*, someone who denies or disavows the "root", i.e., God. As Urbach makes clear, the phrase does not necessarily indicate someone

[7] Azraqī, *Aḫbār Makka*, ed. Rušdī al-Sāliḥ Malḥas, Beirut 1969, i, 119 ff.

[8] Ibn Hišām, *Sīra*, ed. Muṣṭafā al-Saqā *et al.*, Cairo 1955, i, 80–81 (tr. A. Guillaume, *The Life of Muhammad*, Oxford 1955, 36–37); R. Klinke-Rosenberger (tr.), *Das Götzenbuch*, 27 (text) = 53 (translation). The name of the idol of Ḫawlān is reproduced variantly in different sources. For a discussion and argument in favour of the authenticity of the report, see I. Goldfeld, "ʿUmyānis the idol of Khawlān," *IOS* iii (1973), 108–19.

who denies God out of ignorance but may refer to someone who claims to be a monotheist and yet, by his behaviour or belief, does not in fact merit acceptance as such.[9]

The relationship between those attacked in the Quran as *mušrikūn* and those as *kuffār* (or *kāfirūn* or *kafara*) is somewhat problematic, as is the relationship between that group or groups and the Jews and Christians. It does not seem possible to identify the *mušrikūn* and *kuffār* as clearly distinct groups, but there are passages which seem to distinguish between them and the Jews and Christians. However, Quran 5:72–73, for example, clearly imputes *kufr* to those who believe that Jesus is the Son of God or accept the doctrine of the Trinity, and it uses the verb *ašraka* when referring (apparently) to the belief that Jesus was God. One would hesitate to say, therefore, that the distinction between various groups of opponents in the Quran is always obvious or consistent, and, whatever differences are envisaged in various Quranic passages, other Muslim texts clearly associate *kufr* and *širk* with Christians, Jews and other monotheists. Although it is possible to argue that some distinction in meaning between the two terms is maintained, as terms of abuse in Muslim polemic there is a certain overlap.

* * * *

Širk, therefore, may have connotations both of polytheism and of idolatry. It functions, however, in a way broadly similar to the charge of idolatry in Christianity and to accusations in the Jewish tradition which can be understood in the same way. Just as Muslims might describe people whom they saw as polytheists and idolaters in a real sense as *mušrikūn*, so Jews and Christians have described, for example, the adherents of Graeco-Roman religion or the North American Indians, as idolaters. But in Judaism and Christianity, as in Islam, idolatry is frequently imputed to fellow monotheists and it may be that that is the most common context for the accusation.[10] In such cases the force of the charge is that the opponents are *no better than* idolaters, that their beliefs or practices are inconsistent with monotheism as it ought to be understood and that the opponents,

[9] See E.E. Urbach, *The Sages: Their Concepts and Beliefs*, Eng. tr., 2nd edition, Cambridge Mass. and London, 1979, 26–28.

[10] It seems to be accepted that Rabbinical Judaism, notwithstanding its counting idolatry as one of the greatest sins and incompatible with being a Jew (e.g., B. Talmud, Megillah, 13a), nevertheless did not see "real" paganism as a threat to Judaism. It was envisaged that the tendency of Jews towards idolatry had passed away in the time of the first temple (Midrash Rabba on Song of Songs, 7:8). See further, S. Lieberman, "Rabbinic polemics against idolatry," in his *Hellenism and Jewish Palestine*, (1950) 2nd ed., New York 1962, 115–27; *Encyclopaedia Judaica*, article 'Idolatry', 1235a.

therefore, have made themselves *equivalent to* idolaters. In polemical language phrases such as "no better than" or "equivalent to" tend to be omitted.

Since the charge is most transparent when it is made in one of the European languages, perhaps the most obvious examples occur in the history of Christianity. The Protestant accusations of idolatry against the Catholics at the time of the Reformation in Europe and the Iconoclasts' use of the same term (*eidōlatreia*) against the Iconodules in 8th century Byzantium are perhaps the best known. In the context of this article, the letter of Elizabeth I of England to the Ottoman sultan Murād III in which she refers to Philip II of Spain as the chief idolater is especially interesting.[11]

In the Jewish tradition various circumlocutions are used which, like *širk* in Islam, although they are not semantically equivalent to idolatry, may be said to carry the same weight. The title of the Mishna tractate, ʿAvodāh Zārāh, which is usually translated "Idolatry" means literally "Strange Worship", apparently alluding to a number of biblical passages containing the word *zār* in contexts indicating strange forms of worship or strange gods (Lev. 10:1, Deut. 32:16, Isa. 43:12, etc.).The tractate mainly concerns various problems arising from the contacts between Jews and adherents of Graeco-Roman religion in Palestine in the early Christian period.[12]

If that Mishna tractate is concerned with people who, from the Jewish point of view, could be understood as idolaters in a real sense, the application to the Rabbis by their Karaite opponents of the Hebrew word *gillūlīm* with the sense of 'idols' is an example of the intra-monotheist polemical use of language. The word literally means 'pieces of filth' or 'dung' and reflects the use of the same word to refer to idols in the book of Ezekiel (6:4 and *passim*).[13]

Of course, the charge of idolatry has not been made merely in an abstract or general manner by simply labelling one's opponents as idolaters: it has been achieved too by accusing the opponents of performing rituals or of holding beliefs which are transparently idolatrous. An example

[11] Norman Daniel, *Islam, Europe and Empire*, Edinburgh 1966, 12 (citing *Calendar of State Papers*, Foreign Series, vol. xxi, part 1, p. 508 — 9/2/1588).

[12] M. Halbertal and A. Margalit, *Idolatry*, English tr., Cambridge Mass. and London, 1992, 3–4; G. Stemberger, *Introduction to the Talmud and Midrash*, English tr., 2nd edition, Edinburgh 1996, 115 (*Einleitung in Talmud und Midrasch*, Munich 1992).

[13] N. Wieder, *The Judaean Scrolls and Karaism*, London 1962, 151–53. Another possible circumlocutory expression for idol worshippers in the Jewish tradition is *ʿOvdē kōkhāvīm u-mazzālōth*; see H. Strack, *Introduction to the Talmud and Midrash*, English tr., New York 1931, n. 66 to p. 53. For the idolatrous connotations of Hebrew *aḥer*, see I. Gruenwald, "Anti-Gnostic Polemic in Patristic Literature," in R. van den Broek and M.J. Vermaseren (eds.), *Studies in Gnosticism and Hellenistic Religions*, Leiden 1981, 178–79.

from within Judaism would be the accusation made by the Rabbis that the Samaritans worshipped a dove in their sanctuary on Mount Gerizim,[14] from within Christianity the Catholic claim that the Protestants of Zurich venerated the remains of the dead Zwingli in an idolatrous manner.[15]

The notion of idolatry has been extended to cover various forms of behaviour or belief which are disapproved of, and idolatry itself, especially in the Bible and Jewish tradition, may be referred to by metaphors relating to sexual immorality and marital infidelity (e.g., "whoring after the gods (of the people of the land)" in Ex. 34: 15–16). Pride, anger and the love of money have been described as forms of idolatry, and in the Muslim tradition the sphere of *širk* has been extended in a similar way.[16] Maimonides used the concept of idolatry to refer to the anthropomorphic views of the common people which, he said, threatened true monotheism by endangering the concept of God as a perfect unity; Judah Halevi applied it to incorrect forms of worship; and Nachmanides to the worship of real forces which were not, however, deserving of worship.[17] More recently, Yeshayahu Leibowitz denounced the cult of the Western wall as a Golden Calf. All of these examples come from what may be seen as religious discourse and polemic, but the notion has also been extended to refer to beliefs and practices which would not normally be regarded as within the religious sphere. Thus we commonly talk of idolising film stars, of putting people we love on a pedestal, and of worshipping Mammon. Francis Bacon's analysis in his *Novum Organum* of common intellectual fallacies as the four "idols of the mind" is well known.[18]

Between Judaism and Christianity mutual accusations of idolatry have perhaps been limited. In the case of Jewish polemic against Christianity it may be that political circumstances made it necessary for Jews to be

[14] H.J. Schoeps, *Theologie und Geschichte des Judenchristentums*, Tübingen 1949, 392; J. Fossum, "Samaritan Demiurgical Traditions and the Alleged Dove Cult of the Samaritans," in R. van den Broek and M.J. Vermaseren (eds.), *Studies in Gnosticism and Hellenistic Religions*, Leiden 1981, 143–60.

[15] C.M.N. Eire, *War Against the Idols*, 86. The accusation was a polemical development of the idea that Zwingli's heart had not been destroyed, that "his soul goes marching on".

[16] For pride and anger as idolatry see, e.g., Solomon Schechter, *Aspects of Rabbinic Theology*, (1909) New York: Schocken Books 1961, 223–24; for pride as *širk*, I. Goldziher, *Introduction to Islamic Theology and Law*, (1910), Princeton 1981, 42. (Goldziher notes the identification made by some Muslim scholars of a "lesser *širk*" or a "hidden *širk*" [*al-širk al-aṣġar*, *širk ḫafī*], in Sufism the opposite of *tawakkul*.) For love of money as idolatry, see Matt. 6:24, and Karl Marx cited by Halbertal and Margalit, *Idolatry*, 243. For the sexual metaphor, ibid., 9–36.

[17] Halbertal and Margalit, *Idolatry*, 109–10, 186–90, and 190–97.

[18] See, e.g., Anthony Quinton, *Bacon*, Oxford 1980, 35–38, which links Bacon's language with his Puritan upbringing.

guarded in their use of language when alluding to the religion associated with their rulers, and later Jewish scholars (from Maimonides onwards) developed ideas which seem to envisage that what counts as idolatry for Jews does not necessarily apply to gentiles, and that Christianity and Islam have some positive value.[19] Charges of idolatry have, nevertheless, been made with various degrees of explicitness.

In his discussion of the expression *kōfēr bā-ʿiqqār*, Urbach refers to a statement attributed to Rabbi Ṭarfon (end of 1st century C.E.) which makes the Minim effectively worse than the idolaters: whereas the idolaters (i.e., adherents of Graeco-Roman religion) deny God out of ignorance, the Minim are familiar with the conception of the one God, but introduce other elements into it. The Minim here may be Gnostics, but it is perhaps more likely that they are Christians and that the allusion is to the belief in Jesus as the Son of God.[20]

It is obvious that Jews have seen fundamental doctrines and practices of Christianity, such as the recognition of Jesus as the Son of God or the use of icons in worship, as forms of idolatry, and sometimes that has been made explicit. Thus the 13th century anthology from northern Europe of Jewish apologetic and polemic against Christianity, the *Sefer Niṣṣaḥōn Yāšān*, refers to the idols (*pěsīlīm*) in the Christian houses of abomination/ houses of idolatry (*bātē tarefōtām/ bātē ʿavōdāh zārāh*), and sees the doctrine of the Incarnation as referring to the deification of a human being.[21]

It has been possible for Christian apologists and polemicists to depict Judaism as idolatrous by referring to passages of the Hebrew Bible where the prophets accused the Israelites of idolatry and, above all of course, to the story of the Golden Calf. Chapter 7 of the Acts of the Apostles already reports Stephen's speech in which, among other accusations made against the Jews, reference is made not only to their making the idol of the Calf but also to their worshipping the host of heaven (referring to Amos, 5:25,26). In a similar vein, the 12th century Melkite bishop of Sidon, Paul of Antioch, in the letter addressed to one of his friends among the Muslims of Sidon, portrays the Jews as idolaters, citing the text of Psalm 106 (105):

[19] See, e.g., David Berger, s.v. 'Polemics', in M. Eliade (ed.), *The Encyclopaedia of Religion*, xi, 393.

[20] Ephraim E. Urbach, *The Sages*, 26. For the view that much of the Jewish apologetic which has sometimes been interpreted as directed against dualists should in fact be understood as directed against Christians, see *Encyclopaedia Judaica*, iii, col. 191, s.v. 'Apologetics'.

[21] D. Berger, *The Jewish-Christian Debate in the High Middle Ages. A critical edition of the Niẓẓaḥon Vetus*, Philadelphia: The Jewish Publication Society of America, 1979; see, e.g., sections 67, 210 and 219. For idolatrous connexions of the cross, see too Judah Halevi cited below, p. 125, n. 50.

37–39: *wa-ʿabadū al-aṣnām...wa-arāqū daman zakiyan...allaḏī ḏakkaw li-manḥūtāti* (= Hebrew *ʿāṣāb) Kanʿān.*[22]

It seems clear from such examples that the charge of idolatry is not usually merely an empty or meaningless one, but is made when some aspect of the opponent's belief or practice can be portrayed as weakening the divine unity or uniqueness. Frequently the train of thought is quite obvious: there is no difficulty in understanding how the use of icons or statues in worship, or the claim that Jesus was the Son of God, might be interpreted as idolatry and polytheism by those who reject them. (To say that they are rejected because they are seen as idolatrous and polytheistic would be to oversimplify the problem of the nature and sources of beliefs and practices.)

Sometimes, on the other hand, the logical connexions involved are not so simple and a certain amount of exegesis is necessary to uncover the links. An example might be the way in which the Karaites were able to portray the Rabbis as the idols of their followers since those who accepted the Rabbis' authority, from the Karaite point of view, gave them a share in the authority of God which, according to the Karaites, was revealed only in His written revelation, the Torah.[23] In the case of the imputation of a dove cult to the Samaritans, one element at least seems to be a tendentious interpretation by the Rabbis of Genesis 35:4, which refers to Jacob having buried certain "strange gods" under the oak tree at Shechem, the (later) site of the Samaritan sanctuary.[24] As for the depiction of pride as a form of idolatry or *širk*, the reasoning seems to be that the proud man takes account of the way in which other men see him when he should pay attention only to the way he appears to God. The rationale behind accusations of idolatry may not always be readily apparent, therefore, but there nearly always is one.

A constant problem when dealing with this sort of polemical language is in deciding how seriously the polemicist believes what he is saying. Since the words have some relationship, no matter how tenuous, to reality, there must be a tendency to move from an awareness of the hyperbolic and vilificatory nature of the language to an acceptance of it as literally true. This problem would be especially acute once the original context of the language has been lost, something which might explain the willingness of some modern scholars to think that it is possible to reconstruct the milieu

[22] P. Khoury, *Paul d'Antioche Évêque Melkite de Sidon (XIIe s.)*, Beirut: Imprimerie Catholique 1964, 174 (tr.) = 66 (text).

[23] N. Wieder, *Judaean Scrolls*, 151–53.

[24] H.J. Schoeps, *Judenchristentum*, 392; see Midrash Rabba on Genesis, 81:3, and J. Talmud, ʿAvōdhāh Zārāh, 5:4 (tr. J. Neusner, Chicago 1982, 199).

of the Prophet by a literalist understanding of the Quran. This process could lead to the transformation of polemic into history: what began as a polemical accusation could, in the course ot time, come to be understood literally and taken as a fact which is incorporated into historical description.

It is also a mistake, of course, to assume that works of polemic are the only, or even the most important, reflection of the relations between the various religious communities. Alongside the dismissal and even mockery of opponents, there are theologically and philosophically learned works which can hardly be described as polemic.[25]

* * * *

Among Muslims the polemical use of *širk* and *kufr* parallels that of idolatry in the examples already given. It should not be surprising that a form of the tradition which emerged in opposition to and polemic with existing forms of monotheism would emphasise the purity and absoluteness of God's unity and uniqueness as its defining feature, and would give prominence in arguments with opponents to accusations that they had fallen short and compromised true monotheism.[26] As with the idea of idolatry in the other traditions of monotheism, so in the Islamic, *širk* covered a range of beliefs and practices as well as moral failings such as pride and the belief in premonitions and presentiments.

Goldziher referred to the 5th/11th century mystic Samnūn al-Muḥibb who allegedly had qualms about associating the name of Muḥammad with that of God in the *šahāda*,[27] and this seems to be a frequent theme in the mystical tradition. Rabīʿa (d. 801) is reported to have said that her love of God left no room in her heart for the Prophet, while Abū Bakr al-Šiblī (d. 945), it is said, only included the name of the Prophet alongside that of God in the *aḏān* because it was part of God's law. Annemarie Schimmel argues that others, perceiving a danger of antinomianism in such an attitude, stressed the importance of the second part of the *šahāda*. The

[25] E.g., that against the Trinity by al-Warrāq, ed. and tr. David Thomas, *Anti-Christian Polemic in Early Islam*, Cambridge 1992; and see the comments of Saʿadya Gaon prefacing his critique of the doctrine of the Trinity in his *Kitāb al-Āmanāt wa-l-iʿtiqādāt* (tr. S. Rosenblatt, 1948, 103): he specifies that his critique is not addressed to the uneducated Christians who have a corporealist and gross understanding of the doctrine, but to the educated who claim that it rests on "rational speculation and subtle understanding". The passage is cited in *Encyclopaedia Judaica*, s.v. 'Apologetics'.

[26] Cf. I. Goldziher, "Le monothéisme dans la vie religieuse des Musulmans," *RHR*, xvi (1887), 157–65 (= *Gesammelte Schriften*, ii, 173–81).

[27] I. Goldziher, "Le culte des saints chez les Musulmans," *RHR*, ii (1880), 262–63 (= *Gesammelte Schriften*, vi, 67–68).

extent to which anything which might deflect the believer from God could be labelled as *širk* is evident in two other Sufi dicta cited by Schimmel: "the essence of *širk* is that you think you are without *širk*"; and even Sufism may be called idolatry "since it is the safeguarding of the heart from the vision of the other, and there is no other".[28]

Leaving aside the Quran, one of the earliest examples of the accusation of *širk* against other monotheists is that said to have been made by the Ḫāriǧites against ʿAlī, at the time of the First Civil War, an accusation presented as arising out of ʿAlī's agreement to appoint the two "arbitrators" to settle his dispute with Muʿāwiya. From the point of view of the Ḫāriǧites this was giving men a share in a decision which belonged to God alone (*lā ḥukma illā li-llāh*) and thus ʿAlī and his supporters were *mušrikūn*. The chain of ideas here, and some of the terminology, is similar to that of Karaite polemic against the Rabbis, and it may be that the Muslim reports about the argument of the Ḫāriǧites against ʿAlī reflect a similar dispute in early Islam about the relative importance as sources of authority of scripture and extra-scriptural materials.[29]

The letters issued by the caliph al-Maʾmūn in connexion with the beginning of the Miḥna accuse the opponents, those who insist that the Quran is uncreated, of *širk* and *kufr*. Their position is compared with that of the Christians who hold that Jesus is the uncreated Word of God. In their doctrine that the Quran is uncreated, it is said, the ignorant have put God on the same level with what He has revealed; they have abandoned the truth for what is vain (*bāṭil*); they have taken an intimate (*walīǧa*) apart from God, who leads them into error (cf. Quran 9:16); they have fallen short in their monotheism and they are called to absolute monotheism (*iḫlāṣ al-tawḥīd*) — "there is no *tawḥīd* in those who do not accept that the Quran is created"; "their doctrines are pure *kufr* and clear *širk* in the eyes of the Commander of the Faithful."[30]

[28] Annemarie Schimmel, "The Sufis and the *shahāda*," in R.G. Hovannisian and Speros Vryonis Jr. (eds.), *Islam's Understanding of Itself*, Malibu California 1983, 103–25, especially 112 and 117.

[29] G.R. Hawting, "The Significance of the Slogan *lā ḥukma illā lillāh*...," *BSOAS* xli (1978), 453–63; idem, "Two citations of the Qurʾān in 'historical' sources for early Islam," in G.R. Hawting and A. Shereef (eds.), *Approaches to the Qurʾān*, London: Routledge 1993, 260–68. For a survey of the evidence regarding scripturalism in early Islam, see M.A. Cook, "ʿAnan and Islam," *JSAI* ix (1987), 165 ff.

[30] Ṭabarī, *Taʾrīḫ*, Leiden, iii, 1112–1132, *passim*. Cf. J. van Ess, *Theologie und Gesellschaft im 2. und 3. Jahrhundert Hidschra*, Berlin, New York 1992, iii, 452–56. See too I. Goldziher, "Materialen zur Kenntniss der Almohadenbewegung in Nordafrika," *ZDMG* xli (1887), 68–69 (= *Gesammelte Schriften*, ii, 229–30). Goldziher refers to an accusation of *širk* made by al-Maʾmūn against the poet al-ʿAkawwak for his excessive eulogy of Abū Dulaf, an accusation which justified killing the poet and tearing out his tongue. According to the

The debate about whether the Quran may be regarded as created or uncreated was an aspect of the theological dispute concerning the divine attributes, whether or not the divinity may be analysed in terms of attributes distinct from the divine essence, the number and nature of the attributes, the relationship between them and the essence, etc. The Muʿtazilī position on such questions was adopted in the 11th century Maġrib by Ibn Tumart and his followers, and the accounts of their polemic against their Mālikī opponents is similar to that made by the Muʿtazila against the traditionalists. Although the accusation of *kufr* rather than that of *širk* seems predominant, the charge against the opponents centres on the claim that their acceptance of eternal divine attributes independent of the divine essence in effect introduced multiplicity into the divine being. They did not, therefore, maintain true monotheism and, as *kuffār*, were subject to the *ǧihād*.[31]

In the polemic of the Wahhābīs against the generality of their fellow Muslims, *širk* again takes a central place. Behind this charge lay the doctrine of *tawḥīd al-ulūhiyya* developed by Ibn Taymiyya (d.728/1328) and his neo-Ḥanbalī followers, the doctrine that worship must be directed to God alone and that anything which could be interpreted as worship of any other being, whether a prophet, saint, leader of a brotherhood, or temporal ruler, was a form of idolatry.[32] The final pages of the anonymous biography of Ibn ʿAbd al-Wahhāb, the *Lamʿ al-Šihāb*, contain a summary of the bases of his doctrines, presented as his own words, and it is worth quoting this passage quite fully here since it shows how the Quranic vocabulary and concepts were used with little discernible adaptation in a polemic clearly directed at people who saw themselves as monotheists.[33]

"Everything which is worshipped before (*min dūni*) God is vain and idolatrous (*bāṭil wa-ṭāġūt*)...Today the generality of people are not

account of the poet's life by Ibn Ḫallikān, which was Goldziher's source, the caliph indeed told the poet that he was going to kill him *bi-kufrika fī šiʿrika...fa-ašrakta bi-llāh al-ʿaẓīm wa-ǧaʿalta maʿahu mālikan qādiran* (*Wafayāt al-aʿyān*, ed. Iḥsān ʿAbbās, Beirut n.d., iii, 352–53). Ibn Ḫallikān's source, Ibn al-Muʿtazz, however, reads: *bi-kufrika wa-ǧurʾatika ʿalā llāh an taqūla fī ʿabd mahīn tusawwī baynahu wa-bayna rabb al-ʿālamīn* (*Ṭabaqāt al-šuʿarāʾ*, ed. ʿAbd al-Sattār Aḥmad Farrāǧ, Cairo 1956, 172).

[31] I. Goldziher, "Mohammed Ibn Toumert et la théologie de l'Islam dans le Maghreb au XIe siècle," Introduction to J.D. Luciani (ed.), *Le Livre de Mohammed Ibn Toumert*, especially 55–56, 61–62, 63ff., 71–73, 79ff; idem, "Almohadenbewegung," *ZDMG* xli (1887), 69 (= *GS*, ii, 230) for a poem in which Goldziher interprets *mušrikūn* as referring to non-Almohad Muslims, *ahl al-kufr* to Christians.

[32] H. Laoust, *Essai sur les doctrines sociales et politiques de Taḳī-d-Dīn Aḥmad b. Taimīya*, Cairo: Imprimerie de l'Institut Français d'Archéologie Orientale 1939, 472, 531.

[33] A.M. Abū Ḥākima (ed.), *Lamʿ al-šihāb fī sīrat Muḥammad ibn ʿAbd al-Wahhāb*, Beirut n.d. (1967?), 187–90.

upholders of monotheism (*ġayru muwaḥḥidūn*), because they worship entities other than God. Because of this they deserve to be killed just as the infidels among the Arabs deserved it when God sent the Prophet. Among the signs of the people's infidelity and polytheism (*išrāk*) is that they seek to draw near to (*yataqarrabūna ilā*) God by visiting the tombs of pious men, whether prophet or saint, and some of them address others with prayers which should be reserved for God. Thus they seek the procurement of benefits and the prevention of evils over which He alone has power. God's words, 'Say: I have no power, neither beneficial nor harmful, myself, except as God wills',[34] show that their drawing near to God and their prayers are polytheism (*širk*)... Part of the forbidden polytheism is to include the name of a prophet, a saint, or an angel in prayers to God — for example, if someone says, 'O God, I ask you through (*bi-ḥaqqi*) Muḥammad, or ʿAlī, or Gabriel', or some similar being."

Having cited Quran 18:110, which insists on good works and the worship of the Lord without associating any other being with Him, Ibn ʿAbd al-Wahhāb argues that good works are a form of worship. "God does not accept that worship unless you devote yourself exclusively (*tatamaḥḥaḍu*) to Him. But, if any other being is mentioned in prayers made to Him, then he has been given a partner (*ušrika*) in His worship since prayers are the core of worship... One aspect of attributing a partner to God (*al-širk bi-llāh*) is seeking intercession from a being other than Him...Seeking intercession from someone who has no power in it is giving a partner a share in God's sovereignty (*išrāk li-llāh fī mulkihi*)...

"Another aspect of attributing a partner to God is making a vow to something other than Him." Here he cites Quran 22:29 which urges men to fulfil their vows and to perform the circumambulation ritual at the sanctuary, and he draws the conclusion that, just as circumambulation is a form of worship which can be properly addressed only to God, so a vow must be devoted to Him alone: "Anyone who has involved any of God's creatures in a vow has certainly directed God's worship to something other than Him."

Further passages accuse of infidelity (*kufr*) anyone who claims to have knowledge of what is known only to God, anyone who denies divine predestination, and anyone who adheres to the method of figurative interpretation (*ta'wīl*) of the Quran.

As in the Quran, the opposite of *širk* here is not merely monotheism, but pure and absolute monotheism without compromise. Here Ibn ʿAbd al-Wahhāb uses the verb *tamaḥḥaḍa*, which is not Quranic, but he seems to have in mind the same meaning as Quranic *iḫlāṣ*, and elsewhere he does

[34] Quran 7: 188.

use this latter word when elaborating his argument of the need for exclusive devotion to God.[35] The opponents are alleged to argue that they have recourse to other sources of power because they hope that they will be a means of access to God, a defence which is also attributed to them ("those who take *awliyāʾ* other than Him") in the Quran (39:3) and which is used in Christianity by supporters of icons and other such aids to worship.[36] The accusation that the opponents seek to procure benefits and the prevention of ills from beings to whom they resort other than God is a clear reference to the discourse of idolatry: the statement that idols can neither do good nor prevent evil recurs in the Quran, the Bible and other monotheist writings. In Muslim tradition we find ʿUmar addressing the Black Stone of the Kaʿba and insisting that it is merely a stone which can do neither good nor harm.[37]

* * * *

In spite of the apparent distinction between Jews, Christians, *kuffār* and *mušrikūn* in some of the passages of the Quran, it is often impossible to maintain it in other Muslim texts, where *kufr* and *širk* are imputed to Jews and Christians. For example, the *Kitāb ahl al-kitābayn* in the *Muṣannaf* of ʿAbd al-Razzāq has some subheadings referring to the *mušrikīn* but the *ḥadīṯs* which they contain relate to Jews and Christians. Thus the chapter, the title of which indicates that it is concerned with the question of the *mušrik* who converts from one *dīn* to another, has two reports about Jews or Christians who may wish to become Zindīqs and one about a Jew or Christian who may attempt to win his descendants over to Judaism or Christianity (presumably from Islam). Conversely, the chapter which proclaims that it is concerned with the expulsion of the Jews from Medina has a tradition in which the Prophet, in his final illnesss, orders that the *mušrikūn* be expelled from the Arabian peninsula, followed by another in which, again on his deathbed, he commands that no Jew or Christian should remain in the Ḥiğāz.

Even in the Quran itself the distinction seems sometimes dubious: 5:72–73 has already been cited. Commenting on these verses, al-Ṭabarī denounces both groups — those who believe that Jesus was God and those who accept the Trinity — as infidels and polytheists/idolaters (*kilāhumā kafara mušrikūn*).[38] In the context of Muslim polemic against Christians,

[35] Laoust, *Essai*, 531.

[36] Halbertal and Margalit, *Idolatry*, 40, notes 7 and 8.

[37] E.g., Buḫārī, *Ḥağğ*, 50, 57.

[38] Ṭabarī, *Tafsīr*, ed. Šākir, x, 480–82. The equation of *širk* and idolatry when applied to the belief in Jesus as the Son of God gains strength if it is remembered that Christian

širk seems to be associated with reference to the doctrines of the divine sonship of Jesus and of the Trinity, whereas the use of crucifixes and icons tends to be presented as idolatry in a more explicit way by accusing the Christians of worshipping a thing made of wood or stone.

The association of *širk* and Christianity is evident at an early stage in the development of Islam, even leaving aside Quranic texts like that just referred to. In the inscriptions inside the Dome of the Rock and on the east and north entrances, which date from the time of its construction under ʿAbd al-Malik, *šarīk* and *mušrik* both occur once. The former is part of a statement that God has no partner (*šarīk*) in His power, the latter of a proclamation that God has sent His messenger with the guidance and the religion of truth so that He may cause it to triumph over all religion (*ʿalā al-dīn kullahu*), even though the *mušrikūn* resent it. Although there is no explicit linkage of Christianity to the terms, it is clear that a major part of the message contained in the inscriptions is a rejection of Christian claims regarding the status of Jesus and the doctrine of the Trinity.[39]

In his account of the rising of the Banū Nāǧiya against ʿAlī in 38/658–9, a rising which was supported by many Christian Arabs in Fars, al-Ṭabarī gives the text of a letter sent to ʿAlī by one of his commanders reporting a victory. In it is reported that the leader of the rising, al-Ḫirrīt b. Rāšid, had sought help from the *mušrikūn*. It is difficult to know whom this refers to, if not to the local Christians.[40]

Presentation of Christian use of the cross and icons as a form of idolatry, and of its Christology as a form of polytheism and unbelief, is common in Muslim polemic against Christianity in works of the *radd ʿalā al-naṣārā* type, even though explicit use of the terms *širk* and *kufr* do not seem as frequent as one might expect. "You revere the cross and the icon,

theologians like Athanasius and Gregory of Nyssa agreed that Christians would be idolators if Jesus were indeed not the Son of God.

[39] E. Combe, J. Sauvaget, and G. Wiet, *Répertoire chronologique d'épigraphie arabe*, i, Cairo 1931, nos. 9–11; C. Kessler, "ʿAbd al-Malik's Inscription in the Dome of the Rock, a Reconsideration," *JRAS* 1970, 2–14; O. Grabar, "The Umayyad Dome of the Rock in Jerusalem," *Ars Orientalis* iii (1959), 53–55, 59 ; A. Elad, *Medieval Jerusalem and Islamic Worship*, Leiden 1995, 44–46. Most (but not quite all) of the inscriptions occur as passages in the Quran: the passage with *šarīk* is Quran 17:111, that with *mušrikūn* is Quran 9:33 and 61:9.

[40] Ṭabarī, *Taʾrīḫ*, Leiden 1879–1901, i, 3432. Interestingly, in Ṭabarī's *Tafsīr* on the opening verses of Sūra 30 (*Sūrat al-Rūm*), some exegetes wish to distinguish the Christian Byzantines as *ahl al-kitāb* from the Persian Magians who are variously labelled as *mušrikūn* and *ahl al-awṯān*. The insistence on the status of the Byzantines as monotheists arises here because it is necessary to explain why the Believers would rejoice to hear of a Byzantine victory over the Persians.

you kiss them and prostrate before them, but they are man made things which cannot hear or see, can do neither good nor ill; you think that the greatest of them are those made of gold and silver, just as the people of Abraham did with their images and idols (*bi-ṣuwarihim wa-awṯānihim*) ....(The Prophet) commanded us to worship God alone, not to associate anything with Him (*allā nušrika bihi šay'an*), not to make any god with Him, not to worship the sun, the moon, idols, a cross or an icon, and not to adopt one another as lords apart from God."[41]

Ibn Qayyim al-Ǧawziyya ridicules the idea that God would deign to go through the process of gestation in the womb of a woman and suffer all the mockery and torture reported of Jesus, and he takes particular exception to the Christians saying, in justification of the idea of God as the father of Jesus in a real sense, that anyone who does not beget is barren and that barrenness is a defect and a shame — "this is their *kufr* and their *širk* concerning the Lord of the Worlds, and their insulting of Him".[42]

An awareness on the part of the Christians of the accusation of *širk* is evident, it seems, as early as the *De Haeresibus*, attributed to John of Damascus (d. ca. 754) and the ritual of abjuration for those converting to Christianity from the religion of the Saracens. The latter text must be late 9th century at the earliest in the form in which we have it but Cumont argued that it contains materials of a date much earlier than that. In these two texts it is mentioned that the Ishmaelites call the Christians "associators" (*hetairiastas*, a Greek rendition presumably of *mušrikūn*, and one which would carry connotations of prostitution) because of their view that Christ was the Son of God and God, and idolaters (*eidōlolatras*) because of the veneration of the cross.[43]

The attempted refutation of the charge in the *De Haeresibus* is based partly on an unspecific appeal to scripture and the prophets, partly on

[41] D. Sourdel, "Un pamphlet musulman anonyme d'époque ʿabbāside contre les chrétiens," *REI* xxxiv (1966), 17 (tr.) = 29 (text), 25 (tr.) = 33 (text). Only a limited number of the *radd ʿalā al-naṣārā* genre were examined in preparing this article, and it may be that a more extensive survey would alter the conclusions.

[42] Ibn Qayyim al-Ǧawziyya, *Hidāyat al-ḥayārā fī aǧwibat al-yahūd wa-l-naṣārā*, Beirut 1987, 166.

[43] For the text and translation of the *De Haeresibus*, see D.J. Sahas, *John of Damascus and Islam*, Leiden 1972; for the accusations of "association" and idolatry, 134, 136 (text) = 135, 137 (tr.). (There is a new edition in B. Kotter (ed.), *Die Schriften des Johannes von Damaskos. iv Liber De Haeresibus*, Berlin and New York 1981.) For arguments against the attribution of the *De Haeresibus* to John, see A. Abel, "Le chapitre CI du Livre des Héresies de Jean Damascène: son inauthenticité," *SI* xix (1963), 5–25. For the abjuration formula, see E. Montet, "Un rituel d'abjuration des musulmans dans l'église grecque," *RHR* liii (1906), 145–63 (the rebuttal of the "association" charge is at p.154), and F. Cumont, *ibid.*, lxiv (1911), 143–50.

theological arguments which involve the counter charge that the Ishmaelites are "mutilators" (*koptas*) of God in their striving not to associate anything with Him, and partly by turning the tables and accusing them of idolatry. Other Christian apologists reject the implication of *širk* by emphasising their own aversion to any doctrine which supports the idea of plurality in the godhead, and by stressing those Quranic verses which distinguish the Christians from the *mušrikūn*. Paul of Antioch asks, since we Christians regard as *kufr* any implication of plurality or corporeality to God, anything which leads to *širk* or anthropomorphism (*tašbīh*), how can our opponent impute such things to us? If they charge us with *širk* and anthropomorphism, we charge them with corporealism (*taǧassum*) and anthropomorphism (because of their insistence on the literal understanding of those Quranic verses in which God is described anthropomorphically). And he cites Quran 22:17 and 5:69 in an attempt to show that the Muslims' own scripture distinguished between the Christians and the *mušrikūn*: *wa-nafā ʿannā ism al-širk bi-qawlihi.*[44]

Explicit accusations of *širk* against the Jews seem less frequent than against Christians, although the grounds for such an accusation, from a Muslim point of view, are there. One of the main motives for the accusation of *širk* by Muslims was, as we have seen, the view that the opponents were guilty of anthropomorphic and corporealist views of the divinity. These theological errors were associated especially with the Jews, to the extent that we find statements to the effect that "Judaism is corporealism" (*maḏhab al-Yahūd al-taǧsīm*).[45] Goldziher adduced some canonical *ḥadīṯ* in which the association of anthropomorphism with Jews was evident, and recently van Ess has drawn attention to the way in which a *ḥadīṯ* which warns against *širk* in an unspecific way appears in an Ibāḍī source in a context associating *širk* with anthropomorphism and linking anthropomorphism with Jews. In Ibn Ḥanbal's version, Abū Mūsā al-Ašʿarī cites the Prophet's dictum, "Fear this *širk* for it is more secretive than the influx of ants" (*ittaqū hāḏa al-širk fa-innahu aḫfā min dabīb al-naml*) in a context which does not indicate what the word *širk* might be referring to. In the Ibāḍī *ḥadīṯ* collection attributed to Rabīʿ b. Ḥabīb the saying is given, in a slightly different form, as the response of Ibn Masʿūd as he passed a Jew who was teaching that God had gone up to heaven from

44 P. Khoury, *Paul d'Antioche*, text III, sections 22, 53, 54.

45 I. Goldziher, "Monothéisme," 157 (= *GS*, ii, 173); *idem*, "Usages Juifs d'après la littérature religieuse des Musulmans," *REJ* xxviii (1894), 88 (= *GS*, iii, 335); see too *idem*, "Mélanges Judéo-Arabes", *REJ* xlvii (1902), 179–86 (= *GS*, iv, 416–23), especially 182–83 (= 419–20) on polemics between Karaites and Rabbanites on the question of *tašbīh*. The Christian apologetic tract against Islam attributed to al-Kindī also associates the Jews with anthropomorphism (*Risālat ʿAbd al-Masīḥ Ibn Isḥāq al-Kindī*, London 1870, 95).

Jerusalem after the creation, putting His foot on the rock (that over which the Dome of the Rock was built) as He did so.[46]

Elsewhere, alleged Jewish anthropomorphism is designated as *kufr wāḍiḥ*.[47]

* * * *

The attempt in the *De Haeresibus* to turn the tables by insisting that the Ishmaelites are themselves guilty of idolatry in their rubbing and kissing of a stone near their Khabathan, a stone which is the head of Aphrodite, also appears in the abjuration formula required of converts to Christianity and is commonly repeated in Byzantine texts.[48] The portrayal of the *ḥaǧǧ* and the sanctuary at Mecca as idolatrous institutions is frequent. The *Risāla* attributed to al-Kindī draws a parallel between the *ḥaǧǧ* and idolatrous pilgrimages and processions of the Indians, and the author is familar with ʿUmar's address to the Black Stone (in this version together with the stone known as the Maqām) which he uses to substantiate the charge that the Muslim sanctuary rituals are fundamentally idolatrous.[49] Judah Halevi, although the passage as a whole seems to allude both to Muslims and Christians, presumably has the Muslims chiefly in mind when he says that, in spite of their praising the place of prophethood in what they say, they take as their *qibla* places of idolatry (*mawāḍiʿ kānat li-l-awṯān*)...and continue the practices of the ancient worship, the days of its *ḥaǧǧ*, and their rituals (*maʿa ibqāʾihim rusūm al-ʿibādāt al-qadīma wa-ayyām ḥaǧǧihā wa-manāsikahum*). They have merely obliterated the representations of the idols (*al-ṣuwar allatī kānat hunāka*) without abolishing their practices (*rusūm*). He concludes by alluding to several passages in

46 I. Goldziher, "Usages Juifs," *REJ* xxviii (1894), 88 (= *GS*, iii, 335). The Prophet's saying in its shorter form is in Ibn Ḥanbal, *Musnad*, iv, 403; the version quoted by van Ess runs, "There will be a time when *širk* will be more clandestine than ants stepping on a black rock in dark night" (J. van Ess, "ʿAbd al-Malik and the Dome of the Rock. An analysis of some texts," in J. Raby and J. Johns (eds.), *Bayt al-Maqdis: ʿAbd al-Malik's Jerusalem*, part 1, Oxford 1993, 94–95). Uri Rubin points out to me that a version of this *ḥadīṯ* was cited in Edward Lane's *Arabic-English Lexicon*, s.v. *širk*, as an example of the use of that word as the equivalent of hypocrisy. For the anti-anthropomorphist tendency of Rabīʿ b. Ḥabīb's *Musnad*, see Cook, "ʿAnan and Islam," 171.

47 Ibn Taymiyya in his work (*Al-Ǧawāb al-ṣaḥīḥ li-man baddala dīn al-Masīḥ*) against the Christians, cited by Goldziher, "Usages Juifs," 88 (= *GS*, 335).

48 E. Montet, "Un rituel de l'abjuration," *RHR* liii (1906), 153–54. For Muslim worship of Aphrodite in Byzantine polemic generally, A. T. Khoury, *Polémique byzantine contre l'Islam*, Leiden 1972, 275–81.

49 *Risālat ʿAbd al-Masīḥ al-Kindī*, London 1870, 104–5. For the problems of the attribution of this text, see *EI*², s.v. 'al-Kindī'. For the association of the *ḥaǧǧ* and the sanctuary with idolatry in Byzantine texts see A. T. Khoury, *Polémique byzantine contre l'Islam*, 275–81.

Deuteronomy which foretell the worship of "other gods, of wood and of stone", the wood interpreted as the cross worshipped by the Christians, the stone as that worshipped by the Muslims.[50]

The imputation of idolatry to the Muslims in mediaeval European Christian romances and *chansons de geste* is possibly the best known aspect of this polemical exchange of the charge of idolatry between the different traditions of monotheism. In the *Song of Roland* the Muslims (*les paien*) are portrayed as serving Mahum, Apolin, and Tervagant, while other such works provide us with a total of about 30 gods.[51] The anti-Muslim accusation became such a commonplace that in English the word 'mawment', derived from the name of Muḥammad, was used to mean an idol or a vain thing.[52]

In Appendix A of his *Islam and the West*, Norman Daniel discussed the imputation of idolatry to Islam in the romance and *chanson de geste* type of mediaeval European literature. As throughout his book, he seems rather embarrassed and defensive, as much concerned to stress that the imputation has no basis in fact as to explain it. He seems, however, to favour the idea of Henri Grégoire that the charge was invented as part of the propaganda of the Crusade, although possibly related to the idea that Arab idolatry had been preserved in Islam in the *ḥağğ* and the Kaᶜba. Grégoire had suggested that this latter idea may have come into European Christian literature via Petrus Alfonsi from Rabbinic sources, even though he was aware, naturally, that the charge was a topos of Byzantine polemical literature. Daniel, finally, makes the point that "'idolatry' may always be correctly used to describe any mistaken idea of God that men may worship, but that it does not then mean the worship of physical idols".[53]

This last point is one of those which have been laboured in this article. Ideas which in European languages centre on the word idolatry are polemical and part of the monotheist discourse shared by Jews, Christians

[50] Judah Halevi, *Kitāb al-Radd wa-l-dalīl fi-l-dīn al-ḏalīl (K. al-Ḫuzarī)*, ed. D.H. Baneth and prepared for the press by H. Ben Shammai, Jerusalem 1977, 162 (book 4, section 11); partial English tr. by Isaak Heinemann, Oxford 1947, 115. H. Grégoire, "Dieux non moins extravagants" (see n. 52 below), 465.

[51] R.W. Southern, *Western Views of Islam in the Middle Ages*, Cambridge Mass. and London, 1962 (revised reprint 1978), 32; B.Z. Kedar, *Crusade and Mission*, Princeton 1984, 88–89.

[52] Susan Brigden, *London and the Reformation*, Oxford 1989, 94, cites Joan Baker of St. Mary Magdalen Milk Street as wishing, in 1510, that she had never gone on pilgrimage since the images at the shrines were "but mawments and false gods...idols and not to be worshipped or honoured".

[53] N. Daniel, *Islam and the West*, Edinburgh 1960, 309–13; H. Grégoire, "Des dieux Cahu, Baraton, Tervagant...et de maints autres dieux non moins extravagants," *Annuaire de l'Institut de Philologie et d'Histoire Orientales et Slaves*, vii (1939–44), especially 462–66.

and Muslims. In the Muslim tradition they are represented particularly by *širk* and *kufr*. The related charges of idolatry and polytheism rarely seem to be made without any rationale, although it is sometimes a complicated one and difficult now to reconstruct. Because the accusation functions as polemic, it is not legitimate to infer from it that those who made it understood their opponents as idolators in a literal sense. Much less can one infer that the religion or culture as a whole which produced the texts saw those at whom they were directed as really idolatrous — different texts were produced for different purposes and in different circumstances. It is this which makes it so difficult to produce a general statement about the image which one group had of another, even over a relatively short period of time.[54] Nevertheless, there is clearly a danger that polemic, once it is launched, will take on a life of its own and be transformed into an historical reality, and it may be that that has to be taken into account — together with the crusading atmosphere and the tradition of Byzantine polemic against the *ḥağğ* and the Kaʿba — when attempting to explain the depictions of the idolatrous paynim in mediaeval European literature. It may also be important for understanding our image of the religious situation which the Quran addresses.

[54] Cf. R.W. Southern, *Western Views of Islam in the Middle Ages*, which characterizes the whole period until the early 12th century as "the age of ignorance".

ŠAHRASTĀNĪ ON THE MAĠĀRIYYA

STEVEN M. WASSERSTROM

ŠAHRASTĀNĪ AND HIS *BOOK OF RELIGIONS AND SECTS*

Abū al-Fatḥ Muḥammad al-Karīm al-Šahrastānī (d. 528/1153) was arguably the greatest of all pre-modern historians of religions.[1] His contribution to the study of religion has been recognized and properly lauded for over a century. Sir Hamilton A.R. Gibb epitomized the tone of this praise when he remarked that "there are few works in Arabic literature that reflect more credit on medieval Muhammadan [sic] scholarship than Šahrastānī's *Kitāb al-Milal wa-l-Nihal, The Book of Religions and Sects.*"[2] E.J. Sharpe, in his *Comparative Religion, A History* writes: "The honour of writing the first history of religion in world literature seems in fact to belong to the Muslim Shahrastani."[3] And from the specific perspective of the historian of Judaism, S.D. Goitein has observed that "...when we compare Shahrastani's detailed, well-informed and remarkably unbiased accounts with the Greek and Latin texts related to Judaism, we have to

[1] Texts, translations and more detailed analyses of Šahrastānī and other Muslim scholars of foreign religions can be found in my dissertation, *Species of Misbelief: A History of Muslim Heresiography of the Jews* (University of Toronto, 1985) [hereafter: *Species*]. I would like to thank Professor G.M. Wickens for his comments on an early version of the present study. Continued research on Šahrastānī was made possible by a Post-Doctoral Fellowship at the University of Chicago in 1986, granted by the Social Sciences and Humanities Research Council of Canada, for which I am grateful. The Dean's Research Fund of Reed College provided subsequent support, for which I thank Dean Linda Mantel. I would also like to thank Professor Sarah Stroumsa for her comments on the present article, which she generously provided despite her dissent from some of my conclusions. All remaining inadequacies are my own.

I have dealt with Šahrastānī on the *ġālī* Muġīra ibn Saʿīd, in "The Moving Finger Writes: Mughīra Ibn Saʿīd's Islamic Gnosis and the Myths of its Rejection," *HR* (1985): 1–25; and on the ʿĪsāwiyya, in "The ʿĪsāwiyya Revisited," *Studia Islamica* 75 (1992): 57–80. See also my "Islamicate History of Religions?" [A Review Essay of recent translations of Šahrastānī], *History of Religions* 27 (1988): 405–11.

[2] *Arabic Literature*, pp. 126–27.

[3] (London 1975) p. 11.

confess that between Tacitus and Shahrastani, humanity has made a great step forward."[4]

Šahrastānī's *Kalām Summa*, available in Guillaume's translation, is his major theological tract, to which the *Kitāb al-Milal wa-l-Nihal* serves as a kind of outsized appendix.[5] The structure of the *Kitāb al-Milal wa-l-Nihal* (henceforth *Milal*) on the Muslim sects has been analyzed by D. Sourdel.[6] Although Šahrastānī's masterwork has been edited, translated and analyzed, much work remains to be done on this motherlode of the History of Religions. William Cureton's 19th century edition served as the basis both for the complete German translation by Theodor Haarbrücker, and for numerous subsequent editions produced by Muslim scholars.[7] The work has benefited in recent years by the close attention of French scholars, especially those associated with the *École pratique des hautes études*.[8] Its sections on the Muslim sects have recently been translated into English by co-translators A.K. Kazi and J.C. Flynn.[9] UNESCO funded a complete annotated French translation by Gimaret, Monnot, and Jolivet, a major scholarly accomplishment.[10]

[4] "Between Hellenism and Renaissance — Islam, the Intermediate Civilization," *IS* II (1963): 217–33, at pp. 229–30.

[5] *Nihāyat al-Aqdām fī ʿIlm al-Kalām*, ed. and trans. A. Guillaume (London 1934).

[6] "La classification des sectes islamiques dans le *Kitāb al-Milal* d'Al-Šahrastānī," *SI* XXXI (1970): 239–48.

[7] *Kitāb al-Milal wa-l-Nihal*, ed. W. Cureton: *Book of Religius and Philosophical Schools*, two vols. (London 1846); Th. Haarbrücker trans., *Religionspartheien und Philosophen-schulen*, two vols. (Halle 1850–1851); Cairo 1328/1910 (used herein); reedited by Badrān in two vols. (Cairo 1951–1955), and again in three vols. (Cairo 1968). In this article I shall use the Arabic edition of Badrān, referring to it as *Milal*; its pagination is provided in the margins of *Livre des Religions et des Sectes.*

See *GAL* I, pp. 550–51; *GALS* I, pp. 762–63. See also Guy Monnot, "Les écrits musulmans sur les religions non-bibliques," *MIDEO* 11 (1976): 9–48, at p. 36.

[8] See D. Gimaret, *Annuaire, École pratique des hautes études (Ve Sect., Sci. Relig.)* 87 (1978–1979): 261–65; 88 (1979–1980): 277–86; G. Monnot, vol. 90 (1981–1982): 279–81, and Gimaret, pp. 283–88; Monnot, vol. 91 (1982–1983): 318–20 and Gimaret, pp. 321–26; Monnot, vol. 92 (1983–1984): 305–15 and Gimaret, pp. 317–21; vol. 92 (1984–1985) Monnot, pp. 193–303; vol. 101 (1992–1993), Monnot, pp. 198–202.

[9] "The Muʿtazilites," *Abr-Nahrain* 8 (1968–1969): 36–68; "The Jabarites and the Ṣifātīya," 9 (1969–1970): 81–107; "The Khārijites and the Murjiʾites," 10 (1970–1971): 49–75; "The Shīʿites," 15 (1974–1975): 50–98. These were subsequently published as *Muslim Sects and Divisions: The Section on Muslim Sects in Kitāb al-Milal wa-'l-Nihal by Muhammad b. ʿAbd al-Karīm Shahrastānī* (Kegan Paul International: London, Boston, Melbourne and Henley, 1984) [hereafter "KF"]. In the same year there appeared the translation of the same sections by J.C. Vadet, *Les Dissidences de l'Islam* (Paris 1984).

[10] *Livre des Religions et des Sectes, vol. I*, trans. G. Monnot and D. Gimaret (Peeters, UNESCO: Paris 1986), and vol. II, trans. G. Monnot and J. Jolivet (Peeters, UNESCO: Paris 1993) [hereafter "*LRS*"].

At the beginning of the last of five introductions with which Šahrastānī begins *Milal*, he summarizes his work succinctly: "Our treatment shall cover Islamic sects and others who have a truly revealed book, as the Jews and Christians; those with what pretends to be a book, as the Magians and Manicheans; those who have penal laws and statutes but no book, as the ancient Sabaeans; and, finally, those who have neither book nor penal laws nor religious laws, such as the early philosophers, atheists, star-worshippers, idol-worshippers and Brahmins".[11] *Milal* thus is divided into two sections. The first, on the Muslim sects, is considerably shorter than the second, on the non-Muslim sects. In this latter section, sects are set forth in accordance with their respective (ostensible and/or assumed) divergence from the principles and practices of Islam. The first non-Muslim sects addressed are therefore those of the *ahl al-kitāb* ("Peoples of the Book"). These are, in order of Šahrastānī's presentation, Jews, Christians, Zoroastrians, Manicheans, and Hindus, several dozen groups and sub-groups in all.[12] The section of *Milal* on non-Muslim groups begins with Revealed Religions. The first non-Muslim sects addressed in *Milal* are therefore those of the "Scriptuaries," the "Peoples of the Book." In this category Šahrastānī discusses four groups of Jews, and three of Christians. He then continues his magisterial survey with Revealed Religions lacking an authentic Holy Book, possessing scriptures only they themselves (and not Islamic theologians) consider sacred. In this category Šahrastānī includes three subgroups of Magians and five subgroups of "Dualists" (*Ṯanawiyya*): Manicheans, Mazdakites, Bardesanians, Marcionites and Metempsychosists. The remainder of the work comprises a lengthy discussion of Natural Religions. Šahrastānī divides these into three general categories: Sabians, Greek philosophers, and polytheists (pre-Islamic Arabian and Indian religions).

"DIFFERENT NAMES IN DIFFERENT PLACES": ŠAHRASTĀNĪ AS AN HISTORIAN OF JUDAISM, WITH SPECIAL REFERENCE TO HIS STUDY OF "GNOSIS"

A review of *Milal* on Jewish, Samaritan, Mazdakite, Sabian, Manichean and other groups shows that its ostensibly disparate sections illumine each

[11] *Milal*, p. 44; KF p. 31, slightly altered here. As Gimaret and Monnot note, this overview is at once a title, a début of the exposition proper, and a table of contents (*LRS* I, p. 159, n. 1).

[12] The symmetry of this scheme, treating both Muslim and non-Muslim groups with the same methodology, laying out all known groups in the same "tableau," no doubt is responsible for the praise of Muslim historians of religions, who successfully conceptualized the idea of religious multiplicity and studied it as such with this kind of (relatively) equitable balance.

other interactively. Šahrastānī's exposition of "die islamische Gnosis" is therefore relevant to the analysis of his Jewish studies.[13] In his discussion of the early proto-Shīᶜites (to use the phrase of W.M. Watt) commonly known as *ġulāt* ("extremists," also to be translated as "exaggerators," "those who go too far"; Šahrastānī uses the less common form *ġāliya*) Šahrastānī discusses eleven of their subdivisions.[14] He begins by stating that "These erroneous ideas of the *ġāliya* have their origin in the doctrine held by those believing in incarnation and transmigration of souls, or in the beliefs of Jews and Christians, since Jews liken God to man and Christians liken man to God. These ideas so deeply influenced the minds of extreme Shīᶜites that they attributed divine qualities to some of their Imams."[15]

Šahrastānī then introduces the *ġāliya* — whom Halm and others characterize as "Islamic gnostics" — by stating that they "are known by different names in different places."[16] This comment, followed by the specific names and places, is seemingly made almost in passing, yet it expresses Šahrastānī's observation that there may have been certain unifying features — which I am calling "gnostic" — shared by an apparently disparate plethora of sects.

A comparative analysis of the respective sections of *Milal* concerning those and other "extremist" groups may be a useful, if not a necessary approach to the study of a phenomenon as polymorphic as Islamic "gnosis."[17] Multiple embodiments of "gnosis," after all, remained very

[13] H. Halm, *Die Islamische Gnosis* (Zürich and Munich, 1982). S. Lieu's entirely admirable *Manicheanism* (Manchester 1986), which thoroughly covers the history of Manicheanism in the Roman and Chinese empires, leaves aside the history of Manicheanism under Islam. Such work remains a desideratum for the history of religions. G. Stroumsa is one of the few scholars investigating late Manicheanism in the Middle East. See "Monachisme et Marranisme chez les Manichéens d'Egypte," *Numen* 29 (1983) pp. 184–201, esp. pp. 195–97; "Gnostics and Manichaeans in Byzantine Palestine," *Studia Patristica* XVIII vol. I (ed.); Elizabeth A. Livingstone (1986) pp. 273–78.

[14] *Milal I*, pp. 363–410; KF 149–63; V 291–308. For a review of the literature on the *ġulāt* see my "The Moving Finger Writes: Mughīra b. Saᶜīd's Islamic Gnosis and the Myths of its Rejection," *History of Religions* 25 (1985): 1–29.

[15] *Milal I*, pp. 363–64; KF 149–150.

[16] *Milal I*, pp. 365; KF p. 150.

[17] "If it is to be called *a* religion, how do we cope with the facts that it has no unified and identifiable social form, no straightforward *public* life, and that it is consistently parasitic on the mythological conventions of other groups... must we not rather speak of gnosis as — like apocalyptic — a *style*, a rhetoric? It is an exploitation within various traditions of the elements of those traditions that suggest the possibility of living with disjunction and alienation." Rowan Williams, review of Kurt Rudolph, *Gnosis* (San Francisco 1983) in *Journal of Theological Studies* 37 (1986): 202–6, at p. 205. One particular difficulty in

much alive and active in the early Islamicate period.[18] A cross-referenced reading of *Milal* as an integrated whole, and not merely as a catalog of disparate elements, will thus serve to show the depth and richness both of *Milal* and of its multivalent understanding of "gnosis." *Milal* should optimally be utilized as an interactive whole.

I take it as rather indicative of Šahrastānī's instincts as a scholar, and certainly of his preoccupations, that his longest report on any of these eleven "extremist" groups concerns that least known to modern scholarship, the so-called Kayyāliyya.[19] Virtually all the other groups of "extremists" Šahrastānī discusses can be studied at some length from many other sources. But in the case of the Kayyāliyya, almost nothing aside from Šahrastānī's report was known to modern scholarship until the treasure troves of Ismāʿīlī literature began to be published after World War II.[20] With the recovery of that literature, the historicity of the enigmatic al-Kayyāl was corroborated and set into its historical context.[21] This still little-known — and still unfinished — corroboration anticipated subsequent, better-publicized validations of the sources available to Islamicate historians of religion. The best-known of these corroborations is the vindication of Ibn al-Nadīm's report on Manicheanism, which resulted from the publication of the Cologne Mani Codex.[22]

In addition to this corroboration, several features of Šahrastānī's report on al-Kayyāl's doctrine may be usefully adduced to demonstrate the quality of Šahrastānī's scholarship. The first of these features is Šahrastānī's explicit utilization of a variety of primary sources deriving

studying the multiple forms of "gnosis" is that of doctrinally-enjoined *reservatio mentalis* (Arabic: *taqiyya*).

[18] See "The Moving Finger Writes," esp. pp. 14–15.

[19] *Milal I*, pp. 383–95; KF 156–58; V 299–303.

[20] Ismail K. Poonawala, *Biobibliography of Ismaʿili Literature* (Malibu 1977).

[21] V. Ivanow, "Ismailis and Qarmatians," *Journal of the Bengal Branch of the Royal Asiatic Society* 16 (1940): 43–85, at pp. 63–64, discusses this corroborating textual evidence for the history of al-Kayyāl, as found in the important Ismāʿīlī history, *ʿUyūn al-Aḫbār* (not to be confused with a better-known work of the same name by Ibn Qutayba). A review of the sources is given in Madelung, "Al-Kayyāl," *Encyclopedia of Islam* vol. IV, pp. 847–48. More recently the citations on al-Kayyāl and the Kayyāliyya as found in the *Rasāʾil Iḫwān al-Ṣafāʾ* have been discussed in Carmela Baffioni, "Traces of 'Secret Sects' in the *Rasāʾil* of the Ikhwān al-Ṣafāʾ," in *Shiʿa Islam, Sects and Sufism: Historical dimensions, religious practice and methodological considerations*, ed. Fredick De Jong (M. Th. Houtsma Stichting: Utrecht 1993) pp. 10–25.

[22] Itamar Gruenwald, "Manichaeism and Judaism in Light of the Cologne Mani Codex," *Zeitschrift für Papyrologie und Epigraphik* 52 (1983): 29–45; John C. Reeves, "The 'Elchasaite' Sanhedrin of the Cologne Mani Codex in Light of Second Temple Jewish Sectarian Sources," *Journal of Jewish Studies* XLII (1991): 68–91.

from followers of al-Kayyāl himself: "There are still extant many writings in Arabic and Persian expounding his views about the universe. They are full of empty rhetoric and repugnant both to the *Šarīʿa* and to reason."[23] It is noteworthy that Šahrastānī rarely condemns directly the groups whose views he reiterates. That he does so in the case of the Kayyāliyya indicates that al-Kayyāl must have been particularly repellent to Šahrastānī. All the more striking then is Šahrastānī's unusually extended treatment of the primary sources of the Kayyāliyya. Šahrastānī dismisses the doctrines of al-Kayyāl as "erroneous views and empty speculations."[24] Yet he reads al-Kayyāl's writings, and reports on them at length. It is obviously not an exaggeration to suggest that Šahrastānī was acting consciously when he thus filled in lacunae in the literature.

Further evidence that this was his motivation can be found in Šahrastānī's treatment of the Jewish sects. The first point that needs to be made in this connection concerns the ʿĪsāwiyya. The ʿĪsāwiyya are the most important Jewish sect, aside from the Karaites, from the time of the Second Temple until the rise of the Sabbateans in the seventeenth century.[25] In a number of important respects the ʿĪsāwiyya appear to be a kind of "Jewish gnostic" group. This would appear to be all the more likely when one considers the many points of contact, homology, and structural similarity between the ʿĪsāwiyya and contemporaneous, geographically contiguous Muslim gnostics.[26]

I will try to show below that the most striking feature of this section of *Milal* is that Šahrastānī appears to have utilized a primary (oral or written) source deriving (directly or indirectly) from the ʿĪsāwiyya themselves. Several preliminary observations may be made in this connection. First, Šahrastānī seems to have possessed a privileged source concerning the ʿĪsāwiyya alone among Jewish groups. Second, his entire report on the groups of Jews seems to bear a kind of ʿĪsāwite coloration. And finally, these two observations lead to the conclusion that, in his

[23] *Milal I*, p. 387; KF p. 156.

[24] *Milal I*, p. 386; KF p. 156.

[25] *Ibid.*, Appendix I, "Notes Towards a History of the ʿĪsāwiyya," pp. 314–41. S. Pines published a series of articles concerned, *inter alia*, with the ʿĪsāwiyya, in *Jerusalem Studies in Arabic and Islam*. See "Notes on Islam and Judaeo-Christianity," vol. 4 (1984): 1–74; "Studies in Christianity and in Judaeo-Christianity Based on Arabic Sources," vol. 6 (1985): 107–61.

[26] This case is made in great detail by Israel Friedlaender in his "Jewish-Arabic Studies," *Jewish Quarterly Review* n.s. I (1910–1911): 183–215; II (1911–1912): 481–517; III (1912–1913: pp. 235–300. Gil speaks of "Jewish Manichaeans" in "The Creed of Abū ʿĀmir," *Israel Oriental Studies* 12 (1992): 9–57, at pp. 19–20. For the relation of Judaism to Manichaeanism in late antiquity, the fundamental work is now John C. Reeves, *Jewish Lore in Manichaean Cosmogony: Studies in the* Book of Giants *Traditions* (Cincinnati 1992).

chapter on the Jewish sects, Šahrastānī made an effort to subordinate his "secondary sources" to the "primary source" that was his (oral or written) informant. Šahrastānī was markedly source-conscious. Indeed, after the Karaite Qirqisānī, he remains by far the most important surviving source on the ʿĪsāwiyya.

The foregoing demonstrates the remarkable rarity and variety of Šahrastānī's sources. That he also strove to present them accurately has made him perhaps the single most important source for the history of the manifestations of gnosis in the early Islamicate civilization. This assertion may also be tested by a study of Šahrastānī's treatment of Samaritan sects, which he includes with the Maġāriyya and ʿĪsāwiyya among the Jewish groups.

It should be remembered that the hypothesis of a Jewish origination for gnosticism continues to be an important area of research into the history of gnosis.[27] In addition to the notorious difficulties attendant on this hypothesis, some scholars continue to probe the origins and development of gnosis through the rather more problematic Samaritan connection. The literature on this approach has been substantially reviewed and advanced, especially in Jarl Fossum's provocative research.[28] Regarding this area of *gnostica*, as well as those aforementioned, *Milal* provides the modern researcher with tantalizing bits of rare information.

The first point to be made in this regard is that most of Šahrastānī's report on Samaritanism derives ultimately from Christian heresiographies. This indebtedness should be compared to the other reports of Islamicate historians of religion on a still poorly understood Samaritan sect, the Dositheans.[29] The complex question of the identity of this so-called "Samaritan-gnostic" group is magnified by Šahrastānī's manifold contributions to the study of this group. Such complexification may be considered a mark of his excellence as a scholar.

[27] For a useful recent overview, see the articles in *Gnosisforschung und Religionsgeschichte, Festschrift für Kurt Rudolph zum 65. Geburtstag*, eds. H. Preissler and H. Seiwert (Marburg 1994).

[28] R. Pummer, "The Present State of Samaritan Studies: II," *Journal of Semitic Studies* 22 (1977): 27–47, at pp. 27–31 ["Gnosticism"]. An indispensable overview has been published by Jarl Fossum. See his exhaustive chapter "Sects and Movements" in Alan D. Crown (ed.), *The Samaritans* (Tübingen 1989) pp. 293–389.

[29] Stanley Isser, *The Dositheans* (Leiden 1976). Fossum noticed that Isser missed Judah Hadassi's *Eškol ha-Kofer* as a source for the Dositheans. See "The Origin of the Gnostic Concept of the Demiurge," *Ephemerides Theologicae Lovanienses* LXI (1985): 142–52, at p. 150 n. 45. This source was already cited by Goldziher in "La Misasa," *Revue Africaine* 52 (1908): 23–28, at p. 27. For more on Karaite sources on Dositheanism see Saul Lieberman, *Shkiin* שקיעין (Jerusalem 1939; 2nd ed., Jerusalem 1970) pp. 25–26 [Hebrew].

The contributions made by Šahrastānī to the "Dosithean problem" in the history of gnosis include: 1) an evocative report on an obscure sub-sect of the Dositheans known as the *Ilfāniyya*;[30] 2) a parallel report (in the section of *Milal* devoted to the "Dualists") on a pair of quasi-gnostic groups known as the Kantawiyya and the Ṣiyāmiyya, a pairing almost certainly literarily related to the Samaritan "sects," Kūšāniyya and Dūsitāniyya;[31] 3) the ultimate derivation of both these cliched doublets, in turn, from Christian sources such as Theodor bar Khonai, who associates Samaritans with the development of such gnostic groups as the Mandeans.[32]

It may be readily apparent that so far intractable difficulties have faced historians trying to identify more precisely these various gnosticizing groups. At the moment, it seems minimally clear that a vaguely defined range of loosely interrelated gnosticizing groups were active and widespread in the Mesopotamian and Persianate provinces before and after the rise of Islam. Šahrastānī anticipated our understanding of the relationships of these sects. In this regard I turn to Šahrastānī's suggestion that the "extremists" were also known "in Rayy as al-Mazdakiyya."[33]

The first point to be made in regard to Šahrastānī on the Mazdakiyya is that, once again, Šahrastānī here provides us with a precious if not unparalleled account. The importance of this account is such that it has

[30] The earliest source appears to be Abū ʿĪsā al-Warrāq's *Kitāb al-Maqālāt*. See my *Species of Misbelief*, pp. 131–32. Isser was unaware of many of the most important Muslim sources available, such as al-Bīrūnī, concerning this almost unknown sect. See *Dositheans* p. 73 n. 114. Most notably, the "Faniyya" are included in one of the oldest surviving heresiographies, "Le Kitāb al-Radd ʿAlā l-Bidaʿ d'Abū Muṭīʿ Makḥūl al-Nasafī," ed. Marie Bernard, *Annales Islamologiques* 16 (1980): 39–126, at p. 110. Related lists may be found in Ḫālid al-ʿAsalī, *Ğahm b. Safwān* (Baghdad 1965) p. 199, # 8 of the sects of the Ğahmiyya; the version given by al-ʿAsalī was translated a century ago in Thomas Hughes's *Dictionary of Islam* (Delhi 1885; repr. 1977) p. 569: "Faniyah, who say both Paradise and Hell will be annihilated"; ʿUṯmān b. ʿAbd Allāh al-ʿIrāqī, *Al-Firaq al-Muftariqa bayn Ahl al-Zayġ wa-l-Zandaqa*, trans. Yasar Kutluay (Ankara 1962) [Turkish] pp. 84–85.

[31] Additional insights were added by H.H. Schaeder in his "Die Kantäer," *Welt des Orients*, I (1949): 288–98. Scholarship on this subject recently received another important source, that of Abū ʿĪsā al-Warrāq. See Wilferd Madelung, "Abū ʿĪsā al-Warrāq über die Bardesaniten, Marcioniten und Kantäer," *Studien zur Geschichte und Kultur des Vorderen Orients, Festschrift für B. Spuler*, eds. H.R. Roemer, A. Noth (Leiden 1981) pp. 210–24, esp. pp. 221-24.

[32] See these sections of Theodor Bar Khonai's *Scholies*, translated into French by R. Hespel and R. Draguet, part I, *Corpus Scriptorum Christianorum Orientalium*, 431, Scr. Syr. t. 187 (Louvain 1981) pp. 303–4; and part II, *CSCO* 432, Scr. Syr. t. 188, pp. 254–61. I have demonstrated that the heresiographical tradition of Theodor bar Khonai must have been known to al-Maqrīzī in fifteenth-century Egypt: see *Species* p. 246.

[33] *Milal*, p. 365; KF p. 150.

been subjected to close scrutiny for the past half-century.[34] Of all these, the most important commentator remains Erik Peterson, in his rich (if mistitled) study, "Urchristentum und Mandaïsmus."[35] Peterson is one of the few scholars to bring one section of *Milal* to bear on another. In this way Peterson is able to draw the following conclusion: "... the Persian-nationalist groups of Gnostics (Bardesanians and Manicheans) — through Bardesanian intermediation — knew, from a distance, remnants of ancient Valentinean ideas and cultic practice, as we would expect from other information we have about the evolution of sects in the East."[36] Peterson's use of Šahrastānī anticipated the best recent research on gnostic groups under early Islam, such as that of Wilferd Madelung and Heinz Halm.[37]

The foregoing examples illustrate that one cannot fully understand Šahrastānī's report on the gnosticizing Muslim "extremists" without recourse to *Milal* on other, contemporaneous gnosticizing groups. This kind of comparative and integrative use of *Milal* facilitates a multidimensional understanding of the history of gnosis under early Islam. To ignore the testimony of Šahrastānī is to willfully discount unique information concerning several of these groups, including the ʿĪsāwiyya, the Maġāriyya and the Mazdakiyya.

I have not touched on many of the *Milal*'s most important sections on

[34] The *status quaestionis* on the question of the Mazdakites has now been provided by Shaul Shaked, *Dualism in Transformation: Varieties of Religion in Sasanian Iran* (London 1994). An earlier *überblick* may be found in Ehsan Yar-Shater, *The Cambridge History of Iran* 3 (2) (Cambridge 1983) pp. 991–1024. For an excellent analysis of Šahrastānī's report in the light of Ismāʿīlī texts see Heinz Halm, "Die Sieben und die Zwölf, die ismaʿilitische Kosmogonie und das Mazdak-Fragment des Šahrastānī," *Deutscher Orientalistentag* XVIII (1972) (Vortrage) pp. 170–77. See also Werner Muller, "Mazdak and the Alphabet Mysticism of the East," *History of Religions* 3 (1963–1964): 72–82; Franz Altheim and Ruth Stiehl, "Mazdak and Porphyrios," ibid. pp. 1–21. Moshe Gil has discussed this text in connection with his far-reaching arguments for Manichean influences in the origins of Islam: "The Creed of Abū ʿĀmir," *IOS* 12 (1992): 9–57, esp. pp. 23–29, and pp. 46–47 [for a text and translation of the Cureton edition of Šahrastānī's report].

[35] In certain respects some of the best work done on these groups, based largely on a perspicuous reading of Šahrastānī, is Erik Peterson's "Urchristentum und Mandaïsmus," *Zeitschrift für die neutestamentliche Wissenschaft* 27 (1928) pp. 55–98.

[36] Ibid. p. 82 (my translation).

[37] See nn. 38 and 58 above. An important and little-known contribution to this question is the lecture of Michelangelo Guidi, "La gnose et les sectes musulmanes shiʿites," in *Annuaire de l'Institut de Philologie et d'Histoire Orientale* 3 (1935): 199–216. Guidi stresses the Mazdakite connection on p. 213. He also puts up a staunch defence of the Muslim sources: "...je suis très loin de participer à l'attitude si sceptique de beaucoup d'historiens en face des informations de nos sources d'histoire religieuse musulmane, qui sont très souvent beaucoup plus raisonnables que les reconstructions érudites des savants" (p. 210).

gnosticizing groups, such as those treating the Sabians, the Marcionites, the Bardesanians or the Manicheans.[38] However, I have tried to show that it is unsatisfactory to study Šahrastānī on the origins of Shiᶜism, or on the divisions of Judaism, for example, without an understanding of his discussions of numerous other "gnosticizing" groups. Likewise, one cannot

[38] Guy Monnot, "Écrits", reviews the literature on all these questions. Some significant advances have been made in recent years in the study of the Sabians. For a selection of such recent and varied historical studies see: G. Monnot, "Sabéens et idolâtres selon ᶜAbd al-Jabbār," *Mélanges de l'Institut Dominicain...* 12 (1974): 13–48; Gotthard Strohmaier, "Eine sabische Abrahamlegende und Sure 37, 83–93," *Studien zum Menschenbild in Gnosis und Manichaismus*, ed. Peter Nagel (Halle/Saale 1979); and, most importantly, Michel Tardieu, "Sabiens Coraniques et 'Sabiens' de Harran," *Journal Asiatique* CCLXXIV (1986): 2–44. Tardieu's work is an invaluable contribution to the literature of history of religions on this hitherto insoluble historical problem. He makes an appropriately sharp distinction between the two kinds of "Sabians" adduced in his title. Regarding the former he concludes, "Les Sabiens coraniques, correspondant arabe au nom grec de Stratioques, ne sont donc pas autre chose que des Gnostiques au sens strict" (p. 42). See also G. Stroumsa, "Gnostics and Manicheans," pp. 273–74, regarding the same passage from Epiphanius used by Tardieu to make this point. S.M. Stern's strictures regarding any identification of Sabians with gnostics may now need to be revised: see "ᶜAbd al-Jabbar's Account of how Christ's Religion was Falsified by the Adoption of Roman Customs," *Journal of Theological Studies* 29 (1968): 159–64. Tardieu's second identification, of the Platonic Academy of the Sabians of Harran, would seem to be confirmed by direct documentation. See Sebastian Brock, "A Syriac Collection of Prophecies of the Pagan Philosophers," *OLP* 14 (1983): 203–47; idem, "Some Syriac Excerpts from Greek Collections of Pagan Prophecies," *Vigiliae Christianae* 38 (1984): 77–91. Moreover, the possibility of Hermeticism at the Harranian Academy has been underlined by H.J. Drijvers, "Bardaisan of Edessa and the Hermetica," *Jaarbericht/Ex Oriente Lux* 21 (1969–1970): 190–210. Finally, Tardieu has illumined Šahrastānī's report on Manicheanism, by the light of Stoic physics: "La gnose valentinienne et les Oracles chaldaïques," *The Rediscovery of Gnosticism* I, ed. B. Layton (Leiden 1980) pp. 194–237, at pp. 213–14.

For recent work on the Sabians, see the following: M. Tardieu, "Les calendriers en usage à Harran d'après les sources arabes et le commentaire de Simplicius à la Physique d'Aristote," in I. Hadot (ed.), *Simplicius, Sa Vie, Son Oeuvre, Sa Survie* (New York, Berlin, 1987) 40–57; Françoise Hudry, "Le *Liber XXIV Philosophorum* et le *Liber de Causis* dans les Manuscrits," *AHDLMA* 59 (1992): 63–88; David Pingree, "Indian Planetary Images and the Tradition of Astral Magic," *JWCI* 52 (1989): 1–13, at p. 8; Ilsetraut Hadot, "The Life and Work of Simplicius in Greek and Arabic Sources," in Richard Sorabji (ed.), *Aristotle Transformed: The Ancient Commentators and their Influence* (Ithaca, NY, 1990): 275–303; Sarah Stroumsa, "The Barāhima in Early Islam," *Jerusalem Studies in Arabic and Islam* 6 (1985); Binyamin Abrahamov, "The Barāhima's Enigma: A Search for a New Solution," *Die Welt des Orients* XVIII (1987): 72–91; Nick Kollerston, "The Star Temples of Harran," in Annabella Kitson (ed.), *History and Astrology* (London 1989): 47–60; Moshe Gil, "The Creed of Abū ᶜĀmir," *IOS* 12 (1992): 9–57, esp. pp. 13–15; Jürgen Tubach, *Im Schatten des Sonnengottes: Der Sonnenkult in Edessa, Harran und Hatra am Vorabend der christlichen Mission* (Wiesbaden 1986) pp. 142–75; *Moon-Cult of Harran*: T.H. Green, *The City of the Moon God: Religious Traditions of Harran*, Leiden and New York: Brill, 1992.

fully comprehend his discussion of Muʿtazilism without reference to his history of Greek philosophy. In short, given the great philosophical care with which *Milal* is constructed, one must have a firm grasp of its author's thought as a whole in order to properly grasp the purport of its parts.

KITĀB AL-MILAL WA-L-NIHAL ON THE DIVISIONS OF THE JEWS

Šahrastānī's presentation of Jews and Judaism is learned and lucid, though not without its intriguing ambiguities. Its sometimes surprising assessments may be gauged by reference to the proportions of its internal divisions. The following points may be noted initially: 1) The section on Muslim sects is more than eight times as long as the section on Jewish and Christian sects, but is several pages shorter than the treatment of philosophy; 2) The treatment of Avicenna alone is almost four times as long as the treatment of Jews and Christians put together; 3) The treatment of non-Muslim groups is far longer than that of Muslim groups. For good reason, then, Gimaret judges *Milal* to be of "proportions assez choquantes."[39]

Before he presents the sects, Šahrastānī devotes several pages to an analysis of Judaism, with particular concentration on the Torah.[40] He declares that, in regard to the doctrine of predestination, "the Rabbanites are like the Muʿtazilites among us and the Karaites are like the Muǧabbira and the Mušabbiha."[41] After several more pages he abruptly remarks that the Jews broke up into seventy-one sects, of which he declares his intention to recount "the best-known and most prominent of them and will forgo the rest."[42]

The first of these, and thus the very first non-Muslim sect — in his views, the sect closest to Islam — is the ʿAnāniyya. Šahrastānī seems less concerned with the sect than with the heresiarch ʿAnān, particularly with his attitude toward Jesus as prophet. Indeed, there is nothing distinctively Jewish in Šahrastānī's description of ʿAnān's doctrine, which the scholar alleges to have comprised an ascetic ritual praxis. It is rather ʿAnān's attitude toward Christianity which is the focus of this entire section.[43]

39 *AEPHE* (1979) p. 278.

40 See my translation below.

41 P. 495.

42 P. 502.

43 Šahrastānī was equally learned in Christianity. See the study of his section on the Christians by G. Troupeau in "Les croyances des Chrétiens présentées par un hérésiographe musulman du XII siècle," *MFO* L/ii (1984): 671–88.

Šahrastānī claims that ʿAnān, "called ʿAnān ibn Dāwūd, *Raʾs Ǧālūt*," recognized Jesus as a righteous man, not as a prophet, but that other subsections of the ʿAnāniyya believed otherwise. *Contra* Poznanski and Friedlaender, Mainz has argued that Šahrastānī here provides three distinct positions on the Karaite doctrine of Jesus.[44] According to his interpretation of this passage, Šahrastānī says that "Some held that [Jesus] was one of the friends (*awliyāʾ*) of God." A second group is said to have maintained that the Gospel was not divinely inspired, rather it was the biography of Jesus. Another group, according to this view, is said to have rejected Jesus and even to have murdered him.[45]

Šahrastānī follows the ʿAnāniyya with the ʿĪsāwiyya. This report, after that of Qirqisānī, is by far the fullest extant report on this sect. Several elements of Šahrastānī's report are unparalleled, and therefore have long been recognized as possessing some particular importance for the study of the history of Judaism.[46] From the perspective of Muslim heresiography of the Jews, however, Šahrastānī's report provides material pertinent to each of the Jewish sects it discusses.

My first observation about this report is that Šahrastānī's source was an informant in possession of genuine Jewish materials. The voice (or text) of this informant informs this entire section on the ʿĪsāwiyya. Šahrastānī actually quotes Hebrew terms. He says, for example, that "Abū ʿĪsā Isḥāq ibn Yaʿqūb al-Iṣfahānī was called *ʿŪfīd Allūhīm*, that is, *ʿĀbid Allāh*."[47] That Šahrastānī quotes this name "Servant (literally, worshipper) of God" in a Hebrew form suggests that Šahrastānī's informant defined it to Šahrastānī, and one or the other of them transliterated and then transposed it, more or less, into its Arabic equivalent. Similarly, when Šahrastānī gives the (Persianate) name of the ʿĪsāwite continuator Yūḏġān, he adds that "it is said that his name [in Hebrew] was Yehuda."[48]

The apparent "in-group" quality of Šahrastānī's report on the Jewish sects suggests the existence of an informant among the Jews, perhaps among the ʿĪsāwiyya.[49] This hypothesis has never been submitted in modern scholarship. It could help explain several hitherto perplexing features of Šahrastānī's report as well as of other reports which either rely

[44] See Poznanski's review of Graetz, *REJ* LX (1910): 306–12, at p. 308; Friedlaender "Jewish-Arabic Studies" III, p. 243; E. Mainz "Comments on the Messiah in Karaite Literature," *PAAJR* XXV (1956): 115–18.

[45] P. 504.

[46] The question is reviewed in my *Between Muslim and Jew: The Problem of Symbiosis under Early Islam* (Princeton: Princeton University Press, 1995), pp. 68–89.

[47] P. 506.

[48] P. 509.

[49] This conjecture is based solely on internal evidence which I review below.

on Šahrastānī or perhaps on other ʿĪsāwiyya informants. A sectarian origin for the materials on the Jewish sects may be significant for the history of Muslim heresiography of the Jews.

First, some well-known Jewish folkloristic motifs, such as the encirclement with a stick of myrtle, the flight to the Banū Mūsā, and the sand-river (Sambatyon), are mentioned without interpretive comment.[50] The whole report, including its Hebrew terms, is presented with direct authority, as if he were retelling an original account which he had heard or read. We may therefore tend to discount the possibility of a Christian informant. We may also discount the possibility of a Karaite informant.[51] If, then, Šahrastānī had a Jewish informant who was not Karaite, his report could likewise not have been given to him by a Rabbanite. Rabbanite teachings are given short shrift, Talmudic tradition not being addressed at all. The whole of his report on the Jewish groups is informed by a sectarian tendency, for it treats these groups knowledgeably, without criticism, and without regard to the centrality of Rabbinism. When one considers the section on the Jews as a whole, the most plausible conclusion is that Šahrastānī relied on an ʿĪsāwite informant. In addition to the material already presented this argument has, as it were, both a positive and a negative defense. First it is, as stated above, highly likely that Šahrastānī's informant was neither a Rabbanite nor a Karaite. We know, by contrast, that ʿĪsāwites, by their quasi-Islamic doctrine, would have been more likely than other Jews to meet with Muslims. They did in fact meet with Ibn Ḥazm and Nuʿmānī. Šahrastānī's report on the ʿĪsāwiyya, moreover, is fully shaped, with a narrative beginning and an end, unlike his reports on the other Jewish sects. And it contains telling details: the ʿĪsāwite doctrine that Abū ʿĪsā was called *ʿabd, nabī* and *rasūl* is reported without criticism, though these were terms specifically applied to Muḥammad in the daily Muslim prayers and deeply ingrained in the Islamic consciousness.

Several secondary issues could likewise be explained by the assumption of an ʿĪsāwite informant. An ʿĪsāwite informant could also have given Šahrastānī a report on ʿAnān, including three distinct positions on Jesus held by ʿAnānites, for the ʿĪsāwiyya alone of all the major "Jewish" groups maintained the prophethood of Jesus. This hypothesis is further strengthened if Šahrastānī's dating of the ʿĪsāwiyya uprising is construed as correct. The most extensive arguments yet submitted in support of Šahrastānī's dating (as opposed to the earlier dating of Qirqisānī, who

50 P. 506–7.

51 We have no evidence that Šahrastānī knew Qirqisānī's *Anwār* directly. On the rejection of the theory of Karaite origination for Muslim heresiographic treatments of Jews and Judaism, see my *Species*, pp. 35–80.

placed Abū ʿĪsā in the time of ʿAbd al-Malik) are those of Friedlaender.[52] His (admittedly circumstantial and contextual) argument was based on a lengthy analysis of fifteen elements exhibited by both Abū ʿĪsā and the proto-Shīʿī *ġulāt*, whose uprisings culminated in the last years of the Umayyad dynasty, the period in which Šahrastānī places Abū ʿĪsā.

A final argument in support of the possibility of an ʿĪsāwite informant for Šahrastānī's report on the Jewish sects can be derived from Šahrastānī's overall categorization. The first group he describes, the ʿAnāniyya, are ascribed almost exclusively Christian ideals, which characterization the ʿĪsāwiyya alone of the Jewish sects would have had doctrinal reasons for giving. Šahrastānī proceeds to mention four other groups. These are the ʿĪsāwiyya themselves, the two groups of ʿĪsāwiyya continuators, and the Maġāriyya (text has Maqāriba), whom he also lists under the rubric of the ʿĪsāwiyya continuators. This classificatory scheme exhibits a clear ʿĪsāwiyya bias.

It is unlikely, however, that an ʿĪsāwite informant was Šahrastānī's sole source on the Jewish sects. His introduction draws on already established treatments of the etymology of "Jew," *yahūd*; the description of Torah; and the Jewish position on *nasḫ*.[53] Moreover, Šahrastānī used the *Kitāb al-Maqālāt* of Abū ʿĪsā al-Warrāq.[54] Bīrūnī used that same book when discussing the Maġāriyya.[55] Both these authors, as Golb points out, maintain that the Maġāriyya (if they are identified with Šahrastānī's "Maqāriba") believed Passover was incumbent only on those living in Palestine, which would seem to be similar to the Yūḏġāniyya (Šahrastānī's "Yūḏʿāniyya," if this was indeed the form he actually used himself), who said that the festivals were not incumbent on those in exile.[56] Indeed, Šahrastānī places the Maqāriba among the Yūḏʿāniyya and the Mūškāniyya (apparently ʿĪsāwite continuators).

This fact would suggest that Šahrastānī subordinated his "secondary sources" to the "primary source," namely his informant. Likewise, he makes suspiciously similar observations regarding ʿAnān, Abū ʿĪsā and Yūdġān: all three are said to have proscribed alcohol and meat, and enjoined austerity and supererogatory prayers. Later continuators of

52 "Jewish-Arabic Studies" I, pp. 203–4.

53 Pp. 491–502.

54 This assertion is based on the concordance of his report with the report of Bīrūnī, who explicitly states his dependence on Abū ʿĪsā al-Warrāq. See the benchmark review provided by Norman Golb, "Who Were the Maġārīya?" *Journal of the American Oriental Society* 80 (1960): 347–59, at p. 349.

55 See *Species of Misbelief*, pp. 114–53.

56 Golb, "Maġārīya," p. 349.

Šahrastānī, like Faḫr al-Dīn al-Rāzī, read Šahrastānī to mean that the Maġāriyya and the Yūdġāniyya were somehow the same.[57]

ŠAHRASTĀNĪ ON THE MAĠĀRIYYA

It is true, of course, that one can simply mine *Milal* for details relevant to some historical interest (as do the bulk of its medieval and contemporary "users") without bothering to grasp its approach as a whole.[58] Doing so, however, runs the instrumentalist's risk of misconstrual. The case of the Maġāriyya is particularly dangerous in this regard. For this report, short as it is, has generated a strikingly diverse scholarly response. Given its brevity, Šahrastānī's account of the Maġāriyya [translated and annotated below] is indeed remarkable for the diversity of identifications which scholars have tried to find in it.[59] Such theories generally consider a

[57] Thus, he asserts that the "Maʿādiyya" follow a man from Hamadan, which surely is a corrupt conflation of Šahrastānī's report, given together in the same sub-section, on the Maġāriyya and the Yūḏġāniyya, who, Šahrastānī tells us, followed Yūḏġan of Hamadan. I shall return to the linkage of Yūḏġāniyya and Maġāriyya below.

[58] In this sense, the present study emphasizes *Šahrastānī* on the Maġāriyya as opposed to Šahrastānī on the *Maġāriyya*. In particular, I shall not attempt here to harmonize Šahrastānī's report with that of Qirqisānī. With the hardheaded good sense that typifies his work, Baron refused to harmonize these two reports. See *Social and Religious History of the Jews*, vol. V (Columbia University Press and JPS: New York, London and Philadelphia, 1957) pp. 378–80.

[59] In addition to Golb, "Who were the Maġārīya?", see Ernst Bammel, "Höhlenmenschen," *ZNW* 49 (1958): 77–88; Harry A. Wolfson, "The Pre-Existent Angel of the Magharians and Al-Nahawandi," *JQR* 51 (1960): 89–106; Shalom Spiegel, "On the Interpretation of the Polemics of Pirkoi ben Baboi", *H.A. Wolfson Jubilee Volume* (Jeruslaem 1965): 243–74 [Hebrew].

The fullest treatment can be found in Jarl Fossum, "The Magharians: A Pre-Christian Jewish Sect and its Significance for the Study of Gnosticism and Christianity," *Henoch* ix (1987): 303–44. See also the interesting exchange between Yoram Erder and Haggai Ben-Shammai in "When Did the Karaites First Encounter Apocryphal Literature Akin to the Dead Sea Scrolls?" *Cathedra* 42 (1987): 53–86 [Hebrew]. I thank Professor Ben-Shammai for kindly supplying me with an offprint. I tend to disagree with Fossum and Erder on the significance of the Maġāriyya as an "ancient sect": I find Ben-Shammai's reading of Šahrastānī on the Maġāriyya (pp. 82–83) more persuasive, though I disagree with him that Šahrastānī's report is "confused." I have made brief reference to the literature on the Maġāriyya in *Between Muslim and Jew*, p. 39, no. 99.

The oddest, and unlikeliest, report comes from S. Szyszman, in his review of the first volume of the UNESCO French translation of *Milal*. See *Bulletin des Études Karaïtes* 2 (1989) 103–106, where he reports on the purported existence of a "document qui est relativement récente" concerning a Cairene cemetery divided between Karaites, Rabbanites, and Maġārites. Qirqisānī, who had seen some of their books, thought they were extinct in his day. See Golb, "Who were the Maġārīya?", p. 354.

portion of the evidence while ignoring the problematic remainder. I shall try to show that the resulting lack of consensus concerning the Maġāriyya is due in some measure to the plucking of the report out of its appropriate context in *Milal* itself.

These theories have had their champions. Gilles Quispel's insistence on the relevance of the Maġāriyya (Šahrastānī has "Maqāriba," a discrepancy probably due to a corruption in pronunciation and/or orthography), the "Cave-Sect," for the study of the history of Jewish esotericism and gnosis has been pursued by his student, Jarl Fossum.[60] Gedaliahu Stroumsa, likewise, has shown in some detail how the allegation that the Jews worshipped a demiurgic angel, suggested by Šahrastānī in regard to the *Maġāriyya*, bears some substantive relevance for research into the relationship of Judaism to ancient gnosticism.[61] Since the discovery of the Dead Sea Scrolls, one school of scholarship has identified the Maġāriyya as the Essenes, and/or their successors, whose texts were rediscovered in the Judean caves around the year 800C.E.[62] Yet others argued their importance in the study of Karaism.[63]

My approach in this article complements these various interpretations. I maintain that the interpretation of Šahrastānī's text itself demands interpretation.[64] The labors of Gimaret, Monnot, Jolivet, and Vadet,

[60] See Edwin M. Yamauchi, *Pre-Christian Gnosticism* (Grand Rapids, 2nd ed., 1983) pp. 158–59; Gilles Quispel, "The Origins of the Gnostic Demiurge," in P. Granfield and J.A. Jungmann (eds.), *KYRIAKON: Festschrift Johannes Quasten*, vol. I (Münster 1970) pp. 272 ff.; Jarl Fossum, "Gen. 1,26 and 2,7 in Judaism, Samaritanism and Gnosticism," *Journal for the Study of Judaism* XVI (1985): 202–39, at pp. 229–31; idem, "The Origin of the Gnostic Concept of Demiurge," *Ephemerides Theologicae Lovanienses* LXI (1985): 142–52, at p. 143–44; idem, *The Name of God and the Angel of the Lord* (Tübingen 1985) esp. pp. 329–32.

[61] G.G. Stroumsa, "Le couple de l'ange et de l'esprit: traditions juives et chrétiennes," *Revue Biblique* 88 (1981): 42–61, at pp. 49–52; idem, "Form(s) of God: Some Notes on Metatron and Christ," *Harvard Theological Review* 76 (1983): 269–88, at p. 278. Stroumsa here argued influentially that the Maġāriyya could not have been gnostics.

[62] Fossum, "The Magharians."

[63] Fossum, "The Magharians."

[64] Wilfred Madelung suggested that Šahrastānī himself had been an Ismāʿīlī at some point in his life. See "Aš-Šahrastānī's Streitschrift gegen Avicenna und ihre Widerlegung durch Nāṣir ad-dīn aṭ-Ṭūsī," *Akten des VII Kongresses für Arabistik und Islamwissenschaft* (Göttingen 1976) pp. 250–59, and idem, "Nāṣir ad-Din Ṭūsīs's Ethics Between Philosophy, Shiʿism and Sufism," *Ethics in Islam*, ed. Richard G. Hovannisian (Undena: Malibu, CA, 1985): 85–101. I find Madelung's arguments convincing.

For recent discussion of this point, see D. Gimaret, "Šahrastānī šiʿite? ismaélien?" in *LRS*, vol. I, pp. 52–63; Guy Monnot, "L'univers religieux d'al-Shahrastani," in *Annuaire Résumés des conférences et travaux; École Pratique des Hautes Etudes, Ve Section — Sciences Religieuses*, Tome 101 (1992–1993) pp. 198–201; and Angelika Hartman, "Ismâʿîlitische Theologie bei Sunnitischen ʿUlamâʾ des Mittelalters?" in *"Ihr alle aber seid Brüder,"*

among others, show us that Šahrastānī constructed his masterwork carefully and precisely.[65] Much remains to be done in understanding the full dimensions of this great tome. By contrast, evidence that the Maġāriyya was an ancient sect is slim indeed. It consists solely of Šahrastānī's (apparent) claim that they lived 400 years before Arius, and Qirqisānī's (apparent) dating of them to sometime before Jesus Christ. That Qirqisānī would seem to date them to this earlier period has misled scholars who have sought their sectarian identity to assume a particular significance for them, largely on the basis of this presumed antiquity. Yet the only substantial reports flatly contradict each other. Qirqisānī, for example, assigns the Samaritans to a date before the Maġāriyya, while Šahrastānī places them in reverse order. The very failure of our sources to provide adequate evidence for the dating of this sect should alert us to the dangers of such backdating, especially in the absence of external corroboration. Qirqisānī, who scorned the Maġāriyya, did claim to have seen their books: "For most of the rest of the Maġārian books, most of them are of no value and resemble nonsensical tales... their interpretations of some passages in the Scripture are altogether improbable and resemble nonsensical talk (*ḫurāfāt*)."[66] Still, neither report names the founder or any other member of this purported "sect." Šahrastānī, in pointed contrast to his reports on other groups, provides no historical information on the origins, development, or practices of the Maġāriyya, other than to remark that they were "men of abstinence and mortification." In short, the dating of the Maġāriyya from antiquity, is — as the Rabbis said of the Rabbinic laws pertaining to Sabbath observance — "mountains hanging from a hair." Two hairs, to be precise.[67]

Festschrift für A. Th. Khoury zum 60. Geburtstag, eds. L. Hagemann and Ernst Pulsfort (Echter, Oros Verlag: Würzburg 1990) 190–206.

65 See the works of Gimaret, Monnot, and Jolivet cited above. For a searching analysis of the five prefaces to *Milal*, see Jean-Claude Vadet, "Le *Livre des Religions et des Opinions*. A-t-il un sens ou n'est-il qu'un simple répertoire?" *Revue des études islamiques* 54 (1986): 311–26.

66 Note that Qirqisānī, a great scholar, claims to have read rare "Maġārian" books well over a thousand years old. Yet he did not note the obvious oddity: that he knew virtually nothing about the group itself, neither its origins nor any aspect of its history. It is interesting that the style of the *Bahir* struck Meir ben Simeon in much the same way. See the discussion of the former in Elliot Wolfson, "The Tree That is All: Jewish-Christian Roots of a Kabbalistic Symbol in *Sefer ha-Bahir," JJTP* 3 (1993): 31–76, at 40.

67 Among others, Poznanski ("Philon dans l'ancienne littérature judéo-arabe," *Revue des études juives* 50 (1905): 10–31), followed by Bammel (Ernst Bammel, "Höhlenmenschen," *ZNW* 49 (1958): 77–88.), dated them to the 7th–8th century. Golb believed that he had refuted this position.

There seems to be a certain parallel to the study of *Sefer Yeṣira*. There, as here, a certain

It should be emphasized, then, that Šahrastānī's dating is questionable, whether or not one reads it to mean that he saw the Maġāriyya as an ancient sect. He apparently got at least some of his information not from Qirqisānī but from Severus ibn al-Muqaffaʿ. This 10th century bishop of Ašmunayn, like Šahrastānī in his report on the Maġāriyya, repeatedly linked Benjamin al-Nehawandi and Arius with the Jewish doctrine of an Angel-demiurge.[68] Šahrastānī thus knew about both Benjamin and Arius independently of his source on the Maġāriyya. Since, furthermore, he locates the Maġāriyya among the Yūḏġāniyya (eighth-century ʿĪsāwite continuators), it would seem clear enough that he saw them as being a post-Islamic group. His phrase "400 years before Arius" must then be explained in some other fashion.[69]

One heretofore unexplored explanation does present itself. Yet another reason to be wary of Šahrastānī's dating of the Maġāriyya to antiquity is his oblique approbation of this group's teaching.[70] A provocative parallel in Judah Halevi's *Kuzari* gives credence to this point. Halevi's Khazar king and his vizier convert to Judaism after contacting a Jewish group who celebrate the Sabbath in a cave (*maġāra*), where the new converts are *secretly* circumcised.[71] In both cases, moreover, the motif of *400 years* is employed: for Šahrastānī, the Maġāriyya seemingly date from 400 years before Arius, and for Halevi, the events concerning the Khazar king are stated by him to have taken place 400 years before the date of his writing

irony reigns. That is, scholars primarily outside the area of Judeo-Islamic research assert great antiquity on the basis of indirect evidence. At the same time, concerns raised by scholars specializing primarily in the study of the Islamicate texts, which provide the earliest verifiable dating, are routinely underestimated. See my "*Sefer Yeṣira* and Early Islam: A Reappraisal," *JJTP* 3 (1993): 1–30.

[68] I have discussed this point in "A Muslim Designation for Rabbinic Jews" (forthcoming in the papers from the Society for Judeo-Arabic Studies meeting in Princeton). I have since noticed that Gimaret and Monnot name Severus as a source for Šahrastānī's report on the doctrine of the Arians in his section on the Christians (*LRS*, p. 618, n. 36). See also G. Troupeau in "Les croyances des Chrétiens présentées par un hérésiographe musulman du XIIe siècle," *MFO* L/ii (1984): 671–88. Sidney Griffith has since indicated additional references to Severus on Benjamin al-Nehawendi and Jewish Angel-demiurgism. See "The *K. al-Miṣbāḥ al-ʿAql* of Severus ibn al-Muqaffaʿ," *Medieval Encounters* 2 (1996).

[69] See my comments in the annotation below. It may be noted that Šahrastānī does not cite the Maġāriyya in his informed treatment of Arian doctrine (in his section on Christianity). He uses Arius, Benjamin Nehawandi, and the Quran in his report on the Maġāriyya as points of [Christian, Jewish and Muslim] comparison.

[70] Which I shall try to explicate in my commentary below. Vadet does an excellent job of showing how Šahrastānī uses historical "data" as vehicles to convey his own convictions. See "Le *Livre des Religions et des Opinions*. A-t-il un sens ou n'est-il qu'un simple répertoire?"

[71] Halevi's story bears some relation to the famous letter of Hasdai ibn Shaprut, who noted the Khazar worship in caves. See the useful discussion by Baron, ibid., p. 377, n. 50.

the *Kuzari*.[72] Halevi and Šahrastānī, commonly drawing on Hermetic and Ismāʿīlī traditions, thus seemed to have employed the image of a "cave-people" to refer obliquely to a contemporary "true Judaism in hiding."[73] Further evidence in support of this supposition may be found in the fact that both authors draw on the *Iḫwān al-Ṣafāʾ*, who themselves typified their esoterism with the metaphor of *hiding in caves*.[74] That this influential society saw themselves as a metaphoric "cave-people" (*Maġāriyya*) suggests an analysis other than the more literal readings popular in scholarship (as surveyed above).[75] In this alternative reading, Šahrastānī's Maġāriyya were not simply involved with either texts or practices in caves — neither claim having anything but tangential and circumstantial evidence to commend it — but also with the *cave as symbol for secrecy*.[76]

[72] The latter detail, however, is not found in the Judeo-Arabic text, but only in the Ibn Tibbon translation. See *Kitāb al-Radd wa-l-Dalīl fī al-Dīn al-Ḏalīl*, ed. D.H. Baneth and H. Ben-Shammai (Jerusalem 1977) p. 3, n. 5.

In his *Iggeret Teiman*, Maimonides emphasized that the 400-year sojourn of the Israelites in Egypt refers "to the duration of the exile, and not (solely) to the Egyptian bondage." He goes on to make explicit that the 400-year-span carries a Messianic significance. I follow the translation in Isadore Twersky, (ed.) *A Maimonides Reader* (New York 1972) p. 451. The esoteric reading of "exile," as in the *Rasāʾil Iḫwān al-Ṣafāʾ*, was metaphorically represented as "entering the cave": see below, n. 74.

[73] I hope to deal with the relation between Šahrastānī and Halevi at length on another occasion. For now, on Halevi, see my "The Compunctious Philosopher?" in *Medieval Encounters* (forthcoming). The following remarks, to be documented on another occasion, may suffice for the moment. Šahrastānī and Halevi share important features, not the least of which include 1) formative influences from contemporaneous Ismāʿīlī theology of world religions; 2) an embrace of the theory of hierarchy; 3) an angelology, prophetology, and historiosophy congruent with that Ismāʿīlī view of hierarchical differences.

[74] The Iḫwān al-Ṣafāʾ famously characterized themselves this way: "Know oh my brother, that we are the society of the Brothers of Purity, beings who are pure and generous-hearted. We sleep in the cave of our father Adam through a lapse of time during which temporal vicissitudes and calamitous events pass us by... Now is the time to return to our cave, to take refuge in the observation of the arcana and in concealment!" This widely-cited passage is discussed, for example, by Anton M. Heinen, "The Notion of *Taʾwīl* in Abū Yaʿqūb al-Sijistānī's *Book of the Sources (Kitāb al-Yanābīʿ)*," *Hamdard Islamicus* II (1979): 35–45, at p. 35; Corbin, *Temple and Contemplation*, pp. 156–57, and more recently in N. Peter Joose, "An Example of Medieval Arabic Pseudo-Hermetism: The Tale of Salaman and Absal," *JSS* XXXVIII (1993): 279–93, at 292.

[75] And, of course, Šahrastānī says nothing of caves in his report.

[76] Other esoteric traditions, both Jewish and Muslim, current in this period, also used the image of hiding in caves as metaphor for the clandestine elite surviving throughout a dark world-age. This image, for example, is central to the *Haft Paykar* of Niẓāmī, born a few years before Šahrastānī's death. For a short, concentrated discussion of the symbol of the cave in the esoteric literature of this period, see Julie Scott Meisami's introduction to her excellent new translation, *Haft Paykar: A Medieval Persian Romance* (Oxford 1995) pp. xxxiii–xxxiv. For Jewish sources, see the evidence gathered in Martin Plessner, "Hermes Trismegistus and Arabic Science," *SI* 2 (1954): 52–54.

Why, after all, does he use this peculiar designation for this group, when he otherwise refers to sects by the names of their founders?[77] It is surely improbable that a sect would themselves have embraced such an odd self-appellation. The name itself seems chosen to signify the essence of this group. And if this "sect" in fact comprised an esoteric sodality within contemporaneous Judaism, with whom he shared Ismāʿīlī tendencies, then the name "Maġāriyya" served him the double duty of at once highlighting their special status while not otherwise revealing their identity. If this is the case, then Šahrastānī may have seen fit to appropriate this metaphor to apply to some esoteric grouping within Judaism — perhaps one with which he had personal contact.[78]

What can be said about such contacts? As indicated more fully in my notes to the translation below, I believe that the Jewish esoteric traditions represented by Šahrastānī as being "Maġārian" doctrine bears affinities to *Sefer ha-Bahir*, some version of which was circulating through the Muslim world in his day.[79] First, we know that the eighth-century Jewish sects described by Šahrastānī emerged in the proto-Shīʿite milieu.[80] Second, Ismāʿīlīs were familiar with Karaite texts, and vice versa, and they obviously had open lines of contact.[81] More specifically, al-Masʿūdī knew of the son of the Karaite sage Daniel al-Qūmisī.[82] Šahrastānī sometimes relied heavily on Masʿūdī, even, perhaps, in his section on the Jews.[83] Now Daniel al-Qūmisī knew *Raza Rabba*, which obscure text Scholem has shown to have constituted the kernel of *Bahir*.[84] My point is not that this was necessarily the precise chain of contacts through which Šahrastānī learned of such Jewish esoterica. But it does show, at least, that such

[77] To be sure, there is some textual uncertaintly as to whether he even used the name "Maġāriyya." But I follow the consensus of scholarship in agreeing that he did so.

[78] I am suggesting that Šahrastānī may have understood the name, and used it as such, in a sense secondary to that of the "text-discovery-in-a-cave" usage by Qirqisānī.

[79] The Angel-doctrine as such, of course, is not found in the redacted versions of *Sefer ha-Bahir*.

[80] I have demonstrated this point in some detail in *Between Muslim and Jew*, especially pp. 47–93.

[81] Yefet ibn ʿAli was familiar with Ismāʿīlī propaganda, and Abū Ḥātim al-Rāzī knew of some Jewish sectarians. See S.M. Stern, *Studies in Early Ismailism* (Jerusalem and Leiden, 1983) 84–96, and p. 41.

[82] See now the discussion in Camilla Adang, *Muslim Writers on Judaism & the Hebrew Bible* (Leiden 1996) p. 84.

[83] *LRS*, vol. I, pp. 82–83.

[84] It is true that Daniel al-Qūmisī and another unnamed contemporaneous Karaite describe *Raza Rabba* as a Rabbanite book of magic. But Scholem's demonstration of its relation to *Bahir* remains persuasive. See his *Origins of the Kabbala* (Philadelphia and Princeton, 1987) pp. 106–7.

contacts provided interconfessional channels both open and near. This is all to suggest that the best information we have about the whereabouts of *Bahir* in this day places it well within the conceivable reach of Šahrastānī.[85]

Internal evidence from the *Milal*, moreover, suggests that Šahrastānī approved of the doctrines he ascribed to the Maġāriyya.[86] As Gimaret and Monnot noticed, the Yūdġāniyya and the Maġāriyya were the only non-anthropomorphizing Jews presented in *Milal*.[87] That Šahrastānī approves of their solution to the problem of anthropomorphism, moreover, may be seen in his citing verbatim the Maġāriyya's assertion, "God wrote the Torah with His Hand" in his general introduction to the Jews — in the form of a *ḥadīṯ*![88] Since he also concludes his report on the Maġāriyya with further Quranic parallels, the careful reader is left with the impression that the Maġāriyya's angel-centered anti-anthropomorphism must be consonant with Islamic orthodoxy. Moreover, he ascribes the hermeneutics of *ta'wīl* to Yūḏġān, which form of hermeneutics he, as an Ismāʿīlī sympathizer, endorsed.[89]

Now it should be recalled that Šahrastānī, despite his unusually explicit critique of Judaism, positions it as the *closest of all religions in the world*

85 Perhaps the most important avenue for future research on this connection is the work of the (unfortunately) obscure Judah ben Nissim ibn Malka. Judah ben Nissim, whom Idel has now dated to the 13th century, was strongly influenced by the negative theology of Ismaʿilism; he espoused the doctrine of the chief angel Metatron as "Adonai Qaton" [little Lord]; and commented on *Sefer ha-Bahir*. This combination of factors is unique for its day, and suggests a nexus directly pertinent to the present discussion. In the only substantial work done on this author, Vajda recognized that Šahrastānī's description of the Maġāriyya's deflection of divine attributes from the supreme godhead was reminiscient of Judah's Ismāʿīlizing negative theology, but properly concluded that the "contexte de ces spéculations est trop obscur pour autoriser un rapprochement de fond avec l'idéologie de Juda b. Nissim." See Georges Vajda, *Juda ben Nissim ibn Malka: Philosophe juif marocain* (Paris 1954) p. 69, n. 2. For Idel's dating, see M. Idel, "The beginning of Kabbalah in North Africa? A Forgotten Document by R. Yehuda ben Nissim ibn Malka," *Peʿamim* 43 [1990] 4–15 [Hebrew].

86 It is well known that elsewhere in *Milal* Šahrastānī places his own views in the mouths of groups he is ostensibly describing. In the most important such example he speaks through the Ḥunafā' in the "Debate between the Sabeans and the Ḥunafā'." Pines has discussed this section of Šahrastānī at length in his "Shīʿite Terms and Conceptions in Judah Halevi's *Kuzari*," *JSAI* 2 (1980) esp. pp. 190–92, and pp. 196–210. Monnot also stresses that Šahrastānī speaks through the mouth of the Ḥanīf. See "L'univers religieux d'al-Shahrastani," p. 200.

87 *LRS*, vol. I, p. 312, n. 21.

88 *LRS*, vol. I, p. 595.

89 Habib Feki, *Les idées religieuses et philosophiques de l'ismaélisme fatimide* (Tunis 1978) pp. 267–301; I.K. Poonawala, "Ismaʿili *ta'wīl* of the Qur'an," in *Approaches to the History of the Interpretation of the Qur'an*, ed. A. Rippin (Oxford 1988) pp. 199–222; and Anton M. Heinen, "The Notion of *Ta'wīl* in Abū Yaʿqūb al-Sijistānī's *Book of the Sources (Kitāb al-Yanābīʿ)*."

to Islam, in a chapter longer than that devoted to the Christians. The very closest of Jewish sects are those emerging in the early Islamic period, the very first of hundreds of non-Muslim groups explicated in *Milal*. Even the Samaritans, whom he well knows to be very ancient, are addressed after these contemporaneous Jewish groups. There is also something sharply contrastive in the contents of these two chapters. His exposition of the Jewish sects is replete with Shīʿite terminology, preoccupied with the "secrets of holy books," and especially with the messianic promise.[90] This chapter, most strikingly, is framed at beginning and end with a highly charged and profoundly cryptic discussion: the section on the Christians is notable for its data-driven dryness.

None of the foregoing should be construed to imply that the Maġāriyya never existed. But it is important to underscore the way that this author arranged the articulation of his "data" to convey his own doctrinal message. And it seems fairly clear why he should have done so. Šahrastānī's Ismāʿīlī inclinations, it would appear, impelled him to transcend the limited polemic imperative inherent in the Kalām approach to foreign creeds. He seems thus to have discovered the ultimate cover for his Ismāʿīlī claims; he revealed his own passionate intent by means of a dispassionate exposition of others'. *The transconfessional was the mode in which he expressed himself confessionally*.

In summary, three factors lead to the suspicion that Šahrastānī used this report to refer to something more than an ancient Jewish sect. They are 1) his apparent approval of their teachings; 2) his esoteric art of writing; and 3) his use of historical data as vehicles for his own ideas. In short, while one can merely mine it for "facts," as indeed do the preponderance of its contemporary readers, such a "one-eyed" reading was manifestly not the goal of the author.[91] He spared neither labor nor intelligence in the felicitous selection and emphatic finesse he bestowed on his tableau. As such, "facts" in *Milal* are saturated with multiple implications. *Milal* is nothing if not self-consciously overdetermined; its five Introductions, and numerous other forewords, prolegomena, and preliminaries make such authorial care abundantly obvious. Šahrastānī's presentation of the Maġāriyya, then, while quite rightly to be seen as an invaluable historical rarity, says at least as much about Šahrastānī's religious vision of the

[90] The conclusion of the section on the Jews, most especially, has not been analyzed as such. Some insight may be gleaned from the remarks of Vadet, "Le *Livre des Religions et des Opinions*. A-t-il un sens ou n'est-il qu'un simple répertoire?"

[91] Like William Blake after him, Šahrastānī inveighed against an *aʿwar bi-ayyi ʿaynayhi šāʾa*, translated by Gimaret/Monnot as "borgne de l'œil dont il ne veut pas voir," (p. 120), which Kazi/Flynn gives as "a one-eyed point of view" (p. 15).

world as it does about some ostensible historical entity in the Jewish community. To read the *Milal* exclusively one way or the other is to ultimately miss both dimensions; and surely misses its meaning as a whole. Only by reading binocularly, seeing the historical and the philosophical dimensions simultaneously, may we discern that meaning, suddenly alive to us in its three-dimensional roundness.

CONCLUSIONS

Islamicate History of Religions was globally unsurpassed in all of premodern intellectual endeavor in the breadth and relative sophistication of its studies of other religions. To see this complex literature "steadily, and see it whole," however, we cannot disengage our analysis from its contexts of polemic, apologetic, and jurisprudence. Nor should we evade its overarching context in the general political domination of Islamicate civilization over the other religions it so admirably studied. Indeed, even Šahrastānī inevitably had a *Tendenz.* Perhaps most importantly, nonetheless, we must also read it in terms of its sectarian shaping and philosophical framing. I thus would concur with the assessment of Daniel Gimaret: "Il y a aussi, chez Šahrastānī, c'est vrai, une hauteur de vue, un esprit de synthèse... En réalité, Šahrastānī est éminément un philosophe, un théoreticien, beaucoup plus qu'un historien. La stricte relation des faits l'interesse beaucoup moins que leur interpretation et leur mise en système."[92] *Milal* is neither a grab-bag of esoteric tidbits, nor a flatly polemic distortion of the religions of others,[93] but a staggeringly learned and philosophically subtle contribution to the History of Religions. Šahrastānī's *Kitāb al-Milal wa-l-Nihal* has yet to be properly utilized by working historians, and indeed to be studied in its own right — as the first masterpiece of the comparative study of world religions.

[92] *Annuaire, EPHE,* vol. 87 (1978–1979): 265.

[93] A.J. Arberry disparaged it as a "farrago of quotations from older writers, loosely arranged and inconsequently strung together without the slightest acknowledgement," as cited in *KF,* p. 4. Baron, on the other hand, is quite correct to stress that "these stray tidbits do not yet allow for any far-reaching hypotheses concerning the underground links, if any, between the ancient [sic] Magharians or Qumran sectarians and their medieval successors." (*op. cit.*, p. 378, n. 50).

APPENDIX

ŠAHRASTĀNĪ ON THE MAĠĀRIYYA: TRANSLATION OF AND COMMENTARY ON *MILAL*, PP. 509–513

[509] "The Yūḏġāniyya and the Maġāriyya"
The Yūḏġāniyya were named for Yūḏġān of Hamadan; it is said that his name was Yehuda.[94] He used to urge austerity and many prayers. He forbade the consumption of flesh and alcoholic liquors. Among the things said about him was that he exalted the *Dāʿi*.[95] He used to claim that the Torah had an extrinsic [*ẓāhir*] and an intrinsic [*bāṭin*] meaning, and a revealed textual form [*tanzīl*] and an interpretation of that form [*taʾwīl*],[96] but he opposed them in the matter of anthropomorphism, and inclined toward the doctrine of predestination [*qadar*], asserting that act is a reality for man, but that reward and punishment are predestined for him; and he went to extremes to emphasize this.

[510] Among them were the Mūškāniyya, followers of Mūškān.[97] He was of the sect of Yūḏġān except that he used to insist on their going out to fight their opponents. Indeed, he ordained that they should be fought. So

[94] Inasmuch as the present study is devoted to the Maġāriyya, I shall refrain from a review of the scholarship on Yūḏġān and Mūškān, except as it pertains to the Maġāriyya. Yūḏġān is unlikely to be identified with the "Yehudah ha-Parsi" mentioned by Abraham ibn Ezra and Elijah Bashyatchi. See Baron, *op. cit.*, p. 379, n. 54.

[95] Gimaret and Monnot read this as *Rāʿi*, i.e., the "Shepherd" mentioned in the preceding section on Abū ʿĪsā al-Iṣfahānī. However, given the equal emphasis on the function of the *Dāʿi* in that same section, and given, as well, the Shīʿite coloration of the whole, I am inclined to the latter reading. It may not be irrelevant to note that Nāṣir al-Dīn Ṭūsī considered Šahrastānī himself to be the *dāʿī al-Duʿāt*. See Madelung, "Nāṣir ad-Dīn Ṭūsī's Ethics Between Philosophy, Shīʿism and Sufism," p. 95.

[96] These are the typical characteristics of Šīʿī exegesis.

[97] Another report on this sect is found in Baġdādī. A "Sʾdkh" is mentioned by the Ismāʿīlī Abū Ḥātim al-Rāzī. See S.M. Stern, *Studies in Early Ismailism* (Magnes and Brill: Jerusalem and Leiden, 1983) p. 41.

they went out, nineteen strong,[98] and were killed on the outskirts of Qum. It is recounted about a group of the Mūškāniyya that they affirmed the prophethood of Muḥammad for the Arabs and for all the rest of mankind except for the Jews, for they are [already] the people of a recognized religious community and a Book.

One sect of the Maġāriyya [text has *Maqāriba*][99] claims that God spoke to the prophets through the agency of an Angel[100] whom he had chosen and whom He had placed in precedence over all created beings and had made vicegerent [*ḫalīfa*] over them.[101] They say: "Everything, in the Torah and the rest of the books[102] *[511]* describing God refers to this Angel, for otherwise it would not be possible to describe God."[103] They say: "The one who spoke to Moses is that Angel, and the Tree [*šağara*] mentioned in the Torah is that Angel.[104] The Lord is too exalted to speak to mankind in

[98] Cf. Q 74:30, "Over them are nineteen." For useful comments on this number in this passage, see Israel Friedlaender, "Jewish-Arabic Studies," *JQR* II (1912–1913), p. 289. See, more generally, Franz Rosenthal, "Nineteen," *Analecta Biblica* 12 (1959): 304–18, and Kurt Rudolph, "Die Anfänge Muhammad," p. 313. The numerology of nineteen was used by the Judeo-Ismāʿīlī Netanael al-Fayyūmī, contemporary of Šahrastānī — in a commentary on the Šahāda! See Pines, "Nathanaël ben al-Fayyûmî et la théologie ismaëlienne," *Revue de l'histoire juive en Égypte* 1 (1947): pp. 5–22, at p. 19, n. 1. See also Ronald Kiener, "Jewish Ismaʿilism in Twelfth Century Yemen: R. Nethanel ben al-Fayyumi," *JQR* LXXIV (1984): 249–66, at p. 261.

The symbolical shaping of this report suggests that, like the report on the ʿĪsāwiyya, it may have been at least in part generated by criteria other than those of strict verisimilitude. I have demonstrated the close resemblance of the reports on ʿĪsāwiyya to that of a *ġulāt* group, the Manṣūriyya, in *Between Muslim and Jew*, pp. 82–84.

[99] For a useful review of the variations in names see Fossum, "The Magharians." Note that while Šahrastānī explicitly states that Mūškān was of the Yūḏġāniyya, he does not say that the Maġāriyya were part of the Yūḏġāniyya *per se*.

[100] For the literature on Jewish belief in an angelic chief agent, see my *Between Muslim and Jew*, pp. 167–206.

[101] In Q 2:30, God says to the angels, "I am setting up a *ḫalīfa* over you." The ensuing cosmogonic conflict between man and angels provides the backdrop for the third Introduction to *Milal*, an extended allegorical dialogue between Iblis and the angels. See *Milal*, pp. 12–17.

[102] Unclear whether this means other *intra*-Biblical or *extra*-Biblical books.

[103] To this should be compared the statement in *Sefer ha-Bahir*, "Every term of Creation spoken about [in Scripture] takes place through him" [*Bahir* (Margoliot) clxxx; Scholem, *On the Mystical Shape of the Godhead*, p. 96].

[104] In Quran, Sūrat al-Qaṣaṣ, (28:30), God speaks to Moses *min al-šağara* (lit. "from the tree"). The present passage might be taken to confirm the theory of Philonic influence, inasmuch as Philo argued that it was an Angel who spoke in the Burning Bush. See *De Vita Mosis*, I, 66 [=*Life of Moses*], ed. Colson (Cambridge Mass.: Harvard University Press, 1950). I found this reference in Massimo Cacciari, *The Necessary Angel*, transl. Miguel E. Vatter (Albany NY: SUNY Press, 1994) p. 97, n. 13. The fullest theory of Philonic influence on the Maġāriyya was laid out by Poznanski in "Philon." Alexander Altmann subsequently

speech. Everything mentioned in the Torah is referred to in such terms as "seeking to see [God] (*ru'yā*)"[105]; "I spoke to God"; "God came"; "He wrote the Torah with his own hand";[106] "God ascended into the clouds"; "He settled down on the throne firmly";[107] "he has the form[108] of Adam" (*wa-lahu ṣūrat Ādam*);[109] "curly hair and black curls [below the ears]";[110]

went so far as to assert that the Maġāriyya's dependence on Philo was of "no doubt" (in his entry on "Angelology" in the *Encyclopedia Judaica*). For more on a possible Philonic connection see Fossum, "The Magharians," pp. 318–20.

Of greater relevance, with much closer temporal and intellectual proximity, is Judah ben Nissim ibn Malka's philosophical exegesis of the Burning Bush (Ex. 3:2): the Angel in the Bush is the rational soul who speaks to Moses. See Vajda, *Judah ben Nissim ibn Malka*, p. 46, n. 1.

See more generally, Josef van Ess, "The Youthful God: Anthropomorphism in Early Islam," (*Ninth Annual University Lecture in Religion at Arizona State University*, March 3, 1988), p. 4. Idel lists other Jewish sources for the revelation of the Bush being Metatron: "Enoch is Metatron," *The New Testament and Christian-Jewish Dialogue: Studies in Honor of David Flusser*, edited by Malcolm Lowe [= *Immanuel* 24/25, 1990, originally in Hebrew in Joseph Dan, (ed.) *Early Jewish Mysticism* (Jerusalem 1987) pp. 151–70)] pp. 218–40, at p. 232.

[105] See Gösta Vitesam, "At-Tabari and the Seeing of God," *The Arabist. Budapest Studies in Arabic 13–14 (1995) [= Proceedings of the 14th Congress of the Union Européenne des Arabisants et Islamisants, Part 1 (Budapest, 19th August – 3rd September 1988)]*: 147–55.

[106] This exact phrase earlier in *Milal* is placed by Šahrastānī into the mouth of Muḥammad! He cites this *ḥadīṯ* in *Milal*, p. 178. For a general review of the Jewish sources, see Meir Bar-Ilan, "The Hand of God. A Chapter in Rabbinic Anthropomorphism," *RASHI* pp. 321–35. With reference to *Bahir*, "He hewed out the letters of the Torah, and engraved them in the Spirit, and made his *forms* in it," see Idel's extended discussion of "Forms" in *Kabbalah*: *New Perspectives*, (New Haven 1988) Chapter 6.

[107] *Istiwā'*, one of the most important technical terms for understanding Šahrastānī's report. It is discussed at crucial points throughout *Milal*, and a cross-referenced analysis of its usages is in order (see *LRS* vol. I. s.v. *istawā, istiwā'*). For now, it is necessary to note that, in his conclusion of his report on the Jews, Šahrastānī claims that "The Jews are unanimous in saying that God, when he had finished creating the heavens and the earth, set Himself down on His Throne, leaning back, with one leg under the other." [*Milal*, p. 519]. Van Ess comments on this passage in "The Youthful God," p. 19, n. 97.

[108] *"form" (ṣūra)* — Stroumsa (p. 51, n. 42; and "Forms(s)" 272, n. 14), recognizes that *Bahir* is relevant to this aspect of the Maġārian teachings. See also van Ess 17 n. 71; and Idel *in extenso*; note that Metatron becomes identified as the *wāhib al-ṣuwar, dator formarum*. See Vajda, "Pour le Dossier de Metatron" 345, from Aaron ben Elijah, (written ca. 1353).

[109] On the tradition linking Adam and Metatron, see especially Idel, "Enoch is Metatron" (who notes the Maġārian connection on p. 232 n. 45, but only in connection with the revelation of Metatron to Moses, not with reference to Adam); Mopsik, notes to *3Enoch*, 209–10. On Adam in this context, see also Alfred Ivry, "Ismā'īlī Theology and Maimonides' Philosophy," in *The Jews of Medieval Islam. Community, Society & Identity*, edited by Daniel Frank (Leiden 1995) pp. 271–301, at 286–87.

[110] The echoes here of *Daniel*, *Song of Songs*, and *Ši'ur Qomah* are also found in other Muslim heresiographies, which characterize Judaism in terms of an anthropomorphism using such imagery. They are discussed by Josef van Ess, "The Youthful God."

"He wept over the Flood of Noah, until His eyes were sore";[111] "The mighty One [*al-Ǧabbār*] laughed until He showed His teeth"[112]; etc., is attributed [according to the doctrine of this sectarian] to that Angel.

It is possible, in the normal course of events, that he should send an Angel spiritual to the point of having all his attributes, *[512]* and should confer his name upon him[113] saying "This is My messenger [*rasūl*],[114] and his position [*makān*] is as Mine among you,[115] and his utterance [*qawl*] is My utterance, his command [*amr*] is My command, and his manifestation [*ẓuhūr*] before you is My manifestation. Thus is the condition of that Angel."

It is said that inasmuch as Arius said that the Messiah is God, and that he is the choicest [being] in the world (*ṣafwat al-ʿālam*),[116] he [Arius] took his doctrine from them [the Maġāriyya], who preceded Arius by 400 years.[117] They were men of abstinence and [even] mortification.[118]

It is said that an author (*ṣāḥib*) of this doctrine (*maqāla*) was Benjamin al-Nehawandi, who established this school (*maḏhab*) among them[119] and taught them that the ambiguous verses [*mutašābihāt*] in the Torah were interpretable; and that God cannot be described by the descriptions applicable to man; and that He does not resemble anything created; nor

[111] Šahrastānī evokes the same "quotation" in a discussion of the heresy of *tašbīh* [assimilationism]; see *Milal* p. 176. For the weeping of God, see Peter Kuhn, *Gottes Trauer und Klage in der rabbinischen Überlieferung (Talmud und Midrasch)* (Leiden: Brill, 1978).

[112] For *al-Ǧabbar* as the name of God, see Q 53:23.

[113] Ex. 23:21. G. Stroumsa, followed by Fossum, recognized the significance of this phrase for the history of Jewish esoteric traditions. References to the Name of God being carried by the theophoric Angel are found in Fossum, *The Name of God and the Angel of the Lord*, and in Wolfgang Fauth, "Tatrosjah-Totrosjah und Metatron in der jüdischen Merkabah-Mystik," *JSJ* 22 (1991): 80–87, at pp. 80–81.

[114] Some significant background to such a usage of *rasūl* is provided by Geo Widengren, *Muhammad, the Prophet of God, and his Ascension* (Uppsala 1955), esp. Chapter 1, pp. 7–54. In some cases (e.g., pp. 21–22), the *rasūl* is explicitly an angel.

[115] In *Bahir*, as a gloss on Ezekiel 3:12, "Blessed is God's Glory from His place" (S 132).

[116] Gimaret and Monnot reject the reading of this difficult phrase offered by Harry Wolfson: "That he is God in the sense that he is the elect of the world." (*LRS* vol. I, p. 608, n. 75). Widengren, *Muhammad the Prophet*, gives examples in which the notion of the "elect" is coupled with that of the *rasūl*.

[117] This passage is discussed in Rudolf Lorenz, *Arius judaizans? Untersuchungen zur dogmengeschichtlichen Einordnung des Arius* (Vandenhoek & Ruprecht: Göttingen 1980) pp. 174–76. See my discussion above.

[118] Since only the Maġāriyya are mentioned in the plural in the preceding sentence, it seems clear that this sentence refers to them, and not to Arius.

[119] "Them" may refer to the Jews in general, who comprise the subject of this section as a whole. If Benjamin — whose (rough) date was known to Šahrastānī — established this school among the Maġāriyya, then how could they have lived "400 years before Arius"? I prefer the reading which sees an error in the report on the Arians.

does any thing in them resemble Him; and that the referent of the aforementioned passages occurring in the Torah was that Angel honored [by God].[120]

[513] This is as in the Quran where the coming of God is reported as being that of one of the angels. Thus, again, as the Word of God on the subject of Mary: "We have breathed Our Spirit into her" (21:91). And, in another passage: "We have breathed into her with our Spirit." (66:12). The one who does the breathing here is Gabriel (Peace be Upon Him) when he appeared to [Mary] "in the form of a man in all respects" (19:17) to give her "a holy son" (19:19).

[120] Virtually all historians interested in identifying the Maġāriyya with the Essenes, Gnostics, and the like, leave off the translation at this point. What becomes clear by studying the section as a whole, however, is that Šahrastānī concluded his treatment of the Maġāriyya by appending comparisons to three positive parallels, found, respectively, within Christianity, Judaism, and Islam. Only read thus, I believe, do some remarkable implications begin to emerge.

CHRISTIAN SUCCESS AND MUSLIM FEAR IN ANDALUSĪ WRITINGS DURING THE ALMORAVID AND ALMOHAD PERIODS*

MARIBEL FIERRO

1. CHRISTIANS AND MUSLIMS DURING THE ALMORAVID AND ALMOHAD PERIODS

The year 519/1125 was decisive for the situation of Christian communities in al-Andalus. It was then that the king of Aragon Alfonso I "el Batallador" reached Granada with his army. The military campaign was unsuccessful, and its failure caused the emigration towards the North of the Mozarabs who had joined the king.[1] Emigration was an old phenomenon which greatly contributed to the reduction of Christian communities in al-Andalus. Another consequence of the expedition of Alfonso I el Batallador was the eventual expulsion of part of the Mozarabic population which did not emigrate, on the grounds that they had broken the pact of the *ḏimma* by their support for an external enemy. The deportation took place in 520/1126 and it was backed by *fatāwā* of the jurists consulted by the Almoravid *amīr*.[2] But this did not mean the total disappearance of the Mozarabs of Granada, of whom mention continues to be made in the

* I wish to thank Prof. D. Wasserstein for his comments and corrections.

1 See V. Lagardère, Communautés mozarabes et pouvoir almoravide en 519h/1125 en al-Andalus, *Studia Islamica* 67 (1988), pp. 99–119, and especially D. Serrano, Dos fetuas sobre la expulsión de mozárabes al Magreb en 1126, *Anaquel de Estudios Árabes* 2 (1991), pp. 162–82, with a discussion of the extant interpretations of the reasons for the expedition. I use the term "Mozarabs" in the general sense of "arabized Christians" both inside and outside al-Andalus.

2 The most famous *fatwā* is the one given by the judge of Cordoba, Ibn Rušd al-Ǧadd (d. 520/1126), on which the above-mentioned articles by Lagardère and Serrano can be consulted, as well as the article by R. Oswald, Spanien unter den Almoraviden. Die *Fatāwā* des Ibn Rušd als Quellen zur Wirtschafts- und Sozialgeschichte, *Die Welt des Orients* XXIV (1993), pp. 129–31 (includes data about other *fatāwā* dealing with Jews and Christians). The *fatwā* by Ibn Ward (d. 540/1145) is being studied by D. Powers.

sources.[3] A second deportation took place in 533/1138. These deportees, settled in Moroccan towns such as Miknāsa, Salé, Fez or Marrakech, were allowed to build a church in the last town.[4] Some of them joined the Christian militia of the Almoravids in Morocco. The expulsion decrees led other Mozarabs to apostatize for fear of losing their properties in al-Andalus and having to abandon their land.[5] The Christian communities of al-Andalus, therefore, suffered a dramatic decrease in their number through emigration, deportation and conversion.[6] On the other hand, there was also an increase of a special group of Christians living in the *dār al-islām*, the mercenaries.[7]

Almoravid policy against Christian *ḏimmīs* should not be seen as the result of the fanaticism and intolerance that are usually attributed to the Berber dynasty. Among the different stages proposed by Bulliet regarding the relationships between Muslims and Christian *ḏimmīs*, the stage under the Almoravids would correspond to the fourth: "Muslim rule challenged by external non-Muslim force. Muslim rulers fluctuate between utilizing Christians pragmatically and scapegoating them. Muslim thinkers act as in State 2 [Muslim thinkers enunciate a broad spectrum of doctrinal views reflecting responses to convert pressures and the corollary desire to encourage conversion], except when involved in scapegoating. Christians vacillate between conservative desire to maintain accommodation with Muslims in political and social life, and adventurous inclination to risk making common cause with impinging force. Splits in Christian community".[8] For his part, Urvoy considers that the Almoravids would

[3] See P. Guichard, *Les musulmans de Valence et la Reconquête (XIe–XIIIe siècles)*, 2 vols., Damascus 1990–1991, I, 90.

[4] See V. Lagardère, *Histoire et société en Occident musulman au Moyen Age. Analyse du "Miʿyār" d'al-Wanšarīsī*, Madrid 1995, p. 39, no. 131 and p. 66, no. 251. See on the church of Marrakech P. de Cenival, L'église chrétienne de Marrakech au XIIIe siècle, *Hespéris* 7 (1927), pp. 69–83; A. Huici Miranda, *Historia política del imperio almohade*, 2 vols., Tetuán, 1956–7, II, 479, 485, 496, 524; R. Le Tourneau, *The Almohad movement in North Africa in the twelfth and thirteenth centuries*, Princeton 1969, p. 94. On the intellectual activity of the deported Christians, see P. Sj. van Koningsveld, Christian-Arabic manuscripts from the Iberian Peninsula and North Africa: a historical interpretation, *Al-Qanṭara* XV (1994), p. 427.

[5] See Serrano, "Dos fetuas", pp. 174, 180–82.

[6] For an attempt at quantifying this process, see B. Reilly, *The Contest of Christian and Muslim Spain, 1031–1157*, Oxford 1992, pp. 17–21, quoting R.W. Bulliet, *Conversion to Islam in the Medieval Period*, Cambridge 1979.

[7] See Huici, *Historia*, I, 141, and the classical study by J. Alemany, Milicias cristianas al servicio de los sultanes del Al-Magreb, *Homenaje a F. Codera*, Zaragoza 1904, pp. 133–69.

[8] See R.W. Bulliet, Process and Status in Conversion and Continuity, in M. Gervers and R.J. Bikhazi (ed.), *Indigenous Christian Communities in Islamic Lands eighth to eighteenth Centuries*, Toronto 1990, pp. 1–12, p. 8.

have generalized what until then was only sporadic intolerance, by allowing the religious scholars to determine the policy to be followed against the *ḏimmīs*.[9] But J.-P. Molénat has pointed out that the Christians who were deported had chosen not to follow Alfonso I el Batallador out of al-Andalus, indicating that they must have thought it was possible for them to continue living under Muslim rule. At the same time, the fact that the Almoravid *amīr* consulted the jurists proves that he considered himself bound by the *ḏimma* pact.[10] There is no evidence that the Christians were denied the protection they were entitled to as *ḏimmīs*.[11] Even the harsh measures proposed by Ibn ʿAbdūn (fl. between the 5th/11th–6th/12th century) in his *Risāla fī l-qaḍāʾ wa-l-ḥisba* were in agreement with the teachings of Islamic religious law on *ḏimmīs*, as those measures are connected with the maintenance of their condition of humiliation and subservience (*ṣiġār*) or tolerated discrimination: the prohibition of Muslims acting as servants of Jews and Christians; that Muslim women should not enter Christian churches, because of the low morality of the priests; that Christians and Jews should dress in a way that will make it easy to recognize them; that no bells should be rung in Muslim lands; that Muslim books should not be sold to Jews and Christians, because the latter would translate them and attribute them to Jewish and Christian authors; and that Jewish and Christian doctors should not be permitted to have dealings with Muslims.[12] The prohibition on selling to Christians products which could be used against Muslims must have been discussed in al-Andalus as it was in Sicily.[13]

[9] See D. Urvoy, *Pensers d'al-Andalus. La vie intellectuelle à Cordoue et Seville au temps des Empires Berbères (fin XIe siècle — début XIIIe siècle)*, Toulouse 1990, p. 17; idem, Les aspects symboliques du vocable 'mozarabe'. Essai de réinterprétation, *Studia Islamica* LXXVIII (1993), pp. 117–53, pp. 146–47.

[10] See J.P. Molénat, Point de vue sur la permanence et l'extinction de la minorité chrétienne dans l'Occident musulman médiéval, *Colloque International "Les minorités ethniques et religieuses dans le monde arabo-musulman" (Rabat, 28–30 novembre 1995)*, forthcoming, where an extensive survey of previous literature on the subject can be found.

[11] See the *fatāwā* given on their behalf in Lagardère, *Histoire et société*, pp. 65, no. 250, 357, no. 286, as well as pp. 274, no. 224, 365–66, no. 321 (Ibn Ward's *fatwā*), 418, no. 196.

[12] See Ibn ʿAbdūn, *Risāla fī l-qaḍāʾ wa-l-ḥisba*, transl. E. García Gómez and E. Lévi-Provençal, *Sevilla a comienzos del siglo XII. El tratado de Ibn ʿAbdūn*, Madrid 1948; repr. Sevilla 1981, pp. 149–51, 152, 154–55, 157, 168, 172–73 and G. Vajda, A propos de la situation des juifs et des chrétiens à Séville au début du XIIe siècle, *R.E.J.* XCIX (1935), pp. 127–29. The rejection of the services of Jewish and Christian doctors is illustrated in a story regarding the Sufi Abū Yaʿzā, who used to cure women by touching their breasts and bellies, and this was considered reprehensible, until the Sufi Abū Madyan remarked that those who censured it would allow the women to be touched by non-Muslim doctors: Ibn al-Zayyāt al-Tādilī, *op. cit.* in note 99, pp. 231–32.

[13] See Lagardère, *Histoire et société*, p. 194, no. 370 (*fatwā* by the Sicilian al-Māzarī). The

As regards the Almohad period, during the conquest of Sevilla in 541/1147, Christians and Jews were killed, but they were not the only victims.[14] In 566/1170 another deportation of Christians to Morocco took place.[15] The Almohads are generally considered to have put an end finally to the presence of indigenous Christians in al-Andalus through deportations, massacres and forced conversions, so that by the beginning of the 7th/13th century almost all Christians were either captives, merchants or mercenaries. This policy would not have been due only to internal problems,[16] but would have also been influenced by doctrine, as some scholars state that ʿAbd al-Muʾmin (r. 527/1133–558/1163), the first Almohad caliph, forbade the existence of any other religion in the territory under his command, thus abolishing the *ḏimma* status.[17] But as Molénat has recently shown, the texts on which this statement is based are not without difficulties.[18] In any case, from the middle of the 6th/12th century, the survival of Christian communities in al-Andalus and North Africa is only hypothetical. It can be added to the evidence adduced by Molénat that the famous poet Ibn Quzmān (d. 554/1159, thus living in the Almoravid period) mentions Christians in his *Dīwān* only as dangerous soldiers from outside al-Andalus, and he is silent about Christians living in al-Andalus.[19] Ibn Quzmān does mention Jews, who appear as neighbours with whom one deals in daily life.[20] M. Talbi[21] has rightly pointed out that

discussion is well documented in the Naṣrid period: see J. López Ortiz, Fatwas granadinas de los siglos XIV y XV, *Al-Andalus* VI (1941), p. 93.

14 See Molénat, *art. cit.* in note 10.

15 See F.J. Simonet, *Historia de los mozárabes de España*, Madrid 1897–1903 (repr. Amsterdam 1967), pp. 750–55, 770. See also ʿU. Kuḥayla, *Taʾrīḫ al-naṣārā fī l-Andalus*, Cairo 1993.

16 See Urvoy, Les aspects symboliques, pp. 148–49 on the rarity of Mozarab alliances with the Northern Christian kingdoms, and Molénat, *art. cit.* in note 14, on the rarity of Mozarab alliances with rebels against the Almohads.

17 See L. Torres Balbás, Mozarabías y juderías de las ciudades hispanomusulmanas, *Al-Andalus* XIX (1954), p. 175; Huici, *Historia*, I, 188; J.F.P. Hopkins, *Medieval Muslim Government in Barbary Until the Sixth Century of the Hijra*, London 1958, pp. 60–62, 69–70.

18 See *art. cit.* in note 10. Those texts refer more specifically to the Jews.

19 See F. Corriente, Judíos y cristianos en el Dīwān de Ibn Quzman, contemporáneo de Abraham ibn Ezra, *Abraham ibn Ezra y su tiempo = Abraham ibn Ezra and his age. Actas del Simposio Internacional = Proceedings of the International Symposium (Madrid, Tudela, Toledo, 1989)*, Madrid 1989, pp. 73–77.

20 Ibn ʿAbdūn's recommendation of avoiding Jewish doctors was clearly not followed: the Jew Abū Yūsuf Ibn al-Muʿallim was the doctor of ʿAlī b. Yūsuf b. Tāšufīn.

21 See M. Talbi, Le Christianisme maghrébin de la conquête musulmane à sa disparition: une tentative d'explication, in M. Gervers and R.J. Bikhazi (eds.), *Indigenous Christian Communities*, pp. 313–51, especially p. 328. Talbi (pp. 339–46) dates the disappearance of

the disappearance of Christians was not accompanied by that of the Jews, meaning that the reasons which led to the former state must have been more complex than the alleged Almohad fanaticism. For Talbi, Christians from both inside and outside bore their share of responsibility, the former for having been unable to find the intellectual resources necessary for survival and the latter for not having inspired any revival of local Christianity. In any case, Molénat demonstrates that there is no evidence of any Almohad text dealing with and justifying the suppression of the *ḏimma* status, such as we have for later periods,[22] and that if such action took place, it was later considered something reprehensible that had to be silenced. To what extent do we have here a situation similar to the one later produced in Christian territory with the conversion of the *mudéjares*: when a part of the Muslim population living under Christian rule converted to Christianity, the contact that they might continue to have with Muslims, especially relatives, could endanger their new faith, this being one of the reasons that led to a policy of either conversion of all Muslims or their expulsion?[23] The protection of the faith of recent Christian converts to Islam could have been behind the harsher treatment of Christians who clung to their beliefs.

The increasing Muslim territorial losses to the Christians advancing from the North added to the internal factors in bringing about the developments just sketched. Guichard has explored the various reasons for Muslim military weakness, culminating in the first half of the 7th/13th centuries with the Christian conquest of the major towns in the East and the South, with the exception of Granada.[24] Muslim confidence had received a major blow by the capture of Barbastro in 456/1064.[25] Even if Barbastro was reconquered shortly after, Toledo was lost forever in 478/1085. As the Mozarab Sisnando confided to ʿAbd Allāh b. Buluggīn (r. 465/1073–483/1090): "Al-Andalus originally belonged to the Christians. Then they were defeated by the Arabs and driven to the most

Christian communities later than Molénat, but the texts he adduces could refer to Christian foreigners.

22 See S. Ward, A fragment from an unknown work by al-Ṭabarī on the tradition 'Expel the Jews and Christians from the Arabian Peninsula (and the lands of Islam)', *BSOAS* LIII (1990), pp. 407–20, and J.O. Hunwick, The rights of *ḏimmīs* to maintain a place of worship: a 15th century *fatwā* from Tlemcen, *Al-Qanṭara* XII (1991), pp. 133–55.

23 See M.D. Meyerson, *The Muslims of Valencia in the Age of Fernando and Isabel. Between Coexistence and Crusade*, Berkeley/Los Angeles 1991, p. 56.

24 See Guichard, *Les Musulmans de Valence*, I, 92–100 and II, 393–419. See also Reilly's study mentioned in note 6.

25 See an analysis of the literary treatment of this disaster in M. Marín, Crusaders in the Muslim West: the view of the Arab writers, *The Maghreb Review* 17 (1992), pp. 95–102.

inhospitable region, [Ǧillīqiya]. Now that they are strong and capable, the Christians desire to recover what they have lost by force. This can only be achieved by weakness and encroachment. In the long run, when it has neither men nor money, we'll be able to recover it without any difficulty."[26] At the time, most Taifa rulers believed that there was nothing Muslims could do to stop the advance of the Christians, but they were also confident that, when everything seemed to be lost, "God will bring salvation and support to the Muslims."[27]

During the 6th/12th century, the Christian advance was more or less successfully halted by the new North African dynasties, the Almoravids and Almohads. But if Christian incursions were slowed, the disintegration of al-Andalus continued. Valencia was in Christian hands from 487/1094 to 495/1102 and was lost again in 636/1238; Zaragoza was taken in 512/1118, Lisbon in 542/1147, Tortosa in 543/1148, Silves in 586/1190, Ubeda in 609/1212, Cordoba in 633/1236, Murcia in 640/1243, and Sevilla in 646/1248. The Muslim inhabitants of those cities must have felt then the same despair that had been described by the *qāḍī* of Zaragoza before the Christian conquest, urging the Almoravids to put an end to their passivity. His warning that Zaragoza acted as a "retaining wall" which, once broken, would lead to the destruction of the rest, came sadly true.[28] The biographical dictionary of Andalusī scholars written by Ibn al-Abbār (d. 658/1260) can be read as a chronicle of the loss of al-Andalus, as it reflects the emigration of *ʿulamāʾ* from the conquered towns.[29] With few exceptions, Muslim authors show in their writings the acceptance of the inevitability of a process for which no solution was conceived, except intervention from outside. It seemed as though the loss of al-Andalus foretold in Prophetic traditions was to become reality. Some of those prophecies had been circulating since the 2nd/8th century and can be found in the eschatological literature produced in the 6th/12th–7th/13th centuries, such as Ibn al-Ḫarrāṭ's (d. 581/1185) *Kitāb al-ʿāqiba* and al-

[26] ʿAbd Allāh b. Buluggīn al-Zīrī, *The Tibyān Memoirs of ʿAbd Allāh b. Buluggīn, Last Zīrid Amīr of Granada*, transl. A.T. Tibi, Leiden 1986, p. 90. Cf. M. Perlmann, Notes on anti-Christian propaganda in the Mamlūk empire, *BSOAS* 10 (1939–1942), pp. 843–61, where mention is made of a discussion on whether Egypt belongs to the Copts who were its former inhabitants.

[27] ʿAbd Allāh b. Buluggīn al-Zīrī, *Tibyān*, p. 90; G. Martínez-Gros, *L'idéologie omeyyade. La construction de la légitimité du Califat de Cordoue (Xe–XIe siècles)*, Madrid 1992, p. 283.

[28] See M.J. Viguera, *Aragón musulmán*, 2nd ed., Zaragoza 1988, pp. 229–30.

[29] See M. Fierro, "Obras y transmisiones de *ḥadīṯ* (ss. V/XVI–VII/XIII) en la *Takmila* de Ibn al-Abbār", in *Ibn al-Abbār. Potític; escriptor àrab valencià (1199–1260)*, Valencia 1990, p. 209; M. Marín, Des migrations forcées: les savants d'al-Andalus face à la conquête chrétienne, *La Mediterranée occidentale au Moyen Age*, ed. M. Hammam, Rabat 1995, pp. 43–59.

Qurṭubī's (d. 671/1272) *al-Taḏkira fī aḥwāl al-mawtā wa-ʿulūm al-āḫira.*[30] History was fulfilling the belief that al-Andalus had been doomed from the beginning. Nuʿaym b. Ḥammād (d. 228/843) had recorded in his *Kitāb al-fitan* a tradition describing how the inhabitants of al-Andalus would be forced to leave their land, unable to stop the Christians, and how God would then open the sea to allow them to cross the straits and take refuge in North Africa.[31] From the 7th/13th century onwards, the story was often related of how the caliph ʿUmar b. ʿAbd al-ʿAzīz (d. 101/720) had tried to force Muslims to leave the "island" (*ǧazīra*) of al-Andalus, because it was too far from the rest of the *dār al-islām* and because of its isolation, surrounded as it was by sea and by Christians (*rūm*).[32]

2. MUSLIM PERCEPTIONS OF CHRISTIANS DURING THE 12TH–13TH CENTURIES IN AL-ANDALUS

The image of Christians in chronicles and related writings during the Umayyad and Taifa periods has been dealt with in a number of studies.[33] They show how often more attention was paid to the "Arab" ethnic identity of Andalusīs, as opposed to Berber, than to their religious identity as Muslims, as opposed to Christians. Moreover, they also demonstrate how the image of Christians varied according to whether they were *ḏimmī*s or Christians from the Iberian kingdoms, or Christians from kingdoms outside the Peninsula. We lack similar comprehensive studies

[30] See M. Fierro, Mahdisme et eschatologie dans al-Andalus, in A. Kaddouri (ed.), *Mahdisme. Crise et changement dans l'histoire du Maroc. Actes de la table ronde organisée à Marrakech par la Faculté des Lettres et des Sciences Humaines de Rabat du 11 au 14 février 1993*, Rabat 1994, pp. 47–69.

[31] See M. I. Fierro and S. Faghia, Un nuevo texto de tradiciones escatológicas sobre al-Andalus, *Sharq al-Andalus* VII (1990) pp. 99–111, no. 116. This tradition was later recorded by Andalusī authors such as Abū ʿAmr al-Dānī (d. 444/1053) and Ibn al-Faḫḫār (d. 723/1323).

[32] See on this al-Wanšarīsī *al-Miʿyār al-muʿrib*, 13 vols., Rabat 1401/1981, II, 140–41, as well as the *fatwā* by Ibn al-Rabīʿ concerning Muslims living under Christian rule: see note 65.

[33] See M. ʿA. Makki, La España cristiana en el *Dīwān* de Ibn Darrāŷ, *Boletín de la Real Academia de Buenas Letras de Barcelona* 30 (1963–1964), pp. 63–104; R. Barkai, *Cristianos y musulmanes en la España medieval (El enemigo en el espejo)*, Madrid 1984, 2nd ed., Madrid 1990; A. al-Azmeh, "Mortal enemies, invisible neighbours: Northerners in Andalusī eyes", in S.Kh. Jayyusi (ed.), *The Legacy of Muslim Spain*, Leiden 1992, pp. 259–72; B. Münzel, *Feinde, Nachbarn, Bündnispartner. Themen und Formen der Darstellung christlich-muslimischer Begegnungen in ausgewählten historiographischen Quellen des islamischen Spanien*, Münster 1994. See also R.M. Speight, "Muslim attitudes toward Christians in the Maghrib during the Fatimid period", in Y.Y. Haddad and W.Z. Haddad (eds.), *Christian-Muslim encounters*, Gainesville, Fl., 1995, pp. 180–92.

for the Almoravid and Almohad periods. Among the few available, we have seen how Ibn Quzmān's *Dīwān* reflects the disappearance of Christians as *ahl al-ḏimma*, showing them only as *ahl al-kitāb* and as outsiders living in the *dār al-ḥarb* and therefore as enemies, with whom one fights or concludes treaties. The Christians of the North are dangerous external enemies, hated and despised, but also feared. Those Muslims able with God's help to defeat the Christians are to be praised. We are witnessing here the end of the "convivencia" in al-Andalus,[34] and the identification of Christians as constant aggressors towards whom the normal feelings are fear and hatred. Historical writings such as Ibn Ṣāḥib al-Ṣalāt's (d. after 594/1198) *al-Mann bi-l-imāma*, ʿAbd al-Wāḥid al-Marrākušī's (d. after 621/1224) *al-Muʿǧib* and Ibn al-Qaṭṭān's (7th/13th century)'s *Naẓm al-ǧumān*, as well as Ibn ʿIḏārī's (7th/13th century) *al-Bayān al-muġrib*, offer many examples of Christians portrayed almost exclusively as enemies who stimulate feelings of hostility, suspicion and disapproval.

Christians also played an important role in the internal struggles among Muslims, as their alliance was sought by the contending parties. Thus in the chronicles, reflecting the view of central authority, a customary way of attacking Muslim rebels was to point to their alliance with Christians. This is especially so in the case of Ibn Mardanīš.[35] Alliances with the Christians, however, were so widespread among contending Muslim parties that their scandalous nature was usually remembered only in the context of propaganda and ideological struggle. When the murder of the Sufi rebel Ibn Qasī by his followers is explained in the sources as a punishment for his alliance with the Portuguese,[36] it might just be Almohad propaganda or a way of indicating that the alliance was seen as having more negative consequences than positive ones by those who liquidated their former leader.

[34] Intellectual exchanges continued of course to exist. For example, the Christians of Toledo used to visit the scholar ʿAbd Allāh b. Sahl al-Ġarnāṭī (alive in 553/1158) in the town of Baeza to profit from his extensive knowledge in *ʿulūm al-awāʾil*: see Ibn al-Ḫaṭīb, *al-Iḥāṭa fī aḫbār Ġarnāṭa: nuṣūṣ ǧadīda lam tunšar*, ed. ʿAbd al-Salām Šaqqūr, Tiṭwān 1988, no. 82.

[35] See Ibn Ṣāḥib al-Ṣalāt, *al-Mann bi-l-imāma*, ed. ʿAbd al-Hādī al-Tāzī, 2nd ed., Beirut: Dār al-Ġarb al-Islāmī, 1987, pp. 77, 125, 127, 198, 207, 414; transl. A. Huici Miranda, Valencia 1969, p. 17, 39, 40, 77, 84, 217. On the "mudejarismo" of Ibn Mardanīš, see Guichard, *Les musulmans de Valence*, I, 116–22; H. Kassis, The coinage of Muḥammad ibn Saʿd (Ibn Mardanish) of Mursiya. An attempt at Iberian Islamic autonomy, *Problems of Medieval Coinage in the Iberian Area*, ed. M. Gomes Marques and D.M. Metcalf, Santarém 1988, pp. 209–29.

[36] See J. Dreher, L'imamat d'Ibn Qasī à Mértola (automne 1144 – été 1145): Légitimité d'une domination soufie?, *M.I.D.E.O.* 18 (1988), pp. 195–210.

Some nuances can be introduced into this general trend. In the year 566/1170, the Andalusī Abū Muḥammad Sīdrāy b. Wazīr, acting as an Almohad ambassador to the Christians, lost his turban, stolen by some "low caste" Christians (*arḏāl al-naṣārā*), servants in charge of the tents. Once returned to Sevilla, he reported the event to the Almohad *amīr*, laughing at the ways of the Christians.[37] What they had stolen was of little worth, a piece of Muslim wearing apparel. Their act seems not to have been motivated by gain, but rather by the desire to obtain a souvenir and to boast of the risk involved in stealing it, perhaps wearing the turban in front of others, imitating the Muslims' strange manners. And this behaviour does not arouse hostility on the part of Ibn Wazīr, but rather laughter.

Another Andalusī, the historian Ibn Ḥubayš (d. 584/1188), was in Almería when the town was captured by the Christians in the year 542/1147. He said to the commander, Alfonso VIII of León and II of Castille, that he knew of a tradition which traced the king's genealogy to Heraclius, the Emperor of Constantinople.[38] Pleased with the information, the king granted freedom to Ibn Ḥubayš and to all who were with him without payment of a ransom.[39] The message here seems to be that Christians are ignorant and vain, and when their vanity is stirred by the superior knowledge of their adversaries, their behaviour can be turned to the Muslims' advantage.

The famous traveller Ibn Ǧubayr (539/1144–614/1217) describes in his *Riḥla*, undertaken in Almohad times, the events which led up to a shipwreck off Messina. He "unfavourably contrasts the grief stricken behaviour of the Christians with the more pietistic and fatalistic attitude of the Muslim passengers... Yet the salvation from the wreck of many impecunious Muslim passengers, unable to pay their rescuers' fee, is freely attributed to the generosity of the Christian king of Sicily, William II."[40] For his part, the Almohad historian ʿAbd al-Wāḥid al-Marrākušī gives a sympathetic portrayal of king Alfonso VIII for his refusal to massacre the inhabitants of Calatrava after its conquest. Part of the Christian army then decided to abandon the campaign, dissatisfied with the king's

[37] See Ibn Ṣāḥib al-Ṣalāt, *al-Mann bi-l-imāma*, p. 315; transl. Huici Miranda, p. 157.

[38] To the best of my knowledge, there were no attempts at connecting the Spanish royal families with the Byzantines. See P. Linehan, *History and the Historians of Medieval Spain*, Oxford 1993.

[39] See D.M. Dunlop, The Spanish historian Ibn Ḥubaysh, *JRAS* 1941, pp. 359–62, quoting Gayangos, *Muhammadan Dynasties*, II, 312. See also Urvoy, *Pensers*, p. 106.

[40] I.R. Netton, Basic structures and signs of alienation in the *Riḥla* of Ibn Jubayr, *JAL* XXII (1991), pp. 21–37, p. 34.

behaviour towards Muslims.[41] Kings are here favourably contrasted with the rest of the Christians, but their generosity and kindness are sometimes to be attributed more to their regal rank than to their being a special kind of Christian. Ibn Ǧubayr "did not really like Christians or Christianity. It is true that he may, on occasion, admire individual Christian people or their actions, but the Crusading milieu and his own religious upbringing and environment prove too strong to disguise Ibn Ǧubayr's fundamental attitude: Christianity is intrinsically the enemy from every point of view, whether it be moral, spiritual or physical."[42]

The "demonization" of the Christian increased with Christian threat and victories, as shown for example in anecdotes found in a 7th/13th century source, al-Ḥimyarī's *Rawḍ al-miʿṭār*. The protagonist of one of them is Alfonso VI, the conqueror of Toledo. According to this story, the king wanted his wife Constance to give birth in the mosque of Cordoba, on the advice of his priests and bishops who reminded him that in the western part of the mosque a church had stood before.[43] The positive image of Alfonso VI found in earlier sources as protector of the Mudéjar population of Toledo and as opposed to the conversion of its central mosque into a cathedral[44] has now been replaced by that of a king who wants deliberately to defile the purity of a sacred place, the mosque of Cordoba, not only through a Christian presence, but even more through the presence of a Christian woman in labour. It is easy to imagine the horror with which such a story would have been received by a Muslim audience.

3. MUSLIM NARRATIVES OF GOD'S HELP TO THE CHRISTIANS AND OF CHRISTIAN MIRACLES

Muslim chronicles record examples of God's assistance and His intervention to save Muslims from their enemies and to punish those who rebel against Him, especially those who "prefer Trinity to Unity."[45] This is

[41] See ʿAbd al-Wāḥid al-Marrākušī, *Kitāb al-muʿǧib fī talḫīṣ aḫbār al-Maġrib*, ed. R. Dozy, 2nd ed., Leiden 1881 (transl. E. Fagnan, *Histoire des Almohades*, Argel 1893; transl. A. Huici Miranda, Tetuán 1955), p. 236/279 (Fagnan) and 266 (Huici).

[42] Netton, *art. cit.*, p. 34.

[43] Al-Ḥimyarī, *al-Rawḍ al-miʿṭār*, ed. and transl. E. Lévi-Provençal, Leiden 1938, p. 84/104–5; ed. I. ʿAbbās, Beirut 1975, p. 288. This story is presented as justifying the decision taken by al-Muʿtamid to kill the ambassador (a Jew) sent by Alfonso VI with this impossible proposal.

[44] See M. Fierro, "Religión", *Los Reinos de Taifas*, t. VIII/1 of the *Historia de España fundada por R. Menéndez Pidal y dirigida por J. M. Jover*, Madrid: Espasa Calpe, 1994, pp. 399–496, pp. 480, 485.

[45] The expression is used by an Almohad *šayḫ* in a letter to the people of Málaga, after the

especially so in Almoravid times, when there seems to have existed a more confident attitude on the part of the Muslims, so that virtue is more clearly described to be on one side (the Muslim) and evil on the other (the Christian). One example is the story about Alfonso VI's dream before the battle of Zallāqa. He saw himself riding an elephant "which was all the time beating a drum with his trunk. His priests and monks could not interpret the dream, so he bribed a Jew to go over to the Muslims to find some interpretation. The interpreter said that Alfonso and his army would have a great calamity befall them. The dream may be explained in those words of the Quran, 'seest thou not how thy Lord has dealt with the people of the elephant?'. The Jew did not tell Alfonso this interpretation, but one that he preferred to hear."[46] Before that same battle took place, there was an exchange between the Christians and the Muslims in order to fix the day of the military encounter, with the Christian king proposing either a Saturday or a Monday in order to avoid fighting on Friday or Sunday, the holy day for each of the parties. It was, of course, a stratagem as the Christians did not intend to respect the Muslim holy day. Most sources agree that the battle took place of Friday 12 Rağab 479/ 23 October 1086.[47] On the eve of the battle, the jurist Abū al-ʿAbbās Aḥmad b. Rumayla dreamed that the Prophet Muḥammad told him that he would die a martyr the next morning and that the Muslims would obtain a great victory.[48]

The increasing military power of the Christians, their victories and the inability of Muslim armies to recover lost territories or to produce a significant shift in the balance of power, awoke the old conviction that political and military success was evidence of theological truth and led Muslims to pay attention to the divine help that Christians seemed to be enjoying.[49]

death of the *qāḍī* Ibn Ḥassūn who had asked the help of the Christians against the Almohads: see J. Vallvé, Una fuente importante de la historia de al-Andalus: la *Historia* de Ibn ʿAskar, *Al-Andalus* XXXI (1966), pp. 237–65, pp. 258–60.

[46] R. Messier, The Almoravids and holy war, in H. Dajani-Shakeel, and R.A. Messier (eds.), *The Jihad and its Times: dedicated to Andrew Stefan Ehrenkreutz*, Ann Arbor 1991, pp. 15–29, pp. 23–24. The story is found in al-Ḥimyarī, *Rawḍ*, ed. Lévi-Provençal, p. 89/110; *al-Ḥulal al-mawšiyya*, ed. S. Zakkār and ʿA. Zamāma, Casablanca 1979, pp. 54–55 (transl. A. Huici Miranda, *Colección de Crónicas Árabes de la Reconquista*, vol. I, Tetuán 1952, pp. 67–68). The Quranic verse is CV, 1. See also V. Lagardère, *Les Almoravides jusqu'au règne de Yusuf b. Tashfin (1039–1106)*, Paris 1989, pp. 112–14.

[47] See the different versions of this story in V. Lagardère, *Le Vendredi de Zallāqa (23 octobre 1086)*, Paris 1989; idem, *Les Almoravides*, pp. 116–18.

[48] See al-Ḥimyarī, *Rawḍ*, ed. Lévi-Provençal, p. 91/112.

[49] On the issue of the religious values attached to the "Reconquista" by the Christians, see V. Cantarino, *Entre monjes y musulmanes. El conflicto que fue España*, Madrid 1978;

Ibn Ṣāḥib al-Ṣalāt describes a Christian commander, Ximeno el Giboso, as a sort of supernatural leader whose activity went on undisturbed by rain, cold or heat and who inflicted much damage on the Muslims.[50] More significant is the following story. In the year 567/1172, a disastrous Almohad campaign took place. The Almohad army, under the command of the caliph Abū Yaʿqūb Yūsuf, besieged Huete. The town was on the verge of surrender for lack of food and water. But one night the Christian inhabitants of Huete went out parading their Gospels while priests and monks raised invocations followed by the rest of the population. After a while, it started raining in such measure that soon their cisterns were full and they were able to quench their thirst. As the Christians were now able to resist, the caliph was obliged to lift the siege.[51] The historian who reports this story, ʿAbd al-Wāḥid al-Marrākušī, seems to be admitting that the Christians received help from above, and that their prayers to the deity worked better than those of the Muslims. God's help was obtained by the Christians through their "sacred books", as if their scriptures, for all their corruption and distortion,[52] still retained enough power from their original authenticity. Their holy men (priests and monks) acted as intermediaries, bringing help through their invocations. The whole scene seems to be a Muslim theme turned Christian. We can easily imagine in a similar situation Muslims carrying copies of the Quran and led by *fuqahāʾ*, *ʿulamāʾ* and *zuhhād*, making invocations (*adʿiya*). The scene in Huete would have appeared more Christian had there been a display of the cross or other characteristic Christian symbols.[53] In that same campaign, the Muslims had destroyed the church and removed the bells as booty,[54] but the campaign was nevertheless a disaster. An earlier source like Ibn Ṣāḥib al-Ṣalāt does not mention the episode of parading the sacred books and

Guichard, *Les musulmans de Valence*, II, 393–419. See also J.T. Monroe, *Islam and the Arabs in Spanish scholarship*, Leiden 1970, p. 242.

50 *Mann*, p. 428; transl. Huici, p. 227.

51 See ʿAbd al-Wāḥid al-Marrākušī, *Muʿǧib*, p. 181; transl. Fagnan, p. 217; transl. Huici, pp. 203–4.

52 On the question of *taḥrīf* and *tabdīl*, see I. di Matteo, Il *taḥrīf* od alterazione della Bibbia secondo i musulmani, *Bessarione* XXXVIII (1922), fasc. 158–59, pp. 64–111 and 160, pp. 77–127; N. Roth, Forgery and Abrogation of the Torah. A theme in Muslim and Christian polemic in Spain, *PAAJR* 54 (1987), pp. 203–36.

53 A Christian source describing the Christian conquest of Lisbon in 542/1147 depicts the Almohads accusing the Christians of believing that a human being is God, while displaying "the symbol of the cross before us with mockery, spitting upon it and wiping upon it the filth from their posteriors", and finally urinating on it: N. Roth, *Jews, Visigoths and Muslims in Medieval Spain: Cooperation and Conflict*, Leiden 1994, p. 67, quoting *Expugnatione Lyxbonensi*, pp. 133, 176.

54 See Ibn Ṣāḥib al-Ṣalāt, *Mann*, pp. 406, 413; transl. Huici, pp. 210, 215.

the invocations of Christian holy men, attributing the disaster to sheer incompetence, disorganization and lack of *ǧihād* spirit.[55] It seems that al-Marrākušī[56] is indirectly criticizing the Almohads by means of this episode, hinting that the power of Almohad scholars and their books, such as the *Kitāb* of the founder of the Almohad movement,[57] was less efficacious than the Christians', therefore implying that the Almohads, as heretics, were further removed from God. The criticism against the Almohads becomes stronger if we take into account the important place that miracles seem to have had in Almohad ideology and propaganda.[58]

Ibn Ǧubayr was particularly distressed by "Christian chivalry, courtesy and mores, which are a snare and an exotic delusion from which he is perpetually praying to be delivered, sensing a seduction and the potential for a fall from the true faith of Islam."[59] The following anecdote reflects Muslim anxiety that Christian strength was a tangible threat to Muslim religion. The Almohad caliph al-Ma'mūn (624/1227–629/1232), who had claimed the throne while in the Iberian Peninsula, asked Fernando III for troops to help in conquering Marrakech. The king of Castile answered: "I will give you the force only on condition that you give me ten fortresses of my own choice adjacent to my territory. Then, if by God's grace you enter Marrakech, you will build for the Christians who accompany you a [new] church in the middle of the city in which they may practice their religion and ring bells at the times of their prayers.[60] If one of the Christians should profess Islam, his profession is not to be accepted, and he is to be returned to his brethren, who will judge according to their laws. But should a Muslim profess Christianity, nobody shall have power to interfere with him"; and al-Ma'mūn would have acquiesced in his demands.[61] Fear of

[55] See *Mann*, pp. 398–413; transl. Huici, pp. 208–15 and especially p. 410/213, where mention is made of the rain, uncommon in the month of June, but not "miraculous".

[56] He wrote at the end of the Almohad period, when the belief in the impeccability of Ibn Tūmart and in his doctrines had already been gradually eroded, to be finally renounced by the caliph al-Ma'mūn (624/1227–629/1232).

[57] See the editions by D. Luciani, *Le livre de Mohammed Ibn Toumert, Mahdi des Almohades*, introd. by I. Goldziher, Alger 1903, and ʿAmmār Ṭālibī, Alger 1985.

[58] See M. Fletcher, Al-Andalus and North Africa in the Almohad Ideology, in S. Jayyusi (ed.), *The Legacy of Muslim Spain*, Leiden 1992, pp. 235–58.

[59] Netton, *art. cit.*, p. 36.

[60] The sound of bells is a frequent symbol of Christian domination and Muslim outrage. In a document dated 1325, the "alcaide" of the castle of Segorbe had to pacify the Mudéjar population who protested when the Christian rang the bells in the "arrabal": see V. García Edo, Actitud de Jaime I en relación con los musulmanes del Reino de Valencia durante los años de la conquista (1232–1245) (Notas para su estudio), in *Ibn al-Abbar. Polític i escriptor àrab valencià (1199–1260)*, Valencia 1990, pp. 291–328, p. 300.

[61] Hopkins, *Medieval Muslim Government*, p. 77, quoting a late source, Ibn Abī Zarʿ.

apostasy, already a feature of the Taifa period,[62] increased during the 7th/13th century, when the Christians were immersed in what Burns has described as the "dream of conversion"[63] and Dufouroq "a great illusion",[64] i.e., the christianization of the Muslim inhabitants of the Iberian Peninsula and even of North Africa. Already in the 6th/12th century the danger of Muslim apostasy was not to be dismissed, given the number of Muslims living under Christian rule.[65] Conversions among the Mudéjar population did take place,[66] but others resisted. Muḥammad b. Aḥmad al-Riqūtī, after the conquest of Murcia by the Christians, replied to those who tried to convert him saying that he had lived until then serving one God without being able to fulfil his duties towards Him, so that he was sure of failing even more were he to try to serve three Gods instead of one. He emigrated to Granada.[67]

Starting at the end of the Almoravid period and continuing under the Almohads, a number of Muslim polemical writings against Christianity[68] were written under the fixed form of letters exchanged between a Christian and Muslim, the former having attacked Islam and invited the Muslim to convert. These tracts show an increased interest in Christian miracles[69]

[62] See H. Kassis, Muslim Revival in Spain in the Fifth/Eleventh Century. Causes and Ramifications, *Der Islam* 67 (1990), pp. 78–110 and cf. Fierro, Religión, *Los Reinos de Taifas*, pp. 482–83. The existence of a relativist atmosphere (that there is no way to prove which religion is true) can be detected in al-Andalus since the Taifa period and it might have influenced certain conversions within each community. See for the case of Jews converting to Islam, S. Stroumsa, On Jewish Intellectuals who converted in the Early Middle Ages, *The Jews of Medieval Islam. Community, Society and Identity*, Leiden 1995, pp. 179–97.

[63] See R.I. Burns, Christian-Islamic Confrontation in the West: the Thirteenth Century Dream of Conversion, *American Historical Review* 76 (1971), pp. 1368–1434; repr. (with modifications), Christian–Muslim Confrontation: The Thirteenth Century Dream of Conversion, in R.I. Burns, *Muslims, Christians and Jews in the Crusader Kingdom of Valencia*, Cambridge 1984, pp. 80–108.

[64] See Ch.E. Dufourcq, La Couronne d'Aragon et les Hafsides du XIIIe Siècle, *Analecta Sacra Tarraconensia* 25 (1952), p. 65.

[65] See now for an early legal discussion concerning the dangers threatening Mudéjar communities, P.S. van Koningsveld and G.A. Wiegers, The Islamic Statute of Mudejars in the Light of a New Source, *Al-Qanṭara* XVII (1996), pp. 19–58.

[66] See for the well-known case of the Almohad prince Abū Zayd, E. Molina, *Cayt Abū Cayt: novedades y rectificaciones*, Almería 1977; C. Barceló, El *sayyid* Abū Zayd: príncipe musulmán, señor cristiano, *Awrāq* 3 (1980), pp. 101–9; R.I. Burns, Príncipe almohade y converso mudéjar: nueva documentación sobre Abū Zayd, *Sharq al-Andalus* 4 (1987), pp. 109–123.

[67] See Guichard, *Les musulmans de Valence*, I, 143.

[68] E. Sivan, *L'Islam et la Croisade. Idéologie et propagande dans les réactions musulmanes aux croisades*, Paris 1968, p. 107, remarks the absence of polemical writings against Christianity during the Crusades in the East.

[69] Reference to the miracles of the Christians is also found in Ibn Bāǧǧa's *Tadbīr*

and they reflect the increased awareness that the military advance of the Christians, in both the East and the West, could also mean a religious advance through conversion, apart from the fact that such advance was usually accompanied by polemical attacks against the Muslim religion.[70]

Aḥmad b. ʿAbd al-Ṣamad al-Ḫazraǧī al-Anṣārī al-Qurṭubī (519/1125–582/1187) is the author of the *Kitāb maqāmiʿ al-ṣulbān fī al-radd ʿalā ʿabadat al-awṯān*.[71] Al-Ḫazraǧī lived in Christian Toledo between 540/1145 and 542/1147, it is not clear whether as a captive or a refugee from Cordoba, having abandoned this town after the collapse of Almoravid power.[72] His *Kitāb maqāmiʿ al-ṣulbān* would have been written as a refutation against a Toledan priest, referred to as al-Qūṭī, who used to attack Islam in front of Muslims living in Toledo. These Muslims do not seem to be captives, but Mudéjares. They turned to al-Ḫazraǧī seeking responses to al-Qūṭī's attacks.[73] Al-Ḫazraǧī's arguments against Christianity do not add anything substantially new or original to the already well established repertoire.[74] But he has a small section where he deals with some Christian miracles, using them as a weapon in his attack against Christianity. In this he was reacting to al-Qūṭī, who in his own writing claimed that if al-Ḫazraǧī knew about the miracles of the

al-mutawaḥḥid, when he deals with the category of false spiritual forms (*al-ṣuwar al-rūḥāniyya al-kāḏiba*): see the ed. and transl. by M. Asín Palacios, *El Régimen del solitario por Avempace*, Madrid/Granada 1946, pp. 56–57 (Ibn Bāǧǧa refers also to miraculous facts told by Arabs, but makes no mention of Muslim miracles). Christian miracles are rarely mentioned in previous Muslim writings and that is even so concerning the miracles of Jesus. In a *qiṣaṣ al-anbiyāʾ* book written by the Andalusī al-Ṭarafī (d. 454/1062), no mention is made of the latter: see R. Tottoli, *Le "Qiṣaṣ al-anbiyāʾ" di Ṭarafī*, Ph.D. Thesis, Naples 1996, p. 74.

70 See Fierro, Religión, *Los Reinos de Taifas*, pp. 466–86; J. Sadan, "Identity and Inimitability. Contexts of inter-religious polemics and solidarity in Medieval Spain in the light of two passages by Moše ibn ʿEzra and Yaʿqov ben Elʿazar", *IOS* 14 (1994), pp. 325–47.

71 Edited by ʿAbd al-Maǧīd al-Šarafī, Tunis 1975 (see the review by Kh. Samir in *Islamochristiana* 6 (1981), pp. 242–54) and by M. ʿAbd al-Ġanī Šāma, Cairo n.d.; 2nd ed., *Bayna al-Islām wa-l-masīḥiyya. Kitāb Abī ʿUbayda al-Ḫazraǧī*, Cairo 1979. There is a partial ed. and transl. by F. de la Granja, Milagros españoles en una obra polémica musulmana (el *Kitāb maqāmiʿ al-ṣulbān* de Jazraŷī), *Al-Andalus* XXXIII (1968), pp. 331–65.

72 P.S. van Koningsveld in his article "Muslim slaves and captives in Western Europe during the Late Middle Ages", *Islam and Christian-Muslim relations* 6/1 (1995), pp. 5–23, pp. 12–13, takes it for granted that al-Ḫazraǧī was a prisoner. He seems to ignore the existence of de la Granja's work, where contradictory data concerning the reasons for al-Ḫazraǧī's stay in Toledo are analysed: see pp. 322–24.

73 For the contradictory data about the reasons for al-Ḫazraǧī's writing, see de la Granja, *art. cit.*, pp. 322–24.

74 See for example A. Bouamama, *La littérature polémique musulmane contre le christianisme depuis ses origines jusqu'au XIIIe siècle*, Alger 1988.

Christians, he would be convinced of the truth of their religion. Al-Ḫazraǧī states that he is aware of such miracles but fails to be impressed by them as they are forgeries. He then proceeds to prove it, by analyzing some of those miracles.[75]

The first refers to a specific day, in a Christian sanctuary, when the hand of God appeared behind a veil every year. A Jew was told of that miracle by a Christian leader who wanted to convert him; the Jew replied that he would convert only if the Christian himself could ascertain the veracity of the miracle. The Christian accepted. Once in the sanctuary, and after making a donation, the hand appeared behind the veil. The Christian seized it. The priests claimed that something terrible would happen to him if he persisted and that he was endangering the religion of his ancestors. He insisted that he only wanted to know the secret of the hand, and finally it was revealed to him that the hand belonged to a priest. Meeting subsequently with the Jew, the Christian abandoned his former insistence on conversion, leaving the decision up to him, so that the Jew understood that his challenge had brought the foreseen result. De la Granja, in his study of al-Ḫazraǧī's text, has found no other reference to this miracle. In another sanctuary a cross was suspended in the air (*huwa wāqif bayna al-samāʾ wa-l-arḍ*). A Jew told his Christian master that the alleged miracle was really a stratagem (*ḥīla*), explained by the presence of magnets in the sanctuary walls. The Christian checked what the Jew had told him and found it to be true.[76] De la Granja points out that a similar story is told of an Indian sanctuary and idol by al-Qazwīnī (d. 682/1283) in his *Āṯār al-bilād*, which must have been in circulation before the author's time, probably in the work of the Andalusī al-ʿUḏrī (d. 478/1085).

In the *Kanīsat al-ġurāb*, located in the South-western part of al-Andalus, there was a lamp suspended in the air like the cross already mentioned. Furthermore, the lamp suddenly lit up on a certain day. One of the Umayyad *amīr*s of al-Andalus decided to find out how that happened. A man from Ifrīqiya explained the tricks involved for both suspending the lamp in the air (magnets placed in the walls) and its lighting up (another device hidden in the walls). The Umayyad *amīr* then visited the church and found those tricks to be true, and had those responsible punished. De la Granja indicates that this miracle contains a variant of the second. The part referring to the light has a parallel in a similar story already told of the

[75] They are repeated by al-Qurṭubī (alive in 600/1203) in his polemical work against Christianity entitled *al-Iʿlām bi-mā fī dīn al-naṣārā min al-fasād wa-l-awhām*, ed. A.Ḥ. al-Saqqāʾ, Cairo 1980, pp. 384–87.

[76] De la Granja, *art. cit.*, pp. 341–46, explores later developments of this miracle in Christian writings.

Church of the Resurrection in Jerusalem by al-Ǧāḥiẓ. It seems as though al-Ḫazraǧī himself adapted it to the well-known *Kanīsat al-ġurāb*.[77]

The fourth miracle is a famous miracle connected with Toledo. On the night of August 15th, the Virgin appeared to the bishop of Toledo, the later San Ildefonso, and gave him a head cover and an embroidered mantle or chasuble (*ṯiyāb muzayyana*). This miracle is clearly Andalusī. It was well known since the 8th century A.D. Al-Ḫazraǧī reacts very strongly against it, trying to show why it cannot be taken seriously with arguments that make sense in an Islamic context, not a Christian one. Thus, he asks whether the Virgin appeared to San Ildefonso with the permission of her Husband or without it. If the Christian's answer was that she had His permission, then God's behaviour needs to be explained, because He should instead have chosen one of His angels or servants, and not humiliate His wife and mother of His son sending her to a man. We have to bear in mind here that a Muslim woman should have no direct contact with a man with whom she has no kinship ties which constitute a barrier for their marriage. If the Christian's answer is that she acted of her free will, without the permission of her Husband, that behaviour would make one wonder how God could have chosen her as His wife and mother of His son, as she cheated Him, descending alone to a man without His permission. The conclusion to be drawn from such behaviour is one only (and we have here a word not legible in the manuscript, although the implication is clear). In the following century, another Andalusī author, al-Lablī (d. 691/1292), tells the story of how a Christian referred to the accusation of adultery made against ʿĀʾiša, the favourite wife of the Prophet; and how a Muslim retorted that the same accusation was made against Mary, Jesus's mother, but with a difference, that in the latter case the accused woman bore a child.[78]

Al-Ḫazraǧī concluded[79] by expressing his amazement at what Christians invent concerning God who is really above anything they might say. While the third and fourth miracles are clearly Andalusī, the two others seem to have been taken from a common repertoire of Christian miracles, maybe from the Eastern source used by al-Ḫazraǧī in his own work.[80]

77 See on this Andalusī church Simonet, *Historia de los mozárabes*, pp. 66, 127, 255–57, 524, 768, 814–15.

78 See al-Lablī, *Fahrasa*, ed. Y.Y. ʿAyyāš and ʿAwwād ʿAbd Rabbihi Abū Zīna, Beirut 1988, p. 56.

79 Apart from the four miracles here summarized, al-Ḫazraǧī briefly lists some others, like an olive tree alleged to give flowers and fruits on the same day. About this, see M.C. Jiménez Mata, A propósito del ʿ*aŷāʾib* del Olivo maravilloso y su versión cristiana en el milagro de S. Torcuato, *Cuadernos de Historia del Islam* (1971), pp. 97–108.

80 See on this issue Kh. Samir in *Islamochristiana* 6 (1981), pp. 242–54; M. Epalza, Notes

4. HOW TO COUNTERACT CHRISTIAN POWER

Al-Šaqundī (d. 629/1232) in his *Risāla fī faḍl al-Andalus* boasts of Muslim heroes who fight courageously against Christians. The Muslim warrior Abū ʿAbd Allāh b. Qādis became famous even among Christians, who acknowledged his merits and feared him. A Christian warrior, seeing that his horse was not approaching a trough to drink water, exclaimed: "What is the matter? Is it that you see Ibn Qādis in the water?". Al-Šaqundī's point is that true merit is the one acknowledged by one's enemies.[81] He insisted that he could tell many anecdotes illustrating how frightened Christians were because of those Muslim heroes.[82] The main aim of al-Šaqundī's *Risāla* was to show the superiority of Andalusīs over North African Berbers, and he clearly uses these anecdotes to counteract the Berbers, who chided the Andalusīs for their inability to protect themselves against the Christians and their need of the Berbers' protection and military skills.[83] In this context, al-Šaqundī also boasted of former Andalusī successes against the Christians, pointing out, for example, that the lamps of the mosque in Cordoba were made from the metal of bells taken from the Christians and that the mosque itself was expanded by the famous al-Manṣūr Ibn Abī ʿĀmir with waste remains of churches he destroyed in his campaigns, transported by Christian captives on their shoulders.[84] This image of waste being transported by defeated Christians seems to have been very appealing to contemporary audiences, as it reminded them of past glories, of a time when Christians were losers and Muslims victors. The historian al-Yasaʿ b. Ḥazm (d. 575/1179 or 595/1199) included in his *Kitāb al-muġrib* a forged episode showing Christian captives transporting earth to Cordoba after an expedition

pour une histoire des polémiques anti-chrétiennes, *Arabica* 18 (1971), pp. 99–106, p. 104; Urvoy, *Pensers*, p. 166.

[81] See *Risāla fī faḍl al-Andalus*, partial transl. E. García Gómez, *Elogio del Islam español*, Madrid-Granada 1934, p. 92. The same story is attributed by al-Ṭurṭūšī to his relative Ibn Fatḥūn: see the translation of al-Ṭurṭūšī's *Sirāǧ al-mulūk* by M. Alarcón, *Lámpara de los Príncipes por Abubéquer de Tortosa*, 2 vols., Madrid 1930–31, II, 336. The story clearly belongs to a common stock which can be applied to different people in different periods and regions.

[82] See *ibid.*, pp. 93, 113, 116. See also H. Pérès, Glanes Historiques sur les mouloūk at'-T'awāʾif et les almoravides dans les *Qalāʾid al-ʿIqyān* d'al-Fath' ibn Khāqān, *Mélanges d'histoire et d'archéologie de l'Occident musulman*, t. II (*Hommage à G. Marçais*), Argel 1957, pp. 147–52, p. 149.

[83] On the limited treatment of the "man of the sword" in Muslim literature, see M. Shatzmiller, The Crusades and Islamic warfare — a re-evaluation, *Der Islam* 69 (1992), pp. 247–88.

[84] Al-Šaqundī, *Risāla*, p. 105.

made by the Umayyad *amīr* al-Ḥakam I against Zamora.[85] Al-Yasaʿ's main aim in his chronicle was to prove that Christians were not be trusted, as they could be shown to have systematically broken the treaties concluded with the Muslims.[86]

But for all al-Šaqundī's boasting, Andalusī military power was clearly not adequate. Almoravid and Almohad presence in al-Andalus derived its legitimacy primarily from the Berber dynasties' dedication to *ǧihād* and to the defence of the territories threatened by the Christians. Their inability to perform such duty was dangerous not only in terms of the external enemy, but also in terms of the internal situation. Almoravid defeats produced feelings of despair and hostility against the Almoravids among the population of al-Andalus, and prompted the Andalusī Abū Marwān b. Abī al-Ḫiṣāl, secretary of the Almoravid *amīr*, to write a letter in which he viciously attacked the Berbers.[87] Almohad propaganda insisted on the duty of *ǧihād*, as revealed in many poems.[88] But the *ǧihād* ideology failed to produce the necessary results to fight the powerful feudal Christian societies, which can be described as societies "organized for war".[89]

To whom or to what could one turn for help?

In the episode of the shipwreck mentioned above, Ibn Ǧubayr states "that the (almost miraculous) presence of the Christian king at this shipwreck was an example of God's kindness towards the Muslim passengers."[90] God had to perform miracles to assist the Muslims. For Ibn Ṣāḥib al-Ṣalāt both Almohad victories against Christians and their victories against Muslim rebels are miracles, *āyāt Allāh*.[91] To counteract Christian power, soldiers are needed, but they can achieve nothing without God's help. In the military field those miracles are performed directly by God, but they take place only if the Muslim leaders have deserved them by not deviating from God's path. Otherwise, the result could be what

85 See M. Fierro, La falsificación de la historia: al-Yasaʿ b. Ḥazm y su *Kitāb al-mugrib*, *Al-Qanṭara* XVI (1995), pp. 15–38.

86 This argument is also given in the *fatwā* mentioned in note 61.

87 See Guichard, *Les musulmans de Valence*, I, 91–92; M.J. Viguera, *Los Reinos de Taifas y las invasiones magrebíes*, Madrid 1992, pp. 180–81.

88 See E. García Gómez, Una qasida política inédita de Ibn Ṭufayl, *R.I.E.E.I.* 1 (1953), pp. 21–28; M. Attahiri, *Kriegsgedichte zur Zeit der Almohaden*, Frankfurt am Main 1992. Ibn Ḥubayš wrote his *Kitāb al-ġazawāt* to establish a parallelism between the expeditions of the first caliphs and those of the Almohad dynasty: see Urvoy, *Pensers*, p. 106. See also M. Jarrar, *Die Prophetenbiographie im islamischen Spanien. Ein Beitrag zur Ueberlieferungs- und Redaktiongeschichte*, Frankfurt am Main 1989.

89 See note 24 and especially Guichard, *Les musulmans de Valence*, I, 92–100, 476.

90 Netton, *art. cit.*, p. 34.

91 See Ibn Ṣāḥib al-Ṣalāt, *Mann*, pp. 202, 205, 237, 290 (transl. Huici, pp. 80, 82, 106, 139). See also Ibn al-Qaṭṭān, *Naẓm al-ǧumān*, p. 247.

happened in Huete, where the Christians obtained God's help and the Almohads lost it.

If that was the situation in the military field, what happened when Christian threats affected individuals? Virtuous Muslim men and saints were then needed. It is not by chance that the 6th/12th–7th/13th centuries saw the emergence of an Andalusī hagiographical tradition. Ibn Baškuwāl (d. 578/1183) showed that the religious authority of scholars did not arise only from religious knowledge (*ʿilm*), but also from their ability to manipulate divine forces.[92] The Sufis Ibn Ṭāhir al-Ṣadafī (alive between 552/1157–572/1177) and Muḥyī al-dīn Ibn ʿArabī (d. 638/1240) wrote biographical dictionaries of Sufis and holy men, for which there were few precedents in al-Andalus.[93] Protection of towns was sought through the holy men who had lived in them, as shown, for example, in the work by Ibn al-Ṭaylasān (d. 642/1244 or 643/1245), *al-Tabyīn ʿan manāqib man ʿurifa quburu-hu bi-Qurṭuba min al-ṣaḥāba wa-l-tābiʿīn wa-l-ʿulamāʾ wa-l-ṣāliḥīn*.[94] What could these holy men do to counteract the Christian danger?[95]

They could, for example, release Muslims from captivity. The role attributed to pious men and saints in the miraculous liberation of Muslim captives had been described in previous centuries,[96] but the more abundant material comes from the centuries under study. The most important Andalusī master of Muḥyī al-dīn Ibn ʿArabī, Abū Ǧaʿfar al-ʿUryānī, returning from Sevilla to his native town of Loulé (Southern Portugal) was

[92] See his *Kitāb al-mustagīṯīn bi-llāh (En busca del socorro divino)*, ed. M. Marín, Madrid 1991.

[93] Ibn Ṭāhir al-Ṣadafī is the author of *al-Sirr al-maṣūn*: see F. Meier, Ṭāhir aṣ-Ṣadafīs vergessene Schrift über westliche Heilige des 6/12 Jahrhunderts, *Der Islam* 61 (1984), pp. 14–90; H. Ferhat, *As-Sirr al-Maṣūn* de Ṭāhir aṣ-Ṣadafī: un itinéraire mystique au XIIe siècle, *Al-Qanṭara* XVI (1995), pp. 273–88. Muḥyī al-dīn wrote the *Risālat al-quds* and *al-Durra al-fāḫira*: see the transl. by R.W.J. Austin, *Sufis of Andalusia. The Rūḥ al-quds and al-Durrat al-fākhirah of Ibn ʿArabī*, London 1971.

[94] See M.I. Fierro, Una fuente perdida sobre los ulemas de al-Andalus: el manuscrito del Museo Jalduní de Túnez, *Al-Qanṭara* XII (1991), pp. 273–76.

[95] The motives we shall see (release of Muslims from captivity, conversion of Christians to Islam and participation in *ǧihād*) strikingly echo parallel concerns among Christians. See, for example, M. García Arenal, Los moros en las Cantigas de Alfonso X, *Al-Qanṭara* VI (1985), pp. 133–51, where the themes related to the Muslims are: "las fronteras y costas continuamente amenazados de robos y saqueos; el celo y las posibilidades de conversión al cristianismo; los sufrimientos y peligros, físicos y espirituales, del cautiverio".

[96] For the case of Ibn Bāz and Baqī b. Maḫlad, see M. Marín's study in her edition of Ibn Baškuwāl's *Kitāb al-mustagīṯīn*, pp. 71–73, also dealt with by van Koningsveld, Muslim Slaves and Captives, p. 9, who does not know Marín's study.

> taken captive, along with others, by the Christians. He knew that this would happen before it took place and he accordingly warned the members of the caravan in which he was travelling that they would all be taken captive on the next day. The very next morning, as he had said, the enemy ambushed them and captured every last man of them. To him, however, they showed great respect and provided comfortable quarters and servants for him.

After six months

> he arranged his release from the foreigners for the sum of five hundred dinars and travelled to our part of the country. When he had arrived it was suggested to him that the money be collected for him from two or three persons. To this he replied, "No! I would only want it from as many people as possible; indeed, were it possible I would obtain it from everyone in small amounts, for God has told me that in every soul weighed in the balance of the Last Day there is something worth saving from the fire. In this way I would take the good in every man for the nation of Muḥammad."[97]

For his part, Ibn Ṭāhir al-Ṣadafī recorded similar stories.

> The twelfth century Andalusian ascetic al-Šarafī succeeded in softening iron neckchains and then, with a friend, in completing the full day's march that he had been compelled to make in Christian territory after their capture, in one single hour, but now in reverse, bound for freedom. Another pious Andalusian from the same period, al-Šātibī, offered resistance to one hundred Christian troopers who wanted to catch him, and, at another occasion, caused the seawind to blow a Christian ship with Muslim captives in her hold on to the shore. The Muslims were liberated and the Christians got what they deserved. Al-Šistarī [sic], another holy man from al-Andalus, could call back people from captivity. The person called back could be welcomed in Muslim territory as soon as the next day.[98]

The chronicler Ibn Ṣāḥib al-Ṣalāt had a similar experience. Relatives of

[97] Muḥyī al-dīn Ibn ʿArabī, *Sufis of Andalusia*, pp. 63–64, no. 1 and note 1.

[98] van Koningsveld, Muslim Slaves and Captives in Western Europe during the Late Middle Ages, p. 9, quoting F. Meier, Ṭāhir aṣ-Ṣadafīs vergessene Schrift, pp. 14–90, pp. 32, 61, 63 and Ibn al-Ḫaṭīb, *al-Iḥāṭa fī taʾrīḫ Ġarnāṭa*, ed. M.A. ʿInān, Cairo 1977, IV, 205–19. See Ibn Ğubayr, *Riḥlạ*, transl. F. Maíllo, *A través del Oriente. El s. XII ante los ojos. Riḥla*, Barcelona 1988, pp. 50, 58–59, 74–75 for the distress felt by fellow Muslims at the sight of Muslim captives.

his had been made prisoners by the Christians in al-Andalus and he travelled to Marrakech in order to see how to liberate them. Then he went to Azemmour and entered the mosque of the Sufi Abū Šuʿayb Ayyūb b. Saʿīd al-Ṣanhāǧī (d. 561/1166). Šuʿayb was sitting with his head down, praying. Ibn Ṣāḥib al-Ṣalāt started praying with him and heard a sound like rain falling on the mat on which he sat, but it was the sound of his tears. Ibn Ṣāḥib al-Ṣalāt told him about the captivity of his relatives and Šuʿayb prayed for their liberation. Before a year had passed they were reunited in Marrakech.[99]

What holy men could also do is foresee Muslim victories[100] and to counteract Muslim conversion to Christianity by Christian conversion to Islam. Another teacher of Muḥyī al-dīn Ibn ʿArabī, Abū Muḥammad Maḫlūf al-Qabāʾilī, wanted to

> dig a well in his house and he was brought a foreign prisoner to help him with the operation. The *šayḫ* said, "This man has been sent to help us, so we must pray to God that he embrace Islam." Accordingly, when night came, the *šayḫ* secluded himself to pray for the man. When he came the next morning to do the work he announced that he had become a Muslim. When he was questioned about it he said that the Prophet had appeared to him in his sleep and had ordered him to believe in him and he had obeyed. Then the Prophet had told him that, because of the intercession on his behalf by Abū Muḥammad Maḫlūf, he would accept him into Islam, or words to that effect.[101]

The conversion of a Christian was also attributed to a contemporary of al-Qabāʾilī, the Maghribi Sufi Abū Muḥammad ʿAbd al-Ǧalīl b. Wihlān (d. 541/1146).[102] One day, a man gave him a tunic worth ten dinars and ʿAbd al-Ǧalīl gave it to a Christian. Everybody was scandalized by such action, but before seven days had passed the Christian converted to Islam.

This power to convert is to be contrasted with another trend within Sufism, that of seeing the different religions as equally valid paths leading to the same goal, found especially among the upholders of the doctrine of the *waḥdat al-wuǧūd*. This was the case of al-Ḥarrālī (d. 637/1240), who "is reputed to have addressed himself in an ornate letter to the church

[99] See Ibn al-Zayyāt al-Tādilī, *al-Tašawwuf ilā riǧāl al-taṣawwuf*, trad. Maurice de Fenoyl, *Regard sur le temps des soufis. Vie des saints du Sud marocain des Ve, VIe, VIIe siècles de l'hégire*, n.p.: Editions Eddif, 1995, p. 142.

[100] We have seen earlier the case of Zallāqa. See for the case of Alarcos Ibn al-Zayyāt al-Tādilī, transl., pp. 249, 279, no. 179, 209.

[101] *Sufis of Andalusia*, p. 123, no. 20.

[102] Ibn al-Zayyāt al-Tādilī, transl., pp. 115–18.

authorities in the Spanish town of Taragona [sic], where several members of his family lived in captivity. In his letter he stressed the unity of the human race... He appealed to his Spanish Christian colleagues to see further than the existing religious demarcation lines of which he denied the real religious meaning."[103] A similar doctrine was upheld by Muḥyī al-dīn Ibn ʿArabī (d. 638/1240). For him, Islam is like the sun and the other religions like the stars. Just as the stars remain when the sun rises, so also the other religions remain valid when Islam appears. Perfect human beings accept the truth of every belief, but they have faith only in God as He has revealed Himself to humankind through a particular prophet.[104] Concerning the fact that Ibn ʿArabī's pronouncements on other religions sometimes fail to recognize their validity in his own time, Chittick considers that one reason may be that he had little real contact with the Christians or Jews in his environment and that he had probably "never met a saintly representative of either of these religions, and he almost certainly had never read anything about these two religions except what was written in Islamic sources. Hence there is no reason that he should have accepted the validity of these religions except *in principle*. But this is an important qualification. To maintain the particular excellence of the Koran and the superiority of Muhammad over all other prophets is not to deny the universal validity of revelation nor the necessity of revelation appearing in particularized expression."[105] Another follower of the *waḥdat al-wuǧūd* doctrine, Abū ʿAlī al-Ḥasan b. Hūd al-Ǧuḏāmī al-Mursī (633/1235–699/1300), however, after settling in Damascus where Christians and Jews attended his classes, converted some of the latter to Islam.[106] The Sufi Abū al-ʿAbbās al-Sabtī, who preached charity and renunciation of all wordly possessions, recommended one of his followers to give the money he had with him to the first person he encountered, even if it were a Christian or a Jew.[107]

Another teacher of Muḥyī al-dīn, Abū al-ʿAbbās al-Šaqqāq, met opposition from his father to his entering upon the Way, and when the situation became more difficult, he confided to Muḥyī al-dīn Ibn ʿArabī:

[103] V. van Koningsveld, Muslim Slaves and Captives, pp. 8–9.

[104] W.W. Chittick, *Imaginal Worlds: Ibn al-ʿArabī and the Problem of Religious Diversity*, Albany: SUNY Press, 1994, pp. 123, 124, 125–26, 139, 140, 141, 152, 155.

[105] *Op. cit.*, p. 155. See also Cl. Addas, *Ibn ʿArabī ou La quête du Soufre Rouge*, Paris 1989, p. 278, for a refutation of Asín Palacios' view that the *Futūḥāt* are replete with hatred against Christians.

[106] See L. Pouzet, De Murcie à Damas: le chef des Sabʿiniens Badr ad-dīn al-Ḥasan Ibn Hūd, *Actes du XIe Congrès de l'UEAI*, Evora 1982; J.L. Kraemer, The Andalusian Mystic Ibn Hūd and the Conversion of the Jews, *IOS* XII (1992), pp. 59–73.

[107] Ibn al-Zayyāt al-Tādilī, transl., p. 329.

> "O my brother, things have become very difficult for me; my father has thrown me out to fend for myself. I would very much like to go to the borders of the Muslim lands to fight the enemy and to serve there in the army until I die". In due course he set off for a place called Jerumenha (in Portugal) and is still there to this day. After some time he returned to Seville to collect some effects, but then returned once again to active service.[108]

The Sufi Abū Muḥammad ʿAbd al-Wāḥid b. Tūmart al-Ḥaskurī went to al-Andalus on a military expedition against the Christians and died in the battle of Alarcos.[109] Another Sufi who did not join that expedition felt guilty about it.[110] Voluntary engagement in *ğihād* remained a minority attitude, so that Andalusīs, unable to check Christian advances, kept hoping for help from outside. Ibn al-Muraḥḥal (d. 699/1300), writing in what was left of former al-Andalus, the small Naṣrid kingdom of Granada, addressed one of his poems to the new hope of salvation, once again Berber tribes from North Africa, the Banū Marīn:

> Religion has chosen you as her legitimate defenders,
> Forward! If you protect her, she will be saved.
> Do not betray Islam, brothers, saddle
> and bridle your horses to help her.
> Al-Andalus has put herself under your protection,

invoking

> the ties of religion and how excellent those ties are!
> She has implored your piety. Be compassionate!, as the Merciful
> will not have compassion on those who were not merciful.
> Al-Andalus is part of your land, her people
> are as much your people as you are her people.
> But now she is surrounded by infidels:
> the sea and the non-Arab peoples are her frontiers.
> What misfortune! al-Andalus, a paradise transformed
> into hell by her enemies.[111]

We have here again the old description of al-Andalus as an island surrounded by the sea and by the Christians, a paradise doomed from the start to become a paradise lost.

[108] *Sufis of Andalusia*, p. 127, no. 23.

[109] Ibn al-Zayyāt al-Tādilī, transl., p. 257, no. 183.

[110] Ibn al-Zayyāt al-Tādilī, transl., p. 284, no. 218.

[111] Transl. J.M. Continente, Dos poemas de Ibn Muraḥḥal, poeta malagueño al servicio de los benimerines, *Awrāq* 2 (1979), pp. 44–54.

THE MUSLIMS AND THE GOLDEN AGE OF THE JEWS IN AL-ANDALUS

DAVID J. WASSERSTEIN

Spain, the Iberian peninsula, is home to one of the great exiles of the Jews. Along with Alexandria in the Hellenistic period, Babylon of the gaonic period, with later Ashkenaz and twentieth-century America, the Iberian peninsula may justly lay claim to the first rank among such exiles.[1] The adoption in modern times of the label Golden Age, from a different period in peninsular history, to identify this particular exile serves both to tie it to its peninsular context and to give it a special identity among Jewish exiles. And indeed this exile possesses a number of special characteristics, both in respect of its internal identity and from the point of view of the modern, or not so modern, student of the Jewish past, which make it different from those other exiles.

The special character of Iberian Jewish history was essentially a product of the Islamic presence in Iberia. Nothing in the history of the peninsula as a whole, nor in the history of the Jews there, before the Muslim conquest, in 711 and the years following, might have indicated either the character or the scale of what was to come. During the two centuries of Visigothic rule before the arrival of the Muslims, there seem to have been very few Jews in Iberia; their legal and social situation seems to have been very degraded; so far as we can tell, they had no specific cultural life of their own, with little or no knowledge of Jewish literary material or specifically Jewish linguistic forms; we know nothing of contacts with the outside Jewish world; and even their exercise of their religion seems to have been slight. The rulers of the state, in some degree of alliance with the Roman Catholic Church, sought increasingly during the seventh century to deprive them even of their religious identity and to bring them into the Christian fold; and towards the end, apparently as part of a general atmosphere of paranoia and a search for fifth-columnists, the Jews were accused of

[1] I consider this issue in 'Jews, Christians and Muslims in Medieval Spain', *Journal of Jewish Studies* XLIII, 1992, pp. 175–86.

conspiring with their co-religionists in North Africa and with the Muslims there to deliver the peninsula into their hands. The result seems to have been their enslavement and their forcible conversion to Christianity.[2]

This is the background to the stories relating Jewish involvement in the provision of assistance to the Muslims during their conquest, a conquest which they are supposed to have seen as bringing them release from the persecutions of the Christians. Such stories seem to be at least largely later inventions, and there appears to be little reason to imagine either that the Iberian Jews of the time could have argued persuasively that it would be a sensible idea to lend such support to the invaders or that they might have been seriously in a position to offer any degree of help such as is described in our sources.[3]

The conquest itself, regardless of any part that the Jews may have played in it, changed everything for the Jews in Iberia, as elsewhere. It released the Jews from the legal constraints placed upon them by a government under the influence of a hostile Church, and raised them to the level of second-class subjects, along with the vast majority of the other inhabitants of the new Islamic empire.[4] It gave them the right to the relatively free exercise of their religion. It gave them economic freedoms such as they had not enjoyed in the Mediterranean basin since before the rise of Christianity centuries before. It placed them in contact with their Jewish fellow-subjects of the Islamic empire, most particularly in far-away Iraq. In other words, it established the conditions and provided the Jews with all the elements for a social, an economic and most especially a spiritual revival. As has been seen, the Jews of Iberia were in particular need of such a revival at just this time. Indeed, given the special

[2] See S. Katz, *The Jews in the Visigothic and Frankish Kingdoms of Spain and Gaul*, Cambridge, Mass. (*Monographs of the Mediaeval Academy of America*, no.12), 1937; J. Juster, *La condition légale des Juifs sous les Rois Visigoths*, Paris 1912 (repr. and brought up to date by A.M. Rabello, 'The legal condition of the Jews under the Visigothic kings', *Israel Law Review* XI, 1976, pp. 259–87, 391–414, 563–90, together with a "Tribute to Jean Juster", by A.M. Rabello, *ibid.* XI, 1976, pp. 216–58 [also published separately, Jerusalem 1976]); E. A. Thompson, *The Goths in Spain*, Oxford 1969; B.S. Bachrach, 'A Reassessment of Visigothic Jewish Policy, 589–711', *American Historical Review* 78, 1973, pp. 11–34; J. Gil, 'Judíos y cristianos en la Hispania del siglo VII', *Hispania Sacra* 30, 1978, pp. 9–110; A.M. Rabello, *The Jews in Visigothic Spain in the Light of the Legislation*, Jerusalem 1983 (Hebrew).

[3] See, e.g., E. Ashtor, *The Jews of Moslem Spain*, I, Philadelphia 1973 (repr. with a new introduction by D.J. Wasserstein, 1992), esp. pp. 15–22 and notes 1–10 at pp. 407–08. N. Roth, 'The Jews and the Muslim Conquest of Spain', *Jewish Social Studies* 38, 1976, pp. 145–58 adds nothing.

[4] Cf. A. Fattal, *Le Statut légal des non-musulmans en pays d'Islam*, Beirut (*Recherches publiées sous la direction de l'Institut de lettres orientales de Beyrouth*, X) 1958.

circumstances created for the Jews by the state on the eve of the conquest, it is easy to conceive that Judaism, and Jews with it, might within a short span have died out completely in the Iberian peninsula.

Instead, we find the Golden Age. However, this did not occur overnight. For the first two centuries of the Muslim presence in the peninsula, in fact, we know very little of Jews or of Jewish life there. It is occasionally claimed that the new conditions of life in the huge *oikoumene* of the Islamic empire led to a Jewish emigration westwards from Iraq, to a new demographic situation for the Jewish people, and that one result of this was a large increase in the size of the Jewish population of Spain.[5] There is no evidence to substantiate such a claim. It is true that we hear more of Jews in Iberia following the conquest, or more precisely following the end of the ninth century; and it is true that the nature of what we hear about them is more suggestive of actual Jews than the feeble indications offered by the plethora of anti-Jewish legislation of the preceding period; it is true also that we have indications of Jewish involvement in Spain in international commerce;[6] and it is true that we do have occasional indications of the arrival of Jews from outside (more or less necessarily from the East) in the peninsula, for example, Eldad ha-Dani.[7] But all these do not, with the best will in the world, add up to a numerically significant movement of people. Given what little we do know of such movements, and given too what very little we know of population sizes at this time, in particular of the numbers of Muslims in the area, it would be surprising if such movements of Jews added up to anything meaningful.

Much the same is true of Jewish cultural life and developments in the peninsula during this period. We hear occasionally of contacts with other areas: apart from the strange case of the adventurer Eldad ha-Dani, referred to above, there is also, at about the same time, towards the end of the ninth century, the case of the correspondence between the Jews of Iraq, more exactly the Gaon Amram (died ca. 875) and those of Spain, possibly of Lucena, in the south, over the liturgy.[8] However, these are

[5] E.g., by E. Ashtor, *op.cit.*, I, p. 51.

[6] Cf. now the valuable work of O.R. Constable, *Trade and Traders in Muslim Spain: the commercial realignment of the Iberian Peninsula, 900–1500*, Cambridge (*Cambridge Studies in Medieval Life and Thought*, 4th series, 24) 1994; though what is striking here too is the scarcity, even virtual absence, of such references for the early period.

[7] See D.J. Wasserstein, 'Eldad ha-Dani and Prester John', in *Prester John, The Mongols and the Ten Lost Tribes*, ed. C.F. Beckingham and B. Hamilton, Aldershot (Variorum) 1996, pp. 213–36.

[8] See the exemplary edition of the *Seder Rav Amram*, by D. Goldschmidt, Jerusalem (Mossad Ha-Rav Kook) 1971 (Hebrew); on Amram himself, see *Encyclopaedia Judaica*, Jerusalem (Keter) 1971, II, cols. 891–93.

isolated episodes, and we do not hear of many such. The overall picture, even when painted by the pen of such an eloquent historian as Ashtor, does not really have very much detail for this period.[9]

This last fact adds some mystery to what happened around the middle of the tenth century. At that time we witness the emergence of a Jewish culture in al-Andalus, Islamic Spain, and its growth almost at once to full maturity. The roots of this must lie in the preceding two centuries, but we have almost no evidence to go on to explain these developments. The achievements of the following two centuries were stopped, and largely destroyed, only by the invasions of the Almohads in the middle of the twelfth century.[10] But it is these achievements that gave Iberian Jewry, both in its Islamic phase and, later, in the Christian kingdoms of the peninsula, its special character. That special character is visible in many ways. A great deal, probably more than from other areas, of the literary productivity of this period has survived. Much of it has survived in the liturgy, and in doing so constituted a living part of the tradition of the Jewish people for a millennium. A great deal more survived, much of it in fragmentary form, in the treasures of the Genizah and in other manuscript repositories of various sorts. Alike in range, in quantity and in quality this literary production is unique to the cultural world of Spanish Jewry. Almost all the greatest poets writing in Hebrew in the middle ages were Iberian: Judah ha-Levi, Solomon Ibn Gabirol, Samuel Ha-Nagid, Moses Ibn Ezra, and so on; the list is long (I shall return to this point). If much of their work is lost, much too is still preserved and read to this day. Some of the most important works of Jewish thought are the product of Iberian Jewry: the *Kuzari*, the *Guide for the Perplexed*, and others. Biblical exegesis, Hebrew grammar, philosophy, talmudic commentary, legal responsa, scientific writings of every sort, and much besides, is represented. In addition, we can point to the deep involvement of the Jews in the translation movement which brought so much ancient Greek and later Arabic material into the medieval west.[11] This activity in its turn offers a hint at another special facet of this Jewry, one which differentiates it from

[9] Cf. the situation for Islamic culture in Iberia at this time: although better, there is still great dependence on the East. M. Fierro, 'Religious beliefs and practices in al-Andalus in the third/ninth century', *Rivista degli Studi Orientali* 66, 1992, pp. 15–33.

[10] The real significance of the Almohad invasions for Jewish life in Iberia has been the subject of much debate. The arguments are concisely summarised, with bibliographical references, in Constable, *op.cit.*, p.95, esp. n.58.

[11] Cf. P.Sj. van Koningsveld, 'Andalusian-Arabic Manuscripts from Christian Spain: a comparative intercultural approach', *Israel Oriental Studies* 12, 1992, pp. 75–110; id., 'Christian-Arabic manuscripts from the Iberian peninsula and north Africa: a historical interpretation', *Al-Qantara* 15, 1994, pp. 423–51.

others. Unlike all the other Jewries of the Islamic world, that of Iberia enjoyed a great phase both under the rule of Islam and, later, and drawing on that Islamic heritage, also under the rule of Christendom. This dual character of Iberian Jewries helped the Jewry of Christian Spain to an awareness of a great past and stimulated it to an active participation at a high level in the culture of Iberia under Christian rule. It was the success of that Jewry in this role, along with its strong consciousness of its past, that helped to endow the Expulsion of 1492 with its cataclysmic significance in the history of the Jewish people as a whole.[12]

Any serious account of the cultural achievements of Iberian Jewry, even in its Islamic phase alone, would amount virtually to a catalogue of the cultural achievements of the Jews. We are in a position to draw up such a catalogue today not only because of the fact that so much material has survived, both in the live tradition of the Jews and buried in the Genizah, but also because the Jewries of Iberia themselves seem to have felt something of the special character that they possessed. We have two, even three, works which, produced by Iberian Jews, constitute almost a memorialisation of the achievements of these Jews, a series of historical monuments to their greatest sons. These are the *Sefer ha-Qabbalah* of Ibn Dā'ūd, the *Kitāb al-Muḥāḍara wa-l-Muḏākara* of Moses Ibn Ezra, and the *Taḥkĕmoni* of Judah al-Harizi. It is possible to dispute about the exact character and nature of these works, about the aims of their authors and about the motives that led to their composition, as also about the reliability and the comprehensiveness of the material which they contain (they are not conceived as histories in the narrow sense of that term; they are not presented as catalogues; they are largely limited to poetical writers and to writers on religious subjects; and of course they are limited chronologically by the times at which their writers themselves lived). Nonetheless, these works share several features, among them that no other medieval Jewry produced any such memorialisation or monumentalisation of its cultural life; another such feature is the extreme self-consciousness of their authors, as Iberian Jews, their awareness of writing as Jews in an Iberian context — or contexts, for they were all very much aware of working or living in areas which were no longer under Islamic rule, and which were in consequence no longer fully part of the Islamic cultural *aire*. This indeed helps to inform the motives of these writers, and other motives, especially in the case of Ibn Dā'ūd, related to the specifically Iberian character of Iberian Jewry, are known to have played very significant roles in their work.[13] The

[12] F. Baer, *A History of the Jews in Christian Spain*, 2 vols., Philadelphia 1961–66.

[13] Cf. the valuable study by G.D. Cohen: *A Critical Edition with a translation and notes of The Book of Tradition (Sefer ha-Qabbalah) by Abraham Ibn Daud*, Philadelphia (Jewish

mere existence of these works, however, has helped to give the cultural legacy of Iberian Jewry a far more definite shape and a far more elevated reputation than it might otherwise enjoy, however much it might deserve it.

Much of the foundation for all the success of the tenth and eleventh and twelfth centuries remains unknown and inexplicable. We know too little, and are not likely ever to know much more, of that dark age of two and a half centuries between the conquest and the middle of the tenth century. However, we do know that much of what happened in the following two centuries depended, must have depended, on the existence by the tenth century of a Jewish community or of Jewish communities in al-Andalus which were economically prosperous and able to benefit from the opportunities which participation in a broader Islamic society had created. Two figures above all in the tenth and eleventh centuries seem to have had an important share in this process. The first was Ḥasdai Ibn Shaprut, and the second Samuel ha-Nagid. Each of them has left a remarkable reputation to posterity, and each of them was able to do so not least because of the way in which he straddled the boundaries between the worlds in which he lived and operated, essentially those of Arab Islam, in a political and a cultural sense, and of the Jewries of the Islamic world, in a cultural and a social sense. Samuel ha-Nagid is far better known to us than Ḥasdai, mainly because of the nature and quantity of the source-material available for him, partly also because of his own activity as a writer and poet. I attempted to bring out some of the problematic aspects, problematic perhaps more for the historian than for his own contemporaries, in a study published some years ago.[14] Ḥasdai, however, remains a far more shadowy figure in almost every way. This is historiographically irritating, not least because from the point of view of the history of the Jews, he is arguably of greater significance than the Nagid.

Our picture of Ḥasdai, both as to the information available and as to the resulting picture, is at base a product of the mid-nineteenth century. We have had scarcely any additions to our knowledge since then; the few that we have had, many of them from Genizah materials, have fleshed out what we know a little but have not provided any major new information or changed anything in our understanding very radically. The accounts that

Publication Society of America) 1967, where in a lengthy introduction Cohen analyses in great detail the motives and the aims of Ibn Dā'ūd in writing this work, showing that the author was far from being merely a disinterested historian, but was concerned to establish the primacy of Spain as heir to Iraq in the Jewish world.

[14] D.J. Wasserstein, 'Samuel Ibn Naghrīla ha-Nagid and Islamic Historiography in al-Andalus', *Al-Qantara* XIV, 1993, pp. 109–25.

we find in modern works all draw their material, as also their conclusions, from a single work written a hundred and forty years ago. That work offers a portrait of Ḥasdai as an important adviser to two successive Umayyad rulers of Cordoba, the caliphs ʿAbd al-Raḥmān III al-Nāṣir (912–61) and al-Ḥakam II al-Mustanṣir (961–76), a man of learning and a doctor who was employed on delicate diplomatic missions to Christian rulers in northern Spain, a minister of finance at the Umayyad court and a generous patron of Jewish culture in al-Andalus. The picture that emerges is of something very close to the Court Jew of Christian Europe.[15] The author, Philoxène Luzzatto, paints a vivid picture, and the result is still bright today. Luzzatto was a careful and painstaking young scholar — he had the example of his father, a famous scholar in his own right, before him; and in this particular work he received help both from him and from the doyen of students of Spanish Islam, Reinhart Dozy, himself.[16] The result is fair, but the impression which it leaves is perhaps a little over-burnished. Ḥasdai emerges as a man of great consequence at the caliphal court. True, Luzzatto is careful and honest enough to reject the claim of Carmoly (well known for the unreliability of his scholarship and possibly even the forgery of manuscripts)[17] that Ḥasdai had served as the prime minister, *hāǧib*, of the caliph ʿAbd al-Raḥmān III al-Nāṣir: "cela ne repose sur aucune autorité" (p. 55); but as in other cases of Jews who have served

[15] Philoxène Luzzatto, *Notice sur Abou-Iousouf Hasdaï Ibn-Schaprout, médecin juif du dixième siècle, ministre des khalifes omeyyades d'Espagne ʿAbd-al-Rahman III et al-Hakem II, et promoteur de la littérature juive en Europe*, Paris (Mme Ve Dondey-Dupré) 1852. The author, who was 23 when this little book was published, died two years later. He was a member of the famous Luzzatto family, and a son of Samuel David Luzzatto, who is himself cited several times in the course of this remarkably learned work. There is a useful entry on Philoxène Luzzatto (by Max Seligsohn) in the *Jewish Encyclopedia*, New York (Funk and Wagnalls) 1907, vol. VIII, p. 221; the section on him in the longer entry for the family as a whole in the *Encyclopaedia Judaica*, Jerusalem (Keter) 1971, vol. 11, col. 597, by Umberto Cassuto, is less informative.

[16] On Dozy, see M.J. de Goeje, *Levensbericht van Reinhart Dozy*, Amsterdam 1883; Luzzatto also relies here on the work of Conde, whom Dozy criticized heavily for faulty scholarship. At the time when Luzzatto was writing, there was little else, apart from Conde's work, available on the subject of Spanish Islam, and Conde's faults were not yet fully visible; but Dozy's criticisms effectively destroyed Conde's reputation for ever. See R. Dozy, *Recherches sur l'Histoire et la Littérature de l'Espagne pendant le moyen âge*, Leyden 1849; subsequent editions (1859 and 1881) omit the critical sections. Dozy retained, however, in the preface to the third edition, reference to these sections and to their success. Lately, R. Hitchcock has attempted to rehabilitate Conde: 'Hispano-Arabic Historiography: the legacy of J.A. Conde', in I.R. Netton (ed.), *Arabia and the Gulf: From Traditional Society to Modern States. Essays in Honour of M.A. Shaban's 60th Birthday (16th November 1986)*, London (Croom Helm) 1986, pp. 57–71. The attempt seems misplaced.

[17] See, e.g., what I report in 'Eldad ha-Dani' (supra, n.7), p. 225, n.22.

at the courts of non-Jewish rulers, so in this case we are left with a picture which allows the reader to be more impressed by the importance of the Jewish minister than his actual position demands. As Luzzatto points out (ibid.): "...hadjib, c'est impossible; puisque, s'il l'avait été, son nom paraîtrait dans les historiens arabes, tandis qu'ils gardent sur lui un silence absolu."

This last remark is not quite true, and Luzzatto himself is our earliest modern source for our knowledge of that fact, for he himself cites the Arabic sources on Ḥasdai. But it is true in the sense that nowhere in Arabic sources do we learn anything about Ḥasdai attaining particularly high rank in the service of the Umayyads. We do learn certain facts about him, as will be seen. But that he served as a government minister seems to go beyond the evidence, and also beyond what our knowledge would suggest was possible at the time. There is a difference between a government minister and an official in government employ, even an official who enjoys the confidence of the ruler. The difference is in part one of rank; and in the case of Jews, that difference in rank is related to a fundamental difference of social status.[18] A hundred years later, as the case of Samuel ha-Nagid shows, those differences could, in changed circumstances and under rulers of different types, be overcome, though not completely. In the tenth century, in caliphal Cordoba, they could not be — nor do we have any actual evidence that anyone wanted to overcome them.

We lack such evidence for at least two reasons. First, there is no particular reason to suppose that anyone might have wanted to give a man like Ḥasdai the importance and the status at the court of the Umayyads that Samuel ha-Nagid was to enjoy a century later in Granada, in the service of the Zirids; the rank that he did attain in Cordoba, as some sort of official who could be given certain types of confidential tasks to perform, perhaps somewhat vague as to rank, and possibly also as to title, suited the time and the place. Secondly, if the Umayyads had wanted to do this, the place to look for evidence of it would be in our Arabic sources. As Luzzatto pointed out a century and a half ago, there is very little information in our Arabic sources about Ḥasdai.

This may occasion surprise. Should it? Should we expect to hear more from Arab writers about a Jewish official in the service of the ruler? This question can be generalised, and put in rather different terms. It can be broadened, to concern itself not so much with a Jew interacting via an official career with the overarching society of Islam and more with the

[18] The significance of the social status of Jews in such situations is well brought out by B. Lewis, 'An Ode Against the Jews', in id., *Islam in History: Ideas, Men and Events in the Middle East*, London 1973, pp. 158–65 and 320–23.

status of Jewish culture in that Islamic society. How much should we know about the Golden Age of the Jews in Spain, or in Islamic Spain, if we did not have the materials which have survived from Jewish sources themselves? This may seem a pointless question, if only because these materials have actually survived, but the lack of comparable amounts and types of material for the Christians of al-Andalus, thanks in part at least to the non-survival of material which did at one time exist, shows that the question is not without significance. Given the real importance of the Golden Age — and given, too, the significance of the material from the Genizah for our overall knowledge, material which might easily never have come to light[19] — it is clear that if we did not have the rich material from Jewish sources, and had only (or virtually nothing but) the material in Arabic sources for this period of Jewish history, then our understanding of the period and of its importance would be much poorer and far less adequate to the reality.[20]

So much is clear; but we can put the question just posed in different terms again, terms which relate the Jewish history of the Golden Age in Iberia still more closely to the Islamic society of which the Golden Age was one facet. How much did Muslims in Iberia and elsewhere, but especially in Iberia, know about this Golden Age? How much did they know about the vital and productive cultural life of the Jewish minority in their midst? In what sense and to what degree did the cultural productivity of these Jews really form part of the overall cultural life of the society in which they lived and worked? How far were Muslims aware of the fact that the Jews in their midst (and similarly the Christians) had a cultural existence and life of their own, with interactions and links with that of the Muslims? These questions matter, in the sense that they have something to tell us about the shape of that overarching society.

We are in fact singularly well placed to consider these questions. In this respect al-Andalus is very unlike other areas. Generally, while we do occasionally come across references to Jewish culture, and to Jews active in cultural spheres, in Muslim Arabic sources for other areas, such references are few, and do not add up to any kind of composite picture. One obvious example here is the reference in the *Fihrist* of al-Nadīm to Saʿadya Gaon and to his writings, which occurs in the course of a more general disquisition by the author on the Torah and other Scriptures.[21]

[19] On the difficulties of access to the Cairo Genizah in its original setting, see M. Cohen and Y. Stillman, 'The Cairo Geniza and the Custom of Geniza among Oriental Jewry — an historical and ethnographic study', *Peʿamim* 24, 1985, pp. 3–35 (Hebrew).

[20] A glance at the relative sizes of the modern scholarly literature on the Jews and on the Christians of al-Andalus serves to confirm this.

[21] B. Dodge (ed. and trans.), *The Fihrist of al-Nadim, A Tenth-Century Survey of Muslim*

Despite the interest of the passage, and its usefulness as an index of Muslim awareness of Jewish cultural history and activity, the usefulness of the text lies essentially in the fact that it demonstrates how thin such an awareness was. We also find sporadic references to Jews active in fields and in ways which are less closely tied to their specifically Jewish identity, mainly as scientists of various sorts. But scattered remarks in Muslim sources about scientists who happen to be Jews are not the same thing as sustained accounts of Jewish cultural life.

In the case of al-Andalus, by contrast, we possess a sustained account, in the *Ṭabaqāt al-Umam* of Ṣāʿid al-Andalusī, which enables us to draw a picture of Jewish cultural activity as known to contemporary, or nearly contemporary, Muslim observers. The result is of interest.

The author of the *Ṭabaqāt al-Umam*, Ṣāʿid al-Andalusī, was born in 1029, a member of a family of legal scholars displaced from Cordoba by the political convulsions of the first half of the eleventh century. His father eventually became *qāḍī* of Toledo, where he died in 1057, and Ṣāʿid himself occupied the same post for the last two years of his life, dying in 1070.[22] This work, the only one by Ṣāʿid to survive, is a classification of the nations of the world in accordance with their share in the acquisition and transmission of the sciences. It acquired great authority very early, and is much quoted by Ibn Abī Usaybīʿa. Eight nations are included in Ṣāʿid's classification: the Indians, the Persians, the Chaldaeans, the Greeks, the Rūm, the Egyptians, the Arabs (who occupy nearly half the work) and, almost *en appendice*, the Banū Isrāʾīl, the Jews. Science is seen to travel more or less from East to West, with the Arabs as the final possessors of it, and Spain in particular as its most recent home.

At the end of this text, as noted, the author has a chapter (which is not present in all the manuscripts; and it is not present, as a consequence, in some modern editions of the text either) on the Banū Isrāʾīl and their scientists. This last chapter, on the Jews, blemishes somewhat the schematic geographical neatness of the exposition of a westward movement of the sciences, both because of the geographical dispersion of the Jews following the destruction of the Temple and because of the insertion thus at the end of the work of an account of their scientific activity before the destruction: one would have expected such an account to come much earlier, somewhere closer to the chapters on the Chaldaeans and the Greeks. However, there may be an explanation for this. A substantial portion of this chapter on the sciences among the Jews is

Culture, New York (*Records of Civilization: Sources and Studies*, No. LXXXIII) 1970, 44–45.

22 See *EI*, second edition, VIII, art. 'Ṣāʿid al-Andalusī' (by G. Martinez-Gros).

occupied by a report on Jews who were prominent in the sciences in al-Andalus. It is worthy of note that in the chapter on the sciences among the Arabs, similarly, nearly half is taken up with the share of al-Andalus. The passage was translated into French, by Blachère, in 1935, in his translation of the entire work, but he paid little attention to the information about the Jews.[23] The passage was also translated into English, by Joshua Finkel, some years earlier, with some annotation.[24] Finkel remarked that the 'numerous branches of the immense Arabic literature contain so many data bearing on Jewish faith and culture that, were this material gathered, it would reach the magnitude of a considerable "Bibliotheca"' (p. 45). There seems to me to be room to dispute this judgement; what we can learn from the passage of Ṣāᶜid that he translates in his article, a passage which he offers in illustration of his suggestion, is, I think, the best proof of this. Despite the existence of his translation, it may be of some use to offer here a new version of the section of Ṣāᶜid's chapter on the Jews dealing with Spain (particularly since I differ from him in respect of certain details of the translation):[25]

TRANSLATION

> There were a number of them [scil. of Jews] in al-Andalus. Among those who studied medicine was Ḥasdāy b. Isḥāq the servant of al-Ḥakam b. ᶜAbd al-Raḥman al-Nāṣir li-Dīn Allāh. He was skilled in the practice of medicine, very learned in the legal science of the Jews, and he was the first to open up for those of them who were in al-Andalus their legal and historical and other sciences. Before that they had to have recourse to the Jews of Baghdad in matters connected to the law of their religion and the years of their era and the dates of their feasts; they would get from them the calculation of a number of years, and in accordance with that they would know the start of their [calendrical] cycles and the beginnings of their years.

[23] R. Blachère, *Ṣāᶜid al-Andalusī: Kitāb Ṭabaḳāt al-Umam (Livre des Catégories des Nations)*, Paris (*Publications de l'Institut des Hautes Etudes Marocaines*, t. XXVIII) 1935, pp. 155–60. There is also a recent translation of the whole work into English: Semaᶜan I. Salem and Alok Kumar, *Science in the Medieval World "Book of the Categories of Nations" by Ṣāᶜid al-Andalusī*, Austin, University of Texas Press (*History of Science Series*, no.5), 1991; the passage on the Jews is at pp. 79–82. It is of no value.

[24] J. Finkel, 'An eleventh century source for the history of Jewish scientists in Mohammedan lands (Ibn Ṣāᶜid)', *Jewish Quarterly Review*, N.S., XVIII, 1927–28, pp. 45–54.

[25] I use the text of L. Cheikho (ed.), *Ṭabaqāt al-Umam*, Beirut 1913, pp. 88–90.

And when Ḥasdāy became connected to al-Ḥakam, and received the highest honour from him on account of his talent and his great skill and his culture, and managed thanks to him to obtain access to the Jewish writings that he wanted from the East, then the Jews of al-Andalus came to know what they had been ignorant of before, and were able to do without what had caused them a lot of bother.

Then during the Fitna[26] there was Menaḥem[27] ibn al-Fawwāl, an inhabitant of Saragossa. He was an outstanding practitioner of medicine, and also devoted to the study of logic (Ar. *manṭiq*) and the other philosophical sciences. He composed a book entitled *Kanz al-Muqill*, which he arranged in question-and-answer form, containing a collection of the rules of logic and the principles of natural science (Ar. *ṭabīʿa*).[28]

With him in Saragossa there was Marwān ibn Ǧanāḥ, who was one of those who studied logic and occupied themselves with the science of the languages of the Arabs and the Jews (Ar. *lisānay al-ʿArab wa-l-Yahūd*); he wrote a fine work on the simple medicaments and on the definition of the amounts to be used in medical treatment according to weights and measures.[29]

Another of these was Isḥāq ibn Qisṭār, who served al-Muwaffaq Muǧāhid al-ʿĀmirī and his son Iqbāl al-Dawla ʿAlī.[30] He was skilled in the principles of medicine and understood the science of logic and the opinions of the philosophers; he was of excellent nature and upright manner. I associated with him a good deal and never saw a Jew like him for his learning, his honesty and his perfect character. He was expert in the study of the Hebrew language and skilled in the law of the Jews, (and also) well informed about their history. He

[26] The period of revolutionary chaos at the start of the eleventh century in al-Andalus, following on the fall of the Manṣūrid dictatorship. See D.J. Wasserstein, *The Rise and Fall of the Party-Kings: Politics and Society in Islamic Spain, 1002–1086*, Princeton, Princeton University Press, 1985, ch.3, pp. 55–81.

[27] The correction, from the Arabic *m.n.ǧ.m*, is simple, the removal of a dot, and obvious. The Arabic is simply a *lectio facilior*.

[28] See Ashtor, *Jews of Moslem Spain* (*supra*, n.3), II, pp. 255 and 348, n.193; apart from citing the passage in Ibn Abī Usaybīʿa, which is simply a copy of this, Ashtor adds nothing. Given the hugely extensive learning of that scholar, we may assume that nothing further is known today about Ibn al-Fawwāl.

[29] See *Encyclopaedia Judaica*, Jerusalem (Keter) 1972, vol.8, cols. 1181–86, art. 'Ibn Janāḥ, Jonah' (by David Tene), with bibliographical references; Ashtor, *Jews of Moslem Spain*, III, index, sub nomine Abu ʿl-Walīd Morwan [sic] Ibn Djanāḥ, and esp. 12–29.

[30] For these rulers of Denia see Wasserstein, *Rise and Fall*, index. The son, ʿAlī, died in 1075–76, after Ṣāʿid's own death; the petty state of Denia was then annexed by the Hūdid ruler of Saragossa, al-Muqtadir.

died in Toledo in the year 448 [=1056], aged 75; he never married.[31]

Another of them, also involved in the study of some of the philosophical sciences, was Sulaymān ibn Yaḥyā, called Ibn Ǧabruwāl [i.e., Gabirol], who lived in Saragossa and was devoted to the study of logic; he was very intelligent and had a penetrating mind. He died when he was past the age of 30 close to the year 450 [=1058].[32]

Another of them, one of the young men (Ar. *fityān*, sing. *fatā*) of our own time, was Abū al-Faḍl Ḥasdāy ibn Yūsuf ibn Ḥasdāy, an inhabitant of the city of Saragossa, of a noble family of Jews in al-Andalus descended from Moses the Prophet, peace be upon him. He studied the sciences in an organised way and acquired much varied learning. He excelled in the study of the language of the Arabs, and acquired a great amount of poetry and rhetoric, excelling in the sciences of arithmetic and geometry and astronomy; he understood the science of music and tried his hand at composing it. He studied the science of logic and worked at research and observation. Then he raised himself to the science of physics (Ar. *ṭabīʿa*), and started off in that by listening to the *Kitāb al-Kiyān* of Aristotle until he understood it; then he started on the *Kitāb al-Samāʾ wa-l-ʿĀlam*. I parted from him in the year (4)58 [= 1066] when he had already understood it thoroughly. And if he lives long and if he continues to devote himself to study then he will certainly go very far in philosophy and will understand (all) the branches of learning. This is because he is still very young, not yet fully mature; but God, may He be exalted, confers His blessings on whomever He wishes; He is All-powerful.[33]

These are the famous Hebrews among us who have excelled in the science of philosophy. As for those who are learned in the law of the Jews, they are innumerable, both in the East and in the West [Here follows a list of several learned Jews in the Orient].

And among them in al-Andalus was Abū Ibrāhīm Ismāʿīl ibn Yūsuf the Scribe (Ar. *kātib*), known as Ibn al-Naġrīla,[34] who served Bādīs ibn Ḥabbūs (Ar. Ḥayyūs) al-Ṣinhāǧī, king of Granada and its

[31] On this scholar, known also as Ibn Yashush, see Ashtor, *Jews of Moslem Spain*, II, p. 293 and 364–65 nn.329–32; and *Encyclopaedia Judaica*, Jerusalem (Keter) 1972, vol. 8, col.1211, art. 'Ibn Yashush' (by Ashtor).

[32] This is of course the famous poet Solomon Ibn Gabirol.

[33] Ashtor, *Jews of Moslem Spain*, III, pp. 217–24, and 294–95, nn. 106–22; see also p. 250, n. 84; see also II, pp. 257–58, and 350–51, n.200.

[34] Ar. al-Ġazāl; the correction is obvious, the "tooth" of the *nūn* has dropped out, and the dots of the *nūn* and the *ġayn* have each been displaced to the left.

territory, and administrator of the state.[35] No one in al-Andalus before him had such learning in the law of the Jews and knowledge of how to use it and to defend it. He died in the year 448 [= 1056].[36]

Several features of this text, positive and negative, are of capital interest here. First, as has been seen, Ṣāʿid devotes a large proportion of his chapter on the Jews to those of al-Andalus. I have translated here only those sections which are concerned with Iberia, but the remaining part of this chapter, dealing almost entirely with the ancient period of Israelite history and literature, is scarcely longer than this section. Secondly, Ṣāʿid has remarkably narrow geographical range. With one exception, all his Andalusi Jewish men of learning are connected with Saragossa (or with another state, Denia, closely linked with Saragossa); and the single exception, Samuel Ibn Naġrīla, stands out in peninsular Jewish history so much, in every way, that he scarcely counts as an exception. Ṣāʿid seems to have known only those Jews who were active in Saragossa. Put another way, he seems not to have had any acquaintance even with those of Toledo, where he spent much of the latter part of his career, coming at the end to write the *Ṭabaqāt* in that city. And there is nothing on Jews anywhere else, and this at a time when Jews were to be found scattered all over the peninsula. Thirdly, Ṣāʿid's interest is very limited culturally too: all the Saragossan Jews whom he mentions are described as excelling in a single group of sciences: medicine, "logic", and other broadly secular branches of learning are virtually the only fields with which Ṣāʿid concerns himself here. He does refer to the study of Hebrew, twice, a fact of considerable interest; and beyond this he also ascribes, in fairly general terms, a knowledge of "the law of the Jews" to virtually every Jew whom he lists. Poetry, both in Hebrew and in Arabic, is noticeable for its absence. Ṣāʿid makes no mention of poets, as poets, at all. Of course he does mention Ibn Gabirol, and Ibn Naġrīla, both of them among the greatest of all Hebrew poets, but not in their quality as poets.

The people whom Ṣāʿid mentions, Ḥasdāy Ibn Shaprut, Menaḥem ibn al-Fawwāl, Marwān Ibn Ǧanāḥ, Solomon Ibn Gabirol, Ḥasdāy ibn Yūsuf ibn Ḥasdāy, Ibn Qisṭār, and Samuel Ibn Naġrīla, are an interesting group. Four of them are very well known to us from Jewish sources: Ḥasdāy ibn Shaprut is known to us from Jewish sources as an associate of al-Ḥakam

[35] For this ruler, see Wasserstein, *Rise and Fall*, index.

[36] For Samuel Ibn Naġrīla see, besides my article cited earlier (supra, n.14), J. Schirmann, 'Samuel Hannagid, the man, the soldier, the politician', *Jewish Social Studies* 13, 1951, pp. 99–126; Wasserstein, *Rise and Fall*, pp. 197–205; R. Brann, *The Compunctious Poet, Cultural Ambiguity and Hebrew Poetry in Muslim Spain*, Baltimore (Johns Hopkins University Press) 1991, index, esp. pp. 49–58.

II al-Mustanṣir and as patron of Jewish learning in al-Andalus; Marwān ibn Ǧanāḥ is very well known indeed as an early grammarian of importance, and most of his works survive to this day. It is interesting, however, in the present context, and especially in view of what has already been noted about Ṣāʿid's interest in medicine, that the only work by Ibn Ǧanāḥ that Ṣāʿid actually mentions by name should be a medical text, and that this is not actually known to us otherwise at all (Ibn Abī Usaybīʿa, who generally depends faithfully on Ṣāʿid, also mentions this text, but under a different name, which is puzzling; it would be very good to have some independent confirmation of the existence of this text). Solomon Ibn Gabirol is well known both as a writer on philosophical themes and as a Hebrew poet — though this side of his activity is not noted by Ṣāʿid. And Samuel Ibn Naġrīla is extremely well known in a wide variety of ways. But the other three are, at least in terms of what we know from Jewish sources, decidedly minor characters.

These are not the only features which make this short text interesting. Ṣāʿid also tells us, almost in passing, that his young friend Abū al-Faḍl Ḥasdāy ibn Yūsuf ibn Ḥasdāy was a member of a noble Jewish family in Saragossa. It is noteworthy that he gives us the names of both his father and his grandfather: such detail is all too rare for Jews in this period, and is to be valued all the more when we find it. In general, Jews about whom we know anything for this period did not come from families with long lists of ancestors. This was both because long lists of this sort were not customary (fathers' names were often known, but the Arab Muslim practice of listing ancestors for several generations backwards is not, in the main, part of the Jewish tradition), and because a Jew known to us from this period was generally the only member of his family to achieve renown. Ṣāʿid tells us more than this: he adds that the family was descended from "Moses the Prophet, peace be upon him". This is probably an error by Ṣāʿid: Jews wishing to lay claim to distinguished ancestry in the Middle Ages usually asserted that they were descendants of the house of David. In doing so, they were able at once to claim royal ancestry and a link with the future Messiah. Moses is not otherwise known as an alleged ancestor of distinguished medieval Jews; the error is likely to lie in a confusion by Ṣāʿid, or his source, in imagining that the Jewish parallel to descent from Muḥammad, the Prophet of Islam, would necessarily involve Moses, the Prophet of Judaism.

What these features of Ṣāʿid's text suggest is very interesting. The most interesting and valuable part of the report, and of the picture which it gives us, is the section at the beginning, on Ḥasdāy ibn Shaprut. Here we have a picture of a successful Jew in royal employ; a Jew who is able to use his royal connections in order to obtain books and other material (information about the operation of the Jewish calendar, of great importance for calculations of the dates of festivals, and the like); of a Jew who is able thereby to cut the local Jewish dependence on the Jewry of Baghdad. There is virtually nothing here that we do not know from other sources. However, what makes this report different is its context. It occurs in a Muslim text, from not so long after the event, and in a form which tends to suggest that Ḥasdāy, in thus cutting the umbilical cord with Iraq, was acting in concert with his employer, the caliph of Cordoba. This is of significance in a quite different context.

One of the concerns of the Umayyads in Spain, especially in the decades following the re-establishment of the caliphal institution in Cordoba in 929, was to create an adequate identity, especially in ideological and cultural terms, for al-Andalus within the Islamic world. We have evidence for this in the structure and patterning of the great mosque in the Umayyad capital, Cordoba; and in the whole career of al-Ḥakam II al-Mustanṣir, the patron of Ḥasdāy, I have argued elsewhere that we have much more than that.[37] Al-Ḥakam's patronage, I tried to suggest, had a purpose, and that purpose was the establishment of al-Andalus as a state, with Umayyad caliphal rulers, with a distinctive cultural identity, one separate from that of the ʿAbbāsid-ruled East, Iraq. Ḥasdāy's work, in separating the Jews of al-Andalus from those of Iraq, and in offering the patronage and creating the conditions in which a distinctive Jewish cultural identity came into being in the Iberian peninsula, parallels that of his own patron, al-Ḥakam II al-Mustanṣir, in which exactly the same happened, at exactly the same time, for the Muslims of al-Andalus. It is asking a lot to see in this parallellism pure coincidence. However, Ṣāʿid is the only author who seems to make explicit a link between Ḥasdāy's work and his dependence on his patron. Given the position of Ṣāʿid outside the Jewish cultural ambit, and after, but not long after, the end of the Umayyad dynasty's existence, we should attach very great significance to this report.

The rest of Ṣāʿid's report, interesting as it is, is in fact very thin. What he has to tell us about Samuel Ibn Naġrīla does not amount to very much. We hear much more about him in other sources, Muslim and Jewish alike; it is a shame that we do not hear more in this case, given that the author was a contemporary of the Nagid. Ṣāʿid's account of the other Jewish men of letters in al-Andalus, as the Saragossan link joining them all shows, is simply a report of the few Jewish scientists with whom Ṣāʿid had happened to have some contact during his career. It is limited to his personal

[37] D.J. Wasserstein, 'The library of al-Ḥakam II al-Mustanṣir and the culture of Islamic Spain', *Manuscripts of the Middle East* 5, 1990–91, pp. 99–105.

experience, by the localities in which he had been active, and to the range of his own professional interests.[38]

Does this, then, tell us anything about the Golden Age? Does this single sustained account of Jewish cultural life in al-Andalus during the Golden Age from the pen of a contemporary non-Jew show us any awareness of the degree, the range or the quality of that achievement? The answer must be negative. And there is very little that can be added to Ṣāᶜid. While we do have quite a lot of material attesting to Muslim awareness of the existence of Jews, to their presence in al-Andalus, to their participation in the political life of the peninsula, and so on, there is scarcely anything else attesting to knowledge of their cultural activity. The main body of information which can be added here is the scattered pieces of poetry in Arabic, by Jewish poets (and one Jewish poetess, Qasmūna, the daughter of Samuel Ibn Naġrīla), which we find quoted here and there, mainly in the *Muġrib* of Ibn Ṣāᶜid. Samuel Stern studied these a generation ago.[39] But his concern was with the social conditions which led to the production of such poetry, and to the relative rarity of such production. He was less directly concerned with the interest in or awareness of it that Muslim littérateurs might have had. And once again, what we see in this poetry is material which has only tangential connection with the real matter of the Golden Age, material which stands half-way outside the cultural life of the Jews as Jews. It is precisely because, and only because, of that facet of it that it could come to be noticed by outsiders.

Gabriel Martinez-Gros argues for a view of Ṣāᶜid's *Ṭabaqāt* according to which the author was a "conciliator of two classes of the sciences which he knew well, as a judge by day and an astronomer by night", with a "privileged place of the Jews at the end of the chain of nations".[40] This

[38] For these latter aspects M. Plessner, 'Der Astronom und Historiker Ibn Ṣāᶜid al-Andalusī und seine Geschichte der Wissenschaften', *Rivista degli Studi Orientali* 31, 1956, pp. 235–57 (with valuable corrections to the text); and especially L. Richter-Bernburg, 'Ṣāᶜid, the *Toledan Tables*, and Andalusī Science', *From Deferent to Equant: A Volume of Studies in the History of Science in the Ancient and Medieval Near East in Honor of E.S. Kennedy*, ed. D.A. King and G. Saliba, New York (= *Annals of the New York Academy of Sciences*, vol.500) 1987, pp. 373–401.

[39] S.M. Stern, 'Arabic Poems by Spanish-Hebrew Poets', in *Romanica et Occidentalia Etudes dédiées à la mémoire de Hiram Peri (Pflaum)*, ed. M. Lazar, Jerusalem (Magnes Press) 1963, pp. 254–63. For Qasmūna see J.M. Nichols, 'The Arabic Verses of Qasmūna bint Ismāᶜīl Ibn Bagdālah', *International Journal of Middle East Studies* 13, 1981, pp. 155–58; J.A. Bellamy, 'Qasmūna the Poetess: Who Was She?', *Journal of the American Oriental Society* 103, 1983, pp. 423–24.

[40] See especially his article in *EI*, second edition, cited *supra*; id., 'Classification des sciences et classification des nations, trois exemples andalous du Ve/XIe siècle', *Mélanges de la Casa de Velazquez* 20, 1984, pp. 83–114; id., 'La première histoire andalouse des sciences', *Autrement, Tolède XIIe–XIIIe siècles*, fév. 1991, pp. 200–17.

seems to me exaggerated. It calls for the author to have inserted his account of the Jews in general, and of the Jews of al-Andalus in particular, with a very clear aim in mind; this is what Martinez-Gros is arguing. But this in its turn calls for Ṣāʿid to have had some clear understanding and informed knowledge of the character of Jewish cultural life there. From what we have seen of it, that is scarcely a description that would fit Ṣāʿid's account of the cultural life of the Jews.

Should this surprise us? Perhaps less than our knowledge of the Golden Age might encourage us to permit it to. The cultures of Islam, especially of Arabic Islam, had by the tenth century almost completely ceased to have much interest in the outside. Until the tenth century, there is plenty of evidence of interest in what other cultures had to offer, and this takes visible form in translation into Arabic of works from Greek and other languages. But by the time of Ḥasdāy, Arabic Islam has become far more closed and self-sufficient, less interested in the outside. It is noteworthy in this connection that Ṣāʿid should mention, as he does, the work of some of these Jews in Hebrew linguistic studies, for an interest in non-Arabic languages is noticeably absent in the middle ages of Islam. In this sort of context, it is scarcely surprising that the only Jews whom Ṣāʿid should mention are ones whose activity had an impact outside their own cultural community.

EXCERPTS FROM THE ABRIDGMENT *(AL-MUḪTAṢAR)* OF *AL-KITĀB AL-KĀFĪ* BY ABŪ AL-FARAǦ HĀRŪN IN ARABIC SCRIPT

NASIR BASAL

1. INTRODUCTION

1.1. In the tenth and eleventh centuries the Jewish centers in Palestine,[1] North Africa and Spain were under the rule of Islam.[2] During this period Arabic culture was almost at its peak in all the areas of science and the interaction between Arab and Jewish cultures was very intense.

In fact, it was natural for Jewish authors to be influenced by Arabic culture, since it was predominant at that time. This influence mark on all types of literary work and is reflected in various aspects of Hebrew literature, e.g., the themes of the works, the methods used, the basic premises and professional terminology. Furthermore, Arabic compositions were even copied outright; for example, Jewish grammarians copied entire chapters from Arabic grammar treatises and adapted them to Hebrew grammar;[3] physicians and other intellectuals copied entire chapters from various books in Arabic into Judaeo-Arabic (in Hebrew characters) in order to make them accessible to potential Jewish readers;[4] and even grammar books dealing with the Arabic language were copied in their entirety into Hebrew characters for the same purpose.[5] This is an

1 A list of bibliographical abbreviations can be found at the end of the article.

2 On this period in Palestine see: Gil, II, p. 490 ff; in North Africa see: H. Z. (J. W) Hirschberg, *A History of the Jews in North Africa*, Leiden (1974); in Spain see: D. Wasserstein, *The Rise and Fall of the Party-Kings Politics and Society in Islamic Spain, 1002–1086*. Princeton (1985).

3 See, e.g., D. Becker, "Yona Ibn Ǧanaḥ u-tluto ba-medaqdeqim ha-araviyyim", *Lešonénu* 57 (1993), pp. 138–39.

4 For a detailed review of this topic, see: T. Langermann, "Arabic Writing in Hebrew Manuscripts", *Arabic Sciences and Philosophy* 6 (1996), pp. 137–60.

5 See, e.g., a manuscript from the collection of Firkovich II at the National Library of

indication of the profound effect that Arabic culture had on Jewish culture in the period under discussion.

From the historical point of view, the assimilation of Arabic into the system of Jewish written languages in the Orient was in essence the replacement of Aramaic, the language used by the Jews in both writing and speech before the adoption of Arabic. This changing of the guard was not a parallel process in which Aramaic was gradually discarded and Arabic began to function in its place in those areas which had previously been the stronghold of Aramaic; instead the absorption of Arabic into Hebrew writing was part of a wider process of interaction through which new functions and new patterns of writing, which had not been used in Hebrew writing prior to contact with Arabic culture, entered the Hebrew system. In essence, Arabic functioned in a different literary system than did Aramaic, and therefore some of the old Aramaic writing patterns were abandoned.

We know that the Karaites discarded Aramaic long before the Rabbanites and that Arabic was adopted to fill the vacuum produced by the decline of Aramaic. However, it is worthwhile noting that, even in the early stages of the development of Karaite literature, a language other than Arabic was proposed for use as the language of literature, viz. Hebrew,[6] and Qirqisānī's[7] remarks indicate that the option of speaking Hebrew, which had been raised by Benjamin al-Nahawandī,[8] also existed: **ופי הדא איצ̇א רד עלי בנימין פי קולה אנה לא יג̇וז לנא אן נתכלם פימא ביננא אלא בלגה̈ אלעבראני**[9] ("Thus, there is also an answer for Benjamin [al-Nahawandī] who said that it is not possible to speak among ourselves in any language other than Hebrew"). In contrast, it is well-known that most of the Karaite authors who lived and worked in the tenth and eleventh centuries, such as Salmon b. Yeruḥim, Sahl b. Maṣliaḥ, Yefet b. ʿAlī and later Ibn Sāqawayh, David b. Abraham al-Fāsī, Joseph b. Noaḥ, Abū al-Farağ Hārūn and Joseph b. Baḫtawayh wrote in Arabic and not in Hebrew.[10]

Interpretation of the Bible was the main subject of Karaite writing, but

Russia in St. Petersburg, no. Evr.-arab. I, 290. 2) It is my intention to publish these excerpts (? texts) in the near future.

[6] See, e.g., Daniel al-Qumisī (who was born in Persia but lived in Jerusalem in the first half of the tenth century) wrote most of his work in Hebrew. For a detailed review of al-Qumisī and his works, see Gil, II, pp. 784–87.

[7] For a detailed review of him and his works, see: L. Nemoy, *Karaite Anthology (Yale Judaica Series, III)*, New Haven (1952), pp. 42–68.

[8] For a detailed review of him and his works, see: ibid., pp. 20–29.

[9] See: L. Nemoy (ed.), *Kitāb al-Anwār wal-Marāqib by Yaʿqūb al-Qirqisānī*, Vol. III, New-York (1942), p. 645, lines 19–20.

[10] On these authors see, e.g., Gil, II, pp. 787–819.

works were also writen on the *halakhah* and grammar, a dictionary was compiled, and so forth.

1.2. It is well known that in the Middle Ages Jews used the Hebrew script when writing Arabic. Blau is of the opinion that this usage indicates that Judaeo-Arabic culture was partially detached from its surroundings. True, Jews did occasionally use the Arabic script as well in those days, but apparently much more sparingly.[11]

Blau points out that it is quite reasonable to assume that Judaeo-Arabic literature was at first written in Arabic characters, and that there are indications to the effect that Rav Saadya Gaon wrote some of his Arabic essays in Arabic characters. But the evidence available to us is insufficient, in his opinion, for arriving at a definitive conclusion as to which script he used in general for writing his essays, and in particular for writing his translation of the Bible.[12]

In the British Library (formerly the Library of the British Museum), in the Genizah Collection of the Cambridge University Library and in the Russian National Library in St. Petersburg (formerly the Saltykov-Schedrin Public Library in Leningrad) are to be found Judaeo-Arabic manuscripts written in Arabic characters. These manuscripts have their origin in Palestinian and Egyptian Karaite circles of the tenth and eleventh centuries. They contain transcriptions of the Hebrew Bible,[13] liturgical texts and some grammatical treatises.

Some prominent scholars have attempted to explain why these Karaite writers composed their Arabic works using Arabic characters and why they transcribed the Bible in this manner as well.[14] Opinions are divided on this issue and the explanations given to solve it do not adequately account for the practice of transcription and the distribution of the transcriptions in the Karaite manuscripts.[15]

11 Blau, Emergence, p. 38.

12 For a discussion of this issue, see ibid., pp. 39–41.

13 For descriptions of these Old Testament transcriptions into Arabic, see, e.g.: Hoerning; Khan (1987), (1990) — the introduction, (1992), (1993) and Harviainen (1993_1), (1993_2), (1994).

14 See: H. Hirschfeld, in a review of *A Commentary on the Book of Daniel by Jephet ibn Ali the Karaite*, edited and translated by D. S. Margoliouth, *Semitic Series* vol. I, Part III, Oxford; *ZDMG* 45 (1891), p. 332; "Early Karaite Critics of the Mishnāh", *JQR* n.s. 8 (1917–1918), p. 169; S. Poznanski, "Aus Qirqisânî's 'Kitâb al-ʾanwâr wa'l-marâqib'", in: G.E. Kohut (ed.), *Semitic Studies in Memory of Alexander Kohut*, Berlin (1897), p. 439; Z. Ankori, *Karaites in Byzantium*, New-York (1959), pp. 417–18; Blau, Emergence, p. 43; A. Ben David, "Minnayin ha-ḥaluqqah li-tnuʿot qeṭannot u-gdolot?", *Lešonénu* 22 (1958), p. 134; A. Dotan, "Masorah", *Encyclopaedia Judaica* vol. 16, col. 1466.

15 For an additional discussion which sums up the issue, see Khan (1992), p. 159–61.

Many of these Arabic manuscripts written in Arabic characters contain Hebrew words and Biblical quotations in Arabic transcription, as mentioned above, while in some of them the Hebrew words and Biblical quotations appear in Hebrew characters.[16]

1.3. The Arab.-Evr. series of the Firkovich II collection in the Russian National Library in St. Petersburg contains manuscripts written in Judaeo-Arabic using Arabic characters. Most of these manuscripts contain exegetical material, while others contain transcriptions of Biblical texts into Arabic and grammatical essays.

One of the few grammatical works is Ms. 300, which contains two pages of Judaeo-Arabic in Arabic characters, including the transcription of Biblical texts into Arabic with Tiberian Hebrew vowel signs.

These pages contain short chapters and parts of chapters which have the same structure as those of Abū al-Farağ's[17] *Muštamil*[18] and *Kāfī*.[19]

The first three lines of page 1 are the end of the chapter on the subject of the adjective functioning as a *nomen agentis*. This is followed by a chapter on the passive voice and one on word-order within the sentence. At the bottom of the page begins a discussion on the various types of patient and the opening remarks on the absolute patient. Page 2 contains a part of a chapter on the two kinds of Hebrew verbal conjugation, apparently indicated by the word mark עֲדִי,[20] as well as certain exceptional conjugations which are given no particular sign. The last chapter on page 2 concerns the criteria for determining patterns of the verbal forms.

Each page consists of twenty-two lines. Page 1 is complete and presents no problems of decipherment. Page two is torn on top and in the middle, contains many erasures, and thus presents many difficulties to the reader.

The two pages are not contiguous in the manuscript, but they are doubtless part of the same work and have been copied by the same hand. This conclusion has been reached by the present author after a thorough examination of the text, in which similarities in writing were found, such as the manner of connecting letters and the form of the letter ز.

[16] On the two types of manuscripts see, e.g.: G. Margoliouth, *Catalogue of the Hebrew and Samaritan Manuscripts in the British Museum*, part I, London (1899), p. 189; part II (1905), p. 172; H. Ben-Shammai, "Hebrew in Arabic script — Qirqisānī's view", in S. R. Brunswick (ed.), *Studies in Judaica, Karaitica and Islamica presented to L. Nemoy*, Ramat-Gan (1982), p. 121, n. 32.

[17] See Maman, pp. 119–21.

[18] On this work see, e.g., Bacher; Maman, pp. 119–21.

[19] On this treatise, see M. Steinschneider, *Die arabische Literatur der Juden*, Frankfurt a. M. (1902), p. 88 and Zislin (1962), p. 178.

[20] On the meaning of this sign and of those that mark the conjugations, see below in the commentary on the text, § 5.5.

As is the case with many Karaite manuscripts written in the Arabic alphabet, numbers in this manuscript are indicated by letters, a practice which is not commonly encountered in Muslim writings. We thus propose that this indicates an analogy and affinity to Judaeo-Arabic manuscripts written in Hebrew characters.[21]

The manuscript uses the following transliteration of Hebrew letters into Arabic:

א=ا; ב=ب; גּ=ج; ג=غ; ד=د; ד̄=ذ; ה=ه; ו=و; ז=ز; ח=ح; ט=ط; י=ي;
כ=ك; כ̄=خ; ל=ل; מ=م; נ=ن; ס=س; ע=ع; פ, פּ=ف; צ=ص; ק=ق; ר=ر; ש=ش;
שׂ=س; תּ=ت; ת̄=ث.

This article aims at providing a decipherment of the original text, an English translation and commentary, and an analysis of the contents, which are compared to the two aforementioned works by Abū al-Farağ Hārūn (*Muštamil* and *Kāfī*).

Since it is well-known that there are two additional works in Hebrew grammar by Abū al-Farağ: *al-Muḫtaṣar* and *Kitāb al-ʿuqūd fī taṣārīf al-luġa al-ʿibrāniyya*[22] and there is within hand short extracts from *Kitāb al-ʿuqūd* (assuming that the identification of the extract is correct), we can compare certain passages (the section which deals with the conditions for determining patterns of word-formation) from *Kitāb al-ʿuqūd* with the respective section in the text published in this article. And, certainly, comparison of this sort may prove beneficial in deciding to which treatise the passage published here belongs.

I shall also discuss the method used by the author for transcribing Hebrew Bible texts into Arabic characters.

2. THE TEXT

1a

[في الفاعل وبالواو واليا]

[الفاعل ؟؟؟ على مقتَضاَ القياس نحو صيدَيلق وجنّاب][23]

اذ لو جا على القياس لكان صوذيق وجونيب لكنه جا[ ]

[21] On this issue, see Ben-Shammai (1986), p. 62; Khan (1992), p. 169.

[22] Hirschfeld has published two Genizah fragments belonging to the British Library. The author of these fragments states in the beginning (ibid., p. 5) that he produced a compendium to *Kitāb al-Kāfī* under the title *al-Muḫtaṣar* and he also adds that he wrote a more condensed compendium, *Kitāb al-ʿuqūd*, of which the following fragment are a part of: קד כנת אכׄתצרת אלכאפי פי אללגה ... וסאל סאיל אן אכׄתצר מכׄתצר אכׄר אוגׄז מן אלמכׄתצר אלמדׄכור.

[23] The completion of the first word is certain, but the second one is doubtful. See below in the commentary on the text.

باب في الفعل الذي لم يسمَّ فاعله
الفعل المبني للمفعول مضموم الاول نحو اشارّ لا سپفيار لاهپم
يسپفيار ليپلدور هپكّپا افرايم ويپكّو شوطري صپوّا ييے
اشار يصپوا هوقپام همشكان والفعل الغير مسَما
فاعله لا يحسن ان يجي فاعل بعده كما لا يحسن مجي مفعول بعد
الفعل المسَمَى فاعله. وقد يجي من فعل الانفعال ما هو
بمعنى ما لم يسم فاعله نحو ولا يشپافخ پام نپاقي المقارّب لمعنى
وشُپفّاخ پامپام وتّلاقپاح استيرّ الذي هو بمعنى وتُپقاح هپاإشپا
بيث فرعو وقوله وإتپا هپشپلإخپتپا مقبرّخپا هو بمعنى
هپشپلإخپتپا ومثله كپاليل تپقبطپارّ بمعنى تپقطپار واما
الفعل المبني للفاعل فانه لا يجي علي طريقة واحدة كما يجي الفعل
المبني للمفعول بالضَمّ على [الاشهر][24] وكما لا تكمل فايدة
الفعل المبني للفاعل الا [بمجي][25] الفاعل كذلك الفعل المبني
للمفعول لا تكمل فايدته الا [بمجي المفعول][26] ولهذا اذا كان من باب ما
يتعدّى الى مفعولين لم يحسن ان يقتصر على احدهما كقوله يپتّان
اث ابيشاغ هشونميث لاأذنپيپاهو المفعول الاول ابيشاغ والثاني اذونيپاهو[27]
باب في الفعل والفاعل والمفعول
اذا اجتمع ذلك في الكلام فالاولى تقديم الفعل على الفاعل والمفعول
[مع] جواز التاخير والذي يبين الفاعل من المفعول هو دخول

1b

[اث على المفعـ][28]ـول مثل ويّكپا فشحور إث [يرا]ميپاهو واث
عمپاسا سپام ابشپالوم واذا ارتفعت [اث] عنه [حصـ]ـال الـ[تبـ]اس[29]
ونحتاج في تمييز احدهما من الاخرّ الى امرّ من خارّج نحو وپيّاعپبير

[24] There are numerous stains on the letters, making it difficult to read this word. My reading is based on the available parts of letters as well as a comparison with *Kāfī* Ms. II, 24a, line 17.

[25] The manuscript has a stain here, and the text has been filled in according to the context.

[26] This reading is compatible with the remnants of the letters and the context.

[27] This word is written on the left margin.

[28] This word is illegible in the manuscript, and has been reconstructed in accordance with *Kāfī* Ms. II, 24b, line 12.

[29] واذا ... التباس. There are stains on the manuscript, and the text has been reconstructed according to *Kāfī* Ms. II, 25a, line19; *Kāfī* Ms. III, 7a, line 7: **פאלתבס אחדהמא באלאכֿר ענד ארתפאע את** (= one is confused with the other when the word 'את' is deleted).

يشاي شيمّا بپانپاو يرصّو ذليم والفعل والفاعل
والمفعول اذا تقدم بعضهم على بعض تجي على ستة وجوه آ
تقدم الفعل على الفاعل والمفعول مثل وَيَكِا فشحور اث يرميّاهو
وهو اشهرها ب تقدم الفاعل على فعله ومفعو[له]
نحو وييح فپاقياذ اث سپارا وهو مشهور ايضا ج تقدم
المفعول على الفعل والفاعل نحو هيقاسپل نپاسياخ حپاراش
اث اذوني صبوّا ييح د تقدم الفاعل على مفعوله وفعله
نحو وارّص رفپا يم تفيل ييح بپاعير صلمام تبزا ه تقدم
المفعول على الفاعل والفعل نحو روش مسبّاي عمال سفپاثيمو
يخيسّيمو و تقدم الفعل على المفعول والفاعل نحو وَيّار
اوثام ناعر لإخين كااخول قاش لشون[30] إيش بحيث يجعل اخول بتقدير الفعل
باب في اقسام المفعول
اقسام المفعول خمسة آ [المفعول المط]لق[31] ب مفعول به ج مفعول فيه
د مفعول [له][32] ه مفعول معه
فصل في المفعول المطلق
ذلك هو المصدر لانه المفعول الحقيقي الصادر من الفاعل
وذلك مثل وبهاعلوث اهرّون اث هينّيروث الذي
مفعول اهرّون المطلق [هو][33] الاصعاد الذي هو مصدر
مسما في العبراني هاعلوث والمفعول به هو النيروث[34]

2a

را[ ]

فورا [ ]

من [ ]

[30] This word and the preceding one are written on the right margin of the page.

[31] The context makes the reconstruction of the missing part certain, as does the text of *Kāfī* Ms. II, 25a, line 19; III, 7a, lines 1–3; IV, 17a, line 14; *Muštamil* Ms. I, 46a, line 10.

[32] Illegible in the manuscript, but the reconstruction is certain both from the context and by comparison with *Kāfī* Ms. II, 25b, line 1; III, 7b, line 3; IV, 17a, line 14; *Muštamil* Ms. I, 46a, line 11.

[33] There is a stain on the manuscript, and the word has been inserted according to the context as well as *Kāfī* Ms. II, 26a, line 4; III, 7b, line 19; IV, 18a, line 1. In *Muštamil* there is no discussion of ובהעלת אהרן את הנרות (see § 5.4).

[34] Here begins a lacuna whose size is difficult to determine. In addition, there is no continuity between the subject matter on this page and on the following one.

والمفعول [ ] على [ ]
] عندي [ ]
آ الامر[35] [هيليل بروش بنقطتين][36] والماضي هيلبيل بنقطة واحدة من][37]
كلّو ييلبيل بّ هوريز عاريخ] امر [والماضي هوريز][38]
والفاعل موريز شاول [ويّپاعيل][39] والمفعول مورّاز [مثال المفعول] من
هاشيب][40] واعلم انه قد تبقت [تصاريف لم تدخل تصاريفها
في شي من العلامات منها ما لا ماضي له [ولا فاعل]
من نفس الامر مثل شيب وداع وكل هذا الوزن
ومنها ما لا [يسمى][41] فاعله من نحو هاجيد] هجياذ شلاخ
هشلخ وما جرى [هذا المجرى ليس منه][42] امر ومنها
ما هو شاذ في الاستعمال] وهم يذشّنّا
سلّا وإقبرّا لخبا [ ]وث وام هيبامين
واسمبايلا ميفا؟ [ ] وعل بركايم تشاعشاعو
الى غير ذلك مما يجري هذا المجرى] الذي لا وجه لوضع علامة له
من حيث انه لم يشتهر تصريفه [ا]شتهارًا يقطع عليه
باب في الشروط المراعاة في اوزان
الالفاظ بعضها على بعض
شروط اوزان الافعال سبعة آ ان تكون صيغة
[اللفظة كصيغة اللفظة الموزونة بها] حتى يكون خروجهما من الفمّ

[35] This reading is compatible with the extant for remnants of the letters as well as with the context.

[36] This reconstruction is required by the context.

[37] This is missing in the manuscript and has been filled in according to the context and *Kāfī* Ms. I, 277a–b.

[38] This reconstruction is certain, both because of the context and in comparison with *Kāfī* Ms. I, 277b, line 1.

[39] The word is erased in the manuscript, save remnants of the letter lamed, but the reconstruction is certain.

[40] The reconstruction is certain. See *Kāfī* Ms. I, 277b, line 3.

[41] There is a stain here in the manuscript, and the text has been filled in according to the context.

[42] The context makes this reconstruction certain, since the topic is conjugations lacking an overt marker, and passive forms, lacking an imperative, certainly have no marker for it.

2b

[خروجا واحدا ويرٚدان على حاسة السمع مورٚدا واحدا مع]

[اختلاف حرٚوفهما وذلك مثل عپاسپا وعپالپـ[43]]

] [

] [

] [

] [

] [

] مثل يپاسوب[

اوثـ[ـو][44] الذي هو فعل يپارٚوذ يپارادنو الذي هو مصدرٚ

ومثل وهوليخ مـهـيـرٚا [الـ]ـذي هو امرٚ وهوليخ

لبوقر صلماوث الذيّ هو اسم ومثل يوليخ يـيـ

اوثخپا فعل يوعيص بساخل اسم ومثل حپاشياب

انوش فعل حارٚاش عيصبيم اسم جٚ [هو

اتفاقهما في وصـ[ـف واحد فهو][45] انه ان كانت

الواحد ة فعلا [ماضيا كانت الاخرٚى][46] كمثل او مستقبلا

فكمثل او امرٚا [فكمثل ولولا ذلـ]ـك لساغ وزن

قپارٚبو رٚيبخپام يومارٚ [الذي هو امـ]ـرٚ على إربو لنفشي

الذي هو فعل ماضي [ولساغ وز]ن وقپارٚاب اوثپام الذي

هو امرٚ على وقپاذارٚ [عل]ـيهـپام الذي هو فعل ماضي

وكذلك تپافياس يوا[ش][47] هو فعل ماضي على تپالا[ن

عيني وهو فعل مستقبل دٚ كون

عدد الاحرٚف الجوا[هـ]ـرية في الواحدة كالاخرى

[43] Missing in the manuscript, and filled in accordance with *Kāfī* Ms. I, 279a, line 9.

[44] Filled in following *Kāfī* Ms. I, 279b, lines 5–6.

[45] Filled in following *Kāfī* Ms. I, 280a, line 1.

[46] Filled in following *Kāfī* Ms. I, 280a, line 3.

[47] يواش , The manuscript reads يواب , apparently by mistake, as in *Kāfī* Ms. I, 280a, line 9 (= יוֹאָב). The form used by the present author is certainly the correct one.

3. TRANSLATION OF THE TEXT

1a
[in the *nomen agentis* and with *waw* and *taw* and *yod*]
the *nomen agentis* [ ] as necessitated by analogy as in צַדִּיק (Gen 6, 9) [and גַּנָּב (Jer. 2, 26 and elsewhere)]
since if it had been formed by analogy it should have been like צוֹדֵק and גּוֹנֵב (Deut. 24, 7) but instead it appeared as [ ]

A Chapter concerning the Passive Verb

Verbs in the passive voice have u/o as their first vowel, e.g. אשר לא־סֻפַּר להם (Is. 52, 15);
יְסֻפַּר לאדני לדור (Ps. 22, 31); הֻכָּה אפרים (Hos. 9, 16); וַיֻּכּוּ שטרי (Ex. 5, 14); צֻוָּה ביהוה (Num. 36, 2);
אשר יְצֻוֶּה (Ex. 34, 34); הוּקַם המשכן (Ex. 40, 17). The passive verb should not be followed by an agent <noun>, just as a patient <noun> should not follow
an active verb. Sometimes a verb appears in the *nif'al* form, which has the same function as a passive verb, e.g. ולא יִשָּׁפֵךְ דם נקי (Deut. 19, 10), with a meaning close to that
of וְשֻׁפַּךְ דמם (Zeph. 1, 17); וַתִּלָּקַח אסתר (Est. 2, 8 & 16); וַתֻּקַּח האשה בית פרעה (Gen. 12, 15); ואתה הָשְׁלַכְתָּ מקברך (Is. 14,14) means the same as הָשְׁלַכְתָּ, and likewise כליל תָּקְטָר (Lev. 6, 16) means תָּקְטַר. And as
to the verb in the active voice, it does not appear in one form only, as does the verb
in the passive voice, which has the vowel u/o [in most cases].[48] And just as the complete meaning
of the verb in the active voice needs the presence of the agent, so also the verb in the passive voice
needs [a patient noun] for the completion of its meaning. Thus, if it belongs to the class of <verbs> which
are doubly transitive, it is not appropriate for it to be limited to one object only, for as it is written יֻתַּן
את־אבישג השנמית לאדניהו (1K. 2, 21), the first patient is אבישג while the second one is אדניהו.

[48] In most cases, but not all, since in his opinion the *nif'al* form serves occasionally as a passive.

A Chapter concerning Verb, Agent and Patient

If these appear in an utterance, it is appropriate for the verb to precede the agent and the patient,
with the possibility of preceding and delaying. What differentiates agent from patient is the addition of
['את' to the patient], as in ויכה פשחור את ירמיהו (Jer. 20, 2); ואת עמשׂא שׂם אבשלום (2 Sam. 17, 25). If ['את'] is absent <the utterance> is vague, and we would have need of something external in order to know which is which, as in ויעבר
ישי שמה (1 Sam. 16, 9); בניו ירצו דלים (Job 20, 10). Verb, agent and patient can precede each other in six ways: a.
The verb precedes both agent and patient, as in
ויכה פשחור את ירמיהו (Jer. 20, 2).
This is the most common one; b. The agent may precede its verb and agent, as in ויהוה פקד את־שׂרה (Gen. 21, 1). This one is also common; c. The precedence
of the patient, before verb and agent, as in הפסל נסך חרש (Is. 40, 19); את־אדני צוה יהוה (Gen. 36, 2); d. The agent precedes the patient and the verb,
as in וארץ רפאים תפיל (Is. 26, 19); אדני בעיר צלמם תבזה (Ps. 73, 20); e. The precedence
of the patient, before agent and verb, as in ראש מסבי עמל שׂפתמיו יכסימו (Ps. 140, 10); f. The verb precedes patient and agent, as in וירא אתם נער (2 Sam. 17, 18); לכן כאכל קש לשון אש (Is. 5, 24), in which case the word אכול has the status of a verb.

A Chapter on the Classification of Patients

Patients are divided into five kinds: a. absolute patient; b. direct patient; c. adverbial patient;
d. causative patient; e. concomitant patient.

A Section on the Absolute Patient

This is the infinitive, since it is the real patient, which originates from the agent,
as in ובהעלת אהרן את־הנרת (Ex. 30, 8), in which
the absolute patient of אהרן is *ʾiṣʿād* (=raise),[49] which is the infinitive, which in the Hebrew text is the word העלות, while the direct patient is הנרת.

[49] I.e., *ʾiṣʿād* (= raise) is the actual action which the agent is performing (see below § 5.4).

2a

ר[ ]

פורה [ ]

from [ ]

and the patient [ ] on [ ]

[ ] by me [ ]

a. The imperative [הֵילֵל בראש] (Zach. 11, 2) with *ṣere*], and perfect הֵלִיל (Jer. 47, 2 — הֵילִיל) [with *ḥireq*, originating from]
כלה יְיֵלִיל (Is. 15, 2); b. הוֹרֵד עריך (Ex. 33, 5) is an imperative, the perfect form is הוֹרַד (2R. 16, 17)
the active participle is מוֹרִיד שאול ויעל (1 Sam. 2, 6) and the passive participle is מוּרָד, like the passive participle
[derived from הָשֵׁב]. And you should know that some verbs are not inflected in accordance with
any of the <usual> signs. Some have no past <form>, and no [active participle] derived
from the imperative itself, as in שֵׁב (Gen. 20, 15 *et al.*) also דַּע (ibid., 20, 7) and all of this form.
Some of them are passive forms, as in הֻגֵּד הֻגַּד (Josh. 9, 24); שֻׁלַּךְ (unattested in the Bible);
הֻשְׁלַךְ (Dan. 8, 11 — וְהֻשְׁלַךְ). These that behaved [in this manner have no] imperative. Some are
anomalous in their use [ ] יְדַשְּׁנֶה ; והם
סלה (Ps. 20, 4); וָאֶקְרָאֶה לך (1 Sam. 28, 15) [ ] ות
ואם־הימין ;
וְאַשְׂמְאִילָה (Gen. 13, 9); [ ] מֵפַּ; ועל־ברכים תְּשָׁעֳשָׁעוּ (Is. 56, 12)
and others that behave in this manner, so that it is not possible to define a sign for them,
since they are inflected in a way that is not common enough to be able to be defined <by a sign>.

A Chapter on the Conditions that Should be Considered When <Determining> the Pattern of One Form by Comparing it to Another
The conditions (for determining verbal patterns are seven in number: a. The form of
the word must be like that of the word whose pattern is being compared to it, so that their pronunciation

2b

[will be similar, and they will reach the ear in a similar manner,]
[despite the dissimilarities in their letters, as in עָשֹׂה and עָלֹה...

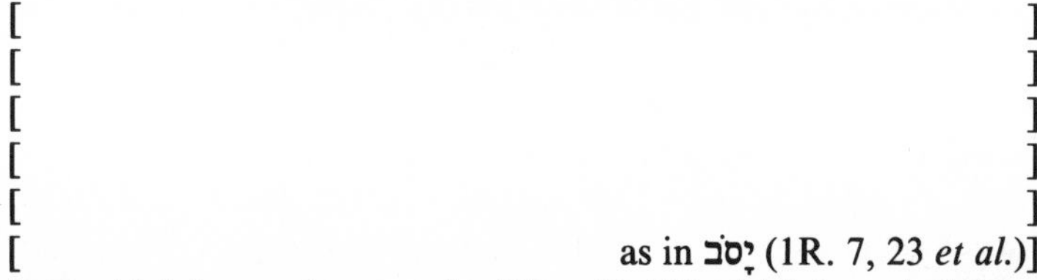

[as in יָסֹב (1R. 7, 23 *et al.*)]
[אתו which is a verb, יָרֹד ירדנו (Gen. 43, 20) which is an infinitive, and like וְהוֹלֵךְ מהרה (Num. 17, 11) which is an imperative, וְהֹלֵךְ לבקר צלמות (Amos 5, 8) which is a noun. Another <example is> יוֹלֵךְ יְיָ אתך (Deut. 28, 36) which is a verb, <while> יוֹעֵץ בשׂכל (1Ch. 26, 14) is a noun. And also חָשַׁב אנוש (Is. 33, 8), which is a verb, <while> חָרַשׁ עצים (Is. 44, 13) is a noun. c. [Their one shared attribute, viz.]: If one is a perfect verb, the other one should be so as well, and if it is future or imperative, <the other verb> should be the same, for otherwise it would be permissible to determine the pattern of קָרְבוּ ריבכם יאמר (Is. 41, 21) [which is an imperative] according to אָרְבוּ לנפשי (Ps. 59, 4), which is a verb in the perfect, [and one could determine the pattern of] וְקָרַב אתם (Ez. 37, 17), which is an imperative, according to וְקָדַר עליהם (Mi. 3, 6), which is a perfect verb. In the same manner, תָּפַשׂ יואש (2Ch. 25, 23), which is a perfect verb <could be compared to> תָּלַן עֵינִי (Job 17, 1), which is a future verb. d. Since the number of basic letters in the one is identical to that in the other.

4. TRANSCRIBING HEBREW BIBLE TEXTS WITH ARABIC CHARACTERS[50]

In the present text the Bible excerpts transcribed in Arabic characters represent only the *qere* form. The transcription itself is based on an Arabic writing convention in which only those vowels that were pronounced as long are represented by the *matres lectionis* ا و ي.

An analysis of the text indicates that all vowels within stressed syllables and all vowels in open syllables (except for *šewa* and *ḥaṭaf*) were marked by means of quiescent letters. This method of marking leads to the conclusion that the length of the vowel was not an independent variable, but rather that it was conditioned by stress and syllable structure.

[50] On six different methods of transcribing the Old Testament in Arabic characters, see, e.g., Khan (1993), pp. 50–51.

Since the Arabic script has only three *matres lectionis*, while the Tiberian vocalization recognizes seven vowel qualities, it is clear that this transcription cannot accurately reflect vowel quality as pronounced by the author of the text or by the scribe.

In any case, the seven Hebrew vocalic signs were matched with the three Arabic *matres lectionis* in the following manner: *qameṣ*, *pataḥ* and *segol* =ا ; *ḥolem*, *šureq* = و; *ḥireq*, *ṣere* = ي. Below are some examples:

Qameṣ gadol is usually transcribed by *mater lectionis* *ʾalif.*

Open syllable: لاهم (לָהֶם — Is. 52, 15. la, line 13); هااشا הָאִשָּׁה — Gen. 12, 15. la, line 11); واقراا لخا (וָאֶקְרָאֶה לְךָ — 1 Sam. 28, 15. 2a, line 15).

Stressed syllable: همشكان (הַמִּשְׁכָּן — Ex. 40, 17. 1a, line 7); تقطار (תָּקְטָר — Lev. 6, 16. 1a, line 13); مساي (מִסִּבָּי — Ps. 140, 10. 1b, line 12).

The *qameṣ* occurs after consonantal *ʾalef* in وارص (וָאָרֶץ — Is. 26, 19. 1b, line 11) and the *mater lectionis ʾalif* is omitted.

Pataḥ is usually represented by *mater lectionis ʾalif*:

Open syllable: وياعبير (וַיַּעֲבֵר — 1 Sam. 16, 9. 1b, line 3); لاادنياهو (לַאֲדֹנִיָּהוּ — 1K 2, 21. 1a, line 19); وبهاعلوث (וּבְהַעֲלֹת — Ex. 30, 8. 1b, line 20).

Stressed closed syllable: سفار (סֵפֶר — Is. 52, 15. 1a, line 5); هشلاخ (הִשְׁלַךְ — Dan. 8, 11 וְהִשְׁלַךְ. 2a, line 13); حاراش (חָרַשׁ — Is. 44, 13. 2b, line 12).

Pataḥ in open and unstressed syllable is not transcribed by *mater lectionis ʾalif* when it occurs after consonantal *ʾalif* in: اهرون (אַהֲרֹן — Ex. 30, 8. 1b, line 20).

Segol is usually transcribed by *mater lectionis ʾalif*:

Open syllable: كاالخول (כֶּאֱכֹל — Is. 5, 24. 1b, line 14); سالا (סֶלָה — Ps. 20, 4. 2a, line 15).

Stressed closed syllable: اشار (אֲשֶׁר — Is. 52, 15. 1a, line 5); هفاسل (הַפֶּסֶל — Is. 40, 19. 1b, line 9); رييخام (רִיבְכֶם — Is. 41, 21. 2b, line 17). In (לָהֶם — Is. 52, 15. 1a, line 5) *segol* is not represented by *mater lectionis ʾalif* in stressed closed syllable.

Ṣere is always transcribed by *mater lectionis yāʾ*:

Open syllable: هنيروث (הַנֵּרֹת — Ex. 30, 8. 1b, line 20); مهيرا (מְהֵרָה — Nu. 17, 11. 2b, line 10); عيصيم (עֵצִים — Is. 44, 13. 2b, line 13).

Stressed closed syllable: لاخين ... ايش (לָכֵן ... אֵשׁ — Is. 5, 24. 1b, line 14); وياعبير (וַיַּעֲבֵר — 1S 16, 9. 1b, line 3); استير (אֶסְתֵּר — Est. 2, 8,16. 1a, line 11).

Sometimes, the *ṣere* is left unrepresented by *mater lectionis yā'* in closed stressed syllable: يشافخ (יְשָׁפֵךְ — Dt. 19, 10. 1a, line 10); وهوليخ (וְהוֹלֵךְ — Nu. 17, 11. 2b, line 10); يولخ (יוֹלֵךְ — Dt. 28, 36.2b, line 11).

Ḥolem is transcribed always by *mater lectionis wāw* including most cases where MT has *scriptio defectiva* of *ḥolem*: لدور (לְדוֹר — Ps. 22, 31. 1a, line 6); شوطري (שֹׁטְרֵי — Ex. 5, 14. 1a, line 6); كااخول (כֶּאֱכֹל) — Is. 5, 24. 1b, line 14); شاول (שָׁאוּל — 1 Sam. 2, 1. 2a, line 8).

Ḥireq is transcribed by *mater lectionis yā'*:

Open syllable: بيشاي (יִשַׁי — 1 Sam. 16, 9. 1b, line 4).

Stressed closed syllable: كاليل (כָּלִיל — Lev. 6, 16. 1a, line 13); رفايم (רְפָאִים — Is. 26, 19. 1b, line 11); موريذ (מוֹרִיד — 1S 2, 6. 2a, line 8).

Šureq is transcribed by *mater lectionis wāw* including cases where MT has *qibbūṣ* without *mater lectionis wāw* in an open syllable:

Open syllable: هوقام (הוּקַם — Ex. 40, 17. 1a, line 7); موراذ (מוּרָד — unattested in the Bible. 2b, line 8); هشونميث (הַשֻּׁנַמִּית — 1K 2, 21. 1a, line 19).

Stressed closed syllable: فشحور (פַּשְׁחוּר — Jer. 20,2. 1b, line 1).

Final *mater lectionis he* of the Hebrew orthography transcribed by *'alif* when the preceding vowel is *qameṣ* or *segol*:

Qameṣ: هكا (הֻכָּה — Hos. 9, 7. 1a, 6) سارا (שָׂרָה — Gen. 21, 1. 1a, 8); واسما ايلا (וְאַשְׂמְאִילָה — Gen. 13, 9. 2a, 16).

Segol: ويكا (וַיַּכֶּה — Jer. 20, 2. 1b, line 1); تبزا (תִּבְזֶה — Ps. 73, 20. 1b, line 11); يذ شنا (יְדַשְּׁנֶה — Ps. 20, 4. 2a, line 13).

But the final *mater lectionis he* is not transcribed when it is preceded by a consonantal *'alif*: واقرا (וָאֶקְרָאֶה — 1 Sam. 28, 15. 2a, line 15).

When the preceding vowel is *ḥolem* the final *mater lectionis he* is transcribed by *wāw*: فرعو (פַּרְעֹה — Gen. 12, 15. 1a, line 12); كلّو (כֻּלֹּה — Is. 15, 2. 2a, line 7).

Quiescent *'alef* preceded by *ḥolem* in the middle of the word is transcribed by *wāw*: روش (רֹאשׁ — Ps. 140, 10. 1b, line 12); يومار (יֹאמַר — Is. 41, 21. 2b, line 17).

It is transcribed by *'alif* in the transcription of the word לֹא: (לֹא — Is. 52, 15. 1a, line 5); (וְלֹא — Dt. 19, 10. 1a, line 10).

The unpronounced final *'alef* in the Hebrew orthography of the MT is omitted in the transcription: ويار (וַיַּרְא — 2S 17, 18. 1b, line 13).

The otiose *yod* in pronominal suffixes attached to the plural noun בָּנִים is transcribed by *'alif*: باناو (בָּנָיו — Job. 20, 10. 1b, line 4).

*Šewa na*ʿ is transcribed twice by *pataḥ*: واتا (וְאַתָּה — Is. 14, 19. 1a, line 13); وشفاخ (וְשֻׁפַּךְ — Zeph. 1, 17. 1a, line 12).[51]

Segol and *pataḥ* twice:[52]
Segol instead of *pataḥ* هشللختا (הָשְׁלַכְתָּ — Is. 14, 19. 1a, line 13).
Pataḥ instead of *segol*: هفّاسل (הַפֶּסֶל — Jes. 40, 19. 1b, line 9).

Sometimes there are Arabic vowel signs in addition to the Hebrew ones: ويّكّو (וַיֻּכּוּ — Ex. 5, 14. 1a, line 11); وشُفّاخ (וְשֻׁפַּךְ — Zeph. 1, 17. 1a, line 11); يرصّو (יְרַצּוּ — Job. 20, 10. 1b, line 4). وتقّاح (וַתֻּקַּח — Gen. 12, 51. 1a, line 11).

5. COMMENTARY ON THE TEXT AND ANALYSIS

5.1 ADJECTIVE THAT MAY BE LIKENED TO THE *NOMEN AGENTIS*

As mentioned previously,[53] only the bottom three lines of this chapter are extant, and of those one-and-a-half lines are illegible because of many erasures. Still, there is no doubt that these lines form a part of the chapter on *al-ṣifa al-mušabbaha bi-ism al-fāʿil* (= adjective that may be likened to the *nomen agentis*).

The remnants of this chapter allow us to gather that forms such as צַדִּיק (Gen. 6, 9 *et al.*) and גַּנָּב (Jer. 2, 26 *et al.*) are indeed examples of adjectives that may be likened to the *nomen agentis*, and that had they been formed according to the paradigm of the *nomen agentis*, the result should have been צוֹדֵק (unattested in the Bible) and גּוֹנֵב (Deut. 24, 7).

When we compare the remnants of this chapter with the corresponding

[51] This vocalization, with *pataḥ*, reflects the pronunciation of *šewa* mobile: in the word וְאַתָּה the *šewa* mobile is pronounced like the vowel of following guttural ʾ*alef*, viz. as *pataḥ*. In the word וְשֻׁפַּךְ it is pronounced as *pataḥ*, which is its basic pronunciation. On the pronunciation of *šewa* in Tiberian Masorah, see: Sh. Morag, *ha-ʿivrit še-be-fī yehudei Teman*, Jerusalem (1963), pp. 160–66. On the alternation, based on pronunciation, of *šĕwa* mobile and *pataḥ* in manuscripts, see, e.g., Sharvit (1974), p. 552; (1986), p. 121 and Y. Yevin, *Masoret ha-lašon ha-ʿivrit ha-mištaqqefet ba-niqqud ha-bavli*, Jerusalem (1985), p. 416.

[52] On this issue see, e.g., Sharvit (1974), p. 552; (1986), pp. 121–122; "ʿIyyunim be-niqqudam šel qiṭʿei tefillah mi-gnizat Qahir" in: *Meḥqarim ba-lašon 5–6 — Israel Yevin Festschrift*, Jerusalem (1992), p. 502; Sh. Morag, "Mišnayot min ha-pereq 'bamme madliqin' bi-šnei kitvei-yad šel genizat Qahir", in: *Studia Orientalia Memoriae D. H. Baneth Dedicata*, Jerusalem (1979), pp. 118–20.

[53] See above, § 1.2.

chapters in *Muštamil*[54] and *Kāfī*,[55] we see that the form צַדִּיק is to be found in the latter, but not the form גַּנָּב, which is an innovation in our text. It thus appears that the author was of the opinion that the latter form indicated a vehemence of action lacking in the regular *nomen agentis* form, גּוֹנֵב, since according to *Kāfī*, adjectives that may be likened to the *nomen agentis* indicate an increased intensiveness.[56]

5.2. THE PASSIVE VERB

The passive verb in this chapter is called: *allaḏī lam yusammā fāʿiluhu* (= the verb whose agent has not been named) as is usual in medieval Arabic[57] and Hebrew[58] grammatical literature.

The following issues are raised on this topic:

a) The beginning of the passive verb is <vocalized with> *u/o* (= *maḍmūm al-ʾawwal*). In this the author does not deviate from the path trodden by medieval Arabic and Hebrew grammarians, who saw this vowel as a mark of the passive voice.[59] The active verb, in contrast, does not have one characteristic vowel.

From a perusal of the actual passive forms used by the author as examples, one may conclude that the expression *ʾawwal al-fiʿl* (= the beginning of the verb) means either the first radical or the prefix of forms in *hufʿal*:[60]

1) The vowel *u* following the first radical: סֻפַּר (Is. 52, 15. 1a, line 5); יְסֻפַּר (Ps. 22, 31. 1a, line 6).

2) The vowel *u* following the initial *he* of *hufʿal*: הֻכָּה (Hos. 9, 16. 1a, line 6); הוקם (Ex. 40, 17. 1a, line 7).

[54] E.g. Ms. I, 43b–45a.

[55] E.g. Ms. II 23a.

[56] Ms. II, 23a, line 12: לכן צדיק ושליט ואמיץ גׄאת מן אלמבאלגה̈ וצודיק ואוזאנה ליס כדלך כקולהם פי אלערבי אכיל ושריב אלדי יפידאן אלמבאלגה̈ עלי אֵכל ושארב (= but the <forms> צַדִּיק (Gen. 6, 9 et al.), שַׁלִּיט (Eccl. 8, 8) and אַמִּיץ (2 Sam. 15, 12 et al.) indicate intensiveness, while <the form> צוֹדֵק (unattested in the Old Testament) and those formed on the same paradigm do not. In the same way one says in Arabic *ʾakīl* [= a hearty eater] and *šarīb* [= a heavy drinker], forms which indicate an excess of eating and drinking). It is noteworthy that the word אֵכל in the preceding Arabic text is vocalized with *ṣere*, indicating a pronunciation with *ʾimāla*, i.e. *ā>ē: ʾākil>ʾēkil*. On this phenomenon in Judaeo-Arabic, see, e.g., Blau, Emergence, pp. 72, 73, 125, 135 and note 3.

[57] See, e.g., Ibn al-Sarrāğ, I, p. 77, line 14 and cf. Wright I, 50 B.

[58] See, e.g., Ḥayyūğ, pp. 30, line 1; 41, line 17; 80, line 2 and cf. W. Bacher, *Grammatische Terminologie des Jehûdâ b. Dâwîd Ḥayyûğ*, Wien (1882), p. 31.

[59] Cf. *Kāfī* Ms. II, 23a, lines 17–18; *Muštamil* Ms. I, 45a, line 11; Ms. II, 11a, line 21; Ibn al-Sarrāğ, I, p. 73, line 5.

[60] The actual examples of *hufʿal* in our text are all perfect forms with prefixed *he*.

b) It is not proper for a passive verb to be followed by a *nomen agentis*, just as it is not proper for a *nomen patientis* to follow an active verb. This means that a passive verb is followed by a noun signifying the patient, not the agent, while an active verb is followed by the agent. The reason for this is that the meaning of a verb in the active voice is completed through the following *nomen agentis*, just as the meaning of a verb in the passive voice is completed through the following patient.[61]

The use of the term *mafʿūl* (*nomen patientis*) indicates that the noun following a passive verb has the status of an object. Therefore, whenever a verb which subcategorizes for two objects appears in the passive voice, it is to be expected that the two objects follow it, as in: יֻתַּן את־אבישג השנמית לאדניהו (1K. 2, 21). The first object is אבישג, and the second one is לאדניהו.[62] In other words, יֻתַּן = יִתְּנוּ, without a specific subject, and the underlying meaning of the clause is 'let (someone unspecified) give *Abishag* to *Adoniyyahu*'. This latter formulation clearly indicates that the verb נתן takes two objects: 1) אבישג, 2) אדניהו. This clause is thus underlyingly similar to one which precedes it in the same chapter: וְיִתֶּן־לי את־אבישג השנמית לאשה (1K. 2, 17).[63]

It is worth noting that beginning with the end of his discussion of this topic[64] the author copies from *Kāfī* almost word for word, until the end of the first page.

c) It has already been stated above that the *nifʿal* form may occasionally take on a passive meaning. In other words, such a meaning is a possible, context-dependent, use of this form, but certainly not the only one. Indeed, in order to demonstrate that the *nifʿal* does at times have a passive meaning, the author compares those forms in which this occurs to others which are unambiguously passive, as in יִשָּׁפֵךְ (Deut. 19, 10) = וְשֻׁפַּךְ (Zeph. 1, 17); וַתִּלָּקַח (Est. 2, 8 & 16) = וַתֻּקַּח (Gen. 12, 15).[65]

In dealing with *nifʿal* in this manner, our author remains within the consensus of medieval Hebrew grammarians, who did not see it as merely

[61] It should be pointed out that this is the accepted view within Arabic grammar, for the noun which follows a passive verb is called *mafʿūl lam yusamma man faʿala bihi* (= a *nomen patientis* appearing without the mention of who did the action to it). See, e.g., Ibn al-Sarrağ, I, p. 76, 19.

[62] *Kāfī* II, 23b line 9. Cf. *Muštamil* Ms. I, 45b, line 19.

[63] See *Kāfī* Ms. II, 24b, lines 1–5, *Muštamil* Ms. I, 45b, lines 15–18. It is worth noting that in *Muštamil* there is another example, not mentioned either here in our text or in *Kāfī*: יֻתַּן־נא לעבדך משא צמד פרדים (2K. 5, 17).

[64] See above note 58.

[65] For a discussion in a similar vein, but more at length, see *Kāfī* Ms. II, 23b, lines 15 ff. In contrast, this issue receives no mention at all in the respective chapter of *Muštamil* Ms. I, 54b.

a passive form,[66] but rather considered its uses as an active verb,[67] a passive verb,[68] a verb denoting intensiveness,[69] etc.

To sum up, we have found that every example found in this section can be found as well in the corresponding chapter in *Kāfī*, while there is only a partial overlap with the examples adduced in *Muštamil*. The role of *nifʿal* as an occasional passive is not mentioned at all in *Muštamil*. Furthermore, nearly half of the relevant chapter here in our text is copied word for word from *Kāfī*.

5.3. SENTENTIAL WORD ORDER

This section will deal with word order within a clause: verb (predicate), agent (subject) patient (object). This order is considered to be the most appropriate (*al-ʾawlā*).

The author points out that since both subject and object are nouns, the two functions are differentiated through the particle את which appears before the object, as in ויכה פשחור את ירמיהו (Jer. 20, 2); ואת עמשׂא שׂם אבשלום (2 Sam. 17, 25). It follows that whenever this particle is missing the clause will be ambiguous, and only some external factor will be able to help us clarify its meaning, as exemplified by the following: ויעבר ישי שמה (1 Sam. 16, 9); בניו ירצו דלים (Job 20, 10).

The treatise enumerates six possible clause-internal constituent orders:

Verb, agent, patient: ויכה פשחור את ירמיהו (Jer. 20, 2). This is the most common order.

Agent, verb, patient: ויהוה פקד את־שׂרה (Gen. 21, 1). This order is common as well.

Patient, verb, agent: הפסל נסך חרש (Is. 40, 19).

Agent, patient, verb: וארץ רפאים תפיל (Is. 26, 19).

Patient, agent, verb: ראש מסבי עמל שׂפתימו יכסימו (Ps. 140, 10).

Verb, patient, agent: וירא אתם נער (2Sam. 17, 18); לכן כאכל קש לשון אש (Is. 5, 24).

[66] See Ibn Ǧanāḥ, *Lumaʿ*, p. 162.

[67] It is, for example, Ḥayyūǧ's opinion (See P. Kokovcov, *Novye materialy dlja kharakteristiki Yekhudy Khajjudzha, Samuila Nagida* ... Vol. II, Petrograd (1916), p. 46 ; Basal, § 3.4.5.1) and Ibn Ǧanāḥ's view (See J. & H. Derenbourg, *Opuscules et traités d'Abou'l-Walid Merwan Ibn Djanah*, Paris (1880), p. 6; *Lumaʿ*, p. 162.).

[68] It is worth noting that Rav Saadia Gaon looks upon *nifʿal* forms as אצ̇טראר (= constraint), as against *hifʿil* forms, which are אכ̇תיאר (= preference). Cf. S. L. Skoss, *Saadia Gaon, The Earliest Hebrew Grammarian*, Philadelphia (1955), pp. 38, 47.

[69] Ḥayyūǧ, for example, translates the form נִדְבַּרְנוּ (Mal. 3, 13) *mukālama* (= a talk). See: I. Eldar, "Qeṭaʿ min 'Kitāb al-Nutaf' le-rabbi Yūdah Ḥayyuǧ litrei ʿaśar", *Lešonénu* 43 (1979), pp. 256, 258 and cf. Basal, § 3.4.5.1.

The author points out that the form כֶּאֱכֹל in the last example is an infinitive serving as a finite verb.[70]

A comparison of this chapter with its counterpart in *Kāfī*[71] reveals, unsurprisingly, that the latter is longer and more detailed. The author of the present work begins the chapter in the same way as in *Kāfī*, but unlike the latter, does not include a comparison of the ways of distinguishing between subject and object in Hebrew and Arabic.[72] The author then returns to *Kāfī*, in which it is pointed out that in Hebrew the two are distinguished by means of the particle את, in order to prevent confusion in interpreting the clause. Here I should like to point out that the lacunae in our manuscript can all be filled in by comparing the text to *Kāfī*.

The six structures given here are identical with those given in *Kāfī*, and so are the examples. Furthermore, one example for the sixth order, viz. לכן כאכל קש לשון אש (Is. 5, 24), is accompanied by the comment that the form אכול (an infinitive) has the status of a finite verb, as mentioned also in *Kāfī*, but not in *Muštamil*.[73] This provides further support to the view that the present work is a synopsis of *Kāfī*.

5.4. THE PATIENT

The present treatise classifies patients into five categories: 1) *mafʿūl muṭlaq* (= absolute patient); 2) *mafʿūl bihi* (= direct patient); 3) *mafʿūl fīhi* (= adverbial patient, accusative of time and place); 4) *mafʿūl lahu* (= causative patient, accusative of cause and reason); 5) *mafʿūl maʿahu* (= concomitant patient, the patient in connection with which something is done).

This classification is not novel; it is known from medieval works on Arabic[74] and Hebrew[75] grammars.[76]

After the introduction there is a detailed discussion on the *mafʿūl muṭlaq*, which as the infinitive is considered to be the true patient, i.e., the actual action initiated by the agent. In other words, the infinitive can always represent the action performed by the agent. Consequently, this

[70] See below, § 5.4.

[71] See Ms. II, 24b–25a; Ms. III, 7a; Ms. IV, 17a.

[72] Abū al-Farağ Hārūn points out that this distinction is made in Arabic by the *ʾiʿrāb* (= inflection).

[73] Ms. I, 46a.

[74] See, e.g., Ibn al-Sarrāğ, I, p. 159, lines 8–9.

[75] E.g. in *Kitāb al-Muwāzana* by Ibn Bārūn, as published in P. Kokovcov, *Kniga sravnenija evrejskogo jazyka s arabskim Abū Ibragima (Isaaka) Ibn Bārūna ispanskago...*, Petrograd (1893), p. 20.

[76] I will not deal here with this issue to which I intend to dedicate a separate article in the near future.

form is similar to a verb and as such may govern an object. In this respect it differs from other patients. This treatment of the *mafʿūl muṭlaq* as *maṣdar* (= infinitive) is in line with the way this form is treated in medieval Arabic[77] and Hebrew[78] grammars.

The example used by the author is ובהעלת אהרן את הנרת (Ex. 30, 8). The word ובהעלת is translated into Arabic as *ʾiṣʿād* (=raise) and treated as indicating the action which the agent, Aaron in this case, performs. In other words, Aaron caused or performed the action of raising the candles.

This example and its explanation may be found also in *Kāfī*,[79] but not in *Muštamil*.[80] However, the discussion of this issue in *Kāfī* is much more lengthy than in our treatise, since Abū al-Farağ treats the concept of *mafʿūl muṭlaq* rather at length from the point of view of the Arabic language.[81]

5.5 TWO VERBAL CONJUGATIONS MARKED AS עֶדִי AND OTHER, UNMARKED, CONJUGATIONS

The beginning of this chapter is missing in the manuscript, but it is clear from the examples and from a comparison with *Kāfī*[82] that the subject it

[77] See, e.g., Ibn al-Sarrāğ, I, p. 159, line 11: *al-mafʿūl al-muṭlaq, wa-yuʿnā bihi al-maṣdar ...huwa al-mafʿūl fī al-ḥaqīqa li-sāʾir al-maḫlūqīn ... wa-ʾiḏā qulta: ḍarabtu fa-ʾinnamā maʿnāhu ʾaḥdaṯta ḍarban wa-faʿalta ḍarban fa-huwa al-mafʿūl al-ṣaḥīḥ* (= The absolute patient, by which is meant the infinitive ... indicates the actual action with respect to all creatures ... so that if one says *ḍarabtu* (= I hit) it means that the speaker has initiated and performed the action of hitting, and thus it (i.e. the hitting) is the real patient). I would like to take this opportunity to point out that the foundations of Abū al-Farağ's grammatical theory, and his syntax in particular, are to be found in medieval Arabic grammar, and specifically in Ibn al-Sarraj's *Kitāb al-ʾUsūl*. We are referring to the structure of the chapters dealing with syntax, their theoretical background and to the examples from the Arabic language. I am now in the process of completing an article which will clarify this point.

[78] So, e.g., in *Kitāb al-Muwāzana* by Ibn Bārūn, cf. note. 72 above. Cf. also Maman, p. 125.

[79] See: Ms. III, 7b, lines 9–23; Ms. IV, 17b, lines 4–18. A manuscript in the Russian National Library in St. Petersburg (Firk. II, Evr.-arab. I, no. 2374), which is a grammatical treatise very similar to *Kāfī*, also contains a discussion in this vein.

[80] In part b of *Muštamil*, Abū al-Farağ discussed the form and usage of the infinitive. In his Chapter 4 (Ms. III, 33a) he quotes the example of ובהעלת אהרן (Ex. 30, 8) in a section which does not deal with the same issue as the one dealt with here by our author and in *Kāfī*, but rather as an example of an infinitive which governs a subject or an object. The Biblical text quoted makes it very clear that the infinitive form ובהעלת in this case governs a subject, viz. אהרן, and this of course is clearly incompatible with the analysis in our treatise and in *Kāfī*.

[81] For a recent comprehensive and instructive discussion of the infinitive in Hārūn's *Muštamil*, see Maman.

[82] Ms. I, 277a.

deals with is verbal conjugations marked as עֲדִי. In order to understand the chapter it is necessary first to clarify the nature of the marking system in Karaite grammar.

The marking system[83] was developed by Karaite grammarians as a method for classifying verbal forms according to the 'constant letters' that are overt[84] throughout the inflection.

This method is known from the writings of two grammarians: 1) Abū al-Farağ Hārūn, who at the beginning of the chapter mentions the fact that the four marks הָבֵא, גַּנִּי, פְּרָת, שׁוּעָל were designated by an earlier grammarian (= אעלם אן בעץ̇ מן תקדם מן אלדקדוקיין עלי מא חכי וצ̇ע מן הד̇ה אלעלאמאת הבא גני פרת שועל).[85] 2) The author of *Me'or ʿayin*, who wrote in Hebrew.[86]

The method can be summarized as follows: Hebrew verbs may be classified into patterns of conjugation (=*taṣārīf*).[87] Each such pattern consists of the basic forms of a verb in the following order: imperative masculine singular, perfect 3rd person masculine singular, and other forms, such as active and passive participles (if any). For classifying the various conjugations marks were introduced, each mark specifying one or more pattern. For example, the mark הָבֵא specifies four patterns of conjugation: a) הָשֵׁב — הֵשִׁיב. b) זָרֵה — זֵרָה. c) הָשֵׁב — הֵשַׁב d) בָּרֵךְ — בֵּרַךְ. The mark itself consists of a bisyllabic word. The vowel of the first syllable indicates the vowel of the first syllable of the imperative, while the vowel of

[83] For more information on this system, see Becker, pp. 250–57.

[84] Ḥayyūğ (p. 21) is the first grammarian, to our knowledge, to have classified Hebrew verbs into conjugations (= *Binyanim*) and strong and weak classes. This classification was entailed by his claim that no Hebrew verb consists of fewer than three radicals (Cf. Basal, § 3.1). Before his time there were two systems in use: a) The system of Rav Saadia Gaon, according to which the basic form is the uninflected and indivisible form of the noun, as e.g. מַחֲנֶה, which is basic, and from which are derived יַחֲנֶה, חָנָה and other forms. For a comprehensive description of this method, see: E. Goldenberg, "ʿIyyunim ba-egron lĕ-rav Saadya Ga'on", *Lešonénu* 37 (1973), pp. 117–36; 275–90; 38 (1974), pp. 78–90; "Luaḥ ha-neṭiyyah ha-ʿivri ha-rišon". *Lešonénu* 43 (1979), pp. 86–7. b) The system of constant letters, by which a radical is defined as a letter which appears overtly in all forms of the inflection (for a survey of all these systems, see, e.g., Basal § 3.1.1.).

[85] See Zislin (1965), p. 170.

[86] See Zislin (1990), pp. 119–39.

[87] Abū al-Farağ writes quite explicitly that it is not his intention to explain conjugations entirely by means of the marking system, but merely to mark in this way the forms of the imperative, the perfect and the active and passive participles. The reason given is that Karaite grammarians in Iraq had already exhausted the subject: לאנה ליס דלך אלגרץ̇ ההנא בל אלאמר ואלמאצ̇י ואלפאעל ואלמפעול ולאן ד̇לך קד תקצאה בעץ̇ אלדקדוקיין מן משאיכנא אלעראקיין רחמהם אללה.

the second syllable indicates the vowel of the first syllable of the perfect form.[88]

As has already been indicated above, this chapter presents two patterns of conjugation, whose mark is עֵדִי. Both here and in Abū al-Farağ Hārūn's *Kāfī*,[89] this mark indicates the vowel of the second syllable of the imperative, *ṣere*, which is replaced by *ḥireq* in the perfect and imperfect forms:[90]

a) הֵילֵל (Zach. 11, 2), imperative; הֵילִיל (Jer. 47, 2 — וְהֵלִיל), perfect.

b) הוֹרֵד (Ex. 33, 5), imperative; הוֹרִיד (2R. 16, 17), perfect; מוֹרִיד (1 Sam. 2, 6), active participle; מוּרָד (unattested in the Bible), passive participle, equivalent to a passive participle of class הָשֵׁב.

In addition to these two classes of conjugations, some others are mentioned that have no particular mark:

a) Verbs whose perfect form cannot be derived from the imperative: שֵׁב (Gen. 20, 15 *et al.*); עֵד (ibid. 7 *et al.*) and the like.

It follows from these examples that the perfect forms יָרַד (Ex. 19, 18 *et al.*); יָדַע (Gen. 4, 1) are not derived from the imperative forms שֵׁב and רֵד, since according to the *marking system* the first letter of both imperative and perfect forms, whose vowel is contained in the mark, must appear in an equivalent manner in both forms, as in שְׁמֹר — שָׁמַר, unlike רֵד — יָרַד; שֵׁב — יָשַׁב.

This conclusion is in complete accord with *Kāfī*,[91] which adds that these verbs are not transitive:[92] מא הו גיר מתעדי ולא יוג̇ד ללאמר מנה עבר מן נפס אלאמר ולא אסם פאעל נחו שֵׁב ואוזאנה ודע ואוזאנה (=which is not transitive and there is no perfect or active participle which is formed from its imperative).[93]

b) Conjugations of passive verbs, e.g. הֻגַּד (Josh. 9, 24); שֻׁלַּךְ (unattested in the Bible); הֻשְׁלַךְ (Dan. 8, 11 — וְהֻשְׁלַךְ).

Passive forms have no marks, since they lack an imperative, which is the basic form for deriving verbal inflections, according to Karaite grammarians.[94]

[88] See also Zislin (1965), p. 170; Becker, p. 251.

[89] Ms. I, 277a.

[90] For another opinion as to the mark of the variable second-syllable vowel, see Becker, p. 253.

[91] See Zislin (1965), at the end of the section. Cf. also Becker, p. 264, lines 17–20 (in the Cambridge manuscript: T-S Ar. 31.147).

[92] This remark is intrinsically interesting, but will not be discussed further here. For a brief explanation, see Becker, p. 254.

[93] The author of *Me'or ʿayin* also mentions (Zislin [1990], p. 138) imperatives that have no perfect, citing examples such as קַח, תֵּן, גַּשׁ, רֵד and others.

[94] See, e.g. S. Munk, "Notice sur Abou'l-Walid Merwan Ibn Djanah...", *JA* 15 (1850), p. 317, n. 1.

c) Inflections of irregular forms whose inflections cannot be assigned a mark because they are so uncommon: יְדַשְּׁנֶה (Ps. 20, 4); וְאַשְׂמְאִילָה (Gen. 13, 9); וָאֶקְרָאֶה (1Sam. 28, 15); תְּשָׁעֳשָׁעוּ (Is. 66, 12).

It is noteworthy that neither this chapter nor the following has a parallel in any of the manuscripts of *Muštamil* in the Russian National Library, photographs of which can be found at the Institute for Photographs of Hebrew Manuscripts in Jerusalem. This fact lends further support to the contention that the present treatise is a synopsis of *Kāfī*.

5.6. THE CONDITIONS FOR DETERMINING PATTERNS OF WORD-FORMATION

At the beginning of this section in *Kāfī*,[95] Abū al-Farağ Hārūn declares that only nouns and verbs are formed to a pattern, but not particles, although the latter are a part of speech. The reason he gives is that nouns have in common the fact that they have plural, singular, connective and pausal forms, and what verbs have in common is the fact that they conjugate (according to the *marking system*). He next enumerates the seven conditions and then goes on to specify each condition in detail, adding examples as well. But the present text is briefer than *Kāfī*,[96] and begins immediately to list the seven conditions together with examples:

a. Two words have a similar shape but consist of different letters. They are pronounced similarly and sound similar, as in עָשָׂה (Gen. 1, 31 *et al.*) — עָלָה (Gen. 19, 15 *et al.*); יַעֲשֶׂה (Gen. 18, 25 *et al.*) — יַעֲלֶה (Gen. 2, 6 *et al.*). שָׁמַר (Gen. 37, 11 *et al.*) — זָכַר (Gen. 40, 23 *et al.*); יִשְׁמֹר (1Sam. 2, 9 *et al.*) — יִזְכֹּר (Jer. 14, 10 *et al.*).[97]

In other words, the two verbal forms that are compared are similar to each other with respect to their vocalization and syllable structure, they belong to the same conjugation and share tense and person. Only the letters are different.

b. Two words whose form is similar should also be related in their meaning.

Since the page is torn here, we will add to the surviving examples in the manuscript the examples in the corresponding chapter of *Kāfī*,[98] which are the same as in our text.

This condition stipulates that two forms which are similar in form and

[95] Ms. I, 278a, lines 3–10.

[96] Ibid.

[97] As mentioned above, all the examples in this chapter are taken from *Kāfī* Ms. I, 279a, lines 11–12.

[98] Ms. I, 279b.

are being compared in order to determine whether or not they share the same pattern, should belong to the same part of speech, i.e., both of them must be either verbs or nouns. Therefore the following pairs are not of the same pattern: יָסֹב (1K. 7, 23) is a finite verb, while יָרֹד (Gen. 43, 20) is an infinitive. וְהוֹלֵךְ (Num. 17, 11) is an imperative, while וְהֹלֵךְ (Amos 5, 8) is a noun. יוֹלֵךְ (Deut. 28, 36) is a verb, while יוֹעֵץ (1Ch. 26, 14) is a noun. חָשַׁב (Is. 33, 8) is a verb, while חָרַשׁ (Is. 44, 13) is a noun.

c. The two forms being compared should share the same nature (*waṣf wāḥid*). This means that two verbs that are being compared should share the same tense. This condition is needed to prevent two forms that have a similar vocalic and syllabic structure but differ in their tense from being considered as belonging to the same pattern.

The examples of this chapter of our text are identical to those of *Kāfī*:[99] קָרְבוּ (Is. 41, 21) is an imperative, and is not of the same pattern as אָרְבוּ (Ps. 59, 4) which is in the perfect. Similarly: וְקָרַב (Ez. 37, 17) is an imperative, and וְקָדַר (Micah 3, 6) is in the perfect. תָּפַשׂ (2Ch. 25, 23) is a perfect form, while תָּלַן (Job 17, 1) is an imperfect form.

It is worth noting here that the present work mistakenly quotes תפש יואב instead of תפש יואש (2Ch. 25, 23). It appears that this mistake originates with *Kāfī*,[100] a fact which once more strengthens the claim that our text is dependent on the latter.

However, there is a considerable difference between the surviving fragment from this section in the published extract and the surviving fragment in the same section in *Kitāb al-ʿuqūd* both in terms of the presentations of the rules and in terms of the Hebrew examples. This fact confirms the affinity between the surviving remnant published here and the *Muḫtaṣar* of *al-Kāfī*.

6. SUMMARY AND CONCLUSIONS

There is no doubt that the two non-contiguous manuscript pages dealt with here are the remains of a single Karaite grammatical treatise, written in Judaeo-Arabic, using the Arabic script even for quotations from the Hebrew Bible, but using Tiberian Hebrew vowel signs.

An analysis of the transcription of Hebrew Bible texts into Arabic leads to the conclusion that only the *qĕre* forms are represented. The system of writing is based on a style of Arabic in which only those vowels that are

[99] Ibid. 280a.

[100] Ms. I, 280a, line 9.

pronounced as long are represented by the *matres lectionis* ي و ا. Vowel length is determined by stress and syllable structure.

The fact that twice in our manuscript *segol* is replaced by *pataḥ* appears to indicate that the manuscript was perhaps copied by a scribe with a Babylonian accent, who may have copied the text for Babylonian Jews.

The comparative analysis of the extant parts of our manuscript with their counterparts in Abū al-Farağ's two books, *Kāfī* and *Muštamil*, has yielded the following results:

a. Corresponding chapters in all three works display a common structure.

b. The present work contains some examples which appear in neither of the others.

c. *Muštamil* contains examples which are found neither in the work under discussion nor in *Kāfī*.

d. Our work contains examples that are to be found in *Kāfī* but not in *Muštamil*.

e. Certain issues are treated briefly here and at length in *Kāfī*, while receiving no mention at all in *Muštamil*.

f. We have occasionally found that all the examples dealing with a certain issue in our manuscript are to be found in *Kāfī* as well, while only some of them appear in *Muštamil*.

g. Several lacunae in our manuscript have been filled in by corresponding texts in *Kāfī*.

h. There are entire lines in our manuscript that are nearly word-for-word copies of lines in *Kāfī*.

i. A single error in the copying of a Biblical text is common to our manuscript and to *Kāfī*.

j. The comparison between our work and *Kitāb al-ʿuqūd* reveals that there is considerable difference between them both in terms of the presentations of the rules and in terms of the Hebrew examples.

These findings all imply that the manuscript we have been considering contains remains of a Karaite grammatical treatise which is an abridgment (*Muḫtaṣar*) of *Kitāb al-Kāfī fī al-luġa al-ʿibrāniyya* by Abū al-Farağ Hārūn in Arabic characters.

Finally, the present study cites some sections from the remnants, written in Arabic characters, of Judaeo-Arabic writing, which is an example of the work of Karaite authors who were steeped in Arabic culture. Thus, these and other similar works apparently prove the assimilation of their authors into the dominant culture in the tenth and eleventh centuries, viz. the Arabic culture. And although the segments are very short, they indicate that the effects of working in the shadow of Arabic grammar were significant.

Undoubtedly, the fact that Hebrew grammar was formed under the influence of Arabic grammar and according to the Arabic method reveals the extent of cultural coexistence at this stage of Jewish history in the Orient; moreover, many Jewish authors worked in this milieu and its effects are clearly discerned in many areas other than grammatical texts.

ABBREVIATIONS AND BIBLIOGRAPHY

Bacher: W. Bacher, "Le grammairien anonyme de Jérusalem," *REJ* 30 (1895), pp. 232–56.

Basal: N. Basal, *Torato ha-diqduqit šel Rabbi Yūdah Ḥayyūǧ* Ph.D. thesis (unpublished), Ramat-Gan (1992).

Becker: D. Becker, "Šiṭṭat ha-simanim šel 'dark̲ei ha-poʿal ha-ʿivri' lefi ha-medaqdeqim ha-qaraʾim Abū al-Faraǧ hārūn u-ḇaʿal 'Meʾor ha-ʿayin' (= 'Meʾor ʿayin'), *Teʿuda* 7 (1991), pp. 250–57.

Ben-Shammai (1986): H. Ben-Šammai, "Lešonot ha-Qaraʾim be-ʾarṣot dovrei ʿaravit (ha-ʿaravit u-masoret ha-ʿivrit): maṣav ha-meḥqar", *Massorot* 2 (1986), pp. 57–64.

Blau, Emergence: J. Blau, *The Emergence and the Linguistic Background of Judaeo-Arabic*, Jerusalem (1981).

Gil: M. Gil, *A History of Palestine, 634–1099*, Cambridge (1992).

Harviainen (1993_1): T. Harviainen, "A Karaite Bible Transcription with Indiscriminate Use of Tiberian pataḥ and segol Vowels Signs" (*Semitica Serta Philologica Constantino Tsereteli Dicata* curaverunt Riccardo Contini, Fabrizio A. Pennachietti, Mauro Tosco, Silvio Zamorani editore), Torino (1993), pp. 83–97.

—, (1993_2): T. Harviainen, "Karaite Arabic Transcriptions of Hebrew in the Saltykov-Schedrin Public Library in St. Petersburg", *Estudios Masoréticos (X Congreso de la IOMS) En Memoria de Harry M. Orlinsky*, Editados por Emilia Fernández Tejero, Madrid (1993), pp. 63–72.

—, (1994): T. Harviainen, "A Karaite Bible Transcription with Indiscriminate Counterparts of Tiberian *qameṣ* and *ḥolam* (Ms. Firkovitsh II, Arab-Evr. 1)", in: *Proceedings of the Eleventh Congress of the International Organization for Masoretic Studies (IOMS)*, Jerusalem (1994), pp. 33–40.

Ḥayyūǧ: M. Jastrow, *The Weak and Geminative Verbs in Hebrew by ... Ḥayyûǧ*, Leiden (1897).

Hirschfeld: H. Hirschfeld, "An Unknown Grammatical Work by Abū al-Faraj Harun", *JQR*, n.s. 13 (1922–1923), pp. 1–7.

Hoerning: R. Hoerning, *Six Karaite Manuscripts of Portions of the Hebrew Bible in Arabic Characters*, London (1899).

Ibn al-Sarrāǧ: Abū Bakr Muḥammad ibn Sahl ibn al-Sarrāǧ, *al-ʾUṣūl fī al-Naḥw*, edited by A. al-Fatly, 3rd edition, I–III, Beirut (1988).

Ibn Ǧanaḥ, *Lumaʿ*: J. Derenbourg, *Le Livre des Parterres Fleuris, Grammaire Hébraïque en Arabe d'Abou'l-Walid Merwan Ibn Djanah de Cordoue*, Paris (1886).

Kāfī: *al-Kitāb al-Kāfī fī al-luġa al-ʿibrāniyya* by Abū al-Farāğ Hārūn. Mss. in the National Library of Russia, St. Petersburg, Russia.

Kāfī Ms. I: Firk. II, Evr.-arab. I, 2437.

Kāfī Ms. II: Firk. II, Evr.-arab. I, 2441.

Kāfī Ms. III: Firk II, Evr.-arab. I, 2475.

Kāfī Ms. IV: Firk. II, Evr.-arab. I, 2702.

Khan (1987): J. Khan, "Vowel Length and Syllable Structure in the Tiberian Tradition of Biblical Hebrew", *JSS* xxxii (1987), pp. 23–82.

—, (1990): J. Khan, *Karaite Bible Manuscripts from the Cairo Genizah*, Cambridge (1990).

—, (1992): J. Khan, "The medieval Karaite Transcriptions of Hebrew into Arabic Script", *Israel Oriental Studies* xii (1992), pp. 157–76.

—, (1993), 'The Orthography of Karaite Hebrew Bible Manuscripts in Arabic Transcription', *JSS* xxxviii (1993), pp. 49–70.

Kitāb al-ʿuqūd. see Hirschfeld.

Maman: A. Maman, "Ha-Maqor wĕ-šem ha-pĕʿullah bi-tfisat Abū-l-Farağ Hārūn", in: *Studies in Hebrew and Jewish Languages presented to Shĕlomo Morag*, edited by M. Bar-Asher, Jerusalem (1996), pp. 119–50.

Muštamil: *al-Kitāb al-Muštamil ʿalā al-ʾuṣūl wa-al-fuṣūl fī al-luġa al-ʿibrāniyya* by Abū al-Farağ Hārūn. Mss. in the National Library of Russia, St. Petersburg, Russia.

Muštamil Ms. I: Firk. II, Evr.-arab. I, 2388.

Muštamil Ms. II: Firk. II, Evr.-arab. I, 2283.

Muštamil Ms. II: Firk. III, Evr.-arab. I, 2287.

Sharvit (1974): Š. Šarvit, "Heʿader niggud ben qameṣ le-ḥolem u-ḇen segol le-pataḥ (bi-ḵtav-yad še-hagiyyato bavlit)", in: *Sefer Zikkaron le-Henoch Yalon*, edited by E.Y. Kutscher and others, Jerusalem (1974, pp. 547–55.

Sharvit (1986): Š. Šarvit, "Niqqud 'Bavli-Tavrani' bi-Gnizat Qahir", *Massorot* 2 (1986), pp. 119–35.

Wright I–II: W. Wright, *A Grammar of the Arabic Language*[3], London (1955).

Zislin (1962): M. Zislin, "A Chapter from the Grammatical Work of Abū-l-Farağ Harūn Ibn al-Farağ 'al-Kāfī'" (Russian), *Palestinskiy Sbornik* 7 [70] (1962), pp. 178–84.

Zislin (1965): M. Zislin, "Abū-l-Farağ Hārūn on the inflection of the Hebrew verb" (Russian), *Kratkiye Soobshcheniya Instituta Narodov Azii* 86, Moskva (1965), pp. 164–77.

Zislin (1990): M. Zislin (ed.), *Meʾor ʿAyin...*, Moskva (1990).

JEWISH CONVERTS TO ISLAM IN THE MUSLIM WEST[1]

MERCEDES GARCÍA-ARENAL

Research into the process of religious conversion can reveal much about the construction of cultural, social and political identities. From its first centuries, Islam has shown great flexibility in its accommodation of communities of converts from diverse backgrounds. In this regard the recent study of the period known as the "Age of Conversions" has yielded most interesting results. Although the delimiting dates of this phenomenon have been successively revised backward and new explanations have been offered for it,[2] once the point has been defined at which Muslims became a majority in different regions, scholarly interest in subsequent conversions seems to diminish.

Mediterranean Islam is a mother lode for the study of ethnic and religious group formation, interaction, coexistence, tension and conflict.[3] Numerous studies have treated the diversity of groups, the antiquity of the phenomenon and its transformations, but this variety has not often been considered in terms of the mechanisms by which these groups are built, interact, and mingle or fuse with each other. Also little studied are the mechanisms through which certain groups fade away discretely, not because of political measures of expulsion or forced conversion but through erosion, attrition or simple emigration.

Through his well known work on ethnic groups, Barth[4] has changed many points of view by focusing his investigation on the ethnic *boundary*

[1] This paper was read at the Near Eastern Department of Princeton University in the Mellon Seminar, February 1995, and has benefited from the discussion with its participants.

[2] M.G. Morony, "The Age of Conversions: A Reassessment," in Gervers and Bikhazi (eds.), *Conversion and Continuity: Indigenous Christian Communities in Islamic Lands* (Toronto 1990) pp. 135–50.

[3] L. Valensi, "La tour de Babel: groupes et relations ethniques au Moyen Orient et en Afrique du Nord," *Annales, E.S.C.* 441, 4 (1986): 817–38.

[4] See his introduction in F. Barth (ed.), *Ethnic Groups and Boundaries: The Social Organization of Culture Difference*, Boston 1969.

that defines the group, not the cultural stuff that it encloses. According to Barth, if a group maintains its identity when members interact with others, criteria exist for determining membership and ways of signaling membership and exclusion. It is clear that boundaries persist despite a flow of persons across them and that social processes of exclusion and incorporation coexist with this mobility. Discrete categories are maintained despite changing levels of participation and membership in the dominant society. On the other hand, interaction in a multi-ethnic social system does not lead to liquidation of a given ethnic group through change and acculturation; cultural differences can persist despite inter-ethnic contact and interdependence.

In this view (Barth's) of a multi-ethnic society, focusing on the boundaries between the different religious groups, the question of conversion is of the utmost importance, as it can act as an index of the integrative force of the hegemonic culture, an axis through which processes of acculturation and assimilation are more clearly put to the test. Religion, in the time and area we are dealing with, appears to be an important (but not the only) ingredient in the construction of group identities. Conversion, a way of crossing boundaries, is therefore inseparable from the very complex processes which achieve integration and paradoxically include phenomena of exclusion and stigmatization by the dominant group. The reduction of cultural distance (acculturation) does not always lead to a reduction of social distance (assimilation). Strategies of converts, such as accommodation, false assimilation, and adherence to specific or sectarian religious movements, can be the other face of the coin, aspects on which I shall not dwell here. As I intend to focus more on converts than on conversion, I am mainly interested in how the convert is perceived socially and in the mechanisms which deter the disappearance of the difference, such as the stigmatization of solidarity networks or the maintenance of the stereotypes accorded to the group of origin. Furthermore, of what importance are origin and lineage? In times of crisis and social disruption, what causes or permits the dominant society to absorb and assimilate others by, for example, administrative measures designed to do away with a minority (i.e., forced conversion)? And after the minority has disappeared as such, what specifically causes the impulse of repulsion, of differentiation and rejection of converts? I shall consider the mechanisms by which a people wishing to be part of a society might be excluded from it as conspiratorial and impure, and the moments when successful assimilation becomes the real target: the disappearance of difference precipitates fear in the dominant society.

I am going to focus on two lands of Islam (al-Andalus and the Western Maghrib) in the Middle Ages and Early Modern times. Muslim rule was well established in these areas in spite of internal strife or challenge by external enemies; according to Bulliet,[5] in such circumstances conversion to Islam is exceptionally massive only in times of acute crisis. I shall also deal with moments of acute crisis in which conversion can be both massive and enforced, as well as the conversion of individuals or groups belonging to elites; there is a tendency to conform to new religious values when these reaffirm the position of the elite in the social structure.[6] Among individuals dedicated to an intellectual activity there is also a longing to participate in a world of ideas regarded as superior, to be admitted to the cultured world, i.e., another type of elite.[7]

The societies of both al-Andalus and the Maghrib had religious minorities whose legal situation was one of submission and dependence defined by the *ḏimma*. They suffered civil and legal discrimination but enjoyed security as "protected peoples." This juridic status guaranteed their religious liberty, communal autonomy and liberty to choose and practice their professional dedications. The last was limited by their situation of submission and dependence; they were excluded not only from power, but from any exterior manifestation which implied superiority over Muslims and an implied rupture of the *ḏimma* pact. Muslim society, recognizing the autonomous status of religious minorities, enhanced cultural autonomy as well. The Jews of al-Andalus experienced a rapid acculturation, but not as a result of exterior pressures or political deliberation. Their role in the society did not depend on the acceptance or refusal of the majority culture.

In times of social disintegration, in general, the *ḏimmīs* were politically important. They were able to achieve political power (as in the case of the Jewish viziers of the Zirids of Granada, or of the Marinids of Fez) on the whim of the governing group or the dynasty which they served. Often, they were entrusted to carry out the most unpopular tasks of government, such as tax collection, making of them a lightning rod for the wrath and uprisings of the people in moments of political crisis. The rulers welcomed a defenseless, easily taxable, economically specialized group, bound to them by a strictly sustained and reinforced vulnerability. In times of economic crisis or opposition to the dynasty, the rulers could assuage a

[5] R. Bulliet, "Process and Status in Conversion and Continuity" in Gervers and Bikhazi (eds.), *Conversion and Continuity*, pp. 7–8.

[6] See A. Banani, "Conversion and Conformity in a Selfconscious Elite," in A. Banani and S. Vryonis, *Individualism and Conformity in Classical Islam*, Wiesbaden 1977.

[7] S. Stroumsa, "On Jewish Intellectuals who Converted in the Early Middle Ages," in D. Frank (ed.), *The Jews of Medieval Islam: Community, Society and Identity*, Leiden 1995, 179–97.

great deal of discontent in the wider population by scapegoating, dispossessing and persecuting the minority.

The *ḏimmī* pact provided the group with reasonable security and autonomy, while imposing a ceiling to limit its social mobility. In times of stability, the guarantees were maintained; in times of tension or social disruption, the discriminatory aspects of the pact were accentuated. In general the population did not covet the minority role which was in any case stigmatized, but in times of economic crisis or of recession, the prosperity of certain Jewish groups, or their control over certain sources of economic power, produced resentment and it was argued that contrary to the pact, the *ḏimmī*s had been elevated over Muslims.[8]

In al-Andalus, persecution of the *ḏimmī*s occurred when the state was seen as incapable of imposing the dictates of the law. This contrasts with the situation in the peninsular Christian kingdoms, where repression tended to be a political instrument of the state whose severity was clearly related to economic factors.

The Muslim majority both in al-Andalus and in the Maghrib was divided into groups that we can call ethnic or quasi-ethnic since the only way to belong to them was by birth. These groups emphasized their respective "myths of origin." Among them were Arabs, Berbers, and Hispano-Romans, using lineage as a basis for social prestige.[9]

Increasingly, historians are attempting to apply to pre-modern societies the theoretical notions with which the social sciences examine ethnic relations in colonial and post-colonial societies. Glick, for example, has examined ethnic relations in the medieval Iberian peninsula (both Christian and Muslim territories)[10] in three specific areas of inquiry: the emergence of ethnic stratification systems, the typology of such systems, and the interdependence of cultural and socio-economic forces in intergroup relations. The systems of ethnic relations that he uses fall broadly within two types described by Van den Berghe as paternalistic and competitive.[11] Paternalistic ethnic relations are characterized by a

[8] For a discussion of *ḏimma* applied to Jewish communities, see M.R. Cohen, *Under Crescent and Cross*, chapt. IV, pp. 52–74; "Diaspora, Galut, Alienation: The Jews of the Islamic Middle Ages," in N. Zemon Davis and Y. Kaplan (eds.), *Peoples in Diaspora: 18th International Congress of Historical Sciences*, Montreal 1995.

[9] See, for example, M. Shatzmiller, "Le mythe d'origine berbère, aspects historiographiques et sociaux", *ROMM* 35 (1983): 145–56; E. Terés, "Linajes árabes de al-Andalus según la 'Yamhara' de Ibn Hazm," *Al-Andalus* 22 (1957): 55–111 and 337–76.

[10] T. Glick, *Islamic and Christian Spain in Early Middle Ages: Comparative Perspectives on Social and Cultural Formation*. New Jersey 1979.

[11] P. van den Berghe, "Paternalistic Versus Competitive Race Relations: An Ideal-typus Approach," *Race and Ethnicity* (1970), pp. 21–41.

horizontal bar between upper and lower castes, scant intercaste mobility, a legal system favoring the ethnic status quo, sharply structured ethnic roles, and adaptation by the lower castes to their inferior status. There is little conflict between the castes. In competitive systems, the bar between castes tilts toward the vertical. The status gap between castes narrows, and increases within castes. Friction is more patent and conflict surfaces readily. The two types are distinguished by institutional features regulating or limiting access to political power by subordinate groups. Glick concludes that the two systems are applicable to the case of al-Andalus: competitive relations between members of the same religion who exhibit social or cultural differences, in particular between Arabs, Berbers and Muslims of Hispano-Roman stock; and paternalistic relations between the religion of the groups which are legally entitled to power — the dominant majority — and the Christian and Jewish minorities. The only way a group in a paternalistic subsystem could shift to the competitive mode was by conversion.

Paternalistic relations fit into what Gellner calls "an agrarian society,"[12] where the ruling class forms a small minority, a caste rigidly separated from the great majority in turn subdivided into a number of more specialized layers: warriors, priests, merchants, and peasants. For Gellner the most important point in this society is this: both for the ruling stratum as for the various sub-strata, there is a great stress on cultural differentiation. The more differentiated the various strata are, the less friction and ambiguity there will be between them. The whole system favors horizontal lines of cultural cleavage, and it may invent and reinforce them when they are absent. Gellner's most interesting proposition for us is that genetic and cultural differences are attributed to what were in fact merely strata differentiated by function, so as to fortify the differentiation and endow it with authority and permanence.

JEWISH CONVERTS IN AL-ANDALUS

The medieval Iberian peninsula, prior to the 17th century (when the last Muslim minority, the Moriscos, was expelled), is a particularly rich field for the study of conversion and resistance in the process of the construction of groups. The changing territorial frontiers did not always entail population displacements. For the most part, populations remained stable despite new political and religious rule. This led not only to conversions of

12 E. Gellner, *Nations and Nationalism*, Oxford 1994, Ch. 2, "Culture in an Agrarian Society."

Christians and Jews to Islam, and of Muslims and Jews to Christianity, but also to resistance (**Mozarabs**, for instance, i.e., Arabized Christians living under Muslim rule, **Mudejars**, i.e., Muslims living in Christian lands, and **Moriscos**). The different reactions and levels of tolerance or accommodation in the dominant societies should also be compared. As the territorial frontiers were gradually modified, Arabized Christians and Jews from al-Andalus now in Christian territory constituted new and differentiated groups (distinct from the Christians and Jews living in Christian lands) who would prove on occasion that common religious beliefs alone were insufficient for group articulation. This is the case in what is known as the Neo-Mozarabs, who were in fact Mudejars assimilating or forming a community with Mozarabs.[13]

Of the conversions which took place in the Iberian peninsula during the Middle Ages, that of the Jews to Islam has received the least attention.[14] Sources in this regard offer little, and we must avail ourselves of very dispersed data, found in literary sources of dubious historical value. They are sufficient, as the tip of an iceberg, to deduce that the phenomenon was widespread and caused a considerable impact on the groups concerned.

It is generally agreed that in all of the conquered territories in the first century of the Hijra, there was a wave of mass conversion of Jews to Islam.[15] As for al-Andalus, it is difficult to imagine that the conversion to Islam of the Hispano-Roman population, which grew in exponential progression throughout the whole of the 10th century, did not include a percentage of Jews. According to the estimates of Bulliet,[16] conversion would have affected some eighty per cent of the population by the year 1100. Unfortunately, on this point the sources are mute; both Lévi-Provençal and Pérès[17] asserted that a high percentage of Jews converted to Islam in al-Andalus in the 10th century, but did not cite any sources on which to base their statements. Hirschberg has demonstrated,[18] based on the study of medieval Maghribi responsa, that the movement of Jews to

[13] M. de Epalza, "La islamización de al-Andalus: mozárabes y neo-mozárabes," *Revista del Instituto Egipcio de Estudios Islámicos* 23 (1985–86): 171–79.

[14] M. García-Arenal, "Rapports entre les groupes dans la Péninsule Ibérique: La conversion des Juifs à l'Islam (XII–XIII siècles)," *Revue du Monde Musulman et de la Méditerranée* 63–64 (1992) 91–102.

[15] Among others, S.W. Baron, *Social and Religious History of the Jews*, New York 1975, vol. III, 96–111.

[16] R. Bulliet, *Conversion to Islam in the Medieval Period.* London 1979, 114–27.

[17] E. Lévi-Provençal, *L'Espagne musulmane au Xe siècle*, Paris 1932, 38, 111–12; H. Pérès, *La Poésie andalouse en arabe classique au XI siècle: ses aspects généraux et sa valeur documentaire*, Paris 1937, p. 264.

[18] H.Z. Hirschberg, *A History of the Jews in North Africa*, Leiden 1974, vol. I, pp. 191 et seq.

Islam was particularly high in the Islamic West. The responsa clearly reflect the scale of the controversy caused by problems which the converts created in Jewish communities over rights of succession, inheritance, and *ḥaliṣa* (release of a widow from the requirements of levirate marriage). Among the documents of the Geniza, Goitein has also found ample evidence of conversions to Islam, independent of periods of political repression.[19]

The documentation of the question in al-Andalus is still more scarce, although Andalusian notarial compendia of the 10th century contain specific formulas for the legal conversion of Jews to Islam[20] as well as *fatwā*s on problems produced by conversions.[21] In general, however, in al-Andalus before the 12th century, we must content ourselves with individual cases, often notorious, and with persons who bore the nisba *al-Islāmī.*

I begin with Abū-l-Faḍl Ibn Ḥasday, whose conversion paved the way for him to become a vizier in the Taifa of Zaragoza under al-Muqtadir (1046–81), al-Mu'tamin (1081–85) and al-Mustaʿīn (1085–1110).[22] A similar position was attained in the court of Ḥusām al-Dawla, prince of the Sahla, by another convert, Abū Bakr Ibn Sadray,[23] and in Granada, Ibn al-Qarawī al-Islāmī was the *ḥāǧib*.[24] In all three cases, conversion was necessary in order to perform a certain function,[25] for individuals who were members of an elite, and moreover, were deeply Arabized.[26] Nevertheless, neither their acculturation nor conversion appear to have been sufficient for their contemporaries to have forgotten their previous

[19] S.D. Goitein, *A Mediterranean Society*, vol. II, 299–303.

[20] P. Chalmeta, "Le passage à l'Islam dans al-Andalus au X siècle," *Actas del XII Congreso de la U.E.A.I. (Málaga, 1984)*, Madrid 1986, 161–83; M. Abumalham, "La conversión según formularios notariales andalusíes," *Miscelánea de Estudios Arabes y Hebráicos* 34:2 (1985), 71–84.

[21] D. Wasserstein, "A *fatwa* on Conversion in Islamic Spain," in R. Nettler (ed.), *Studies in Muslim-Jewish Relations*, vol. I, Oxford 1993, 178–87.

[22] H. Pérès, *Poésie andalouse*, 264; N. Roth, "Some Aspects of Muslim-Jewish Relations in Spain," *Estudios en homenaje a D. Claudio Sánchez Albornoz: Anejos de Cuadernos de Historia de España*, vol. II, Buenos Aires 1983, p. 195.

[23] H. Pérès, op. cit., p. 265.

[24] H. Pérès, op. cit., p. 270; for a parallel to the famous Fāṭimī vizir Ibn Killis, see S.D. Goitein, *Mediterranean Society*, vol. I, 33–34; M.R. Cohen and S. Somekh, "In the court of Yaʿqūb Ibn Killis: A Fragment from the Cairo Geniza," *Jewish Quarterly Review* LXXX (1990): 283–314.

[25] For other examples of prerequisite conversion for Jewish courtiers to achieve promotion see *Ibn Marzuq, El "Musnad". Hechos memorables de Abu l-Hasan, sultán de los Benimerines*, trans. of the Marīnid chronicle by M.J. Viguera, Madrid 1977, p. 135.

[26] See the excellent opinion that Ṣāʿid al-Andalusī had of Ibn Ḥasday's science, in N. Roth, op. cit., p. 196.

status, nor to prevent other Muslims in the same milieu, who also aspired to power, from resenting their access to it. Especially significant in this regard is the letter of Ibn al-Dabbāg to Ibn Ḥasday included in the *Qalā'id* of Ibn Ḫaqān, which I cite from Pérès' translation:[27]

> "I have known a time where you would not refuse to have a laugh with whomever would make jest with you, and where you would not have disdained to respond to whom addressed you... What happened to you: maybe you have seen that the capital city is in need of a *qāḍī* and you want the post. But surely you must be now on the point of trying to learn Muslim law... Go back to your humility, pretend ignorance when in front of an ignoramus, when you are with fools pretend to be a fool even if you are intelligent."[28]

The humiliation and subservience deemed proper for the *ḏimmī* were also demanded of the convert, who was required to exhibit an everlasting wish to win the good will of his contemporaries (feigning ignorance if an uncouth person approached him). Any sign of pride or elevation in the convert, including intellectual superiority, were intolerable. This letter is similar in content to some verses written by Ḥasan ibn al-Ǧadd, secretary of the converted Jew, Ibn al-Qarawī al-Islāmī, and directed to the same, which made a contemptuous allusion to his "co-religionists," making it very clear that no one was likely to forget his origins.[29]

Although less numerous, there are references in sources to converts who belonged to lower social classes, such as craftsmen. The *al-Ḏaḫīra*, which includes biographies of 11th century Andalusians, recounts the incident between Abū Rabīʿ Sulaymān ibn Aḥmad al-Quḍāʿī and the converted Jew, Yūsuf al-Islāmī, who had denied the former some carpentry tools.[30] More interesting, however, are descriptions provided by an anonymous and undated source, which appears to have been composed in Fez in the 15th century, the *Ḏikr Mašāhir Aʿyān Fās fī-l-Qadīm*, a chronicle of noble

[27] Pérès, op. cit., p. 267.

[28] "Je t'ai connu à une époque où tu ne refusais pas plaisanter avec ceux qui te plaisantaient et où tu ne dédaignais pas de répondre à ceux qui t'adressaient la parole. Fais moi connaître — puis-je te servir de rançon — ce qui t'est arrivé: peut-être as-tu vu que la capitale manquait de *qāḍī* et aspires tu à exercer cette fonction. Assurément, pour l'instant, tu dois être en train d'étudier les sentences et tu te mets au courant de la loi musulmane. Admettons que tu sois revêtu de cette dignité après t'être bien preparé à occuper cette charge: que feras-tu quand on t'interrogera sur la légende du sabbat (*qiṣṣat al-sabt*)? Laisse donc ce caractère affecté (*taḫalluq*), reviens à tes capacités naturelles (*aḫlāq*) et retourne à ton humilité. Feins l'ignorance si un ignorant s'approche de toi et fais l'imbécile avec les sots alors que tu es intelligent..."

[29] Pérès, op. cit., p. 271.

[30] Pérès, op. cit., p. 266 and n.1.

families of Fez. This work contains numerous historical accounts of al-Andalus which appear to have been taken from much earlier sources,[31] and thus are relevant to the present topic.

For example, in its narrative of the conquest of al-Andalus and of the groups of peoples who came to live there, it states: "there are Jews who settled in this country [al-Andalus] before the Conquest, and who converted during the Conquest, or were made prisoners and converted, or came to the country after the Conquest and then converted to Islam."[32]

It continues to describe the professional activities introduced by the different groups of the population in al-Andalus, and among them cited as a group apart the Jews converted to Islam, who cultivated the arts of embroidering draperies and precious textiles, encrusted with pearls and lined in cotton; weaving and lining headdresses, dyeing them with different colors. They also worked as moneychangers in the market, as sellers of coagulated milk, and as cobblers. Evidently, in general, they professed the same trades as Jews and it is logical to deduce from this that, if not dwelling near them, they must at least have worked closely with their former co-religionists. In Fez, as we are going to see, neo-Muslims of Jewish origin constituted an important group, and perhaps this fact made the author of the chronicle more sensitive to a topic which is generally unmentioned.

Later, in al-Andalus as in the Maghrib, the conversion of Jews to Islam was related to the Almohad conquest and persecution. All of the textbooks mention it as a matter of course, and pass over it as something well-proven: around 1146, in the early Almohad period, a violent persecution of the Jews took place, and the Caliph ʿAbd al-Mu'min decreed their mandatory conversion to Islam. The current version also states that with the Almohad dynasty's loss of power, they were permitted to return to their former religion without suffering the charge of apostasy.[33]

Upon perusing the sources, one is at a loss to explain the dearth of material related to an episode of similarly extraordinary proportions. The only known precedent is the persecution embarked upon by the Fāṭimid Caliph al-Ḥākim against Christians, and later Jews, which produced numerous conversions from 1015. The character of the Caliph, who by all accounts suffered from a diminished mental capacity, the violence and

[31] According to M. Shatzmiller, "Professions and Ethnic Origin of Urban Labourers in Muslim Spain," *Awraq* 5–6 (1982–83): 149–60.

[32] Shatzmiller, op. cit., p. 151.

[33] A recent revision of this version is J.P. Molenat, "Point de vue sur la permanence et l'extinction de la minorité chrétienne dans l'Occident musulman médiéval (Maghreb et al-Andalus)," *Colloque Minorités ethniques et religieuses dans le monde arabo-musulman*, Rabat 1995.

brevity of the persecution, and the fact that immediately afterward the converts were allowed to return to their former religions without suffering the consequences usually meted out to apostates, may have been influential in the attitudes of the Jewish communities of the western Islamic world upon confronting Almohad pressures.[34]

We possess more information about the lives, deeds and preaching of the Mahdi Ibn Tumart, and of his successor ʿAbd al-Mu'min. Leaving behind doctrinal questions, the former, a messianic personality, took it upon himself to establish the Kingdom of Justice upon Earth before the coming of the end of the world. He seemed devoted to the militant religion proper to the *murābiṭ*, pledged to "order the good and prohibit the bad." His instruments of political propaganda, like those of so many later *murābiṭ*, included such actions as the smashing of musical instruments or amphorae of wine in the markets, the humiliation of the *ḏimmī*s, and the practice of *ǧihād* against the infidel (by infidel he meant anyone not devoted to the movement). The Jewish communities were thus to suffer conspicuously during the Almohad conquests. I do not deny that actions were taken specifically against the Jews, but those were more the effect of the "exploits fondateurs" of the Almohad movement than of new and enforced legislation.

The lack of information about persecution or forced conversions in al-Andalus in Jewish sources is, in a way, more surprising. The basic and most cited source is a poem of Abraham ibn Ezra, a lament (*qina*) over the Almohad calamity, in which he lists the destroyed communities: Sevilla, Córdoba, Jaen, Almería in al-Andalus, Sijilmasa, Marrakesh, Fez, Tlemcen, Ceuta, Meknes and Darʿa.[35] However, Ibn Ezra had travelled to Europe years before these events (considered to have taken place around 1146), and his composition is poetic, full of rhetoric and literary flourishes, without any attempt at factual precision. As a historical source it is thus problematic.[36] Furthermore, his own son, Isḥāq Ibn Ezra, had converted to Islam, giving the poet a personal interest in emphasizing the cataclysm.[37]

The only document which can be considered as such is a letter by a certain Solomon Cohen of Fusṭāṭ to his father, dated January of 1148, which gathered together information from Maghribi witnesses who took refuge in Egypt, Muslims and Jews alike. The father was a native of Sijilmasa and later lived in Aden. The letter makes particular reference to

[34] S.D. Goitein, *Mediterranean Society*, vol. II, p. 300.

[35] I used the translation by Millás Vallicrosa, *La poesía sagrada hebraico-española*, Madrid 1940, 306–7. See also R. Brann, "Taḇniyot šel galut bĕ-qinot ʿiḇriyot vĕ-ʿaraḇiyot bi-Sĕfarad", *Sefer Yisrael Levin*, 1994, 45–61.

[36] As stated by Hirschberg, op. cit., vol. I, 125–26.

[37] S.D. Goitein, op. cit., vol. II, p. 302.

the events which occurred in this locality (Sijilmasa), describing the aftermath of the Almohad conquest during which two hundred Jews were forced to flee. The authorities tried to convince the rest of the community to convert through debates and persuasion lasting more than seven months. At the end of this period, a new governor arrived in the city who killed one hundred and fifty Jews, with the result that the *dayyan* converted, and with him, the rest of the community.[38]

Solomon Cohen also mentioned the cases of Marrakesh and Bougie but was silent on the subject of al-Andalus. The case of Sijilmasa seems to have been particularly notorious and exemplary.[39] It is worth keeping in mind that the majority of violent acts against the Jews, in the Almohad period and later, took place in key commercial cities involved in the gold trade with the Sudan, in which the Jewish communities filled an important role.[40]

The other two extant Jewish historical sources are equally imprecise and quite late: one is the *Šeḇeṭ Yehuda* of Salomón ben Verga, a Sevillian writer of the 15th century. He reiterated the debates and attempts at persuasion which he attributed to Ibn Tumart himself, and explained how the Jews countered them for months. The Sultan ultimately decreed that they must convert, which they tried to avoid, without success, by paying with their property. The Sultan died a month later and his successor allowed the Jews to return to their religion.[41] Ben Verga appears to have confused events which occurred under the Almohads with the episode concerning the Caliph al-Ḥakim.

The account included by Yosef Ha-Cohen, in the 15th century, in his *ʿEmeq ha-Baḵa* is similar, although more brief.[42] Another Hispano-Hebrew historian, Abraham ibn Daud ha-Nasī, wrote of the Jewish *almojarife* of Alfonso VI (1126–1157), the king of Castile, called Yehuda ibn Ezra, who was a member of the famous Grenadine family, and who sheltered the fleeing Jews of al-Andalus in the fortress of Calatrava.[43]

38 The letter, in Judeo-Arabic, has been edited and translated and is included by Hirschberg, op. cit., vol. I, 127–29. The *dayyan* of Sijilmasa, Yosef ben ʿAmran, is a well known figure, who returned to Judaism some years later.

39 Hirschberg, op. cit., vol. I, pp. 352 sq.

40 Such as Tuwāt, cf. J.O. Hunwick, "The Right of *ḏimmīs* to Maintain a Place of Worship: A 15th Cent. *Fatwā* from Tlemcen," *Al-Qantara* XII (1991): 133–55. On the importance of the Jewish communities in commerce with the Sudan and the Crown of Aragon, see Ch.E. Dufourcq, *L'Espagne catalane et le Maghreb*, Paris 1966, pp. 141–42 on Sijilmasa.

41 *Chebet Yehuda (La Vara de Judá)*, trans. F. Cantera, Granada 1927, pp. 48–49 and 137.

42 Spanish trans. by P. Leon Tello, 2nd ed., Barcelona 1989, pp. 62–63.

43 Abraham ben Daud, *Sefer ha-Qabbalah*, ed. and trans. G.C. Cohen, Philadelphia 1967, p. 71; P. Leon Tello, *Judíos de Toledo*, Madrid 1979, pp. 31 sq.

Although we have very few accounts in either Arabic or Jewish sources of the events which occurred under the early Almohads, and fewer still regarding their policy toward the Jews (there is no trace of such a thing as a *ẓāhir* ordering the conversion to Islam of the *ḏimmīs*, which in any case would be against the *Šarīʿa*), there is no doubt of the appearance in that period of a large convert community or of their consequential emigration from al-Andalus and the Maghrib. However, we cannot establish what percentage of this community remained Muslim once the converts were able to legally return to Judaism, although we have evidence from some parts of the Almohad empire that they did.

Al-Marrākušī stated that "The pact of protection (*ḏimma*) has not been signed between us and the Jews nor with the Christians since the arrival of the Masmuda power, nor is there in the whole of the Maghrib a synagogue or a church. The Jews among us only assume Islam, praying in the mosques and their children read the Quran, following our religion and our *sunna*; but God knows what is in their hearts or what they hold behind closed doors in their houses."[44]

Nonetheless, he and other contemporary chroniclers made reference to the different vestments which the Almohad Caliph Abū Yūsuf Yaʿqūb al-Manṣūr imposed on the Maghribi Jews, among many other restrictions on their professional and social contacts with Muslims.[45] But al-Marrākušī also stated that the distinctions in dress were extended to the converts, and he wrote, "What moved Abū Yūsuf to that which he made to separate them by this costume and to distinguish them by it, was his doubt as to their Islam, and he used to say: 'If I were certain of your Islam, I would leave you to mix with the Muslims in their marriages and in their other business, and if I were certain of your infidelity, I would kill your menfolk, make captive your children and make your property as booty for the Muslims, but I have doubts about your case.'"[46]

Another famous passage comes from the Almohad chronicle *al-Mann bi-l-Imāma* of Ibn Ṣāḥib al-Salā. It recounts the betrayal of ʿAbd al-Muʾmin by Ibrāhīm ibn Hamušk, and how he allied himself with the islamicized Jews who lived in the city of Granada. Together, they took over the city and offered it to Ibn Mardaniš.[47]

[44] Al-Marrākušī, *Kitāb al-Muʿŷib fī talkhīṣ akhbār al-Maġrib*, Sp. trans. A. Huici, Tetuan 1955, p. 252. Ed. Dozy, *The history of the Almohads*, Leiden 1881, p. 224.

[45] Al-Marrākušī, ed. Dozy, op. cit., p. 224; Ibn Iḏārī, *Al-Bayān*, trans. A. Huici, Tetuan 1953, vol. I, pp. 203–4; E. Fagnan trans., *Chronique des Almohades et des Hafçides*, Constantine 1895, 19; Ibn ʿAbdūn, *Sevilla a comienzos del siglo XII: El tratado de hisba de Ibn ʿAbdun*, Madrid 1948, paragraphs 153, 157, 164, 169 and 206.

[46] Al-Marrākušī, ed. Dozy, op. cit., p. 224.

[47] *Al-Mann bi-l-Imāma*, trans. A. Huici, Valencia 1969, p. 38.

I am not going to detail any of the prominent figures who had to convert to Islam or pretend to do so, as in the case of Maimonides, who tried to console and advise his co-religionists in the same situation in his letter, the *Epistle of Forced Conversion.*[48] This piece of writing openly disputed an intransigent theologian who, unlike Maimonides and his family, had never been persecuted. In addition, Maimonides' letter expressed with absolute clarity that there never had been a systematic intention to convert *ḏimmīs* by decree. His emigration from Córdoba to Fez, in the heart of Almohad territory, further indicates that persecution was not systematic, nor had it reached the same fervor in all areas.

Another noteworthy convert was Maimonides' beloved disciple, the Rabbi of Ceuta, Yosef ibn ʿAqnīn. In his chief work, the *Ṭibb al-Nufūs*, written in Arabic, he described the distress suffered by the converts to Islam owing to the discrimination by other Muslims, and the prohibitions against them, such as not being allowed to be tutors or testamentary executors, to marry Muslims or hold slaves, etc.[49]

The result of these and other discriminatory practices was the massive emigration of Jews and Jewish converts to Islam to the Christian kingdoms of the Peninsula, not only from al-Andalus, but also from the Maghrib. In particular, Jaime I of Aragon created a general policy of sheltering Jews in his territories, granting "*guidage*," safe-conduct, and letters of naturalization to all Jews who, by land or sea, were able to come and establish themselves in the states of Mayorca, Catalonia and Valencia.[50] Among these documents are preserved the safe-conduct passes granted to two Jewish families from Sijilmasa, dated June 1247, in Valencia. For some time prior to this, Jewish converts to Islam had been permitted to return to their former religion if they so wished.

It is well known that the Jews of al-Andalus were deeply immersed in Arabo-Islamic culture, and that their participation in this culture included the fields of science and literature. Also well-known is the trauma experienced by some Andalusian Jews upon their exile to the Northern kingdoms, a phenomenon profusely described by the poet Moshe ibn Ezra, who spoke in harsh terms of his place of refuge.[51] There are numerous indications that the spontaneous conversion of Jews to Islam came to be a serious problem in the territories of the Crown of Aragon during the 13th

[48] I use the Spanish trans. by M.J. Cano and D. Ferre in *Cinco Epistolas de Maimonides*, Barcelona 1988, 49–76.

[49] Hirschberg, op. cit., vol. I, p. 356.

[50] Regné, "Catalogue des Actes de Jaime I," *Revue des Etudes Juives* LIX (1910) no. 36; also ibid. LXIV (1912) no. 847.

[51] Y. Baer, *History of the Jews in Christian Spain*, Philadelphia 1961, vol. I., 63–64.

and 14th centuries.[52] Among the known cases are Jews who had converted in al-Andalus and emigrated north in their capacity as Jews in order to enjoy the protection afforded by the Aragonese Crown, and once established there, reverted to Islam. There were also Jews who came from al-Andalus and, being deeply Arabized, preferred to take shelter among the Muslim communities, once they arrived in Christian territory.

Rina Drory, studying the works of Moshe ibn Ezra and Yehuda al-Harizi, both Andalusian Jews who emigrated to Christian lands, has concluded that it was this emigration and the immersion in a different Jewish context that was responsible for their conscious use of Arabic models. "Confronting in Christian Spain a Jewish cultural atmosphere so different from that of al-Andalus caused Ibn Ezra to examine his own cultural identity and formulate it in such a way as to define it in opposition to the local Jewish one... Representing the 'Andalusian cause' within the Jewish community of Northern Spain made the Arabic component a marked part of Ibn Ezra's Jewish identity".[53] The opposite case is embodied by Petrus Alfonsi, who emigrated from al-Andalus to Christian Spain and converted from Judaism to Christianity in 1106: he subsequently wrote a treaty *adversus judaeos*.

In any case, in the Council of Tarragona of 1234–35, Jaime I directed that a decision be taken which would prohibit the Jews from converting to Islam under penalty of death. D. Romano[54] has studied various cases of Jewish conversion to Islam within the Crown of Aragon in the final years of the 13th century, who suffered capital punishment as a result. More than a few editors of documentary material have been disconcerted when confronted with cases such as that of Mahomat Alondí Iudei, who appears listed in the text of the *Repartimiento* of Valencia among the Muslim residents of the city.[55]

In this regard, a *quaestio* included in a 15th-century Aragonese manuscript, recently studied and published by W.C. Stalls, is a useful illustration of the problem of Jewish conversion to Islam.[56] The proposals of this *quaestio*, which respond to the question as to whether a Jew who converts to Islam should be punished, are notably different from the

[52] Regné, op. cit., *Revue des Etudes Juives* LIX (1910), no. 9.

[53] R. Drory, "Literary Contacts and Where to Find Them: On Arabic Literary Models in Medieval Jewish Literature," *Poetics Today* 14,2 (1993): 277–302, esp. 288–98.

[54] D. Romano, "Conversión de judíos al Islam (Corona de Aragón, 1280–1284)," *Sefarad* XXXVI (1976): 333–37.

[55] R.I. Burns, "Jaime I and the Jews of the Kingdom of Valencia," *Jaime I y su época*. Zaragoza 1980, vol. I, p. 262.

[56] W.C. Stalls, "Jewish Conversion to Islam: The Perspective of a Quaestio," *Revista Española de Teología* 43 (1983): 235–51.

policy adopted by the Crown towards the problem: They maintain that the Jews and the Muslims were tolerated by the Catholic Church and remained outside the compass of its legal authority. The *quaestio* further explains that only the Christian apostate was obliged to remain within the Church, so to speak, and the Jew converted to Islam was solely an apostate to his own religion and could not be punished by the Catholic Church. By choosing Islam, it says, the Jew has chosen a less evil religion and cannot be punished for his choice. The authors of the *quaestio* consider Islam less dangerous than Judaism.

This was not the policy followed by the Crown, which without doubt wished to maintain its non-Christian communities in watertight compartments and well under control. It must be kept in mind that during the same period in Aragon, the conversion of Muslims to Judaism was also punished, a rather curious phenomenon which may have had its origins in the emigration of Andalusian Jews nominally converted to Islam.[57]

In any case, I believe that there are sufficient indications from the 13th century to argue that a phenomenon similar to the Neo-Mozarabs occurred among Jews, who as neo-Muslims came to form a part (or tried to do so) of the *mudejar* communities in Christian territories. Both cases indicate that in some circumstances, when communities are uprooted or transplanted into a foreign medium, acculturation may have more impact on the definition of their social identity than religion.

JEWISH CONVERTS IN THE MAGHRIB: THE *BILDIYYĪN* OF FEZ

The *bildiyyīn*, still known as such, are a group of inhabitants of the city of Fez considered to be descendants of Jewish converts to Islam.[58] It is difficult to confirm that all of the so called *bildiyyīn* are of Jewish origin, but they were considered so, and that is what matters. The same could be said of its rival group, the *šurafā*ʾ, whose prophetic descent is, at best, difficult to prove in many cases and was, in fact, challenged by other groups.

Until the seventeenth century these neo-Muslims were designated by the

[57] J. Boswell, *The Royal Treasure: Muslim Communities under the Crown of Aragon in the Fourteenth Century*. New Haven and London 1977, 351–52 and 379–81.

[58] I am summarizing part of a more extensive study of the *bildiyyīn*: M. García-Arenal, "Les *Bildiyyīn* de Fès, un groupe de néo-musulmans d'origine juive," *Studia Islamica* LXVI (1987), 113–44.

pejorative name of *muhāğirūn*, those who have performed the *hiğra* from one religion to the other. Their origins are uncertain. As a community they first emerge from the forced conversions that took place in the twelfth century under the Almohads, and from those resulting from the pogroms in the city in Marīnid times, especially during the reign of Abū Yūsuf Ya'qūb (1258–1286).[59] The Marīnids had Jewish stewards and courtiers in important financial positions. Jews also held high positions in intellectual and commercial circles. The enhanced position of some of these courtiers inevitably aroused much jealousy and hostility among the people of Fez, which broke forth on several occasions, especially in 1276.

However, the convert community seems to have become consolidated and both numerically and socially important in the fifteenth century due to the events surrounding the creation of the Mellah in Fez. In spite of the fact that the information available in the sources is often contradictory, Corcos and Hirschberg have reasonably established[60] that the movement of Jews from the district of Fundūq al-Yahūd in Fās al-Bālī to the Mellah in Fās al-Ğadīd took place towards 1438. The beginning of Šarifism as a political movement and the ascent of the *šurafā'* in the city as a preponderant group, which ascent crystallizes precisely in 1438 with the "discovery" of Idrīs's tomb,[61] were decisive in provoking the removal of Jews from the Madīna of Fez, from then on considered *ḥarām*.

The Jews had, however, been victims of the confusion and conflicts that Fez had suffered during the first decades of the fifteenth century. In 1438 numerous families of wealthy Jewish merchants preferred to convert to Islam rather than abandon their district in Fās al-Bālī and the privileged site of their commercial transactions. This displacement to the Mellah, which the Jews experienced as a veritable calamity, produced a wave of conversions that contributed to the consolidation of an important convert community in Fez, mainly settled in the area known as Fundūq al-Yahūd. The new converts were far from well-received by other sections of the population. Both Jews and Muslims mistrusted the competition of these converts in certain forms of business.

The first news extant regarding this convert community reveals their rivalry, at first only in commercial matters, with the leading group in the city, the *šurafā'*. This group of noble blood, formed by families considered

[59] D. Corcos, "The Jews of Morocco under the Marinids," in *Studies in the History of the Jews of Morocco*, Jerusalem 1976.

[60] H.Z. Hirschberg, *A History of the Jews in North Africa*, Leiden 1974, vol. I, pp. 389 ff.; D. Corcos, "Les Juifs du Maroc et leurs Mellahs," in *Studies*... pp. 73 ff.

[61] G. Salmon, "Le culte de Mulei Idris et la mosquée des Chorfa à Fez," *Archives Marocaines* III (1905): 415; H.L. Beck, *L'image d'Idris II, ses descendants de Fās et la politique sharifienne des sultans marinides (656–869/1258–1465)*, Leiden 1989, pp. 228 ff.

descendants of the Prophet and therefore of considerable social and religious prestige, had enjoyed the protection of the Marīnid dynasty that had elevated them as a means to legitimize their own power.[62] The other group with which they competed were the *andalusiyyūn*, or people from al-Andalus, who had emigrated to Fez since the thirteenth century but mostly in the second half of the fifteenth century. Both, therefore, were ethnic or quasi-ethnic groups in the sense that membership was only possible by birth. Both viewed their preponderant role in the life of the city and privileges as their right owing to their origin (Arab descent, Prophetic descent) and lineage.

Commercial rivalry was centered around the Qaysariyya of Fez because the *šurafā*ʾ (among whom were to be found some of the bigger merchant families of the city) aspired to monopolize it. In their view, the sanctity of their origin made them the only ones suitable for posts in a place that was, after all, holy ground. From the beginning they accused the converts of fraudulent practices, of "buying" with money and bribes privileges not rightly theirs and of recruiting the help of their former coreligionists. Unlike the *marranos* of Spain, their contemporaries, the *bildiyyīn* were never accused of hypocrisy or of not being good Muslims. They were, however, suspected of not being reliable or trustworthy, and so the duty of the *šurafā*ʾ was to safeguard the *qubba* of the Qaysariyya from fraud, swindling and dishonest practices. The *bildiyyīn* had neither honor nor reputation (*tawātur*), and were considered dishonest and corrupt in commerce.

According to the anonymous *Ḏikr qiṣṣat al-muhāǧirīn al-musammīn al-yawm bi-l-bildiyyīn*, in principle a history of the guilds of Fez, but written to the detriment of the converts,[63] the *bildiyyīn* had been forbidden to practice certain trades and to establish their business in the Qaysariyya since the time of Abū Yūsuf Yaʿqūb. This sultan had banned them from all the metiers except "those who do not imply a presumption of trustworthiness and of those which by their own nature are trades which offer limited possibilities of swindling."[64] The list of trades forbidden to the converts as reproduced by the *Ḏikr* includes the most noble and lucrative and indicates the aim of excluding all trade permitting access to the Qaysariyya. The events described thereafter in the same source show that the enjeux is the monopoly of the Qaysariyya.

Once the *bildiyyīn* were forbidden access to the Qaysariyya, the situation

[62] M. Kably, *Société, pouvoir et religion au Maroc à la fin du Moyen Age*, Paris 1986, p. 291 ff.

[63] Bibliothèque Général de Rabat, Ms. K.270.

[64] *Ḏikr*, f. 471.

remained stable and free of conflict until the time of ʿAbd al-Ḥaqq, the last Marīnid sultan, who appointed various Jews to important posts. One of them, whom the *D̲ikr* calls Ḥusayn al-Yahūdī, was given the post of *qāʾid al-šurṭa*. The *bildiyyīn* then asked permission of Ḥusayn to reenter the Qaysariyya. It was the time of the *ʿĪd* and the *bildiyyīn* offered to pay a *hadiyya*, a present, every year to the sultan if they were admitted. The sultan, ever in need of money, consented. The following *ʿĪd*, according to the *D̲ikr*, the *bildiyyīn* asked that the other merchants in the Qaysariyya also pay the *hadiyya* as a condition of plying their trades there. Once they had the other merchants paying the *hadiyya* with them, the *bildiyyīn* went to the *nāẓir al-aḥbās* and, with Ḥusayn's help, obtained his consent to sell them the exclusive *ǧulūs* (right to sit) to the shops. The *bildiyyīn* bought the *ǧulūs* of all the shops in less than two months, and anyone wishing to occupy a shop had to pay them rent. The *D̲ikr* accused the *bildiyyīn* of a plot for collective promotion and of connivance with their former coreligionists.[65] All this implies a transgression of the rules of stratification taken for granted by a society which had well established ways of transmission of social status.

The *bildiyyīn* remained masters of the shops until the rebellion of the Muslims of Fez, in what was really a coup of the *šurafāʾ* of Fez. The sultan ʿAbd al-Ḥaqq was killed and replaced by the *mizwar al-šurafāʾ* al-Ǧūtī, who expelled the *bildiyyīn* from the Qaysariyya in 886/1481. The *D̲ikr* seems to indicate that the rivalry between the *šurafāʾ* and the *bildiyyīn*, and the latter's transgression against the social order, were the reasons for the coup against ʿAbd al-Ḥaqq al-Marīnī.[66] The *bildiyyīn* regained access to the Qaysariyya in the time of Aḥmad al-Waṭṭāsī (1526–1549). According to the *D̲ikr*, this sultan had as tax collector a convert, Manǧur al-Islāmī, from whom the *bildiyyīn* bought the right to reenter the Qaysariyya. The civil war between Waṭṭāsids and Saʿdīs forced the sultan to accept the subsidies of the *bildiyyīn*.[67]

But the conflict between *šurafāʾ* and *bildiyyīn* did not end with this episode. On the contrary, it continued on, both groups trying to influence the reigning sultan. We need to keep in mind that this battle originated in the fifteenth century struggle over the monopoly for the Qaysariyya and its key sector, sumptuous and imported fabrics; a struggle which intensified

[65] The same process is described by D. Little, "Coptic Converts to Islam During the Bahri Mamluk Period," in M. Gervers and R.J. Bikhazi (eds.), *Conversion and Continuity: Indigenous Christian Communities in Islamic Lands*, Toronto 1990.

[66] See M. García-Arenal, "The Revolution of Fas in 869/1465 and the Death of Sultan ʿAbd al-Ḥaqq al-Marīnī," *BSOAS* XLI (1978): 43–66.

[67] *D̲ikr*, f. 475.

with the increasing use of these fabrics and the growing importance of European imports.

From the beginning of the seventeenth century, the *bildiyyīn* acquired an ever increasing importance in the life of the city, becoming a dominant group.[68] Over a period of two centuries they had not only secured their economic position, they had also produced eminent judicial and religious figures. As the *bildiyyīn* distinguished themselves in different fields, it became less tolerable for them to suffer any kind of discrimination. The ideological justification other groups (mainly the *šurafāʾ* and *andalusiyyūn*) employed in order to maintain such discrimination weakened correspondingly. During the first half of the seventeenth century the merchants of the Qaysariyya managed (as they had in the past) to expel the *bildiyyīn* from the *qubba*. The latter appealed to the Crown Prince and then Governor of Fez, Muḥammad al-Maʾmūn al-Saʿdī. In 1010/1601 al-Saʿdī made public a *ẓāhir* in which he stated that it is contrary to the *šarīʿa* to raise pride of lineage to the point of segregating the convert, be he of recent or ancient conversion, because religion is one. He decreed as well that the Muslim markets did not exclusively belong to anyone. The *ẓāhir* thereby allowed the *bildiyyīn* to reopen their shops in the Qaysariyya. But in the confusion that followed the death of Aḥmad al-Manṣūr a few years later, the *bildiyyīn* were once again expelled. The question resurfaced in 1051/1641 and a true movement was organized against the measures that caused discrimination against converts. As a reaction to this movement, *bildiyyīn* shops were plundered and bands of people rose in arms so that the Governor of Fez, Abū Bakr al-Tamlī, was forced to take measures and request the support of the *ʿulamāʾ*. We know of these events and of the polemic that followed through a work called *Naṣīḥat al-muġtarrīn*,[69] a compendium of *fatwā*s, diverse legal documents and correspondence regarding the *bildiyyīn* and accompanying a polemical text in their favor by Maḥamad Mayyāra.[70] He was a member of a well-known Bildī family that had already produced eminent scholars. He was born in Fez in 999/1591 and died in the same city in 1072/1662. Although a jurist, theologian, and one of the most reputable scholars of his time, he never held public office due to his origin.[71]

[68] N. Cigar, "Societé et vie politique à Fez sous les premiers ʿalawites," *Hespéris-Tamuda* XVIII (1978–79): 93–172.

[69] See M. García-Arenal, "*Naṣīḥat al-Muġtarrīn* of Maḥamad Mayyāra (d.1072/1662): A Collection of Fatwàs on the Bildiyyīn of Fez," *The Maghreb Review* 16, 1–2 (1991): 84–94.

[70] E. Lévi-Provençal, *Les historiens des Chorfa*, Paris 1922, p. 258; Ibn Sūdā, *Dalīl muʾarriḫ al-Maġrib al-Aqṣā*, Casablanca 1960, vol. I, p. 111. There are at least two copies at the Bibliothèque Générale de Rabat. I use and quote Ms. K.923.

[71] Al-Qādirī, *Našr al-Maṯānī*, French trans. by Michaux-Bellaire, *Archives Marocaines* XXIV (1917) pp. 123–26; al-Kattanī, *Salwat al-anfās*, Fez 1316/1898, vol. I, pp. 165–67.

The fundamental idea of the *Naṣīḥat al-Muġtarrīn* is that personal merit and piety determine a person's value and not his origin, and that it is not legal according to holy law to discriminate among Muslims because of their origin. The writing of this work brought upon Mayyāra the enmity of a large part of the Fāsī aristocracy, as well as popular aversion so widespread that he was forced to seek the sultan's protection.

The violence and intensity of the polemic at this point are recorded in the *Taqrīẓ* of al-Awfī, written in support of Mayyāra by one of his fellow scholars.[72] Also taking his side in the polemic is another Bildī scholar, Ibn Zakrī. According to al-Qādirī,[73] Mayyāra's work, as well as those of his two supporters, caused a true scandal and they thus became the target of harsh criticism by some of the contemporary *ʿulamāʾ*. Mayyāra defended the primacy and superiority of the *ʿaǧam* over the *ʿarab* but nevertheless cast doubt on the Arab lineage of those groups that flaunted it, namely the *šurafāʾ* and the *andalusiyyūn*. He is particularly harsh to the latter. He accuses them of considering themselves superior even to the *šurafāʾ*. Their onomastic conceit and the *nisba*s intended to commemorate their places of origin in al-Andalus seemed ridiculous and offensive to Mayyāra. He refuses to acknowledge their Arab origin by making references to Berber, Hispano-Roman and Slavic elements within Andalusian society, and states that the greater part of the *andalusiyyūn* are themselves descended from converts.[74] Regarding the *šurafāʾ* Mayyāra seems to assimilate some of their arguments as he prides himself on the fact that the *bildiyyīn*, as Banū Isrāʾīl, also have *nabiyyūn*, that is, prophets, among their ancestors. However, Mayyāra insists, the *karam* does not depend on *nasab* but on individual worth, on the knowledge and observance of religion.[75] It is worth conveyed by blood versus worth conveyed by personal behavior: in his work Mayyāra clearly shows, in terms of the social emergence and rivalry of both groups, the extent to which the *bildiyyīn* form part of the mold in which the *šurafāʾ* are cast, and how they finally establish themselves as the concave mark of this mold appropriating the claims (prophetic descent) that the *šurafāʾ* glorify.

From an ideological point of view, the polemic raised by the *bildiyyīn* is a match for what French historians used to call "crise maraboutique." According to C. Geertz's interpretation of this crisis,[76] in the seventeenth

[72] See M. Hajji, *L'activité intellectuelle au Maroc à l'époque Saʿdide*, Rabat 1976, vol. I, p. 210.

[73] Al-Qādirī, *Našr al-Maṯānī*, Ms. Bibliothèque du Palais Royal, Rabat, Ms. n. 1418, pages not numbered and not to be found in the translation of *Archives Marocaines*.

[74] Mayyāra, *Naṣīḥa*, pp. 48–51.

[75] Mayyāra, *Naṣīḥa*, p. 53.

[76] C. Geertz. *Islam Observed: Religious Development in Morocco and Indonesia*, Chicago 1968, p. 45.

century we are witness to a social and cultural stabilization of Moroccan Maraboutism that arose from the fusion of the genealogical concept of saintliness as authorized through miracles and good deeds. For Geertz, the establishment of the *šurafāʾ* dynasties, in particular the ʿAlawī dynasty, still the reigning family of Morocco, represents the affirmation of "the genealogical view of the basis of *baraka* over the miraculous; of the proposition that, though sainthood is naturally enough accompanied by wonders, it is, conveniently enough, conveyed by blood." As opposed to the emergence of an alternative principle of the legitimacy of power, the *bildiyyīn*, in social and economic rivalry with the leading group, fight for the validity of the principle of personal worth and honor through good deeds and observance of religious law. Mayyāra nevertheless exemplifies the concept of lineage acquiring such unquestionable weight that the *bildiyyīn*, rather than holding to their own arguments, use the theoretical principles of their adversaries, basing their defense on their own prophetic lineage (versus *šurafāʾ*) or on discrediting the origin of their rivals (versus *andalusiyyūn*).

CONCLUSION

As Gellner has stated[77] culture and ethnicity can be used to identify and distinguish privileged groups as well as underprivileged or ambivalent groups. It is socially most useful to have such groups because they can be entrusted with tasks that are a source of social power such as bureaucracies, finances (not only Jews, but Greeks or Armenians in the East), elite military corps (Mamluks, *ʿabīd*, renegades) and any kind of key specialization that may confer dangerous power to the specialist with access. The way to neutralize this danger is to insist that the group be easily identifiable culturally, marked for avoidance and contempt, and excluded from political office (at least from the ultimate control of the tools of coercion), and from honor.

The handling of large sums of money obviously confers great power, and if that power is in the hands of someone precluded from using it for his own advancement, because he belongs to a category excluded from high and honorable office and from being able to command obedience, then so much the better. All this changes dramatically if they convert, as they become dangerous owing to their previous professional tools and specialization. Hence, the majority fears the disappearance of particularity. Their background prepares them for competition but also contains a

[77] E. Gellner, *Nations and Nationalism*, pp. 102–5.

tradition of political impotence, and of surrender of the communal right to self-defense. That, after all, had been the price of their entering the profession in the first place: they had to be politically and militarily impotent so as to be allowed to handle tools potentially so very powerful and dangerous. As we all know from modern societies, the conjunction of economic superiority and cultural identifiability with political and military weakness can be disastrous, though in the times and regions we are dealing with, it never reached genocide or general expulsion.

Returning to Glick's theoretical framework which I presented in the first part of this paper, the material examined here leads us to the following conclusions:[78]

— Acculturation will not lead to social assimilation in a paternalistic system where subordinates are legally denied access to power.

In theory, the sole manner of moving from the paternalistic to the competitive system is by means of conversion, but conversion does not necessarily mean assimilation. Acculturation and conversion cannot signify true assimilation when the minority group is a menace (economic or political) to the dominant group. In other words, conversion is accepted with reluctance when it implies socio-economic competition. Therefore acculturation will be a prerequisite of assimilation in competitive systems, but will not lead to a reduction of social distance so long as the subordinate group is regarded as a social, economic or political threat to superordinates.

A shift from paternalistic to competitive modes requires of the groups which made the change, that they acquire the institutionalized right to a share of political power. Inevitably this shift involves ideological ambivalence on the part of the superordinates arising from:

— an unwillingness to validate the acculturation of a lower caste owing to resentment of socio-economic competition,[79]

— difficulty in shedding stereotypes and biases formed in the period of paternalistic relations.

Translated into a new and different paternalistic system, as in the case of the Christian kingdoms of the north of the peninsula, where the dominant group had certain characteristics and a different religion, minority groups may give more weight to acculturation to their previous milieu than to their own religion when defining their social identity.

[78] T.F. Glick, "The Ethnic Systems of Premodern Spain," *Comparative Studies in Sociology* I (1978): 157–71.

[79] L. Broom and J.I. Kitsuse, "The Validation of Acculturation: A Condition to Ethnic Assimilation," *American Anthropologist* 57 (1955): 44–48.

Book Reviews

Igor Diakonoff, *Archaic Myths of the Orient and the Occident*, Orientalia Gothoburgensia 10. Acta Universitatis Gothoburgensis. Västervik, AB C O Ekblad & Co., 1995.

Despite the serious objections I have to Diakonoff's approach, and the warnings I give voice to *infra*, I can not deny that this slim volume of Diakonoff's is praiseworthy in virtue of the valuable tales he has included in it, one of which is the tale of Enki and Ninhursang, from the second millennium B.C.E. (p. 127). I have three objections: the first is to Diakonoff's basic presuppositions, the second to the presentation of his claims, and the third to the way the book has been produced.

To begin with the third and last, the book is written in poor English. This is something that hampers the reader. A partial list of Diakonoff's errors in English includes the following impossible words and locutions, left uncorrected by the editors at Gothenburg University: unaccessible 33, profylactically 24, the possibility to read 16, ever since the invention of writing his memory receives 17, necessity to express 42, incapable to achieve 64, his working place is lighted 42, may sound as an anecdote 21. If the editors have not done their job here, neither have they in cross-referencing; for when Diakonoff writes, on p. 42, "the above information," referring to something he has presented two pages earlier, the lack of a cross-reference necessarily sends the reader searching.

A particular problem is posed by the use of the word "archaic" in the book's title; for it begs the question. This expression has significance only for someone who knows and accepts Marxist anthropology and cultural history as once taught throughout the former Soviet Union; without recourse to such preconceived notions we have no way of distinguishing easily between one period of creation of myth and another in ancient Greece.

For instance, Diakonoff dismisses, virtually out of hand, the conclusions of the late Georges Dumézil, on the grounds that the divisions he found in Indo-European society and myth belong to the age of agriculture, in his view a late stage in the development of myth. However, it does not appear that Diakonoff himself has succeeded in isolating a truly archaic stratum of myth. That is because a living genre, like myth, adapts to changing social patterns so long as it survives as a vital thing and does not petrify or expire. Diakonoff, however, is sure of each stage of the development of archaic society in ancient Greece, from its most primitive stage in which society contained two sectors, in line with the Marxist view of social development. Today this view has been discredited, at least as far as archaic Greece is concerned, in Karl-Wilhelm Welwei, *Athen: vom neolithischen Siedlungsplatz zur archaischen Grosspolis* (Wiss. Buchg., Darmstadt 1991), who discusses the contradictions between the archaeological record and Marxist theory. In Diakonoff's book there is no hint of any such contradictions.

Indeed, when Diakonoff states that the myth of Orestes is evidence of a wish to preserve the "gentilic body" inviolate (pp. 78–79), he does not show himself aware that such a wish itself may betray a period posterior to the archaic period he is so anxious to illuminate.

The book's first objective is to demonstrate the independence of myth from logical thought, regardless of its provenance. Here there comes into play Diakonoff's great store of knowledge in the field of ancient Near Eastern civilizations, of which the world became aware for the most part in the course of the twentieth century. Its next objective is to employ the tools of anthropology and sociology, which Diakonoff classes together under the name of social psychology, in order to determine just how archaic people were led to believe in the existence of elements possessing a will of their own. These Diakonoff characterizes by means of the Latin phrase *principia volentia*, "first principles that possess a will of their own," by which he means spirits, gods and goddesses, whom he terms *tropes*, employing a word borrowed from rhetoric to designate figurative language. Diakonoff (p. 89) has borrowed from the field of social psychology the list of common human impulses (p. 89) which he asserts are associated with such tropes (or principia volentia), i.e., with spirits, gods and goddesses: 1. social standing, 2. information (otherwise termed correlation), 3. power or authority (otherwise called control), 4. respect and love, 5. health, 6. hunger and the sexual urge.

Diakonoff is not entirely consistent when he attacks, legitimately enough (e.g., on p. 113), the tendency of those who write about mythology to characterize a particular divinity as god of war, or goddess of love, since he falls into the same trap on p. 81 when he calls Apollo the god of light. With this assertion he also betrays ignorance of the work of the well-known American scholar, Joseph Fontenrose, who showed that Apollo was identified with light and the sun only at the end of the fifth century B.C.E. or the beginning of the fourth. Indeed Diakonoff cites Russian authors on mythology exclusively, a fact which detracts from the value of his work, and raises the question of why he published this volume which appears to be notes for many years of lectures, in English rather than in Russian; for his primary concern here is to confront the nineteenth and twentieth century myths he inherited from Soviet policy and from the Soviet education he received.

Diakonoff neglects English language publications, save those adopted by the Bolsheviks, like the work of Lord Sherington, the physiologist whose work on the human nervous system was published in 1927. On the same lines, Diakonoff stresses that "belief prevailed over logical analysis" in the archaic period. This may not go without saying for those educated in the former Soviet Union, but it strikes a bizarre note in a work written, as it were, in English. He also felt himself constrained to treat the various meanings of the word "myth," in modern usage, which he has divided into three groups: 1. primary, or archaic, myth, 2. secondary, or rationalistic, myth, and 3. tertiary myth, or falsehood. The most deplorable lacuna in this work is perhaps the absence of any reference to the substantial phenomenon in the study of myth and religion which we in the West have learned from the late Renato Poggioli to use the Russian term *dvoeverie* to refer to, that is the faculty people have of holding both mythic and rational beliefs at one and the same time.

This book also evinces a tendency to reductionism so far as the interpretation of myth is concerned. Thus myths appear simpler than they actually are. For example, Diakonoff claims the Indian myth, in the Rigveda, of the struggle between Indra and Vritra deals entirely with rain and thunderstorms, whereas a most interesting interpretation of this myth was given by P.V. Pathak of Thane, India, at the International Conference on Sanskrit Studies held at Melbourne, Australia in 1994, who explained the story in the Rigveda, which contains no intimation of rain at all, on the basis of tectonic changes in the bed of the Indus River in high antiquity. Moreover, certain archaeological findings, of importance for the interpretation of Greek mythology, are unknown to Diakonoff. Thus he writes of Artemis Iphigenia that "she may be a goddess of midwifery," all unaware that her role as a goddess who helps and saves women in childbirth was established beyond the shadow of a doubt by the excavations conducted over thirty years ago at Brauron in Attica by John Papadimitriou, published as "The Sanctuary of Artemis at Brauron," *Scientific American* (June 1963) 110–120. The association of the dog with Hades has long been understood as well, and there is no need to write that the reason for the connection is unknown. Another strange lacuna is a reference to the seer Tiresias in the context of the association between blindness and wisdom, where the poet Homer is cited (p. 141 note 31).

Ritual, he declares, with no further discussion, is institutionalized magic (p. 116).

It is unclear to what audience this book is directed. Lacking, as it does, a table of contents and an index, it is hard to believe it is meant for a scholarly audience, and students, too, will have trouble with its defective language and its lack of clear divisions. It is divided into two great sections only, with no indication of the particular topic treated at any point. As remarked above, the impression the book leaves with the reader is one of notes put to press at long last.

DANIEL E. GERSHENSON

Watson, J.C.E., *Ṣbaḥtū! A Course in Ṣanʿānī Arabic, Semitica Viva-Series Didactica*, Vol. 3, Harrassowitz, Wiesbaden 1996, xxvii + 324pp.

The English readership of Ṣanʿānī Arabic (hereafter ṢA) dialect has long been in need of (a) an overall description of ṢA phonology, morphology, and syntax to set on it (b) an updated, scholarly course in the dialect — a double task successfully undertaken by Dr. J. Watson: her *Syntax of ṢA*, Semitica Viva, Vol.13, Harrassowitz, Wiesbaden 1993 has been practically qualified as a reference work in conjunction with *Ṣbaḥtū!* which is primarily intended for students of Yemeni Arabic, and is of interest to Arabic dialectologists and to linguists with a general interest in Arabic. A survey of it is appropriate hereto.

Following an introduction to the sounds of ṢA and pronunciation practice, *Ṣbaḥtū!* includes twenty lessons patterned as follows: 1. Dialogues, 2. Vocabulary, 3. Grammar, 4. Thematic vocabulary, 5. Exercises, followed by a concluding Glossary, Bibliography, and a grammatical Index. The 'Dialogues' include various themes, e.g., greetings and familiarity, orientation and communication, life-cycle customs, the house, food, clothing, health, work and leisure, local tours, Yemeni walks of life, and culture. The texts, mostly from recordings, are real, fluent, and updated. Theme, vocabulary, grammar, and exercise go hand in hand, in adequate portions, except lessons 18 through 20 which are long, preferably divided.

Acquisition and internalisation of ṢA are obtained in *Ṣbaḥtū!* by exposing the student to vocabulary and grammar, pace by pace. While 'Vocabulary' is limited to the text of this or that 'Dialogue', 'Thematic vocabulary' widens the scope of the theme under discussion, thereby enriching word-power relating to Yemeni life and culture as a whole. On the other hand, a non-linguist may, at first sight, deem the 'Grammar' in *Ṣbaḥtū!* overdosed, in some cases superfluous. This false impression is mitigated by well thought out, illustrative, simplified explanations of structures, and introducing the literal translation of ṢA structures throughout, matched with their English counterparts. Idiomatic and other ṢA expressions are grammatically analysed. So are the morphophonemics. Moverover, new Complex sentences are analysed for simplification into two-level constituents: the lower one representing the 'base', and the higher — the 'surface' structure, hence transformed into single (complex) structures, e.g., Indefinite Relative Clauses (pp. 182f.). For further examples and clarification of grammar, the student is referred to the parallel paragraph in *A Syntax of ṢA*. For grammatical exercises, see *infra*.

The 'Exercises' include various skills, e.g., word-stress, word reordering, application of rules, gap-filling, matching, inflections, translations from and into ṢA, conditioned by the usage of specific ṢA words and structures, sentence formation, word substitution, morphologic and syntactic substitution, summary of an ṢA text; greetings and replies to greetings and, starting from lesson 17, comprehension of an ṢA text by questions in English, and phrase identification while reading a text.

The ṢA-English 'Glossary' (pp. 295–321) draws together the 1400 vocabulary items from the dialogues and the thematic vocabulary, and an additional vocabulary used to illustrate grammatical points only if required for the exercises. An additional alternative English-ṢA 'Glossary' would not be out of place, depending on whether *Ṣbaḥtū!* is primarily intended for students of Yemeni Arabic (a) who wish *only* to acquire a wide *knowledge* of ṢA themes and structures, fully supplied in the Course, or (b) who, *in addition*, wish to acquire a fluent command of, and proficiency in ṢA *speech*.

Students answering to group (b) need in addition to *Ṣbaḥtū!* an adequate supply of audio-visual electronic aids, preferably staying in a Ṣanʿānī milieu where they can practice and master the dialect — tasks to be fulfilled beyond the book. Yet, such interests might have been advanced within the limits of *Ṣbaḥtū!* had it included (a) the English-ṢA glossary assisting the student, as a tool for translating inwardly from English to the target dialect, in the early stages of practicing ṢA speech; (b) intensified exercises relating to the lessons or otherwise, in addition to repetition of sentences, question and answer formation, activating memory, etc., exercises simulating topics for reporting, description, conversation, discussion, argumentation, and theatrical performance, as a means of activating the student towards correct and adequate or fluent speech under the guidance of his competent teacher.

However, in order for the teacher to perform satisfactorily the suggested tasks in the class-room, a Teacher's Booklet is to be attached to *Ṣbaḥtū!* provided with pedagogical instructions ensuring steady learning and internalisation of the subject-matter and proper fulfillment of exercises by the students. It should also include layouts for the teacher, instructing how to motivate, activate, and guide the student towards speaking ṢA adequately or proficiently. This booklet would hopefully consolidate the teacher's competence when at stake.

Proof-reading has regrettably failed in the following instances: p. 41, l.7, read *baṭaṭ* for *bṭaṭ*, as on p. 42, l.1; pp. 62, l. -15, and 297, l.18, *ʿasid* stands for *ʿaṣīd* (?); p. 115, l. -13, read *bi-ḍabṭ* for *bi-ḏabṭ*, as on p. 114, bottom l.; p. 115, l. -9, read 'diarrhoea' for 'diarrheoa', as on p. 273, l.7; p. 131, l.17, and p. 301, l. -14, read 'pistachios' for 'pestachios'; p. 172, l.8, read *šahay* for *šay*, as on p. 55, l.7; p. 182, ll.4 and 15, read 'referent' for 'referant'; p. 206, l.9, and p. 309, l. -18, read 'vertical' for 'verticle'; to p. 221, l.20, add a closing bracket; p. 260, l.9, read *anā* for *nā*; p. 313, l. -3, delete *šakkam-yišakkim*, see p. 314, l.2.

None the less, *Ṣbaḥtū!* is welcomed as an outstanding course in modern Arabic dialectology, widely opening a window to ṢA in particular, and to Yemeni Arabic in general for the English readership. I warmly congratulate Dr. Watson on it, Semitica Viva — Series Didactica for this successful choice, and Harrassowitz Verlag for publishing the course in an aesthetic volume.

MOSHE PIAMENTA